ULTIMATE

GERMAN

BEGINNER–INTERMEDIATE

ULTIMATE

GERMAN

BEGINNER–INTERMEDIATE

INGEBORG LASTING, PH.D.

HEIDI SINGER, PH.D.

EDITED BY
HELGA SCHIER, PH.D.

Previously published as *Living Language® German All the Way™*

Published by Living Language, A Random House Company,
New York, New York. Living Language is a member of the
Random House Information Group.

Random House, Inc. New York, Toronto, London, Sydney, Auckland

www.livinglanguage.com

Living Language and colophon are registered trademarks of Random House, Inc.

Printed in the United States of America

Library of Congress Cataloging-in-Publication Data is available upon request.

ISBN 1-4000-2106-5

10   9   8   7   6   5   4

ACKNOWLEDGMENTS

Thanks to the Living Language team: Tom Russell, Elizabeth Bennett, Christopher Warnasch, Zviezdana Verzich, Suzanne McQuade, Amelia Muqaddam, Denise De Gennaro, Linda Schmidt, John Whitman, Alison Skrabek, Helen Kilcullen, Heather Lanigan, Fabrizio La Rocca, Guido Caroti, and Sophie Chin. Special thanks to everyone who assisted in the writing and development of this book: Clifford Browder, Walter Kleinmann, Edward G. Fichtner, and Peter Kellersmann.

CONTENTS

ULTIMATE
GERMAN
BEGINNER–INTERMEDIATE

INTRODUCTION

Living Language® Ultimate German is a practical and enjoyable way to learn German. The complete course consists of this text and eight hours of recordings. You can, however, use the text on its own if you already know how to pronounce German.

With *Ultimate German,* you'll speak German from the very beginning. Each lesson starts with a dialogue about common situations that you are likely to experience at home or abroad. You'll learn the most common and useful expressions for everyday conversations.

Key grammatical structures introduced in the dialogue are clearly explained in a separate section. The lessons build on one another. The material you've already studied is "recycled," or used again, in later lessons as you learn new words, phrases, and grammatical forms. This method helps you gradually increase your language skills while reinforcing and perfecting material learned previously.

In addition, brief notes on cultural topics will add to your understanding of German and German-speaking people.

COURSE MATERIALS

THE MANUAL

Living Language® Ultimate German consists of forty lessons, eight review sections, and four reading sections. The review sections appear after every five lessons, and the reading sections after every ten lessons.

Begin each lesson by reading and studying it in the manual before listening to the recordings.

DIALOG (DIALOGUE): Each lesson begins with a dialogue presenting a realistic situation in a German-speaking locale. The dialogue is followed by a translation in colloquial English. Note that while there are many regional dialects and accents, we will be using standard German grammar and vocabulary throughout the course.

AUSSPRACHE (PRONUNCIATION): In lessons 1 through 10, you will learn the correct pronunciation of vowels and diphthongs, as well as consonants and consonant combinations.

GRAMMATIK UND GEBRAUCH (GRAMMAR AND USAGE): This section explains the major grammatical points covered in the lesson. The heading of each topic corresponds to its listing in the table of contents.

VOKABELN (VOCABULARY): In this section you can review the words and expressions from the dialogue and learn additional vocabulary.

ÜBUNGEN (EXERCISES): These exercises test your mastery of the lesson's essential vocabulary and structures. You can check your answers in the *LÖSUNGEN* (ANSWERS) section.

KULTURNOTIZ (CULTURAL NOTE): These brief notes about German, Austrian, and Swiss customs put the language in its cultural context. Cultural awareness will enrich your understanding of German and your ability to communicate effectively.

WIEDERHOLUNGSAUFGABE (REVIEW QUIZ): Review quizzes appear after every five lessons. These quizzes are similar to the exercises in format, but they integrate material from all the lessons you have studied to that point.

LESESTÜCK (READING PASSAGE): The four reading passages are not translated. However, the material covered in the preceding lessons, along with the vocabulary notes that accompany the reading, will enable you to infer the meaning, just as you would when reading a newspaper abroad.

APPENDIXES: There are three appendixes: a glossary of continents, countries, and languages; charts of German grammar and verbs; and a section on letter writing.

GLOSSARY: Be sure to make use of the two-way glossary in the back of the manual to check the meanings of new words and connotations.

INDEX: The manual ends with an index of all the grammar points covered in the lessons.

The appendixes, glossary, and index make this manual an excellent source for future reference and study.

RECORDINGS (SETS A & B)

This course provides you with eight hours of audio instruction and practice. There are two sets of complementary recordings: the first is designed for use with the manual, while the second may be used without it. Listening to and imitating the native speakers, you'll be able to improve your pronunciation and comprehension while learning to use new phrases and structures.

RECORDINGS FOR USE WITH THE MANUAL (SET A)

This set of recordings gives you four hours of audio practice in German only, with translations in the manual. The dialogue of each lesson, the pronunciation sections of lessons 1 through 10, the vocabulary section, and parts of the grammar section are featured on these recordings. All the words and expressions that are recorded appear in **boldface** in your manual.

You will hear native German speakers read the complete dialogue without interruption at a normal conversational speed. Then you'll have a chance to listen to the dialogue a second time and repeat each phrase in the pauses provided.

Next, listen carefully to learn the sounds from the pronunciation sections. By repeating after the native speakers, you will gradually master the sounds.

Finally, the most important and commonly used vocabulary words will also be modeled by the native speakers for you to repeat in the pauses provided.

After you study each lesson and practice with Set A, you can go on to the second set of recordings (Set B), which you can use on the go—while driving, jogging, or doing housework.

RECORDINGS FOR USE ON THE GO (SET B)

The "On the Go" recordings give you four hours of audio practice in German and English. Because they are bilingual, Set B recordings may be used without the manual wherever it's convenient to learn.

The 40 lessons on Set B correspond to those in the text. A bilingual narrator leads you through the four sections of each lesson.

The first section presents the most important phrases from the original dialogue. You will first hear the abridged dialogue at normal conversational speed. You'll then hear it again, phrase by phrase, with English translations and pauses for you to repeat after the native German speakers.

The second section reviews and expands upon the most important vocabulary in the dialogue. Additional expressions show how the words may be used in other contexts. Again, you are given time to repeat the German phrases.

In the third section, you will explore the lesson's most important grammatical structures. After a quick review of the rules, you can practice with illustrative phrases and sentences.

The exercises in the last section integrate what you've learned and help you generate sentences in German on your own. You'll take part in brief conversations, respond to questions, transform sentences, and occasionally translate from English into German. After you respond, you'll hear the correct answer from a native speaker.

The interactive approach on this set of recordings will teach you to speak, understand and *think* in German.

PRONUNCIATION CHART

While the rules of German pronunciation will be introduced and practiced in the first ten lessons of this course, this chart serves as a quick reference guide.

LETTERS AND SOUNDS

DAS ALPHABET (The Alphabet)

The German alphabet has 26 regular letters. They are pronounced as follows:

German Spelling	Approximate Sound in English	Example
a	f<u>a</u>ther	<u>A</u>nna, <u>A</u>lbert
b	<u>b</u>ed	<u>B</u>ank, <u>B</u>erlin
c	nu<u>ts</u>	<u>C</u>elsius
d	<u>d</u>ate; <u>t</u>iger	<u>D</u>rama, Ba<u>d</u>
e	May; f<u>ai</u>ry	<u>E</u>rich, <u>E</u>nde
f	<u>f</u>ly	<u>F</u>ilm, <u>F</u>abel
g	garden	<u>G</u>as, <u>G</u>ustav
h	<u>h</u>ouse	<u>H</u>otel, <u>H</u>unger
i	p<u>i</u>zza	<u>I</u>dee, <u>I</u>ris
j	yes	<u>j</u>a, <u>J</u>aguar
k	<u>k</u>eep	<u>K</u>arl, <u>K</u>anal
l	<u>l</u>and	<u>L</u>ampe, <u>L</u>inie
m	<u>m</u>ile	<u>M</u>aschine, <u>M</u>artha
n	<u>n</u>ew	<u>N</u>ation, <u>N</u>atur
o	al<u>o</u>ne	<u>O</u>per, <u>O</u>fen
p	price	<u>P</u>roblem, <u>P</u>aul
q	quality	<u>Q</u>ualität, <u>Q</u>uiz
r	<u>r</u>ice	<u>R</u>ose, <u>R</u>eis
s	rai<u>se</u>; bo<u>ss</u>	<u>S</u>ignal, <u>S</u>ee, Rei<u>s</u>, Hau<u>s</u>
t	<u>t</u>ea	<u>T</u>ee, <u>T</u>elefon
u	r<u>oo</u>m	<u>U</u>topie, g<u>u</u>t

v	f<u>ai</u>r	*Vers, Vater*
w	<u>v</u>ain	*Willi, Wolf*
x	a<u>x</u>	*Xylophon, A<u>x</u>t*
y	n<u>ew</u>	*typisch, Lyrik*
z	nu<u>ts</u>	*Zoo, Zone*

DIE UMLAUTE UND ß (The Umlauts and ß)

The letters *a, o,* and *u* can also appear with two dots above them, called umlauts; these letters have a different sound. The *ß* (called "ess-tsett") is a ligature of the letters *s* and *z*.

German Spelling	Approximate Sound in English	Example
ä	f<u>ai</u>r	*Bär*
ö	b<u>ur</u>n	*Öl*
ü	n<u>ew</u>	*grün*
ß	hi<u>ss</u>	*wei<u>ß</u>*

DIPHTHONGE (DIPHTHONGS)

German Spelling	Approximate Sound in English	Example
ai	l<u>i</u>ke	*K<u>ai</u>ser, <u>Ei</u>s*
äu, eu	b<u>oy</u>	*H<u>äu</u>ser, d<u>eu</u>tsch*
au	h<u>ou</u>se	*H<u>au</u>s, M<u>au</u>s*

DIE KONSONANTENVERBINDUNGEN (CONSONANT COMBINATIONS)

German Spelling	Approximate Sound in English	Example
ch	lo<u>ch</u>	*Ba<u>ch</u>, Bu<u>ch</u>,*
	<u>h</u>ue	*i<u>ch</u>, Mün<u>ch</u>en, Mil<u>ch</u>, Kir<u>ch</u>e*
sch	<u>sh</u>oe	*<u>Sch</u>uh, <u>Sch</u>iff*
sp	<u>sh</u> + p (fi<u>sh</u> + pool)	*<u>Sp</u>ort, <u>Sp</u>anien*
st	<u>sh</u> + t (fi<u>sh</u> + tank)	*<u>St</u>uhl, <u>St</u>ern*

LEKTION 1

BEGRÜSSUNG UND VERABSCHIEDUNG.   Greetings and Good-byes.

A. DIALOG I

Im Büro.

HERR BERGER: Guten Tag, Frau Steiner. Wie geht es Ihnen*?

FRAU STEINER: Guten Tag, Herr Berger. Gut, danke.

HERR BERGER: Und wie geht es Ihrer* Tochter Monika?

FRAU STEINER: Sehr gut, danke.

HERR BERGER: Wo ist sie?

FRAU STEINER: Sie ist jetzt in Berlin.

HERR BERGER: Berlin ist interessant. Auf Wiedersehen, Frau Steiner.

FRAU STEINER: Auf Wiedersehen, Herr Berger.

In the Office.

MR. BERGER: Hello, Mrs. Steiner. How are you?

MRS. STEINER: Hello, Mr. Berger. Fine, thanks.

MR. BERGER: And how is your daughter Monika?

MRS. STEINER: Very well, thank you.

MR. BERGER: Where is she?

MRS. STEINER: She's in Berlin now.

MR. BERGER: Berlin is interesting. Good-bye, Mrs. Steiner.

MRS. STEINER: Good-bye, Mr. Berger.

* These dative forms of the personal pronouns will be discussed in detail in lesson 10. For now, learn them as vocabulary.

B. DIALOG II

Zwei Freunde in der Schule.

JÖRG: Tag, Steffi. Wie geht's?

STEFFI: Ach Jörg, mir* geht's nicht so gut.

JÖRG: Was ist los, Steffi?

STEFFI: Ich bin krank.

JÖRG: Das tut mir leid.

STEFFI: Tschüs Jörg, bis Montag.

———————

Two Friends at School.

JÖRG: Hello, Steffi. How are you?

STEFFI: Oh, Jörg, I'm not feeling so good.

JÖRG: What's the matter, Steffi?

STEFFI: I'm sick.

JÖRG: I'm sorry.

STEFFI: Bye, Jörg, see you Monday.

C. AUSSPRACHE (Pronunciation)

German spelling is more consistent with its pronunciation than English. Once you've mastered the sounds, it will be easy to pronounce German correctly just by reading it.

German sentence intonation, the rise and fall of the voice pitch, is similar to English.

German words are generally stressed on the first syllable or, if they begin with an unaccented prefix, on the root syllable.

---

* These dative forms of the personal pronouns will be discussed in detail in lesson 10. For now, learn them as vocabulary.

German is spoken crisply and clearly, that is, every word is pronounced distinctly and words are rarely run together as they are in English.

There are no gliding vowel sounds as in the English word "main." Most vowels are pronounced as a single pure sound. The vowels are generally long when followed by an *h* or by a single consonant, and short when followed by two or more consonants.

The vowels *o* and *u,* as well as the consonants *r* and *ch,* have no real equivalent in English and should receive special attention.

In this and the following lessons the individual German sounds will be introduced and practiced.

VOWELS

a	long like the a in father	Vater, Tag
	short like the a in cat or the u in cut	Katze, krank
e	long like a in day	Ende, Erich, geht
	short like the e in best	Bett
	unstressed like the e in the	bitte
i	long like the ee in feet	Iris, Berlin
	short like the i in bit	bitte, ich
o	long like the o in note	Oper, oder
	short like the o in lost	Post
u	long like the oo in moon	gut
	short like the u in put	Mutter, Hunger
y	like the ew in new	typisch

D. GRAMMATIK UND GEBRAUCH
(Grammar and Usage)

1. SUBJECT PRONOUNS

SINGULAR			PLURAL	
I	*ich*		we	*wir*
you (fam.)	*du*		you (fam.)	*ihr*
he/it	*er*		they	*sie*
she/it	*sie*		you (pol.)	*Sie*
it	*es*			

Ich bin krank.
 I am sick.

Sie ist in Berlin.
 She is in Berlin.

Note: Never capitalize *ich* except at the beginning of a sentence. *Sie* (polite) is always capitalized.

Sie is the formal form of address, used when addressing one or more strangers or adults with whom the speaker is not on intimate terms. *Sie* is both singular and plural.

The familiar forms *du* and *ihr* are used when addressing relatives, close friends, and persons under fifteen years of age. *Du* and *ihr* are also frequently used among members of a group such as students, laborers, and soldiers. *Du* is singular, *ihr* is plural.

2. THE VERB *SEIN*

The important verb *sein* (to be) is irregular, as in English. It is conjugated in the present tense as follows:

SEIN TO BE

I am	*ich bin*
you are (fam.)	*du bist*
he is	*er ist*
she is	*sie ist*
it is	*es ist*

we are	*wir sind*
you are (fam.)	*ihr seid*
they are	*sie sind*
you are (pol.)	*Sie sind*

In the preceding dialogues you have seen some forms of the verb *sein:*

Sie ist jetzt in Berlin.
 She is in Berlin now.

Ich bin krank.
 I am sick.

Other examples are:

Wo bist du?
 Where are you? (fam.)

Sie sind in Amerika.
 They are in America.

3. COGNATES

Many German words are similar to or even the same as English ones. These words are called "cognates." Here are some cognates you will recognize immediately, although their German spelling may differ from the English.

das Bett	bed
der Fisch	fish
das Ende	end
der Hunger	hunger
der Mann	man
der Titel	title
die Lampe	lamp
der Sommer	summer

die Adresse	address
das Telefon	telephone
die Universität	university
das Haus	house
das Hotel	hotel
der Film	film

4. THE DEFINITE ARTICLE AND GENDER

As you have seen in the list of cognates above, every German noun is preceded by either *der, die,* or *das.* These are the definite articles. While English uses only one definite article, *the,* for all nouns, German needs three different forms of the definite article to distinguish three different genders:

the man	*der Mann* (masculine)
the woman	*die Frau* (feminine)
the child	*das Kind* (neuter)

Since it is not always possible to guess the gender of a noun by any logical means, you will need to learn each noun with its definite article. As we go along, we will give you some rules of thumb for determining gender.

5. PLURAL FORMATION

German makes no gender distinction in the plural. The definite article *die* is used with all plural nouns, whether masculine, feminine, or neuter. The nouns themselves form their plurals in a number of ways. Study the following chart:

SINGULAR		PLURAL
der Titel	+ -	*die Titel*
der Sommer		*die Sommer*
der Vater	+ ¨	*die Väter*
die Mutter		*die Mütter*

das Hotel	+ *-s*	*die Hotels*
der Film	+ *-e*	*die Filme*
die Hand	+ *(¨)e*	*die Hände*
das Haus	+ *¨er*	*die Häuser*
der Mann		*die Männer*
die Adresse	+ *(e)n*	*die Adressen*
das Bett		*die Betten*

From now on, when you encounter a noun, learn its plural form as well. Plural endings will be indicated in the vocabulary section as well as in the glossary. Nouns without change in the plural will be indicated thus: *der Sommer, -.* Nouns that take both an ending and an umlaut will be indicated thus: *das Haus, ¨er.* Nouns that take just an umlaut will be written thus: *der Vater, ¨.* Nouns that take an ending only will be written thus: *die Adresse, -n.*

VOKABELN (VOCABULARY)

Guten Tag.	Hello.
Guten Morgen.	Good morning.
Guten Abend.	Good evening.
Tschüs.	Bye. (fam.)
Auf Wiedersehen.	Good-bye. (pol.)
bis morgen	until tomorrow, see you tomorrow
bis Montag	until Monday
Wie geht es Ihnen?	How are you? (pol.)
Wie geht's?	How are you? (less formal)
Danke, sehr gut.	Thank you, very well.
Was ist los?	What's the matter?
Ich bin müde.	I'm tired.
Ich bin kaputt.	I'm exhausted.
Mir geht's nicht so gut.	I'm not feeling so good.
Ich bin krank.	I'm sick.
Es geht mir schlecht.	I'm not feeling well.

Das tut mir leid.	I'm sorry.
der Morgen, -	morning
der Abend, -e	evening
die Nacht, ⸚e	night
morgens	mornings, in the morning
abends	evenings, in the evening
nachts	night, at night
jetzt	now
der Tag, -e	day
der Herr, -en*	gentleman, mister (usually used only in address)
die Frau, -en*	woman, wife, Mrs., Ms. (used as form of address)
das Fräulein, -*	unmarried woman (up to age of about 17; thereafter women are addressed as *Frau)*
der Mann, ⸚er	man, husband
die Tochter, ⸚er	daughter
gut	good, well
ausgezeichnet	excellent
danke	thank you
wie	how
was	what
wo	where
wer	who

ÜBUNGEN (EXERCISES)

A. *Formen Sie die Sätze um. Benutzen Sie die richtige Form von "sein" für das Subjektpronomen in Klammern.* (Transform the sentences. Use the correct form of *sein* for the subject pronoun in parentheses.)

BEISPIEL: *Ich bin krank. (er)*
        Er ist krank.

---

* When used as form of address, *Herr, Frau,* and *Fräulein* are used without the article: *Herr Schmidt, Frau Berger, Fräulein Sommer.*

1. *Monika ist in Berlin. (wir)*
2. *Die Männer sind krank. (ich)*
3. *Berlin ist interessant. (du)*
4. *Wir sind in Amerika. (Sie)*
5. *Wo bist du? (er)*

B. *Nennen Sie den bestimmten Artikel.* (Give the definite article.)

BEISPIEL: *Mann/der Mann*

1. *Mutter*
2. *Sommer*
3. *Tag*
4. *Kind*
5. *Bett*

C. *Nennen Sie den Plural.* (Give the plural.)

BEISPIEL: *das Haus/die Häuser*

1. *die Tochter*
2. *der Vater*
3. *die Frau*
4. *der Tag*
5. *das Telefon*
6. *das Hotel*

D. *Suchen Sie die richtige deutsche Übersetzung.* (Choose the correct German translation.)

1. Hello, Mr. Schüler.
2. What's the matter?
3. I'm sorry.
4. She is in Germany now.
5. How are you? (pol.)
6. How are you? (less formal)
7. I'm sick.
8. Fine, thanks.
9. Oh, I'm not feeling so good.
10. Bye.

a. *Das tut mir leid.*
b. *Wie geht es Ihnen?*
c. *Ich bin krank.*
d. *Sie ist jetzt in Deutschland.*
e. *Was ist los?*
f. *Ach, mir geht es nicht so gut.*
g. *Gut, danke.*
h. *Wie geht's?*
i. *Guten Tag, Herr Schüler.*
j. *Tschüs.*

15

E. *Bringen Sie die Sätze in die formale Form.* (Change the sentences to the polite form.)

1. *Wie geht's?*
2. *Wo bist du?*
3. *Tschüs!*
4. *Bist du krank?*
5. *Seid ihr in Amerika?*

KULTURNOTIZ (CULTURAL NOTE)

In German-speaking countries people commonly greet each other with a handshake. Close friends and relatives, if they have not seen each other for a while, usually embrace.

Depending on the time of day, people say *Guten Morgen* (good morning), *Guten Abend* (good evening), or *Guten Tag* (literally: good day), which is used from about 11 A.M. until 4 or 5 P.M. *Gute Nacht* (good night) is used when somebody is going to bed to retire for the night. Less formal greetings used among young people are *Morgen* (morning), *Tag* (literally: day), or *Abend* (evening). Some younger people might simply say *Hallo* (hello).

In southern Germany and Austria many people greet each other with *Grüß Gott* (literally: God's greeting) throughout the day and evening. In the German-speaking part of Switzerland people say *Grüezi* (literally: greet you).

When saying good-bye formally, people shake hands and say *Auf Wiedersehen* (literally: Until we see each other again). Informal ways of saying goodbye reserved for family and friends are *Tschüs* and *Tschau*.

In Austria people usually say *Servus* (literally: [your] servant) when they say good-bye; in Switzerland and the south of Germany you hear *Ade*.

LÖSUNGEN (ANSWERS)

A. 1. *Wir sind in Berlin.* 2. *Ich bin krank.* 3. *Du bist interessant.* 4. *Sie sind in Amerika.* 5. *Wo ist er?*
B. 1. *die Mutter*   2. *der Sommer*   3. *der Tag*   4. *das Kind*   5. *das Bett*
C. 1. *die Töchter*   2. *die Väter*   3. *die Frauen*   4. *die Tage*   5. *die Telefone*   6. *die Hotels*
D. 1.—i 2.—e 3.—a 4.—d 5.—b 6.—h 7.—c 8.—g 9.—f 10.—j
E. 1. *Wie geht es Ihnen?* 2. *Wo sind Sie?* 3. *Auf Wiedersehen!* 4. *Sind Sie krank?* 5. *Sind Sie in Amerika?*

LEKTION 2

VORSTELLUNGEN.   Introductions.

A. DIALOG I

Auf einer Konferenz.

HERR BREUNIG: Gestatten Sie, ich heiße Breunig, Fritz Breunig. Ich komme aus München.

HERR WIRKNER: Freut mich. Mein Name ist Eugen Wirkner. Ich wohne in Hamburg.

HERR BREUNIG: Angenehm, Herr Wirkner. Nette Leute hier, nicht wahr?

HERR WIRKNER: Ja, das ist wahr. Aber leider habe ich morgen viel Arbeit. Deshalb verabschiede ich mich.

HERR BREUNIG: Wie schade!

HERR WIRKNER: Entschuldigen Sie. Ich wünsche noch viel Vergnügen.

HERR BREUNIG: Danke.

At a Conference.

MR. BREUNIG: May I introduce myself? My name is Breunig, Fritz Breunig. I'm from Munich.

MR. WIRKNER: Nice to meet you. My name is Eugen Wirkner. I live in Hamburg.

MR. BREUNIG: Pleased to meet you, Mr. Wirkner. There are some nice people here, don't you think?

MR. WIRKNER: Yes, that's true. But unfortunately I have a lot of work tomorrow. That's why I'm saying good-bye.

MR. BREUNIG: Too bad!

MR. WIRKNER: Excuse me. Enjoy yourself.

MR. BREUNIG: Thank you.

17

B. DIALOG II

An der Universität.

SABINE: Tag, du bist Kirsten aus Schweden, nicht?

KIRSTEN: Nein, das stimmt nicht. Ich komme aus Kanada.

SABINE: Verzeihung.

KIRSTEN: Das macht nichts.

SABINE: Ich heiße Sabine.

KIRSTEN: Tag, Sabine.

At the University.

SABINE: Hello, you're Kirsten from Sweden, aren't you?

KIRSTEN: No, I'm not. I'm from Canada.

SABINE: Excuse me.

KIRSTEN: It doesn't matter.

SABINE: My name is Sabine.

KIRSTEN: Hello, Sabine.

C. AUSSPRACHE (Pronunciation)

UMLAUTE

An *Umlaut* is a vowel modified by an umlaut.

ä	long as the ay in day	spät
	short as the e in let	hätte
ö	long or short as the u in fur	schön
ü	long or short as ew in few	Tür

D. GRAMMATIK UND GEBRAUCH
(Grammar and Usage)

1. THE PRESENT TENSE OF REGULAR VERBS

In the preceding dialogues you saw the verbs *heißen, kommen, gehen, wohnen,* and *wünschen.* These verbs appear with different endings; for example: *ich wohne; sie wohnt.* These endings depend on the subject. As in English, subject and verb must agree. The basic form of a verb (the form you find in the dictionary) is the infinitive. In German, the infinitive of a verb consists of a stem and the ending *-en* or sometimes only *-n: wohn + en → wohnen; tu + -n → tun.* Here is the present tense of the verb *kommen* (to come):

KOMMEN TO COME

I come	ich komm<u>e</u>	we come	wir komm<u>en</u>
you come	du komm<u>st</u>	you come	ihr komm<u>t</u>
he comes	er* komm<u>t</u>	they come	sie komm<u>en</u>
		you (pol.) come	Sie komm<u>en</u>

The verb endings are added to the infinitive stem *komm-.*

Ich komme aus Kanada.
I come/am from Canada.

Herr Breunig kommt aus München.
Herr Breunig comes/is from Munich.

If the stem of a verb ends in *-d* or *-t,* the endings *-st* and *-t* become *-est* and *-et,* respectively. Thus the verb *arbeiten* (to work) will have these forms:

---

* From now on *er* (he), *sie* (she), and *es* (it) will be used alternately to represent the third person singular in the verb charts.

ARBEITEN TO WORK

I work	ich arbeit_e_		we work	wir arbeit_en_
you work	du arbeit_est_		you work	ihr arbeit_et_
she works	sie arbeit_et_		they work	sie arbeit_en_
			you work	Sie arbeit_en_

Ich arbeite in München.
   I work in Munich.

Sie arbeiten in Hamburg.
   You work in Hamburg.

If the stem of a verb ends in a sibilant *(s, ss, ß, z)*, the *-st* ending of the second person singular (fam.) contracts to *-t*; thus the verb *heißen* (to be called) will have these forms:

HEIßEN TO BE CALLED

I am called	ich heiß_e_		we are called	wir heiß_en_
you are called	du heiß_t_		you are called	ihr heiß_t_
it is called	es heiß_t_		they are called	sie heiß_en_
			you are called	Sie heiß_en_

Ich heiße Breunig, Fritz Breunig.
   My name is Breunig, Fritz Breunig.

Meine Tochter heißt Monika.
   My daughter is called Monika.

Note: German has only one present tense form. *Sie kommt* can be translated as "she comes," "she is coming," or "she does come." The present tense is frequently used to express the future tense. In the preceding dialogue you have seen:

Ich habe morgen viel Arbeit.
   I have a lot of work tomorrow.

2. THE VERB *HABEN*

Haben (to have) is another important irregular verb.

HABEN TO HAVE

I have	*ich habe*	we have	*wir haben*
you have	*du hast*	you have	*ihr habt*
he has	*er hat*	they have	*sie haben*
		you have	*Sie haben*

In the preceding dialogue, *haben* was used thus:

Ich habe morgen viel Arbeit.
    I have a lot of work tomorrow.

Other example sentences are:

Wir haben ein Kind.
    We have a child.

Er hat eine nette Frau.
    He has a nice wife.

3. NUMBERS FROM 0 TO 10

DIE ZAHLEN	NUMBERS
null	0
eins	1
zwei	2
drei	3
vier	4
fünf	5
sechs	6
sieben	7
acht	8
neun	9
zehn	10

21

If they appear in writing, the numbers one to ten have to be spelled out.

Ich habe drei Töchter.
I have three daughters.

Fünf und vier sind neun.
Five and four are nine.

VOKABELN (VOCABULARY)

heißen	to be called
kommen	to come
wohnen	to reside, to live
gehen	to go, to leave
stimmen	to be correct, to be true
wünschen	to wish
vorstellen	to introduce
gestatten	to allow, to permit
machen	to make, to do
entschuldigen	to excuse
verabschieden	to say good-bye
Angenehm.	Pleased to meet you.
Freut mich.	I'm glad (to meet you).
kommen aus	to come from (with locations)
(Es) macht nichts.	(It) doesn't matter.
Das stimmt.	That's right.
Das ist wahr.	That's true. Right.
Ich verabschiede mich.	I'm saying good-bye.
Wie schade!	Too bad!
Gestatten Sie.	Permit me; may I introduce myself.
viel	much, a lot
wenig	little
nein	no
woher	from where
die Entschuldigung, -*en*	excuse
der Name, -*n*	name
das Vergnügen, -	pleasure

viel Vergnügen	enjoy yourself
die Arbeit, -en	work
die Leute	people (always plural)
die Länder*	countries
Deutschland	Germany
Österreich	Austria
Frankreich	France
Italien	Italy
England	England
Kanada	Canada
die Schweiz	Switzerland
die U.S.A.	the U.S.A.
Amerika	America
ich komme aus . . .	I come from . . .
mein Heimatland ist . . .	my homeland is . . .

ÜBUNGEN (EXERCISES)

A. *Beantworten Sie die Fragen. Benutzen Sie dabei den Tip in Klammern.*
(Answer the questions. Use the hint in parentheses.)

BEISPIEL: *Wer kommt aus Amerika? (ich)*
Ich komme aus Amerika.

1. *Wo wohnen Sie? (Chicago)*
2. *Wo wohnt Herr Wirkner? (Hamburg)*
3. *Wer kommt aus Kanada? (Kirsten)*
4. *Wer kommt aus München? (Herr Breunig)*

B. *Setzen Sie die Endungen ein.* (Fill in the endings).

1. *ich komm___*
2. *sie* (she) *arbeit___*
3. *wir wohn___*

* Most countries are neuter, but some are feminine, and *die U.S.A.* is plural.

4. *es stimm___*
5. *du heiß___*
6. *ihr komm___*

C. *Setzen Sie die richtige Form von "haben" ein.* (Give the appropriate form of haben.)

1. *Herr Wirkner _____ morgen viel Arbeit.*
2. *Du _____ Probleme.*
3. *Das Jahr _____ vier Jahreszeiten.*
4. *Die Leute _____ viel Vergnügen.*

D. *Suchen Sie die richtige deutsche Übersetzung.* (Choose the correct German translation.)

1. Pleased to meet you.
2. Enjoy yourself.
3. Excuse me.
4. May I introduce myself?
5. I have a lot of work.

a. *Viel Vergnügen.*
b. *Gestatten Sie.*
c. *Entschuldigen Sie.*
d. *Ich habe viel Arbeit.*
e. *Angenehm.*

KULTURNOTIZ (CULTURAL NOTE)

German is spoken in Germany, Austria, Liechtenstein, and parts of Switzerland. There is a great variety of dialects. People from one region may have some trouble understanding people from another region, if they communicate in their respective dialects. But all German-speaking people learn *Hochdeutsch* (High German, Standard German) in school. Newspapers, television, and radio use *Hochdeutsch,* unless it is a decidedly regional publication or broadcast. *Hochdeutsch* is what this book is teaching.

LÖSUNGEN (ANSWERS)

A. 1. *Ich wohne in Chicago.* 2. *Herr Wirkner wohnt in Hamburg.* 3. *Kirsten kommt aus Kanada.* 4. *Herr Breunig kommt aus München.*
B. 1. *komme*　2. *arbeitet*　3. *wohnen*　4. *stimmt*　5. *heißt*　6. *kommt*
C. 1. *hat*　2. *hast*　3. *hat*　4. *haben*
D. 1.—e　2.—a　3.—c　4.—b　5.—d

LEKTION 3

A. DIALOG

Am Telefon.

Es ist Montag. Herr Kraft ist im Büro. Er telefoniert.

SEKRETÄRIN: Hier Meyer und Ullmann.

HERR KRAFT: Meyer und Ullmann? Ist dort siebenundzwanzig dreiunddreißig fünfundfünfzig?

SEKRETÄRIN: Nein, hier ist einundzwanzig dreiunddreißig fünfundfünfzig.

HERR KRAFT: Entschuldigen Sie. Falsch verbunden.

Herr Kraft telefoniert noch einmal.

SEKRETÄRIN 2: Alfred Meyer, Frankfurt.

HERR KRAFT: Herr Meyer, bitte.

SEKRETÄRIN 2: Wer ist am Apparat?

HERR KRAFT: Karl Kraft.

SEKRETÄRIN 2: Moment, bitte. Die Leitung ist besetzt. Bitte, bleiben Sie am Apparat.

HERR KRAFT: Aber das ist ein Ferngespräch. Dauert es lange?

SEKRETÄRIN 2: Nein, ich verbinde jetzt.

HERR KRAFT: Danke sehr.

On the Telephone.

It is Monday. Mr. Kraft is in the office. He is on the phone.

SECRETARY: This is Meyer and Ullmann.

MR. KRAFT: Meyer and Ullmann? Is this twenty-seven thirty-three fifty-five?

SECRETARY: No, this is twenty-one thirty-three fifty-five.

MR. KRAFT: Excuse me. Wrong number.

Mr. Kraft calls again.

SECRETARY 2: Alfred Meyer, Frankfurt.

MR. KRAFT: Mr. Meyer, please.

SECRETARY 2: Who is on the phone?

MR. KRAFT: Karl Kraft.

SECRETARY 2: One moment, please. The line is busy. Please hold.

MR. KRAFT: But this is a long-distance call. Will it take long?

SECRETARY 2: No. I'm connecting you now.

MR. KRAFT: Thank you very much.

B. AUSSPRACHE (Pronunciation)

VOWEL COMBINATIONS

ai, ay, ei, ey	like the i in bite, ice	sein
	like eye, rye	drei, Mayer
au	like the ow in now	braun, Haus
eu	like the oy in boy	heute
ie	like the ee in feet	nie

C. GRAMMATIK UND GEBRAUCH
(Grammar and Usage)

1. WORD ORDER AND FORMING QUESTIONS

In an affirmative statement, the finite verb (the verb that has the endings) is in the *second* position. Here are some statements you encountered before:

Sie ist jetzt in Deutschland.
She is in Germany now.

Ich komme aus München.
I am from Munich.

Ich habe viel Arbeit.
I have a lot of work.

When you form a question that requires a yes-or-no answer, the verb moves into the first position and the subject follows the verb. Here are yes-or-no questions from the preceding dialogue:

Ist das siebenundzwanzig dreiunddreißig fünfundfünfzig?
Is this twenty-seven thirty-three fifty-five?

Dauert es lange?
Will it take long?

You can also turn a statement into a yes-or-no question by raising your voice at the end of the sentence, just as in English. In these cases, the word order does not change. Compare:

Er kommt aus Kanada.
He is from Canada.

Er kommt aus Kanada?
Is he from Canada?

Finally, you can form a yes-or-no question by adding *nicht* or *nicht wahr* to the end of the sentence and raising your voice.

27

Nette Leute hier, nicht wahr?
　　Nice people here, aren't there?

Du bist Kirsten aus Schweden, nicht?
　　You are Kirsten from Sweden, aren't you?

When you want to get specific information, you use question words. The question word is in the first position, followed by the verb and then the subject. Here are some examples:

Wie geht es Ihnen?
　　How are you?

Was wünschen Sie?
　　What would you like?

Woher kommt er?
　　Where does he come from?

Wer ist am Apparat?
　　Who is calling (on the phone)?

2. THE INDEFINITE ARTICLE

The English indefinite article *a* or *an* is expressed in German by *ein* or *eine; ein* is used with masculine and neuter nouns, *eine* with feminine nouns. There is no plural form.

der Mann	*die Frau*	*das Telefon*
ein Mann	*eine Frau*	*ein Telefon*

3. NUMBERS ABOVE 10

DIE ZAHLEN	NUMBERS
elf	11
zwölf	12
dreizehn	13
vierzehn	14
fünfzehn	15

sechzehn	16
siebzehn	17
achtzehn	18
neunzehn	19
zwanzig	20
einundzwanzig	21
zweiundzwanzig	22
dreiundzwanzig	23
dreißig	30
einunddreißig	31
zweiunddreißig	32
dreiunddreißig	33
vierzig	40
fünfzig	50
sechzig	60
siebzig	70
achtzig	80
neunzig	90
hundert	100
hunderteins	101
zweihundert	200
tausend	1,000
eine Million	1,000,000

Note: *Sechs* loses the *s* and *sieben* loses the *en* when combined with *zehn*. Numbers in the twenties, thirties, and so on follow the pattern of the nursery rhyme "four and twenty blackbirds." *Eins* becomes *ein* when combined with the twenties, thirties, and so on: *einundzwanzig, einunddreißig. Dreißig* ends in *-ßig* instead of the usual *-zig*.

4. THE DAYS OF THE WEEK

der Tag	day
die Wochentage	days of the week

Montag*	Monday
Dienstag	Tuesday
Mittwoch	Wednesday
Donnerstag	Thursday
Freitag	Friday
Samstag, Sonnabend	Saturday
Sonntag	Sunday

Die Woche hat sieben Tage.
The week has seven days.

5. THE MONTHS OF THE YEAR

der Monat	month
die Monate des Jahres	months of the year

Januar*	January
Februar	February
März	March
April	April
Mai	May
Juni	June
Juli	July
August	August
September	September
Oktober	October
November	November
Dezember	December

Das Jahr hat zwölf Monate.
The year has twelve months.

VOKABELN (VOCABULARY)

läuten	to ring
wählen	to dial

---

* Note that both the days of the week and the months of the year are masculine in German: *der Tag, der Montag, der Monat, der Januar.*

antworten	to answer
hören	to hear, to listen
auf Wiederhören	good-bye (on the telephone)
der Hörer, -	receiver
bleiben	to stay, to remain
Bitte, bleiben Sie am Apparat.	Please hold.
auflegen	to hang up
danken	to thank
telefonieren	to call, to telephone
anrufen	to call, to telephone
entschuldigen	to excuse
Entschuldigen Sie!	Excuse me.
verbinden	to connect
falsch verbunden	wrong number
das Telefon, -e	telephone
der Apparat, -e	telephone, apparatus
Wer ist am Apparat?	Who's speaking?
der Moment, -e	moment
Die Leitung ist besetzt.	The line is busy.
Die Leitung ist gestört.	The line is out of order.
der Anschluss, ⸚e	connection
der Anruf, -e	telephone call
das Gespräch, -e	conversation, talk
das Telefongespräch, -e	telephone conversation
das Ferngespräch, -e	long-distance call
das Telefonbuch, ⸚er	telephone book
die Nummer, -n	number
die Telefonnummer, -n	telephone number
die Telefonzelle, -n	telephone booth
der Notruf, -e	emergency call
die Sekretärin, -nen	secretary (female)
besetzt	busy, occupied
das Jahr, -e	year
der Monat, -e	month
die Woche, -n	week
der Tag, -e	day
der Wochentag, -e	weekday

ÜBUNGEN (EXERCISES)

A. *Beantworten Sie die Fragen. Benutzen Sie dabei den Tip in Klammern.*
(Answer the questions. Use the hint in parentheses.)

BEISPIEL: *Wo ist Herr Kraft? (im Büro)*
 Herr Kraft ist im Büro.

 1. *Wer telefoniert? (Herr Kraft)*
 2. *Ist die Leitung besetzt? (ja)*
 3. *Ist das ein Ferngespräch? (ja)*

B. *Übersetzen Sie.* (Translate.)

 1. Who is on the phone?
 2. Excuse me.
 3. Where is a telephone book?
 4. Does Mr. Wirkner have a lot of work?
 5. The people are nice, aren't they?

C. *Schreiben Sie die Zahlen.* (Write the numbers.)

 1.   21
 2.   36
 3.   44
 4.   58
 5.   66
 6.   77
 7.   81
 8.   92
 9. 117
 10. 1185

D. *Nennen Sie den unbestimmten Artikel.* (Supply the indefinite article.)

 1. _____ *Woche hat sieben Tage.*
 2. _____ *Jahr hat zwölf Monate.*
 3. *Wo ist* _____ *Telefonzelle?*

32

E. *Vervollständigen Sie die Sätze.* (Complete the sentences.)

1. *Der Januar hat _____ Tage.*
2. *Wochenende ist am Samstag und am _____.*
3. *Nur der _____ hat 28 Tage.*
4. *Das _____ hat 12 Monate.*
5. *Die Leitung ist _____.* (busy)

KULTURNOTIZ (CULTURAL NOTE)

In German-speaking countries telephone numbers are often given in double digits: 27 33 29. But with an increase in automated systems, there is a tendency for telephone numbers to be given in single digits. Area codes are written thus: 089/27 33 29.

There are separate public telephone booths, usually side by side, for telephones that are coin-operated *(Münzfernsprecher)* and those that accept telephone credit cards *(Telefonkarten)*. The telephone credit cards can be bought in the post office and stationery stores. Telephone books, located in all telephone booths, contain information in five languages, including English.

LÖSUNGEN (ANSWERS)

A. 1. *Herr Kraft telefoniert.* 2. *Ja, die Leitung ist besetzt.* 3. *Ja, das ist ein Ferngespräch.*
B. 1. *Wer ist am Apparat?* 2. *Entschuldigen Sie.* 3. *Wo ist ein Telefonbuch?* 4. *Hat Herr Wirkner viel Arbeit?* 5. *Die Leute sind nett, nicht?*
C. 1. *einundzwanzig* 2. *sechsunddreißig* 3. *vierundvierzig* 4. *achtundfünfzig* 5. *sechsundsechzig* 6. *siebenundsiebzig* 7. *einundachtzig* 8. *zweiundneunzig* 9. *hundertsiebzehn* 10. *tausendeinhundertfünfundachtzig*
D. 1. *eine* 2. *ein* 3. *eine*
E. 1. *einunddreißig* 2. *Sonntag* 3. *Februar* 4. *Jahr* 5. *besetzt*

LEKTION 4

DAS WETTER.   The Weather.

A. DIALOG

Ein Wintermorgen.

FRAU MÜLLER: Guten Morgen, Frau Meier. Heute ist es aber furchtbar kalt und nebelig, nicht?

FRAU MEIER: Ja, das ist wahr. Gestern war es noch so schön.

FRAU MÜLLER: Ja, der Wind ist eisig. Ich denke, es schneit morgen. Das sagt auch der Wetterbericht.

FRAU MEIER: Hoffentlich stimmt das nicht.

FRAU MÜLLER: Was machen Sie denn diesen Winter?

FRAU MEIER: Ich fliege nach Mallorca. Da lebt man gut. Die Sonne scheint oft, und man friert nicht. Und was machen Sie?

FRAU MÜLLER: Vielleicht gehe ich Skifahren in Österreich. Eine Freundin wohnt da.

FRAU MEIER: Auch eine gute Idee. Bis bald.

FRAU MÜLLER: Auf Wiedersehen.

A Winter Morning.

MRS. MÜLLER: Good morning, Mrs. Meier. Today it's terribly cold and foggy, isn't it?

MRS. MEIER: Yes, that's true. Yesterday it was still nice.

MRS. MÜLLER: Yes, the wind is icy. I think it's going to snow tomorrow. The weather report says so, too.

MRS. MEIER: I hope that's not true.

MRS. MÜLLER: What will you be doing this winter?

MRS. MEIER: I'll fly to Mallorca. You live well there. The sun shines often and you don't freeze. What are you going to do?

MRS. MÜLLER: Perhaps I'll go skiing in Austria. A friend of mine lives there.

MRS. MEIER: That's also a good idea. See you soon.

MRS. MÜLLER: Good-bye.

B. AUSSPRACHE

CONSONANTS

b	at the end of a word or between vowel and consonant like the p in up, tap	gel<u>b</u>, O<u>b</u>st
	elsewhere like the <u>b</u> in <u>b</u>ad	<u>B</u>uch, <u>b</u>raun
p	like the English p	<u>P</u>apa, <u>P</u>eter
c	(before e, i, or on its own like <u>ts</u> in fi<u>ts</u>)	<u>c</u>irca, W.<u>C</u>.
	(elsewhere like the <u>c</u> in <u>c</u>at)	<u>C</u>afé, <u>C</u>ogna<u>c</u>

C. GRAMMATIK UND GEBRAUCH (Grammar and Usage)

1. THE SIMPLE PAST OF *SEIN*

The simple past of *sein* (to be) is irregular. It is conjugated as follows:

SEIN TO BE

I was	*ich war*	we were	*wir waren*
you were	*du warst*	you were	*ihr wart*
she was	*sie war*	they were	*sie waren*
		you were	*Sie waren*

Note: the first and third person singular have no ending. In the preceding dialogue you have seen:

Gestern war es noch so schön.
   Yesterday it was so nice.

2. WORD ORDER

A German sentence often starts with a word or a phrase other than the
subject. In this type of sentence the verb is usually in the *second*
position. The subject usually comes next, then all other elements. This
point is very important to remember in order to speak and write
German correctly. If a word or phrase other than the subject is in the
first position, that word or phrase is stressed. In the preceding dialogue
you have seen:

Heute ist es aber schön.
   Today it is really nice.

Hoffentlich stimmt das nicht.
   Hopefully that is not true.

Da lebt man gut.
   There you live well.

3. THE SEASONS

die Jahreszeiten	the seasons
der Winter	winter
das Frühjahr* (der Frühling)	spring
der Sommer	summer
der Herbst	fall (autumn)

Im Winter ist es kalt.
   In winter it is cold.

Im Sommer ist es schön.
   In summer it is nice.

* Note that the seasons in German are masculine, with the exception of *das Frühjahr.*

4. WORD FORMATION

a. THE SUFFIX -IN

The suffix -in added to a noun designating a male, a male profession, or a male resident of a country or a city will give the female equivalent.* In the preceding dialogue you encountered the word die Freundin:

der Freund   + in →   die Freund<u>in</u>
friend   girlfriend, female friend

Der Hamburger designates a male resident of Hamburg, die Hamburgerin a female resident. Der Sekretär designates a male secretary, die Sekretärin a female secretary. The feminine plural is formed by adding -nen: die Freundin, die Freundinnen.

b. NOUN COMPOUNDS

In German you encounter many more noun compounds than in English. So far you have encountered several noun compounds: die Jahreszeit, der Wochentag, and in the preceding dialogue, der Wetterbericht. A compound noun may consist of several nouns or of nouns and other words.

    Note: The gender of the last noun in a noun compound determines its gender.

<u>die</u> Woche + <u>der</u> Tag → <u>der</u> Wochentag†

5. WOHNEN AND LEBEN

Both wohnen and leben are translated into English as "to live." Wohnen usually refers to one's place of residence, leben to the state of being alive.

Ich wohne in Hamburg.
    I live (reside) in Hamburg.

* The vocabulary sections of each chapter and the glossary will give only the masculine form of nouns, unless the feminine form is irregular.
† Compare: das Jahr → das Frühjahr

Da lebt man gut.
    You live well there.

6. *DER MANN* AND *MAN*

Der Mann means "man" or "husband"; *man,* without article, not capitalized and spelled with one *n,* means "one," "you," "they," or "people." *Man* is used frequently in German, and it takes a third person singular verb. In the preceding dialogue you encountered:

Da lebt man gut.
    You live well there.

VOKABELN (VOCABULARY)

denken	to think
sagen	to say
fliegen	to fly
leben	to live, to be alive
scheinen	to shine
schneien	to snow
Es schneit.	It snows. It's snowing.
regnen	to rain
Es regnet.	It rains. It's raining.
stürmen	to storm
Es stürmt.	It's stormy.
frieren	to freeze
Es friert.	It freezes. It's freezing.
laufen	to run, to walk
Ski fahren, Ski laufen	to ski
furchtbar	terrible
schön	beautiful, nice
kalt	cold
heiß	hot
nebelig	foggy
klar	clear
eisig	icy

schwül	muggy
die Jahreszeit, -en	season
der Wetterbericht, -e	weather forecast, weather report
das Gewitter, -	thunderstorm
der Sturm, ̈e	storm
der Regen	rain
die Sonne, -n	sun
das Eis	ice
der Schnee	snow
der Wind, -e	wind
der Freund, -e	male friend, boyfriend
die Freundin, -nen	female friend, girlfriend
vielleicht	perhaps
bald	soon
wann	when (used only in questions)
hoffentlich	hopefully, I hope
nach	to (used with cities and countries)
heute	today
morgen	tomorrow
gestern	yesterday
die Idee, -n	idea
gut	good
dieser, -e, -es	this

ÜBUNGEN (EXERCISES)

A. *Beantworten Sie die Fragen zum Dialog.* (Answer the questions about the dialogue.)

1. *Wie ist das Wetter heute?*
2. *Wie war das Wetter gestern?*
3. *Wer fliegt im Winter nach Mallorca?*
4. *Schneit es morgen?*

B. *Suchen Sie die richtige deutsche Übersetzung.* (Choose the correct German translation.)

1. soon	a. *scheinen*
2. to snow	b. *schneien*
3. to shine	c. *nebelig*
4. skiing	d. *Das ist wahr.*
5. perhaps	e. *vielleicht*
6. That's true.	f. *bald*
7. foggy	g. *Skilaufen*
8. the weather report	h. *der Wetterbericht*

C. *Setzen sir die richtige Form von "war" ein.* (Fill in the correct form of *war.*)

BEISPIEL: *Im Sommer _____ es schön.*
       Im Sommer war es schön.

1. *_____ du gestern krank?*
2. *Nein, ich _____ müde.*
3. *Wo _____ Erika?*
4. *Sie (she) _____ in Berlin.*

D. *Nennen Sie die feminine Form.* (Name the feminine form.)

1. *der Sekretär*
2. *der Berliner*
3. *der Freund*

E. *Schreiben Sie die Sätze noch einmal. Beginnen Sie jeden Satz mit dem Wort in Klammern.* (Rewrite the sentences. Begin each sentence with the word in parentheses.)

BEISPIEL: *Ich war krank. (gestern)*
      Gestern war ich krank.

1. *Es ist furchtbar kalt. (heute)*
2. *Es schneit am Montag. (vielleicht)*
3. *Wir waren in Berlin. (Am Montag)*

F. *Vervollständigen Sie die Sätze.* (Complete the sentences.)

1. *Im _____ ist das Wetter schön. (spring)*
2. *Im Sommer _____ die Sonne. (to shine)*
3. *Im Herbst _____ es. (to storm)*
4. *Im Winter _____ es. (to snow)*

G. *"Wohnen" oder "leben" (to live or to reside)*

1. *Frau Schulz _____ im Hotel.*
2. *In der Schweiz _____ man gut.*
3. *Wir _____ in einem Haus.*
4. *Ich _____ in Amerika.*

KULTURNOTIZ (CULTURAL NOTE)

The weather in Germany varies depending on the different regions. The northern and western parts of Germany have fairly mild winters. There are usually no heavy snowfalls *(Schneefälle)* but a lot of rainy, foggy days. The summers are often sunny but not humid. In the eastern and southern parts of Germany the winters tend to be more severe. Especially the southern Alpine regions see a lot of heavy snowfalls. Usually it is possible to ski there until the end of March. The summers in the east and south tend to be warmer and a bit drier than in the north.

LÖSUNGEN (ANSWERS)

A. 1. *Es ist furchtbar kalt und nebelig.* 2. *Es war schön.* 3. *Frau Meier fliegt nach Mallorca.* 4. *Ja, es schneit morgen.*
B. 1.—f 2.—b 3.—a 4.—g 5.—e 6.—d 7.—c 8.—h
C. 1. *Warst* 2. *war* 3. *war* 4. *war*
D. 1. *die Sekretärin* 2. *die Berlinerin* 3. *die Freundin*
E. 1. *Heute ist es furchtbar kalt.* 2. *Vielleicht schneit es am Montag.* 3. *Am Montag waren wir in Berlin.*
F. 1. *Frühling* 2. *scheint* 3. *stürmt* 4. *schneit*
G. 1. *wohnt* 2. *lebt* 3. *wohnen* 4. *wohne/lebe*

LEKTION 5

DIE FAMILIE.   The Family.

A. DIALOG

Meine Familie.

Sabine zeigt Doris ein Familienphoto.

SABINE: Guck mal, Doris, das ist ein Familienphoto. Hier siehst du meine Eltern, meinen Bruder, meine Schwester, meine Großmutter, meine Tante und meinen Onkel.

DORIS: Oh, das ist deine Mutter, nicht wahr?

SABINE: Ja. Der Mann da ist natürlich mein Vater.

DORIS: Deinen Vater kenne ich doch schon. Aber hier hat er keine Brille.

SABINE: Ach ja, wen kennst du denn noch?

DORIS: Ich kenne den Mann da links. Das ist doch Max, nicht wahr?

SABINE: Ja, das stimmt. Ich hoffe, er kommt wieder zu Besuch. Einen Wagen hat er leider nicht.

DORIS: Deine Familie ist aber groß. Wer sind denn der Mann und die Frau hinten rechts?

SABINE: Oh, das sind unsere Verwandten aus Österreich, meine Tante Gretl und ihr Mann. Leider waren keine Vettern und Kusinen da.

My Family.

Sabine shows Doris a family photo.

SABINE: Look, Doris, this is a family photo. Here you see my parents, my brother, my sister, my grandmother, my aunt, and my uncle.

DORIS: Oh, that's your mother, isn't it?

SABINE: Yes. The man here is of course my father.

DORIS: I already know your father. But he's not wearing glasses here.

SABINE: That's right. Who else do you know?

DORIS: I know the man there on the left. That's Max, isn't it?

SABINE: Yes, that's right. I hope he'll come for a visit again. Unfortunately, he doesn't have a car.

DORIS: Your family is really large. Who are the man and woman on the right, in the back?

SABINE: Oh, those are our relatives from Austria, my aunt Gretl and her husband. Unfortunately, no male or female cousins were present.

B. AUSSPRACHE (Pronunciation)

MORE CONSONANTS

ch	after a, o, u, au, hard like in English ugh or Scottish Lo<u>ch</u>, produced in back of mouth as if clearing your throat	Lo<u>ch</u>, Na<u>ch</u>t, Mittwo<u>ch</u>
	soft like exaggerated h, like the <u>h</u> in <u>H</u>ubert, after e, i, umlaut, consonants	ni<u>ch</u>t, Li<u>ch</u>t
chs	like the <u>cks</u> in ba<u>cks</u>	se<u>chs</u>, La<u>chs</u>

C. GRAMMATIK UND GEBRAUCH (Grammar and Usage)

1. NEGATION WITH *KEIN*

There are two negation words in German: *nicht** and *kein. Kein* means "not a," "not any," or "no." *Kein* negates a noun either without an article or preceded by the indefinite article.

---

* Lesson 6 will deal with the negation with *nicht*.

Kein has two forms in the nominative case: *kein* for masculine and neuter nouns and *keine* for feminine and plural nouns.

Ist das ein Junge?
> Is that a boy?

Nein, das ist kein Junge.
> No, that's not a boy.
> No, that's no boy.

Ist das ein Familienphoto?
> Is that a family photo?

Nein, das ist kein Familienphoto.
> No, that's not a family photo.
> No, that's no family photo.

Ist das eine Kusine?
> Is that a cousin (female)?

Nein, das ist keine Kusine.
> No, that's not a cousin (female).

Sind hier Vettern?
> Are there any male cousins?

Nein, hier sind keine Vettern.
> No, there are no male cousins.
> No, there aren't any male cousins.

2. THE NOMINATIVE CASE

The nominative case is used for the subject of a sentence, i.e., the agent of the verb. You can always find the subject of a sentence by asking *wer* (who?) or *was* (what?).

Der Mann wohnt in Berlin.
> The man lives in Berlin.

Wer wohnt in Berlin?
> Who lives in Berlin?

Die Frau ist Amerikanerin.
The woman is American.

Was ist die Frau?
What is the woman?

The nominative is also used for the predicate nominative. The predicate nominative refers back to the subject:

Der Mann ist ein Amerikaner.
The man is an American.

The predicate nominative is used after the verbs *sein, bleiben* (to remain, to stay), *heißen* (to be called), and *werden* (to become).

Er heißt Bob.
He is called Bob.

The nominative articles are:

DEFINITE	INDEFINITE
der Mann *die* Frau *das* Kind	*ein* Mann *eine* Frau *ein* Kind

3. THE ACCUSATIVE CASE

The accusative is used for the direct object of a sentence, that is, for the person or thing that receives the action of the verb. You can always find the accusative object by asking *wen* (whom?) or *was* (what?).

Die Frau kennt den Mann.
The woman knows the man.

Wen kennt die Frau?
Whom does the woman know?

Der Mann kennt das Haus.
The man knows the house.

Was kennt der Mann?
What does the man know?

The accusative articles are:

DEFINITE

> *den* Mann
> *die* Frau
> *das* Kind

INDEFINITE

> *einen* Mann
> *eine* Frau
> *ein* Kind

Only the masculine articles change:

Ich kenne den Mann.
Ich kenne einen Mann.
Ich kenne keinen Mann.

In German, a direct object may begin a sentence if you want to stress it:

Einen Wagen hat er nicht.
He doesn't have a car. (A car he doesn't have.)

4. WER? WEN? WAS?

The nominative of the question word "who" is *wer.* The accusative form is *wen* (whom). Use *wen* if the direct object is a person. Use *was* (what) if the direct object is a thing.

Die Frau kennt den Mann.
The woman knows the man.

Wen kennt die Frau?
Whom does the woman know?

Den Mann kennt sie.
She knows the man.

Der Mann hat einen Wagen.
   The man has a car.

Was hat der Mann?
   What does the man have?

Einen Wagen hat der Mann.
   The man has a car.

5. POSSESSIVE ADJECTIVES

Possessive adjectives are used to indicate possession and relationship.
Each personal pronoun has a corresponding possessive adjective.

SINGULAR		PLURAL	
my	*ich → mein*	our	*wir → unser*
your	*du → dein*	your	*ihr → euer*
his	*er → sein*	their	*sie → ihr*
her	*sie → ihr*	your	*Sie → Ihr*
its	*es → sein*		

Ist das dein Bruder?
   Is this your brother?

Ich kenne deinen Bruder nicht.
   I don't know your brother.

Meine Tante und ihr Mann wohnen in Österreich.
   My aunt and her husband live in Austria.

Kennst du meine Tante und ihren Mann?
   Do you know my aunt and her husband?

   Note: Like the formal pronoun *Sie*, the possessive adjective *Ihr* is
   capitalized.

Frau Meier, ist das Ihre Tochter?
   Mrs. Meier, is this your daughter?

The possessive adjectives take the same endings as the indefinite article and *kein*. *Ein, kein,* and the possessive adjectives are called "*ein*-words." The *ein*-words change in the accusative if the direct object is a masculine noun.

NOMINATIVE

Das ist ein Mann.
> That's a man.

Das ist kein Mann.
> That's not a man.

Das ist mein Mann.
> That's my husband.

ACCUSATIVE

Ich seine einen Mann.
> I see a man.

Ich seine keinen Mann.
> I don't see a man.

Ich seine meinen Mann.
> I see my husband.

VOKABELN (VOCABULARY)

die Familie	family
der Großvater, ̈	grandfather
die Großmutter, ̈	grandmother
die Eltern, *pl.*	parents
der Vater, ̈	father
die Mutter, ̈	mother
der Sohn, ̈*e*	son
die Tochter, ̈	daughter
der Bruder, ̈	brother
die Schwester, *-n*	sister
der Neffe, *-n*	nephew
die Nichte, *-n*	niece
der Vetter, *-n*	cousin (male)
die Kusine, *-n*	cousin (female)
der Onkel, -	uncle
die Tante, *-n*	aunt
der Schwager, ̈	brother-in-law
die Schwägerin, *-nen*	sister-in-law
der Enkel, -	grandson
die Enkelin, *-nen*	granddaughter
der Verwandte, *-n*	relative (male)

die Verwandte, -n	relative (female)
das Album, -s	album
das Photo, -s	photo
die Brille, -n	eyeglasses
der Wagen, -	car
zu Besuch kommen	to come for a visit
zeigen	to show
kennen	to know
gucken	to look
Guck mal!	Look!
links	left
rechts	right
da	there, here
eigentlich	actually
noch nicht	not yet
du siehst	you see

ÜBUNGEN (EXERCISES)

A. *Beantworten Sie die Fragen zum Dialog.* (Answer the questions about the dialogue.)

1. *Was zeigt Sabine Doris?*
2. *Wen kennt Doris?*
3. *Wie heißt der Bruder?*
4. *Wo wohnen die Tante und ihr Mann?*

B. *Suchen Sie die richtige deutsche Übersetzung.* (Choose the correct German translation.)

1. He has no car.
2. left
3. Look!
4. right
5. Whom do you know?
6. When does she come for a visit?

a. *Wen kennen Sie?*
b. *rechts*
c. *Wann kommt sie zu Besuch?*
d. *Guck mal!*
e. *links*
f. *Er hat keinen Wagen.*

C. *Setzen Sie das fehlende Wort ein. Benutzen Sie dabei den Tip in Klammern.* (Supply the missing word. Use the hint in parentheses.)

BEISPIEL: _____ *Schwester wohnt in Kiel. (his)*
     Seine Schwester wohnt in Kiel.

1. *Sabine hat _____ Bruder. (a)*
2. *Haben Sie _____ Wagen? (no)*
3. *_____ Vater ist sechzig Jahre alt. (my)*
4. *Kennen Sie _____ Mann? (the)*
5. *Hat sie auch _____ Schwester? (a)*
6. *Das sind _____ Eltern. (my)*

D. *Übersetzen Sie.* (Translate.)

1. Our father is here.
2. I don't know your (pol.) mother.
3. He has no car.
4. His friend lives in Austria.

KULTURNOTIZ (CULTURAL NOTE)

In Germany, as in the United States, family photographs are treasured possessions, shown to relatives and friends with pride.

Film and film processing are available in photographic equipment stores and most drugstores *(Drogerien).* Newsstands *(Kiosks)* may also carry film. In smaller towns and villages the local professional photographer usually also sells and processes film. The prices for cameras and especially for film processing are considerably higher than in America.

LÖSUNGEN (ANSWERS)

A. 1. *Sabine zeigt Doris ein Familienphoto.* 2. *Doris kennt den Vater und Max.* 3. *Er heißt Max.* 4. *Sie wohnen in Österreich.*
B. 1.—f 2.—e 3.—d 4.—b 5.—a 6.—c
C. 1. *einen* 2. *keinen* 3. *Mein* 4. *den* 5. *eine* 6. *meine*
D. 1. *Unser Vater ist hier.* 2. *Ich kenne Ihre Mutter nicht.* 3. *Er hat keinen Wagen.* 4. *Sein Freund wohnt in Österreich.*

ERSTE WIEDERHOLUNGSAUFGABE
(FIRST REVIEW QUIZ)

A. *Übersetzen Sie.*

    1. What is your name? (informal)
    2. What is your name? (polite)
    3. Where do you live? (polite)
    4. Where do you live? (informal)
    5. How are you? (polite)
    6. How are you? (informal)
    7. He is working.
    8. We are flying to Germany.

B. *Ergänzen Sie die fehlenden Formen von "haben."* (Fill in the missing forms of *haben.)*

BEISPIEL: *Mein Vater _____ zwei Kinder.*
        Mein Vater hat zwei Kinder.

    1. *Das Telefon _____ zehn Zahlen.*
    2. *_____ du ein Telefon?*
    3. *Ja, ich _____ zwei Telefone.*
    4. *Ihr _____ viel Regen, nicht?*

C. *Ergänzen Sie die fehlenden Formen von "sein" im Präsens.* (Fill in the missing forms of sein in the present tense.)

BEISPIEL: *Horst _____ aus Freiburg.*
        Horst ist aus Freiburg.

    1. *_____ Sie Sekretärin?*
    2. *Nein, ich _____ Direktorin.*
    3. *Wir _____ müde.*
    4. *_____ ihr auch müde?*
    5. *Das Wetter _____ schön.*

D. *Ergänzen Sie die Endungen.* (Fill in the endings.)

BEISPIEL: Ich arbeit___ bei Bosch.
Ich arbeite bei Bosch.

1. *Er telefonier___.*
2. *Sie (she) antwort___.*
3. *Peter und Erika komm___ aus München.*

E. *Schreiben Sie den Satz mit dem Subjekt im Plural. Nehmen Sie alle notwendigen Änderungen vor.* (Write the sentence with the subject in the plural. Make all necessary changes.)

BEISPIEL: Die Direktorin telefoniert.
Die Direktorinnen telefonieren.

1. *Der Mann arbeitet viel.*
2. *Die Frau fliegt nach Österreich.*
3. *Der Freund geht jetzt.*

F. *Setzen Sie das fehlende Wort ein.* (Fill in the missing word.)

BEISPIEL: Ich kenne _____ Mann nicht. (the)
Ich kenne den Mann nicht.

1. *Sehen Sie _____ Bruder Michael? (my)*
2. *Meine Sekretärin zeigt _____ Photo. (a)*
3. *Kennen wir _____ Schwester? (her)*
4. *Habt ihr _____ Verwandten in Österreich? (no)*
5. *Haben Schneiders _____ Wagen oder nicht? (a)*

LÖSUNGEN (ANSWERS)

A. 1. *Wie heißt du?* 2. *Wie heißen Sie?* 3. *Wo wohnen Sie?* 4. *Wo wohnst du?* 5. *Wie geht es Ihnen?* 6. *Wie geht's?* 7. *Er arbeitet.* 8. *Wir fliegen nach Deutschland.*

B. 1. *hat* 2. *Hast* 3. *habe* 4. *habt*

C. 1. *Sind* 2. *bin* 3. *sind* 4. *Seid* 5. *ist*

D. 1. *telefoniert* 2. *antwortet* 3. *kommen*

E. 1. *Die Männer arbeiten viel.* 2. *Die Frauen fliegen nach Österreich.* 3. *Die Freunde gehen jetzt.*

F. 1. *meinen* 2. *ein* 3. *ihre* 4. *keine* 5. *einen*

LEKTION 6

IM RESTAURANT.   In a Restaurant.

A. DIALOG

Abendessen im Restaurant.

BEDIENUNG: Guten Tag, mein Herr. Was nehmen Sie?

GAST: Ich nehme ein Wiener Schnitzel mit Reis und Bohnen.

BEDIENUNG: Tut mir leid, aber es gibt kein Wiener Schnitzel mehr.
Essen Sie gern Huhn?

GAST: Nein, Huhn esse ich nicht gern. Was gibt es denn noch?

BEDIENUNG: Wir haben auch ausgezeichneten Fisch.

GAST: Ist er frisch?

BEDIENUNG: Selbstverständlich. Unser Fisch ist immer frisch.

GAST: Gut, dann geben Sie mir Fisch mit Reis, Bohnen und Salat.

BEDIENUNG: Was trinken Sie? Wir haben Wein, Bier und Mineralwasser.

GAST: Ich nehme ein Bier.

Später.

BEDIENUNG: Essen Sie auch Nachtisch? Wir haben Schokoladencreme,
Torte und Eis.

GAST: Nein, Nachtisch esse ich heute nicht. Aber ich nehme eine Tasse
Kaffee.

BEDIENUNG: Sonst noch etwas?

GAST: Nein, danke. Ich bin in Eile. Die Rechnung bitte!

Dinner in a Restaurant.

SERVER: Hello, sir. What will you have?

GUEST: I'll have a Wiener Schnitzel with rice and green beans.

SERVER: I'm sorry, but we don't have any more Wiener Schnitzel. Do you like chicken?

GUEST: No, I don't like chicken very much. What else is there?

SERVER: We also have excellent fish.

GUEST: Is it fresh?

SERVER: Of course. Our fish is always fresh.

GUEST: All right, then give me fish with rice, beans, and salad.

SERVER: What would you like to drink? We have wine, beer, and mineral water.

GUEST: I'll have a beer.

Later.

SERVER: Would you also like dessert? We have chocolate mousse, tart, and ice cream.

GUEST: No, I won't have dessert today. But I'll have a cup of coffee.

SERVER: Anything else?

GUEST: No, thanks. I'm in a hurry. The bill, please.

B. AUSSPRACHE

AND MORE CONSONANTS

d	at the end of a syllable or a word like the t in bat	Bad, Rad
	elsewhere like the d in does	dunkel, dort, da
t	like the t in tolerate	Tag, nicht, runter
g	at the end of a word like the ck in pick	weg
	after i, softer	richtig, billig
	elsewhere like the g in go	gehen, grau
k	like the k in key	Karte, kalt, Elke

C. GRAMMATIK UND GEBRAUCH

1. *GERN**

In German, the most common way to express that you like or enjoy doing something is to use *gern* + the verb denoting the action.

Huhn esse ich nicht gern.
   I don't like (to eat) chicken.

Er arbeitet gern.
   He likes to work.

2. VERBS WITH STEM VOWEL CHANGE

Some verb conjugations involve a change of the verb's stem vowel in the second and third person singular. All other forms are regular. This change may be from *e* to *i*, or from *e* to *ie*.

a. *e* TO *i*

Geben (to give), *essen* (to eat), and *sprechen* (to speak) are some of the most important verbs that change their stem vowel from *e* to *i*.

ich esse	I eat	*wir essen*	we eat
du isst	you eat	*ihr esst*	you eat
sie isst	she eats	*sie essen*	they eat
		Sie essen	you eat

The verb *nehmen* (to take) has a stem vowel change from *e* to *i* and a change of consonants in the singular. The plural forms are regular.

---

* Please refer to lesson 39 for more information on *gern*.

ich nehme	I take	*wir nehmen*	we take
du nimmst	you take	*ihr nehmt*	you take
er nimmt	he takes	*sie nehmen*	they take
		Sie nehmen	you take

b. *e* TO *ie*

Some verbs change the stem vowel *e* to *ie*. Frequently used verbs of this type are *sehen* (to see) and *lesen* (to read).

ich sehe	I see	*wir sehen*	we see
du siehst	you see	*ihr seht*	you see
es sieht	it sees	*sie sehen*	they see
		Sie sehen	you see

3. *ES GIBT*

The basic meaning of the verb *geben* is "to give." Yet, the commonly used phrase *es gibt* means "there is, there are."

Es gibt kein Wiener Schnitzel mehr.
There is no more Wiener Schnitzel.

Es gibt heute Bohnen.
We have beans today.

Es gibt viele Restaurants in Berlin.
There are many restaurants in Berlin.

4. NEGATION WITH *NICHT*

In lesson 5 you learned that *kein* (no) is used to negate a noun that has no article, or is preceded by the indefinite article. *Nicht* (not) is used to negate a noun, when this noun is preceded by a definite article or a possessive adjective.

Das ist der Mann.
    That's the man.

Das ist nicht der Mann.
    That's not the man.

Das ist meine Frau.
    That's my wife.

Das ist nicht meine Frau.
    That's not my wife.

Nicht may negate both a part of a sentence (verb, adjective, noun) or the whole sentence.

The position of *nicht* within the sentence depends on various elements. *Nicht* always follows the verb. *Nicht* usually precedes the part of the sentence that is to be negated.

Heute ist es nicht kalt.
    It's not cold today.

When you negate a whole sentence, *nicht* is in the last position.

Huhn esse ich nicht.
    I won't have chicken.

Nicht follows general expressions of time.

Nachtisch esse ich heute nicht.
    I won't have dessert today.

5. FLAVORING PARTICLES

Flavoring particles are used in colloquial German to show a speaker's attitude about an utterance. Depending on the choice of particle and the tone of voice, a speaker can express surprise, disagreement, or impatience. Flavoring particles cannot be translated easily. Some of the flavoring particles are *aber, denn, ja, doch.*

Er hat ja nie Zeit.
   He never has time. (conclusion)

Was gibt es denn noch?
   What else is there? (impatience)

Heute ist es doch nicht kalt.
   Today it's not cold. (disagreement)

Aber was hast du denn?
   Well, what's the matter with you? (surprise)

VOKABELN

das Restaurant, *-s*	restaurant
die Speisekarte, *-n*	menu
die Suppe, *-n*	soup
das Fleisch	meat
das Schnitzel, *-*	cutlet
das Huhn, *¨er*	chicken
das Rindfleisch	beef
das Kalbfleisch	veal
das Schweinefleisch	pork
das Gemüse, *-*	vegetables
die Kartoffel, *-n*	potato
die Bohne, *-n*	bean
die Erbse, *-n*	pea
die Möhre, *-n*	carrot
der Salat, *-e*	salad
der Nachtisch, *-e*	dessert
die Torte, *-n*	tart, cake
das Eis	ice cream
das Obst, *-*	fruit
der Apfel, *¨*	apple
die Apfelsine, *-n*	orange
das Getränk, *-e*	drink
das Bier, *-e*	beer
der Wein, *-e*	wine
das Wasser	water

eine Tasse Kaffee	a cup of coffee
das Abendessen	dinner
Sonst noch etwas?	Anything else?
Die Rechnung, bitte!	The check, please.
Ich bin in Eile.	I'm in a hurry.
nehmen *(nimmt)*	to take, to have (food)
essen *(isst)*	to eat
trinken	to drink
mehr	more
frisch	fresh
selbstverständlich	of course
sehen *(sieht)*	to see
geben *(gibt)*	to give
ausgezeichnet	excellent
später	later
die Zeit, *-en*	time

ÜBUNGEN

A. *Beantworten Sie die Fragen zum Dialog.*

1. *Was isst der Gast?*
2. *Was trinkt der Gast?*
3. *Ist der Fisch frisch?*
4. *Isst der Gast Nachtisch?*

B. *Suchen Sie die richtige deutsche Übersetzung.*

1. potatoes	a. *selbstverständlich*
2. menu	b. *Sonst noch etwas?*
3. of course	c. *die Speisekarte*
4. Anything else?	d. *Die Rechnung, bitte!*
5. dessert	e. *der Nachtisch*
6. The check please.	f. *das Fleisch*
7. meat	g. *das Obst*
8. fruit	h. *Kartoffeln*

C. *Verneinen Sie diese Sätze mit "nicht."* (Negate these sentences with *nicht.*)

BEISPIEL: Ich wohne in Hamburg.
   Ich wohne nicht in Hamburg.

   1. *Das Bier ist gut.*
   2. *Wir gehen jetzt.*
   3. *Das ist Frau Häberle.*

D. *Setzen Sie die Formen von "nehmen" ein.* (Fill in the forms of *nehmen.*)

BEISPIEL: _____ ihr noch Kaffee?
   Nehmt ihr noch Kaffee?

   1. *Ich _____ Gemüse.*
   2. *_____ du auch Gemüse?*
   3. *Sie (she) _____ Fleisch.*
   4. *Wir _____ Fisch.*

E. *Übersetzen Sie.*

   1. There is a cup of coffee.
   2. I like (to eat) ice cream.
   3. She likes (to eat) beans.

F. *Setzen Sie die Formen von "essen" ein.* (Fill in the forms of *essen.)*

   1. *Wir _____ nicht gern Fleisch.*
   2. *Sie (she) _____ im Restaurant.*
   3. *Ich _____ gern Salat.*
   4. *Herr und Frau Schmidt _____ nicht viel.*
   5. *Er wohnt und _____ im Hotel.*

G. *Antworten Sie.* (Answer.)

   1. *Wo gibt es viele Restaurants? (in Frankfurt)*
   2. *Was gibt es zu essen? (Huhn)*
   3. *Gibt es hier ein Hotel? (Ja, _____)*
   4. *Was gibt es nicht im Restaurant? (Rindfleisch)*
   5. *Gibt es keinen Kaffee mehr? (Nein, _____)*

KULTURNOTIZ

In Germany all restaurants have to post their menus, including the price of each dish, on or next to the entrance. Since the tip *(das Trinkgeld)* is included in the bill, you may tip the waiter, but you don't have to. But note that in better restaurants an additional tip of 10% is customary and expected.

Breakfast in Germany, Austria, and Switzerland usually consists of breakfast rolls *(Brötchen),* jam or cold cuts, and sometimes hard-boiled eggs. Often people eat cereal or Müsli. The main meal *(das Mittagessen)* is served between noon and 2 P.M. Traditionally, dinner *(das Abendessen)* is rather light and consists of bread, cold cuts, and cheese. However, among the younger generation and professionals it has become more and more common to eat the main meal in the evening.

Fast-food restaurants like snack bars *(Schnellimbisse)* or pizza shops *(Pizzerias)* are usually found near or in railroad stations and airports.

LÖSUNGEN

A. 1. *Er ißt Fisch mit Reis, Bohnen und Salat. 2. Er trinkt Bier und eine Tasse Kaffee. 3. Ja, der Fisch ist frisch. 4. Nein, er isst keinen Nachtisch.*

B. 1.—h   2.—c   3.—a   4.—b   5.—e   6.—d   7.—f   8.—g

C. 1. *Das Bier ist nicht gut. 2. Wir gehen jetzt nicht. 3. Das ist nicht Frau Häberle.*

D. 1. *nehme*   2. *Nimmst*   3. *nimmt*   4. *nehmen*

E. 1. *Es gibt eine Tasse Kaffee. 2. Ich esse gern Eis. 3. Sie isst gern Bohnen.*

F. 1. *essen*   2. *isst*   3. *esse*   4. *essen*   5. *isst*

G. 1. *In Frankfurt gibt es viele Restaurants. 2. Es gibt Huhn. 3. Ja, es gibt hier ein Hotel. 4. Es gibt kein Rindfleisch im Restaurant. 5. Nein, es gibt keinen Kaffee mehr.*

LEKTION 7

LEBENSMITTELEINKAUF.   Grocery Shopping.

A. DIALOG

Eine Einkaufsliste.

ELKE: Mein Freund besucht uns morgen. Unser Kühlschrank ist leer.

ANJA: Was kaufen wir für ihn? Ich mache eine Einkaufsliste für uns.

ELKE: Danke. Zum Frühstück brauchen wir sechs Brötchen, Erdbeermarmelade und Butter. Zum Mittagessen kochen wir Spargel mit Schinken. Zwei Kilo Kartoffeln brauchen wir auch.

ANJA: Und ich backe einen Kuchen für deinen Freund.

ELKE: Ohne dich wäre* ich verloren! Also, dann kaufen wir zwei Pfund Mehl, Zucker und sechs Eier.

ANJA: Und zum Abendessen?

ELKE: Wir essen Butterbrote.

ANJA: Haben wir noch Aufschnitt?

ELKE: Fast gar nichts. Wie wär's mit 100 Gramm Leberwurst und 200 Gramm Käse?

ANJA: Gut. Was fehlt noch?

ELKE: Zwei Liter Milch und fünf Flaschen Bier.

ANJA: Wo kaufen wir alles?

ELKE: Im Supermarkt um die Ecke.

A Shopping List.

ELKE: My friend is visiting us tomorrow. Our refrigerator is empty.

* *Wäre* is the subjunctive of *sein* and will be dealt with at length in lessons 35 and 36. For now treat this as part of a phrase.

ANJA: What shall we buy for him? I'll prepare a shopping list for us.

ELKE: Thanks. For breakfast we'll need six rolls, strawberry jelly, and butter. For lunch we'll cook asparagus with ham. We'll also need two kilos of potatoes.

ANJA: And I'll bake a cake for your friend.

ELKE: Without you I'd be lost! Well, then, we'll buy two pounds of flour, sugar, and six eggs.

ANJA: And for dinner?

ELKE: We'll eat sandwiches.

ANJA: Do we have cold cuts?

ELKE: Almost nothing. How about 100 grams of liverwurst and 200 grams of cheese?

ANJA: Good. What else do we need?

ELKE: Two liters of milk and five bottles of beer.

ANJA: Where will we buy everything?

ELKE: At the supermarket around the corner.

B. AUSSPRACHE

AND EVEN MORE CONSONANTS

h	after a vowel silent as in <u>h</u>onor	se<u>h</u>en, ge<u>h</u>en
	elsewhere like the <u>h</u> in <u>h</u>old	<u>H</u>aus, <u>h</u>alten
j	like the y in yes	<u>j</u>a, <u>J</u>ena
k	like the <u>c</u> in ne<u>c</u>tar	<u>K</u>laus, Ne<u>k</u>tar
qu	like <u>k</u> + <u>v</u>	<u>Qu</u>elle, <u>Q</u>ual
l	like the <u>l</u> in <u>l</u>augh	<u>l</u>achen, <u>l</u>eben, <u>L</u>icht

C. GRAMMATIK UND GEBRAUCH

1. THE ACCUSATIVE OF PERSONAL PRONOUNS

Pronouns used as direct objects are in the accusative case. Five German pronouns have accusative forms that differ from the nominative.

NOMINATIVE SINGULAR

I	*ich*
you (fam.)	*du*
he	*er*
she	*sie*
it	*es*

ACCUSATIVE SINGULAR

me	*mich*
you (fam.)	*dich*
him	*ihn*
her	*sie*
it	*es*

NOMINATIVE PLURAL

we	*wir*
you (fam.)	*ihr*
they	*sie*
you (pol.)	*Sie*

ACCUSATIVE PLURAL

us	*uns*
you (fam.)	*euch*
them	*sie*
you (pol.)	*Sie*

Mein Freund besucht uns.
My friend is visiting us.

Wir kennen ihn.
We know him.

C. ACCUSATIVE PREPOSITIONS

The following prepositions require the accusative:

durch	through
für	for
gegen	against
ohne	without
um	around

Ich backe einen Kuchen für deinen Freund.
   I am baking a cake for your friend.

Ohne dich wäre ich verloren.
   I'd be lost without you.

The prepositions *durch, für,* and *um* are often contracted with the definite article *das* to form *durchs, fürs, ums.*

Der Ober kommt durchs (durch das) Restaurant.
   The waiter comes through the restaurant.

Ich brauche Zucker fürs (für das) Obst.
   I need sugar for the fruit.

Er geht ums (um das) Haus.
   He is going around the house.

3. WEIGHTS AND MEASUREMENTS

In Germany, as in other European countries, the metric system is used for weights. The basic unit of weight is the gram *(das Gramm)*. One thousand grams are a kilo *(das Kilo)*. The term *Pfund* (pound) is sometimes still used for half a kilo or 500 grams, but it hasn't been in official use for several decades now. An American pound, on the other hand, equals only 454 grams. The measurement for liquids is the liter *(der Liter)*. One liter equals 2.11 pints.

Wir brauchen zwei Liter Milch.
   We need two liters of milk.

Wir kaufen zwei Pfund Mehl.
   We'll buy two pounds of flour.

Note: The nouns expressing measurements *(der Liter, das Pfund)* are mostly used in the singular.

VOKABELN

die Lebensmittel (pl.)	groceries
die Erdbeermarmelade, -n	strawberry jelly
das Brot, -e	bread
das Brötchen, -	roll
die Butter	butter
der Spargel	asparagus
der Kuchen, -	cake
das Mehl	flour
der Zucker	sugar
das Ei, -er	egg
das Butterbrot, -e	sandwich
der Aufschnitt	cold cuts
die Wurst, ⁻e	sausage
die Leberwurst	liverwurst
der Käse	cheese
der Kühlschrank, ⁻e	refrigerator
die Einkaufsliste, -n	shopping list
das Frühstück	breakfast
das Mittagessen	lunch (main meal)
das Abendessen	supper, dinner
zum Frühstück/Mittagessen/ Abendessen	for breakfast/dinner/supper
das Kilo, -s	kilo
das Pfund, -e	pound
der Liter, -	liter
die Flasche, -n	bottle
der Supermarkt, ⁻e	supermarket
brauchen	to need
fehlen	to be missing
Was fehlt?	What do we need?
kaufen	to buy
kochen	to cook
backen	to bake
die Ecke, -n	corner
leer	empty
nichts	nothing

Wie wär's mit . . .?	How about . . .?
alles	everything
verloren	lost
machen	to make, to prepare

ÜBUNGEN

A. *Beantworten Sie die Fragen zum Dialog.*

1. *Wer besucht Elke?*
2. *Was brauchen Elke und Anja zum Frühstück?*
3. *Backt Anja einen Kuchen?*
4. *Wo ist der Supermarkt?*

B. *Suchen Sie die richtige deutsche Übersetzung.*

1. to cook	a. *zum Abendessen*
2. How about . . .?	b. *das Butterbrot*
3. cold cuts	c. *kaufen*
4. a pound of ham	d. *Wie wär's mit . . .?*
5. for supper	e. *kochen*
6. to buy	f. *um die Ecke*
7. the sandwich	g. *eine Flasche Bier*
8. around the corner	h. *der Aufschnitt*
9. a bottle of beer	i. *ein Pfund Schinken*

C. *Setzen Sie das fehlende Personalpronomen in der richtigen Form ein.*
(Supply the missing personal pronoun in its correct form.)

BEISPIEL: Kennst du _____? (him)
      Kennst du ihn?

1. *Ich sehe _____. (you, fam. sing.)*
2. *Siehst du _____?* (me)
3. *Er besucht _____.* (her)
4. *Sie besucht _____.* (him)
5. *Wer besucht _____?* (us)
6. *Wen kennen _____?* (you, pol.)
7. *Ich kenne _____.* (them)

D. *Übersetzen Sie.*

1. What do you (fam. sing.) have against me?
2. I have nothing against you (fam. sing.).
3. He bakes rolls for his father.
4. She cooks without sugar.

E. *Ergänzen Sie die richtige Präposition.* (Fill in the correct preposition.)

1. *Ich trinke Kaffee _____ Zucker.* (without)
2. *Der Kuchen ist _____ dich.* (for)
3. *Er geht _____ das Haus.* (through)
4. *Ich gehe _____ das Auto.* (around)

KULTURNOTIZ

Store hours in German-speaking countries are regulated by law. They have been, however, extended in recent years, and exceptions are much easier to obtain than they used to be. In larger cities, many stores and supermarkets are open from eight in the morning until eight at night, some until ten. Bakeries often open at 6:00 A.M. Stores are closed on Sundays and on major holidays. A few stores may have obtained a license to open other times as well. Most bakeries, even in small towns, are also open on Sundays, at least until noon, so you'll always be able to buy fresh rolls for Sunday breakfast.

LÖSUNGEN

A. 1. *Ein Freund besucht Elke.* 2. *Sie brauchen sechs Brötchen, Erdbeermarmelade und Butter.* 3. *Ja, Anja bäckt einen Kuchen.* 4. *Der Supermarkt ist um die Ecke.*
B. 1.—e 2.—d 3.—h 4.—i 5.—a 6.—c 7.—b 8.—f
   9.—g
C. 1. *dich* 2. *mich* 3. *sie* 4. *ihn* 5. *uns* 6. *Sie* 7. *sie*
D. 1. *Was hast du gegen mich?* 2. *Ich habe nichts gegen dich.* 3. *Er backt Brötchen für seinen Vater.* 4. *Sie kocht ohne Zucker.*
E. 1. *ohne* 2. *für* 3. *durch* 4. *um*

LEKTION 8

IM HOTEL.   In a Hotel.

A. DIALOG

Ankunft im Hotel.

EMPFANGSCHEFIN: Guten Abend, mein Herr. Sie wünschen?

GAST: Ich brauche ein Einzelzimmer für eine Nacht.

EMPFANGSCHEFIN: Haben Sie eine Reservierung?

GAST: Leider nicht.

EMPFANGSCHEFIN: Nur ein Doppelzimmer mit Bad ist noch frei.

GAST: Was kostet das?

EMPFANGSCHEFIN: Das macht 62 Euro, inklusive Frühstück.

GAST: Gut, das nehme ich.

EMPFANGSCHEFIN: Sie haben Zimmer Nummer 214. Hier ist Ihr Schlüssel. Bitte füllen Sie das Anmeldeformular aus.

GAST: Vielen Dank. Ich habe eine Menge Gepäck.

EMPFANGSCHEFIN: Ich rufe den Hotelpagen. Nehmen Sie für Ihr Zimmer die Treppe hier links. Der Aufzug fährt leider nicht.

GAST: Wie lange ist das Restaurant geöffnet?

EMPFANGSCHEFIN: Bis Mitternacht.

GAST: Ausgezeichnet. Wecken Sie mich bitte um Viertel vor sieben.

EMPFANGSCHEFIN: Selbstverständlich. Ich wünsche einen angenehmen Aufenthalt.

Arrival at a Hotel.

FEMALE DESK CLERK: Good evening, sir. How can I help you?

GUEST: I need a single room for one night.

FEMALE DESK CLERK: Do you have a reservation?

GUEST: Unfortunately no.

FEMALE DESK CLERK: Only a double room with bath is still available.

GUEST: How much is it?

FEMALE DESK CLERK: That'll be 62 euros, breakfast included.

GUEST: Okay, I'll take it.

FEMALE DESK CLERK: You have room number 214. Here is your key. Please fill out the registration form.

GUEST: Thank you very much. I have a lot of luggage.

FEMALE DESK CLERK: I'll call the bellhop. Take the stairs to the left for your room. Unfortunately, the elevator doesn't work.

GUEST: How long does your restaurant stay open?

FEMALE DESK CLERK: Until midnight.

GUEST: Excellent. Please wake me at a quarter to seven.

FEMALE DESK CLERK: Of course. Have a pleasant stay.

B. AUSSPRACHE

STILL MORE CONSONANTS

m	like the m in money	Mutter, mein, Mann
n	like the n in not	Name, nie, Norbert
r	always rolled when stressed, approximately like the r in rid, either trilled with tongue tip or gargled	Radio, rot, richtig
	when unstressed like the r in western	gestern
s	before or between vowels like the z in zoo	sind
	elsewhere like the s in see	was

C. GRAMMATIK UND GEBRAUCH

1. MORE VERBS WITH VOWEL CHANGE

a. a TO ä

Some verbs change the stem vowel *a* to *ä*. Important verbs of this group are *fahren* (to drive) and *schlafen* (to sleep).

ich fahre	I drive		*wir fahren*	we drive
du fährst	you drive		*ihr fahrt*	you drive
er fährt	he drives		*sie fahren*	they drive
			Sie fahren	you drive

b. au TO äu

Some verbs change the stem vowel *au* to *äu*. A frequently used verb of this group is *laufen* (to run).

ich laufe	I run		*wir laufen*	we run
du läufst	you run		*ihr lauft*	you run
sie läuft	she runs		*sie laufen*	they run
			Sie laufen	you run

2. THE IMPERATIVE

Imperative forms are used for commands, instructions, suggestions, and requests. In English, there is only one form of the imperative, because there is only one word for "you." But since German has three words for "you"—*Sie, du,* and *ihr*—it needs three imperative forms. Depending on whom you address, you use one of the following three forms of *kommen*.

Sie-form: *Kommen Sie, Herr Kraft!*
du-form: *Komm(e), Jürgen!*
ihr-form: *Kommt, Jürgen und Erika!*

The *Sie*-form, or formal imperative, is used when addressing one or more persons whom you address as *Sie*. The *Sie*-imperative is identical with the *Sie*-form of the present tense. The subject *Sie* follows the verb directly. The forms for singular and plural are identical:

Gehen Sie um die Ecke, Herr Müller!
Go around the corner, Mr. Müller.

Fragen Sie bitte das Mädchen, Herr und Frau Dahl!
Please ask the girl, Mr. and Mrs. Dahl.

An exclamation mark is generally used after an imperative. In speech, the voice falls at the end of a command. To soften a command, you may add *bitte*.

b. THE *DU*-FORM

The *du*-form, or singular informal imperative, is inferred from the second person singular form minus its ending. No pronoun is used.

du fragst
you ask

Frag(e) den Mann dort!
Ask the man there.

du isst
you eat

Iss den Fisch nicht!
Don't eat the fish.

Adding an *-e* is optional for most verbs, but it must be added when the stem ends in a *-t, -d,* or *-ig.*

Sag(e) kein Wort!
Don't say a word.

Antworte nicht!
Don't answer.

Entschuldige!
Excuse me.

The ending *-e* is never added to verb stems with a vowel change from *e* to *i* or *e* to *ie*.

Sprich lauter!
Speak louder.

Nimm ein Pfund Kaffee!
Take a pound of coffee.

Verbs with a stem-vowel change from *a* to *ä* and *au* to *äu* have no stem-vowel changes in the *du*-form.

Fahr ohne die Kinder!
Drive without the children.

Lauf nicht zu schnell!
Don't run too fast.

C. THE *IHR*-FORM

The *ihr*-form, or plural informal imperative, is identical to the second person plural present tense. As in English, no prounoun is used.

Hilde und Hans, seht den Schnee!
Hilde and Hans, look at the snow.

Lauft nicht gegen den Wind, Kinder!
Don't walk against the wind, children.

Wartet nicht zu lange!
Don't wait too long.

d. THE *WIR*-FORM

The *wir*-form, or first person plural imperative ("Let's . . ."), is used when the speaker is included. It is identical to the present tense first person plural form of the verb. The subject *wir* follows the verb.

Nehmen wir den Bus!
Let's take the bus.

Fahren wir ohne Gepäck!
Let's travel without luggage.

e. THE IMPERATIVE OF *SEIN*

The imperative forms of *sein* (to be) are irregular.

Seien Sie bitte pünktlich!
Please be punctual.

Sei ruhig, Erik!
Be calm, Erik.

Seid bitte pünktlich, Beate und Erika!
Please be punctual, Beate and Erika.

Seien wir zufrieden!
Let's be content.

3. TELLING TIME

In order to find out the time, you ask:

Wie viel Uhr ist es?
What time is it?

Wie spät ist es?
What time is it? (How late is it?)

Um wie viel Uhr...?
At what time . . .?

There are two ways to answer these questions: conventional time and official time.

a. CONVENTIONAL TIME

Conventional time is used in everyday situations:

Es ist 1.00 Uhr. Es ist eins. Es ist ein Uhr.
It's one o'clock.

Es ist 1.10 Uhr. Es ist zehn *(Minuten)* nach eins.
It's ten after one.

Es ist 1.15 Uhr. Es ist Viertel nach eins.
It's a quarter after one.

Es ist 1.20 Uhr. Es ist zwanzig *(Minuten)* nach eins.
It's twenty after one.

Es ist 1.30 Uhr. Es ist halb zwei.
It's one-thirty.

Es ist 1.40 Uhr. Es ist zwanzig *(Minuten)* vor zwei.
It's twenty to two.

Es ist 1.45 Uhr. Es ist Viertel vor zwei.
It's a quarter of two.

Note: The *-s* of *eins* is dropped before the word *Uhr: Es ist ein Uhr.*

Also note the use of *nach* (after, past), *vor* (to), and *um* (at), relating to time. "Half past" is expressed by *halb* and the following hour.

Es ist halb vier.
It's half past three. It's three-thirty.

Since the A.M. and P.M. notations are not used in German, adverbs of time are often added for clarification:

Es ist sechs Uhr morgens.
It's 6 A.M.

Es ist zehn Uhr abends.
It's 10 P.M.

Es ist zwölf Uhr mittags.
It's 12 noon.

Es ist zwölf Uhr nachts.
It's 12 midnight.

b. OFFICIAL TIME

Official time is based on the 24-hour system. The hours 0.00–12.00 *(null Uhr bis zwölf Uhr)* are equivalent to A.M.; 12.00–24.00 *(zwölf bis vierundzwanzig Uhr)* are equivalent to P.M. This system is used in Europe for broadcasting, transportation, business, and entertainment. Thus 2:15 P.M. would be listed as *14.15 Uhr* and announced as *vierzehn Uhr fünfzehn;* 3:35 A.M. would be listed as *3.35 Uhr* and announced as *drei Uhr fünfunddreißig.*

VOKABELN

das Hotel, *-s*	hotel
der Empfangschef, *-e*	reception clerk
der Hotelpage, *-n*	bellhop
die Reservierung, *-en*	reservation
das Anmeldeformular, *-e*	registration form
der Aufenthalt, *-e*	stay
Ich wünsche einen angenehmen Aufenthalt.	Have a pleasant stay.
das Zimmer, -	room
das Einzelzimmer, -	single room
das Doppelzimmer, -	double room
frei sein	to be available
Was kostet das?	What does it cost?
Das macht 62 Euro.	That'll be 62 euros.
inklusive Frühstück	including breakfast
das Bad, *⸚er*	bathroom
der Schlüssel, -	key
die Nummer, *-n*	number
die Zimmernummer, *-n*	room number
das Zimmermädchen, -	maid
die Treppe, *-n*	stairs
Nehmen Sie die Treppe!	Take the stairs.
der Aufzug, *⸚e*	elevator
das Gepäck	luggage
der Koffer, -	suitcase
wecken	to wake
Wecken Sie mich um . . .	Wake me at . . .
die Zeit	time
die Uhr, *-en*	clock, watch, time of the day
Wie viel Uhr ist es?	What time is it?
Wie spät ist es?	What time is it?
Wie lange bleiben Sie?	How long are you staying?
der Mittag, *-e*	noon

die Mitternacht, ¨e	midnight
die Menge, -n	a lot
rufen	to call
geöffnet	open
geschlossen	closed

ÜBUNGEN

A. *Beantworten Sie die Fragen zum Dialog.*

1. *Was braucht der Gast?*
2. *Wie viel kostet das Zimmer?*
3. *Wie lange ist das Restaurant geöffnet?*
4. *Wann weckt man den Gast?*

B. *Suchen Sie die richtige deutsche Übersetzung.*

1. after 9:00 (conventional time)   a. *um fünfzehn Uhr fünfzehn*
2. reservation   b. *das Einzelzimmer*
3. open   c. *das Gepäck*
4. key   d. *geöffnet*
5. single room   e. *die Reservierung*
6. luggage   f. *nach neun Uhr*
7. at 3:15 (official time)   g. *der Schlüssel*

C. *Setzen Sie die richtige Form der Wörter in Klammern ein.* (Insert the correct form of the words in parentheses.)

BEISPIEL: *Ich _____ nicht gern. (laufen)*
    Ich laufe nicht gern.

1. *Wir laufen, aber du _____. (fahren)*
2. *Ich sehe, ihr _____ einen BMW. (fahren)*
3. *_____ du gern? (laufen)*
4. *Frau Sommer _____ im Winter nach Mallorka. (fahren)*
5. *Ihr _____ viel zu schnell. (laufen)*

D. *Übersetzen Sie.*

1. Tell the following persons to visit the restaurant:
   a. your boss
   b. your friend Peter
   c. your friends Laura and Dieter
2. Wake me at 6:30 A.M., Mr. Schneider.
3. How long is the restaurant open?
4. What time is it?
5. He has a lot of luggage.

E. *Sagen Sie es auf Deutsch. Benutzen Sie (a) Zeit im Alltagsgebrauch, (b) offizielle Zeit.* (Say it in German. Use [a] conventional time, [b] official time.)

1. 1:00 P.M.
2. 6:15 A.M.
3. 2:30 P.M.
4. 4:50 P.M.
5. 9:45 P.M.

F. *Setzen Sie folgende Fragen in den Imperativ.* (Change the following questions to the imperative.)

BEISPIEL: *Lesen Sie das Buch nicht?*
          Bitte, lesen Sie das Buch.

1. *Fragen Sie mich nicht? Bitte...*
2. *Nehmen Sie keinen Kaffee? Bitte...*
3. *Schreiben Sie mir keinen Brief? Bitte...*
4. *Fährst du nach München? Bitte...*
5. *Essen Sie nicht? Bitte...*
6. *Antwortest du mir nicht? Bitte...*
7. *Wartest du auf mich? Bitte...*
8. *Isst du deine Suppe nicht? Bitte...*

KULTURNOTIZ

In German-speaking countries you have to show your passport *(Reisepass)* and fill out a registration form *(Anmeldeformular)* when you stay in a hotel. There are more single rooms *(Einzelzimmer)* available than in most U.S. hotels. Single rooms are relatively more expensive than double rooms *(Doppelzimmer)*. You will find most American hotel chains in German-speaking countries. As a rule, so-called Continental breakfast is included in the price of the room. It consists of coffee, tea, or hot chocolate; breakfast rolls and/or bread; butter, jam, and/or honey; and eggs. The eggs are cooked to order and served in an egg cup. Often you can also choose from an assortment of cold cuts and cheese. The *Frühstücksbrötchen* (breakfast rolls) are available in a variety of tastes and are a real treat.

LÖSUNGEN

A. 1. *Er braucht ein Einzelzimmer für eine Nacht.* 2. *Es kostet 62 Euro, inklusive Frühstück.* 3. *Es ist bis Mitternacht geöffnet.* 4. *Man weckt ihn um Viertel vor sieben.*

B. 1.—f 2.—e 3.—d 4.—g 5.—b 6.—c 7.—a

C. 1. *fährst* 2. *fahrt* 3. *Läufst* 4. *fährt* 5. *lauft*

D. 1. a. *Besuchen Sie das Restaurant!* b. *Besuch(e) das Restaurant!* c. *Besucht das Restaurant!* 2. *Wecken Sie mich um halb sieben, Herr Schneider!* 3. *Wie lange ist das Restaurant geöffnet?* 4. *Wie viel Uhr ist es?* 5. *Er hat eine Menge Gepäck.*

E. 1a. *Es ist ein Uhr.* 1b. *Es ist dreizehn Uhr.* 2a. *Es ist Viertel nach sechs.* 2b. *Es ist sechs Uhr fünfzehn.* 3a. *Es ist halb drei.* 3b. *Es ist vierzehn Uhr dreißig.* 4a. *Es ist zehn (Minuten) vor fünf.* 4b. *Es ist sechzehn Uhr fünfzig.* 5a. *Es ist Viertel vor zehn.* 5b. *Es ist einundzwanzig Uhr fünfundvierzig.*

F. 1. *Bitte fragen Sie mich!* 2. *Bitte nehmen Sie Kaffee!* 3. *Bitte schreiben Sie mir einen Brief!* 4. *Bitte fahre nach München!* 5. *Bitte essen Sie!* 6. *Bitte antworte mir!* 7. *Bitte warte auf mich!* 8. *Bitte iss deine Suppe!*

LEKTION 9

A. DIALOG

Am Bahnhof.

BEAMTER: Ja, bitte.

REISENDE: Eine Fahrkarte nach Klagenfurt bitte.

BEAMTER: Hin und zurück?

REISENDE: Einfach bitte, zweiter Klasse und ein Nichtraucherabteil.

BEAMTER: Wann möchten Sie in Klagenfurt ankommen?

REISENDE: Ich muss morgen früh gegen zehn Uhr in Klagenfurt sein.

BEAMTER: Dann nehmen Sie am besten den Inter-City. Er fährt heute Abend um 19:30 Uhr von Bahnsteig zwölf ab und kommt morgen um 9:45 Uhr in Klagenfurt an.

REISENDE: Muss ich umsteigen?

BEAMTER: Nein, der Zug hat einen Kurswagen nach Klagenfurt.

REISENDE: Kann ich einen Platz im Liegewagen reservieren?

BEAMTER: Einen Augenblick, bitte. Nein, alle Plätze sind schon belegt. Möchten Sie ein Bett im Schlafwagen?

REISENDE: Nein, danke. Das kann ich mir nicht leisten.

BEAMTER: Also dann kostet es 92,00 Euro plus 2 Euro Zuschlag. Gute Reise.

At the Train Station.

CLERK: Yes, please.

FEMALE TRAVELER: A ticket to Klagenfurt, please.

CLERK: Round-trip?

FEMALE TRAVELER: One way, second class, and a nonsmoking compartment, please.

CLERK: When would you like to arrive in Klagenfurt?

FEMALE TRAVELER: I have to be in Klagenfurt tomorrow morning around ten o'clock.

CLERK: Then your best bet is to take the Inter-City. It leaves this evening from Platform 12 at 7:30 P.M. and arrives tomorrow morning in Klagenfurt at 9:45 A.M.

FEMALE TRAVELER: Do I have to change trains?

CLERK: No, the train has a direct coach to Klagenfurt.

FEMALE TRAVELER: Can I reserve a place in the couchette?

CLERK: One moment, please. No, all places are reserved. Would you like a bed in the sleeping car?

FEMALE TRAVELER: No, thanks. I can't afford that.

CLERK: Well then, it's 92.00 Euro plus 2 Euro surcharge. Have a nice trip.

B. AUSSPRACHE

AND STILL MORE CONSONANTS

sch	like sh in shine	schon, schnell
sp, st	at the start of a syllable like the sh in shine + p or t	spät, Stein
ss, ß	like ss	muss, groß
eiß	like ice	weiß
th	like the t in tin	Thema
tsch	like the ch in church	deutsch
tz	like the ts in cats	Platz

C. GRAMMATIK UND GEBRAUCH

1. VERBS WITH SEPARABLE AND INSEPARABLE PREFIXES

German has a large number of verbs that consist of a verb plus a prefix. A prefix changes the basic meaning of the verb.

suchen	to search	*besuchen*	to visit
kommen	to come	*ankommen*	to arrive
stellen	to put	*vorstellen*	to introduce

German has verbs with separable and inseparable prefixes. The prefixes *be-, emp-, ent-, er-, ge-, miss-, ver-,* and *zer-* always remain attached to the verb.

Das bezahle ich nicht.
    I don't pay that.

Ich verbinde Sie.
    I'll connect you.

But many prefixes are separated from the verb in a present tense statement, in a question, and in the imperative. Examples are: *ab-, an-, um-, mit-.* In these cases, the separable prefix is in the last position.

Der Zug fährt von Bahnsteig 12 ab.
    The train leaves from Platform 12.

Wann kommt er an?
    When does it arrive?

Steigen Sie bitte in Berlin um.
    Please change (trains) in Berlin.

It is difficult for a beginning student to know whether a verb has a separable prefix. In the infinitive a separable prefix is always attached. Verbs with separable prefixes will be listed in the vocabulary section with an asterisk between the separable prefix and the verb: *um*steigen*

2. MODAL AUXILIARIES

Both English and German have a group of verbs called modal auxiliaries. Modal auxiliaries express an attitude about the action or condition described by the main verb. German has six modal auxiliaries:

können	to be able to, can (ability)
müssen	to have to, must (necessity)
dürfen	to be allowed to, may (permission)
sollen	to be supposed to, should (obligation)
wollen	to want to (intention)
mögen	to like to (inclination), may (possibility)

The conjugation of modal auxiliaries is irregular in the present tense singular. They have no endings in the first and third person. The plural forms are regular. Five modal auxiliaries have a vowel change.

ich kann	I can	*wir können*	we can
du kannst	you can	*ihr könnt*	you can
es kann	it can	*sie können*	they can
		Sie können	you can

ich muss	I have to	*wir müssen*	we have to
du musst	you have to	*ihr müsst*	you have to
er muss	he has to	*sie müssen*	they have to
		Sie müssen	you have to

ich darf	I may	*wir dürfen*	we may
du darfst	you may	*ihr dürft*	you may
sie darf	she may	*sie dürfen*	they may
		Sie dürfen	you may

ich soll	I should
du sollst	you should
es soll	it should

wir sollen	we should
ihr sollt	you should
sie sollen	they should
Sie sollen	you should

ich will	I want to
du willst	you want to
sie will	she wants to

wir wollen	we want to
ihr wollt	you want to
sie wollen	they want to
Sie wollen	you want

ich mag	I like to
du magst	you like to
er mag	he likes to

wir mögen	we like to
ihr mögt	you like to
sie mögen	they like to
Sie mögen	you like to

Möchte (would like to) is a subjunctive* form of *mögen*. The *möchte* forms are used much more frequently than the indicative forms of *mögen*. In the third person singular the ending is *e*.

ich möchte	I would like to
du möchtest	you would like to
er möchte	he would like to
wir möchten	we would like to
ihr möchtet	you would like to
sie möchten	they would like to
Sie möchten	you would like to

* Lessons 35 and 36 will deal with the subjunctive moods in general.

84

In a sentence that has a modal auxiliary, the modal auxiliary is conjugated, and stands in the appropriate position of the verb. The main verb is in the infinitive form and stands at the end of the sentence.

Ich kann das nicht bezahlen.
I can't pay that.

Er muss um sieben Uhr in Klagenfurt sein.
He has to be in Klagenfurt at seven.

Darf sie das Foto sehen?
May she see the photo?

Wann sollen wir heute kommen?
When should we come today?

Wollen Sie den Schlafwagen sehen?
Do you want to see the sleeping car?

Ich möchte eine Fahrkarte kaufen.
I would like to buy a ticket.

If the main verb has a separable prefix, the prefix must remain attached.

Muss ich umsteigen?
Do I have to change?

Er möchte heute ankommen.
He would like to arrive today.

Sometimes the main verb can be omitted, if it is clearly implied by the context.

Möchten Sie ein Doppelbett (haben)?
Would you like (to have) a double bed?

Ich mag kein Brot (essen).
I don't like (to eat) bread.

VOKABELN

der Bahnhof, ̈e	train station
der Beamte, -n	official, civil servant, clerk
die Reise, -n	trip, journey
der Reisende, -n	traveler (male)
die Reisende, -n	traveler (female)
Gute Reise.	Have a nice trip.
die Fahrkarte, -n	ticket
einfach	simple, one-way
hin und zurück	round-trip
die Klasse, -n	class
erster Klasse	first class
der Zug, ̈e	train
die Bahn, -en	train
der Bahnsteig, -e	platform
der Platz, ̈e	seat
das Abteil, -e	compartment
das Nichtraucherabteil, -e	nonsmoking compartment
der Raucher, -	smoker
der Speisewagen, -	dining car
der Schlafwagen, -	sleeping car
der Liegewagen, -	couchette
der Kurswagen, -	through coach
der Zuschlag, ̈e	surcharge
an*kommen	to arrive
ab*fahren	to depart
um*steigen	to change, transfer
reservieren	to reserve
das Bett, -en	bed
der Augenblick, -e	moment
bezahlen	to pay
gegen zehn Uhr	around ten o'clock
morgen früh	tomorrow morning
sich leisten	to afford

ÜBUNGEN

A. *Beantworten Sie die Fragen zum Dialog.*

1. *Wann fährt der Zug nach Klagenfurt ab?*
2. *Wann kommt der Zug in Klagenfurt an?*
3. *Muss die Frau umsteigen?*
4. *Wie viel muss die Frau bezahlen?*

B. *Suchen Sie die richtige deutsche Übersetzung.*

1. to have to
2. Have a nice trip.
3. around ten o'clock
4. one-way
5. to arrive
6. train ticket
7. round-trip
8. to pay

a. *Gute Reise.*
b. *die Fahrkarte*
c. *ankommen*
d. *hin und zurück*
e. *bezahlen*
f. *müssen*
g. *einfach*
h. *gegen zehn Uhr*

C. *Schreiben Sie die Sätze ohne das Modalverb.* (Rewrite the sentences without the modal auxiliary.)

BEISPIEL: *Sie muss jetzt essen.*
      Sie isst jetzt.

1. *Er muss nach Berlin fahren.*
2. *Sie möchte eine Fahrkarte kaufen.*
3. *Könnt ihr morgen kommen?*
4. *Wer soll das bezahlen?*
5. *Er will morgen ankommen.*

D. *Schreiben Sie die Sätze mit dem Modalverb in den Klammern.* (Rewrite the sentences with the modal auxiliary in parentheses.)

BEISPIEL: *Sie backt einen Kuchen. (wollen)*
      Sie will einen Kuchen backen.

1. *Er steigt in Hamburg um. (mögen)*
2. *Er nimmt den Inter-City Zug (wollen)*

3. *Der Zug kommt um sieben Uhr an. (sollen)*
4. *Das Abteil ist belegt. (können)*

E. *Übersetzen Sie.* (Translate.)

1. Would you like coffee? (pol.)
2. How much do I have to pay?
3. I'd like to see that.
4. May I pay?
5. You can leave (go) now.

KULTURNOTIZ

Trains in German-speaking countries and Western Europe are efficient, clean, and popular. More than 200 cities and the capitals of 13 countries are connected by a network of trains known as Euro-City. Inter-City trains run frequently between all major cities. Both kinds of trains require a surcharge. They are equipped with dining cars *(Speisewagen)*, sleeping cars *(Schlafwagen)*, and couchettes *(Liegewagen)*. A compartment in a sleeping car has from two to four beds, and a private bathroom. A compartment in a couchette has six bunks and no separate bathroom facilities. For commuting, people often use short-distance trains *(Personenzüge, Nahverkehrszüge, S-Bahnen)*.

LÖSUNGEN

A. 1. *Der Zug fährt um 19:30 Uhr ab.* 2. *Er kommt um 9:45 Uhr in Klagenfurt an.* 3. *Nein, der Zug hat einen Kurswagen nach Klagenfurt.* 4. *Sie muss 92 Euro plus 2 Euro Zuschlag bezahlen.*
B. 1.—f 2.—a 3.—h 4.—g 5.—c 6.—b 7.—d 8.—e
C. 1. *Er fährt nach Berlin.* 2. *Sie kauft eine Fahrkarte.* 3. *Kommt ihr morgen?* 4. *Wer bezahlt das?* 5. *Er kommt morgen an.*
D. 1. *Er möchte in Hamburg umsteigen.* 2. *Er will den Inter-City Zug nehmen.* 3. *Der Zug soll um sieben Uhr ankommen.* 4. *Das Abteil kann belegt sein.*
E. 1. *Möchten Sie Kaffee?* 2. *Wie viel muss ich zahlen?* 3. *Das möchte ich sehen.* 4. *Darf ich zahlen?* 5. *Sie können jetzt gehen.*

LEKTION 10

GESCHENKEINKAUF.   Shopping for Gifts.

A. DIALOG

Im Kaufhaus.

ULRIKE: Seit zwei Stunden kaufen wir schon Geschenke ein. Ich werde müde.

ANDREA: Dann sehen wir mal unsere Einkäufe an. Den Regenmantel schenke ich meinem Bruder und die Bluse meiner Schwester.

ULRIKE: Und was schenkst du den Kindern?

ANDREA: Ihnen bringe ich die Handschuhe. Ich hoffe, die Größe passt.

ULRIKE: Sag mal, wem willst du den Schal geben?

ANDREA: Meinem Freund.

ULRIKE: Oh, der Schal gefällt ihm bestimmt.

ANDREA: Ja, er trägt gern rot und blau.

In der Umkleidekabine.

ULRIKE: Hilf mir doch bitte, Andrea! Passt mir das Kleid?

ANDREA: Ja, aber die Farbe ist nicht vorteilhaft. Grün macht blass, glaube mir.

ULRIKE: Gut. Ich kaufe es in blau. So ein Ausverkauf kommt nicht so bald wieder.

In the Department Store.

ULRIKE: We've been shopping for presents for two hours. I'm getting tired.

ANDREA: Then, let's look at our purchases. I'll give the raincoat to my brother and the blouse to my sister.

ULRIKE: And what will you give the children?

ANDREA: I'll bring them the gloves. I hope the size fits.

ULRIKE: Tell me, to whom will you give the scarf?

ANDREA: To my boyfriend.

ULRIKE: Oh, he'll like it for sure.

ANDREA: Yes, he likes to wear red and blue.

In the fitting room.

ULRIKE: Please help me, Andrea. Does the dress fit?

ANDREA: Yes, but the color is not flattering. Green makes one look pale, believe me.

ULRIKE: All right. I'll buy it in blue. There won't be a sale like this again soon.

B. AUSSPRACHE

THE LAST CONSONANTS

v	like the f in four	vier, Vater
	like the v in visa, in words of foreign origin	Visum, Viper
f	like the f in four	fahren
w	like the v in vest	Wert, Wasser, was
z	like the ts in cats	Zahl, zehn, Zoo

C. GRAMMATIK UND GEBRAUCH

1. THE DATIVE CASE

You have used the nominative (subject) and the accusative (direct object) cases. To indicate for whom or to whom the action of the verb is done, German uses the dative (indirect object) case. The indirect object is usually a person, and may be either a noun or a pronoun.

Er kauft Sabine eine Uhr.
> He buys a watch for Sabine.
> He buys Sabine a watch.

Er kauft ihr eine Uhr.
> He buys a watch for her.
> He buys her a watch.

Note that in English a preposition may or may not be used, depending on word order.

In the dative case the *der*-words and *ein*-words change their form:

SINGULAR:

MASCULINE	FEMININE	NEUTER

dem Mann	*der Frau*	*dem Kind*
(k)einem Mann	*(k)einer Frau*	*(k)einem Kind*
meinem Mann	*meiner Frau*	*meinem Kind*

Ich gebe dem Mann ein Buch.
> I give the man a book.

Er gibt seiner Frau Blumen.
> He gives his wife flowers.

Sie bringt einem Kind ein Geschenk.
> She brings a child a present.

PLURAL:

MASCULINE	FEMININE	NEUTER

den Männern	*den Frauen*	*den Kindern*
keinen Männern	*keinen Frauen*	*keinen Kindern*
unseren Männern	*unseren Frauen*	*unseren Kindern*

Some German nouns add an -*n* to their dative plural forms (unless the nominative plural already ends on -*n* or -*s*).

NOMINATIVE PLURAL	DATIVE PLURAL
die Brüder	den Brüdern
die Schwestern	den Schwestern
die Autos	den Autos

Ich gebe meinen Brüdern nichts.
    I give nothing to my brothers.

Er gibt seinen Schwestern auch nichts.
    He doesn't give anything to his sisters, either.

    The dative form of the interrogative *wer?* (who?) is *wem?* (whom?):

Wem gibst du die Krawatten? Meinen Brüdern.
    To whom will you give the ties? My brothers.

Wem schenkt Andrea den Schal? Ihrem Freund.
    To whom will Andrea give the scarf? To her boyfriend.

C. PERSONAL PRONOUNS IN THE DATIVE CASE

SINGULAR

ich → mir
du → dir
er → ihm
sie → ihr
es → ihm

PLURAL

wir → uns
ihr → euch
sie → ihnen
Sie → Ihnen

Sie schenkt ihm einen Schal.
    She gives him a scarf.

Er bringt ihr ein Geschenk.
    He brings her a gift.

3. VERBS THAT TAKE THE DATIVE

Most German verbs take accusative objects. A few verbs, however, take the object in the dative case:

antworten	to answer
danken	to thank
gefallen (gefällt)	to please
gehören	to belong to
glauben	to believe
helfen (hilft)	to help
passen	to fit

Warum antwortest du mir nicht?
    Why don't you answer me?

Er dankt Ihnen.
    He thanks you.

Der Schal gefällt meinem Freund.
    My friend likes the scarf.

Der Regenmantel gehört ihr.
    The raincoat belongs to her.

Ich glaube seinem Vater.
    I believe his father.

Wir helfen unseren Freunden.
    We help our friends.

Helfen Sie mir bitte!
    Please help me!

Die Handschuhe passen den Kindern.
    The gloves fit the children.

Antworten is used only with persons. Use *beantworten* and a direct object for things.

Er beantwortet den Brief.
    He answers the letter.

Antworten Sie mir!
    Answer me!

Gefallen literally means "to please." The German for "I like the scarf" is *"Der Schal gefällt mir"* (The scarf pleases me). In other words, the object in English (the scarf) is the subject in German *(der Schal).*

Der Handschuh gefällt mir.
I like the glove.

Die Handschuhe gefallen mir.
I like the gloves.

The verb in the second sentence is in the plural, because the subject *(die Handschuhe)* is plural.

Glauben takes personal objects in the dative case and impersonal objects in the accusative case:

Ich glaube meiner Freundin.
I believe my girlfriend.

Er glaubt es nicht.
He doesn't believe it.

Meiner Freundin is a personal object and is therefore in the dative case; *es* is an impersonal object and therefore in the accusative case.

4. WORD ORDER WITH DATIVE AND ACCUSATIVE OBJECTS

a. Generally, an object in the dative case precedes an object in the accusative case.

Sie schenkt dem Bruder$_{(dat.)}$ ein Radio$_{(acc.)}$.
She gives a radio to the brother.

Sie schenkt ihm$_{(dat.)}$ ein Radio$_{(acc.)}$.
She gives him a radio.

b. If the direct object is a pronoun, it precedes the indirect object or the indirect pronoun:

Sie schenkt es$_{(acc.)}$ dem Bruder$_{(dat.)}$.
She gives it to the brother.

Sie schenkt es$_{(acc.)}$ ihm$_{(dat.)}$.
She gives it to him.

5. THE COLORS

die Farbe	color
blau	blue
grün	green
rot	red
gelb	yellow
schwarz	black
weiß	white
braun	brown
grau	gray

6. THE VERB *WERDEN*

The forms of the verb *werden* (to become) are irregular:

I become	*ich werde*
you become	*du wirst*
she becomes	*sie wird*
we become	*wir werden*
you become	*ihr werdet*
they become	*sie werden*
you become	*Sie werden*

Es wird schon dunkel.
 It's already becoming dark.

Werden Sie auch schnell müde?
 Do you also get tired quickly?

Ich werde dieses Jahr 33.
 I'll turn 33 this year.

VOKABELN

Einkäufe machen	to go shopping
der Einkauf, ¨-e	purchase

ein*kaufen	to shop
das Kaufhaus, ¨er	department store
der Ausverkauf, ¨e	sale
das Geschenk, -e	present
die Umkleidekabine, -n	fitting room
schenken	to give (as a present)
der Geschenkeinkauf, ¨e	gift purchase
die Größe, -n	size
der Stoff, -e	material
tragen *(trägt)*	to wear
an*sehen *(sieht an)*	to look at
Ich nehme die Bluse in gelb.	I'll take the blouse in yellow.
passen	to fit
Der Mantel passt mir.	The coat fits me.
die Kleidung	clothing
das Kleid, -er	dress
der Regenmantel, ¨	raincoat
die Bluse, -n	blouse
der Rock, ¨e	skirt
der Anzug, ¨e	suit (man's)
die Hose, -n	slacks
das Hemd, -en	shirt
die Jacke, -n	jacket
der Hut, ¨e	hat
der Handschuh, -e	glove
ein Paar Socken	a pair of socks
drei Paar Socken	three pairs of socks
bringen	to bring, to take
einmal	once
noch einmal	once more
vorteilhaft	advantageous; flattering
wieder	again
blass	pale
seit	since, for (time)
Antworten Sie mir bitte.	Please answer me!
Sie können mir glauben.	You can believe me.
Helfen Sie mir bitte.	Please help me.

ÜBUNGEN

A. *Beantworten Sie die Fragen zum Dialog.*

1. *Wie lange kaufen Ulrike und Andrea schon ein?*
2. *Was will Andrea ihrem Bruder schenken?*
3. *Wem gibt Andrea Handschuhe?*
4. *Warum ist grün nicht sehr vorteilhaft?*

B. *Suchen Sie die richtige deutsche Übersetzung.*

1. to shop	a. *müde werden*
2. the blouse	b. *der Mantel*
3. purchases	c. *Er antwortet.*
4. the coat	d. *geben*
5. to get tired	e. *die Einkäufe*
6. Help me.	f. *die Bluse*
7. the present	g. *Helfen Sie mir!*
8. He answers.	h. *einkaufen*
9. to give	i. *Es gefällt mir.*
10. I like it.	j. *das Geschenk*

C. *Setzen Sie das fehlende Wort in der richtigen Form ein.* (Fill in the missing word in the correct form.)

BEISPIEL: Ich antworte _____. (you, fam. sing.)
      Ich antworte dir.

1. *Ich schenke _____ Schwester eine Bluse. (my)*
2. *_____ Bruder gibt sie einen Regenmantel. (her)*
3. *Der Regenmantel gefällt _____. (him)*
4. *Der Ober bringt _____ Gast die Speisekarte. (the)*
5. *Andrea schenkt _____ Pullover. (the children)*

D. *Nennen Sie die fehlende Form von "werden".* (Provide the missing form of *werden*.)

1. *Ich _____ schnell müde.*
2. *_____ du auch schnell müde?*
3. *Es _____ bald kalt.*
4. *Wir _____ krank.*
5. *Ihr _____ bald gesund.*
6. *Sie _____ nicht alt, Herr Jung.*

E. *Übersetzen Sie.*

1. I like the dress.
2. Please buy it for me.
3. Why don't you answer me? (fam. sing.)

F. *Welche Farbe passt?* (Which color?)

1. *Die Banane ist _____.*
2. *Die Tomate ist _____.*
3. *Das Gras ist _____.*
4. *Die Maus ist _____.*
5. *Der Ozean ist _____.*
6. *Das Papier ist _____.*

KULTURNOTIZ

Although German shoppers are not quite as used to paying with credit cards as American shoppers, cash is becoming less and less attractive even in Germany. Other ways of paying without cash frequently used in Germany are bank transfers *(Banküberweisungen)* for large sums of money, or Eurochecks *(Euroschecks)* for limited purchases.

German customers shop carefully and critically, looking for high-quality merchandise. People like to take advantage of the seasonal sales *(Ausverkauf)*, which begin on the last Monday in January *(Winterschlussverkauf)* and on the last Monday in July *(Sommerschlussverkauf)*. Occasional special sales *(Sonderangebote)* are offered at almost all retail stores year-round.

LÖSUNGEN

A. 1. *Sie kaufen schon seit zwei Stunden ein.* 2. *Sie will ihrem Bruder einen Regenmantel schenken.* 3. *Sie gibt den Kindern Handschuhe.* 4. *Die Farbe macht blass.*
B. 1.—h 2.—f 3.—e 4.—b 5—a 6.—g 7.—j 8.—c 9.—d 10.—i
C. 1. *meiner* 2. *Ihrem* 3. *ihm* 4. *dem* 5. *den Kindern*
D. 1. *werde* 2. *Wirst* 3. *wird* 4. *werden* 5. *werdet* 6. *werden*
E. 1. *Mir gefällt das Kleid.* 2. *Bitte kauf es mir.* 3. *Warum antwortest du mir nicht?*
F. 1. *gelb* 2. *rot* 3. *grün* 4. *grau* 5. *blau* 6. *weiß*

98

ZWEITE WIEDERHOLUNGSAUFGABE

A. *Beantworten Sie die Fragen. Sagen Sie "nein", und benutzen Sie "nicht" oder "kein".* (Answer the questions. Say "no," using either *nicht* or *kein*.)

BEISPIEL: *Wohnt Herr Schneider hier.*
    Nein, Herr Schneider wohnt nicht hier.

1. *Ist das der Zug nach Berlin?*
2. *Hat er eine Fahrkarte?*
3. *Essen wir Brot?*

B. *Setzen Sie die fehlenden Endungen ein.* (Fill in the missing endings.)

BEISPIEL: *Haben Sie ein___ Schwester oder ein___ Bruder?*
    Haben Sie eine Schwester oder einen Bruder?

1. *Ich sehe dein___ Vater und dein___ Mutter.*
2. *Wir backen ein___ Kuchen.*
3. *Ich habe kein___ Schlüssel.*

C. *Schreiben Sie die fehlenden Präpositionen.* (Write the missing prepositions.)

BEISPIEL: *Ich kaufe _____ meinem Freund ein. (with)*
    Ich kaufe mit meinem Freund ein.

1. *Wir laufen _____ den Park. (through)*
2. *Dann fahren wir _____ die Ecke. (around)*
3. *Wir gehen _____ meinen Bruder. (without)*
4. *Wir kaufen Gemüse _____ unseren Freund. (for)*

D. *Setzen Sie ein Personalpronomen für die unterstrichenen Wörter ein.* (Replace the underlined words with a personal pronoun.)

BEISPIEL: *Horst kauft seinem Bruder eine Uhr.*
    Horst kauft ihm eine Uhr.

1. *Der Zug kommt um 7 Uhr an.*
2. *Wir sehen meine Eltern.*
3. *Mein Vater hat deinen Koffer.*

E. *Übersetzen Sie.*

1. When will you (fam. sing.) arrive?
2. Around 5 o'clock.
3. Visit me tomorrow. (pol.)

99

F. *Setzen Sie die richtige Verbform ein.* (Fill in the correct verb form.)

BEISPIEL: Sie _____ ihre Schwester oft. (sehen)
     Sie sieht ihre Schwester oft.

1. *Er _____ heute nicht. (laufen)*
2. *Er _____ nach Berlin. (fahren)*
3. *Er _____ einen Inter-City. (nehmen)*
4. *Jetzt _____ er den Zug. (sehen)*

G. *Setzen Sie das Personalpronomen ein.* (Fill in the personal pronoun.)

BEISPIEL: _____ Chef heißt Klaus Berger. (His)
     Sein Chef heißt Klaus Berger.

1. *_____ Mutter kommt heute. (Our)*
2. *Wie alt ist _____ Mutter? (your, pol.)*
3. *_____ Freund ist in Bonn. (My)*
4. *Wo wohnt _____ Freund? (your, fam. sing.)*

H. *Setzen Sie das fehlende Wort ein.*

BEISPIEL: Gefällt es _____ in Deutschland? (you, pol.)
     Gefällt es Ihnen in Deutschland?

1. *Ich schenke _____ Vater eine Krawatte. (my)*
2. *_____ gibst du das Geld? (To whom)*
3. *Der Ober bringt _____ Gästen das Essen. (the)*
4. *Es gefällt _____ gut in Deutschland. (I)*

LÖSUNGEN

A. 1. *Nein, das ist nicht der Zug nach Berlin.* 2. *Nein, er hat keine Fahrkarte.* 3. *Nein, wir essen kein Brot.*
B. 1. *deinen, deine* 2. *einen* 3. *keinen*
C. 1. *durch* 2. *um* 3. *ohne* 4. *für*
D. 1. *Er* 2. *sie* 3. *ihn*
E. 1. *Wann kommst du an?* 2. *Gegen fünf Uhr.* 3. *Besuchen Sie mich morgen.*
F. 1. *läuft* 2. *fährt* 3. *nimmt* 4. *sieht*
G. 1. *Unsere* 2. *Ihre* 3. *Mein* 4. *dein*
H. 1. *meinem* 2. *Wem* 3. *den* 4. *mir*

LESESTÜCK I (Reading Passage I)

Now you're ready to practice your reading skills! While you've been "reading" the dialogues, the four reading passages *(Lesestücke)* offer you the chance to practice reading as you would read a newspaper article or essay. First, read through each passage without referring to the accompanying vocabulary notes. Try to understand the main idea and the main point, inferring the meanings of any new words from the context or from their similarities to English. Don't worry if a passage seems long or if you don't know each word; you can go back and reread it, checking the vocabulary notes to learn the exact meaning of the new words and phrases. Now let's begin.

WOHIN REISEN [1] DIE DEUTSCHEN GERN?

Die Deutschen fahren gern und oft in Urlaub.[2] Besonders gern fahren sie in den Süden—nach Italien, Griechenland, Spanien, und auf die Mittelmeerinseln.[3] Sie suchen Sonne und Meer, denn in Deutschland ist der Sommer oft kühl, und das Land hat nur im Norden eine Meeresküste.[4] Die Deutschen haben vier, fünf, vielleicht auch sechs Wochen Urlaub, und sie verdienen gut.[5] Sie können also eine große Urlaubsreise machen. Den Urlaub plant man schon ein Jahr voraus,[6] denn die beliebten und preisgünstigen Reiseziele im Süden sind schnell ausgebucht.[7]

Reisebüros bieten Gruppenreisen mit Bus, Bahn, oder Flugzeug in alle Länder an,[8] oder arrangieren individuelle Reisen.[9] Viele Deutsche planen ihren Urlaub auch selbst und reisen mit dem eigenen Auto.[10]

Millionen Autos fahren in der Feriensaison von Norden nach Süden.[11] Da gibt es stundenlange Verkehrsstaus auf den Autobahnen.[12] Wenn man aber einmal am Urlaubsziel ist, dann vergisst man die Unannehmlichkeiten und genießt die Sonne und das Meer.[13]

VOKABELN

1. *reisen*	to travel
2. *in Urlaub fahren*	to go on vacation
3. *Griechenland*	Greece
Spanien	Spain
die Mittelmeerinseln	Mediterranean islands

4. *suchen* — to search for, to look for
   das Meer, -e — ocean, sea
   die Meeresküste, -n — seacoast, shore
5. *verdienen* — to earn
6. *planen* — to plan
   voraus — ahead
7. *beliebt* — much liked, popular
   preisgünstig — reasonable
   das Reiseziel, -e — destination
   ausgebucht — fully booked, sold out
8. *das Reisebüro, -s* — travel agency
   an*bieten — to offer
   die Gruppenreise, -n — group tour
   das Flugzeug, -e — airplane
9. *arrangieren* — to arrange
   individuell — individual
10. *selbst* — self, themselves
    eigen — own, their own
11. *die Feriensaison* — vacation season
12. *stundenlang* — for hours
    der Verkehrsstau, -s — traffic congestion
    die Autobahn, -en — highway
13. *das Urlaubsziel, -e* — destination
    vergessen (vergisst) — to forget
    die Unannehmlichkeit — inconvenience, unpleasantness

    genießen — to enjoy, to rejoice in

LEKTION 11

DIE POST.   The Post Office.

A. DIALOG

Auf der Post.

FRAU KLEIN: Jetzt warten wir schon seit einer halben Stunde. Ich muss einen Eilbrief abschicken.

FRAU STORM: Und ich habe ein Einschreiben, deshalb kann ich nicht zum Briefkasten gehen.

FRAU KLEIN: Nach der Mittagszeit dauert es oft so lange. Gehen Sie doch morgens.

FRAU STORM: Schalter fünf macht auf. Jetzt geht es bestimmt schneller.

FRAU KLEIN: Endlich.

Am Schalter.

KUNDE: Zehn Briefmarken für Normalpost, bitte. Haben Sie Sondermarken?

POSTBEAMTER: Sie sind ausverkauft. Sonst noch etwas?

KUNDE: Ich möchte das Paket hier nach Kanada schicken.

POSTBEAMTER: Mit Luftpost? Versichert?

KUNDE: Nein, danke.

POSTBEAMTER: Füllen Sie bitte die Zollerklärung aus. Und Ihre Paketanschrift hat keine Postleitzahl für Toronto.

KUNDE: Muss ich dann wieder Schlange stehen?

POSTBEAMTER: Nein, kommen Sie direkt zu meinem Schalter.

At the Post Office.

MRS. KLEIN: We've been waiting for half an hour now. I have to send an express letter.

MRS. STORM: And I have a registered letter; that's why I can't go to the mailbox.

MRS. KLEIN: After lunch it often takes a long time. Try going in the morning.

MRS. STORM: Window five is opening up. Now it will certainly go faster.

MRS. KLEIN: Finally.

At the Window.

MALE CUSTOMER: Ten stamps for regular mail, please. Do you have commemorative stamps?

MALE POSTAL CLERK: They're sold out. Anything else?

MALE CUSTOMER: I would like to send this package to Canada.

MALE POSTAL CLERK: Airmail? Insured?

MALE CUSTOMER: No, thanks.

MALE POSTAL CLERK: Fill out the customs declaration. And your address on the package has no zip code for Toronto.

MALE CUSTOMER: Do I have to stand in line again?

MALE POSTAL CLERK: No, come directly to my window.

B. GRAMMATIK UND GEBRAUCH

1. PREPOSITIONS THAT TAKE THE DATIVE

The prepositions followed by the dative case are:

aus	out of; from (is a native of)
außer	except for, besides
bei	with, at the home of, at a place of business, near, during, at
mit	with; by means of (transportation)
nach	after; toward, to (with cities, and masculine and neuter countries)

seit	for, since (referring to time)
von	from; by (agent of an action)
zu	to (with people and some places)

Nouns or pronouns that follow the dative prepositions are in the dative case. Dative prepositions can have several meanings in English.

a. AUS

Er kommt aus der Post.
He is coming from the post office.

Er kommt aus Holland.
He is from (a native of) Holland.

b. AUSSER

Außer mir war nur ein Kind da.
Except for (besides) me only a child was there.

c. BEI

Er wohnt bei uns.
He lives with us (in our home).

Sie arbeitet bei Müller & Groß.
She works for Müller & Groß (place of business).

Das Restaurant ist bei der Post.
The restaurant is near the post office.

Er isst bei der Arbeit.
He eats while working.

d. MIT

Er kommt mit seinem Freund.
He comes with his friend.

Er fährt mit dem Zug.
He travels by train.

e. *NACH*

Nach dem Mittagessen schläft er.
He sleeps after dinner.

Sie fährt nach Berlin.
She travels to Berlin.

Er fährt nach Holland.
He travels to Holland.

f. *SEIT*

Seit einer Woche arbeitet sie.
She's been working for a week.

Seit Montag arbeiten wir.
We've been working since Monday.

In German, *seit* is used with the present tense to express an action or condition that started in the past but continues in the present. English uses the present perfect tense (have been -ing) with "since" or "for."

g. *VON*

Ich schicke es von meinem Büro.
I'll send it from my office.

h. *ZU*

Wir fahren zu meiner Schwester.
We are driving to my sister's.

Bei and *mit* both can mean "with," but these prepositions are not interchangeable. *Bei* is used with verbs of non-motion; *mit* is used with verbs of motion.

Nach and *zu* both can mean "to," but they are not interchangeable. *Zu* is used to show movement toward people and many locations. *Nach* is used with cities and masculine and neuter countries.* And don't forget the expressions *nach Hause* (home, "to" home), and *zu Hause* (home, at home).

* *In* is used with feminine countries, such as *die Schweiz*. This preposition will be discussed in lesson 13.

Several dative prepositions contract with *der* and *dem*.

bei dem	→	*beim*
von dem	→	*vom*
zu dem	→	*zum*
zu der	→	*zur*

bei dem Frühstück → *beim Fruhstück*   *zu dem Bahnhof* → *zum Bahnhof*
von dem Bahnhof → *vom Bahnhof*   *zu der Arbeit*   → *zur Arbeit*

2. WORD ORDER WITH EXPRESSIONS OF TIME AND PLACE

When a German sentence has expressions both of time and of place, the expression of time precedes the expression of place. When two expressions of time occur in the same sentence, the general expression of time usually precedes the specific one.

	1 TIME	2 PLACE
Ich bleibe	*heute*	*zu Hause.*

I'm staying home today.

	1 GENERAL TIME	2 SPECIFIC TIME	3 PLACE
Er fährt	*heute*	*um sieben Uhr*	*nach Köln.*

He's driving to Cologne at seven today.

VOKABELN

die Post	post office, mail
das Postamt, ⸚er	post office
die Hauptpost	main post office
der Brief, -e	letter
der Eilbrief, -e	express letter
das Einschreiben, -	registered letter

die Briefmarke, -n	stamp
der Briefkasten, ⸚	mailbox
die Luftpost	airmail
mit Luftpost	by airmail
die Postkarte, -n	postcard
der Absender	return address; sender of mail
die Adresse, -n	address
die Anschrift, -en	address
das Paket, -e	package
die Postleitzahl, -en	zip code
der Pfennig, -e	penny
die Zollerklärung, -en	customs declaration
schicken	to send
ab*schicken	to send off
aus*füllen	to fill out
die Versicherung, -en	insurance
versichert	insured
stehen	to stand
Schlange stehen	to stand in line
lang	long
Es dauert lange.	It takes a long time.
dann	then
warum	why
endlich	finally
ausverkauft	sold out

ÜBUNGEN

A. *Beantworten Sie die Fragen zum Dialog.*

1. *Was muss Frau Klein abschicken?*
2. *Warum kann Frau Storm nicht zum Briefkasten gehen?*
3. *Was ist ausverkauft?*
4. *Schickt der Kunde das Paket mit Luftpost?*
5. *Was muss der Kunde ausfüllen?*

B. *Suchen Sie die richtige deutsche Übersetzung.*

1. postcard
2. It takes a long time.
3. immediately
4. zip code
5. letter
6. to fill out
7. return address
8. airmail
9. to send

a. *die Luftpost*
b. *ausfüllen*
c. *der Brief*
d. *Es dauert lange.*
e. *der Absender*
f. *schicken*
g. *die Postkarte*
h. *sofort*
i. *die Postleitzahl*

C. *Setzen Sie die fehlenden Präpositionen ein.* (Supply the missing prepositions.)

BEISPIEL: *Heute gehe ich _____ Post.* (to the)
            Heute gehe ich zur Post.

1. *_____ dem Frühstück schreibe ich einen Brief.* (After)
2. *Jetzt gehe ich nicht _____ dem Haus.* (out of)
3. *_____ einem Monat arbeite ich _____ Müller & Groß.* (For; at)
4. *_____ mir arbeitet meine Freundin auch da.* (Besides)
5. *Müller & Groß ist _____ einem Restaurant.* (near)
6. *Oft gehe ich _____ ihr.* (to)
7. *Meine Freundin ist _____ Kanada.* (from)
8. *Im Sommer fliegt sie _____ Kanada.* (to)

D. *Setzen Sie folgende Satzteile in die richtige Ordnung.* (Put the following words in the right order.)

BEISPIEL: *schreibe/heute/den Brief/nach Frankfurt/ich (Ich ...)*
            Ich schreibe heute den Brief nach Frankfurt.

1. *geht/er/um 9 Uhr/morgen/ins Büro (Er...)*
2. *sie/nach Deutschland/kommt/heute/um 8 Uhr (Sie ...)*
3. *wir/zu Hause/sind/seit/Freitag (Wir ...)*
4. *ich/um 12 Uhr/esse/im Restaurant/morgen (Ich ...)*
5. *sie/heute/im Hotel/nicht/bleiben (Heute ...)*

E. *Übersetzen Sie.* (Translate.)

1. I'm staying in a hotel.
2. She is at her sister's (house).
3. We are from Munich.

4. I stay (I'm staying) home.
5. Since when are you here? (pol.)

KULTURNOTIZ

Many post offices in German-speaking countries have phone booths. Tell the postal clerk at the window *(der Schalterbeamte, die Schalterbeamtin)* that you would like to make a phone call and he or she will assign you to a booth. When you have finished your call you pay the postal clerk for your call. It's considerably cheaper to call from booths in the post office than from booths on the street.

LÖSUNGEN

A. 1. *Sie muss einen Eilbrief abschicken.* 2. *Sie hat ein Einschreiben.* 3. *Die Sondermarken sind ausverkauft.* 4. *Nein, er schickt es nicht mit Luftpost.* 5. *Der Kunde muss eine Zollerklärung ausfüllen.*

B. 1.—g 2.—d 3.—h 4.—i 5.—c 6.—b 7.—e 8.—a 9.—f

C. 1. *Nach* 2. *aus* 3. *Seit; bei* 4. *Außer* 5. *bei* 6. *zu* 7. *aus* 8. *nach*

D. 1. *Er geht morgen um 9 Uhr ins Büro.* 2. *Sie kommt heute um 8 Uhr nach Deutschland.* 3. *Wir sind seit Freitag zu Hause.* 4. *Ich esse morgen um 12 Uhr im Restaurant.* 5. *Heute bleiben sie nicht im Hotel.*

E. 1. *Ich wohne im Hotel.* 2. *Sie ist bei ihrer Schwester.* 3. *Wir kommen (sind) aus München.* 4. *Ich bleibe zu Hause.* 5. *Seit wann sind Sie hier?*

LEKTION 12

A. DIALOG

Nach der Ankunft auf dem Flughafen.

ANITA: Dieser Flug war ruhig, aber der Rückflug kann stürmisch werden.

GEORG: Mach' dir keine Sorgen, wir können ja kurzfristig umbuchen. Hoffentlich laden sie unser Gepäck schnell aus.

ANITA: Auf welchem Gepäckband kommen unsere Sachen?

GEORG: Band drei. Siehst du diese Tafel da oben? Sie zeigt es an.

ANITA: Ach ja.

GEORG: Wir müssen einen Gepäckwagen finden oder unsere Koffer und Taschen einzeln zum Zoll tragen.

ANITA: Dort drüben stehen Gepäckwagen. Hast du Kleingeld?

GEORG: Ja. Hier ist ein Euro.

ANITA: Mit welcher Buslinie fahren wir zu unserem Hotel?

GEORG: Wir nehmen ein Taxi.

ANITA: Ja. Taxifahrer helfen mit dem Gepäck und kennen jede Straße und jedes Hotel.

GEORG: Dann sind wir bald im Hotel, denn bei der Passkontrolle und dem Zoll geht es schnell. Wir haben keine zollpflichtigen Waren, sondern nur Privatgegenstände.

After Arriving at the Airport.

ANITA: This flight was smooth, but the return flight may get rough.

GEORG: Don't worry, we can change flights at short notice. I hope they'll unload our luggage quickly.

ANITA: On which conveyor belt will our things come?

GEORG: Number three. Do you see that board up there? It shows you.

ANITA: Oh yes.

GEORG: We must find a baggage cart, or carry our suitcases and bags piece by piece to the customs.

ANITA: Over there are baggage carts. Do you have change?

GEORG: Yes. Here is one euro.

ANITA: Which bus line will we take to our hotel?

GEORG: We are going to take a taxi.

ANITA: Yes. Taxi drivers help with the luggage and know every street and hotel.

GEORG: We'll soon be at the hotel, because it will go quickly at the passport control and customs. We have no goods to declare but only personal belongings.

B. GRAMMATIK UND GEBRAUCH

1. *DER*-WORDS

The term *"der*-words" refers to a group of words that take the same endings as the definite articles *der, die,* and *das* according to gender, number, and case of the following noun.

a. MEANINGS OF *DER*-WORDS

dieser	this	*Dieser Flug war ruhig.*
		This flight was smooth.
jener	that	*Jener Tag war stürmisch.*
		That day was rough.
welcher	which	*Welcher Bus fährt heute?*
		Which bus runs today?
jeder	each, every	*Jeder Taxifahrer weiß es.*
		Every taxi driver knows it.

alle	all	*Alle Plätze sind besetzt.*	
		All seats are taken.	
manche	some	*Manche Leute fliegen viel.*	
		Some people fly a lot.	
solche	such	*Solche Koffer sind schön.*	
		Such suitcases are nice.	

The *der*-word *jener* is used only in formal German. In modern spoken German *dieser*, often together with the adverbs *da* or *dort* (there), is preferred:

Dieses Kind dort ist vier Jahre alt.
That child is four years old.

Solch ein is used for the singular expression "such a":

Solch ein Flug ist angenehm.
Such a flight is pleasant.

Solch eine Farbe ist nicht vorteilhaft.
Such a color is not flattering.

b. DECLENSION OF *DER*-WORDS

	MASC.	FEM.	NEUT.	PL.
NOM.	*der*	*die*	*das*	*die*
	dieser	*diese*	*dieses*	*diese*
	welcher	*welche*	*welches*	*welche*
ACC.	*den*	*die*	*das*	*die*
	diesen	*diese*	*dieses*	*diese*
	welchen	*welche*	*welches*	*welche*
DAT.	*dem*	*der*	*dem*	*den*
	diesem	*dieser*	*diesem*	*diesen*
	welchem	*welcher*	*welchem*	*welchen*

Manche Tage waren sehr schwül.
Some days were very muggy.

Wir besuchen diese Familie oft.
We often visit this family.

Mit welcher Fluglinie fliegen wir zurück?
On which airline will we fly back?

2. COORDINATING CONJUNCTIONS

The coordinating conjunctions include:

aber	but, however	*sondern*	but, on the contrary, rather
denn	because	*und*	and
oder	or		

Coordinating conjunctions are used to connect independent clauses. They do not affect word order and are generally preceded by a comma.

Wir nehmen Huhn, denn wir essen es gern.
We order chicken because we like it.

Die Koffer transportieren wir mit dem Wagen, aber die Taschen tragen wir.
We'll transport the suitcases with the cart, but we'll carry the bags.

No comma is necessary before *und* or *oder*. You might choose to use one though, if the context would be unclear otherwise.

Wir fahren mit dem Bus oder nehmen ein Taxi.
We'll go by bus or take a taxi.

Sondern is used for "but" only after a negative, when "but" implies "rather" or "on the contrary."

Wir brauchen kein Einzelzimmer, sondern ein Doppelzimmer.
We don't need a single room but rather a double room.

Sondern is also used in the expression *nicht nur . . . sondern auch* (not only . . . but also).

Man muss nicht nur zur Passkontrolle, sondern auch zum Zoll.
One must go not only to the passport control but also to customs.

VOKABELN

der Flughafen, ¨	airport
der Flug, ¨e	flight
der Rückflug, ¨e	return flight
ruhig	calm, quiet; smooth (of a flight)
stürmisch	rough, stormy
das Flugzeug, -e	airplane
fliegen	to fly
der Fluggast, ¨e	airplane passenger
der Abflug, ¨e	departure
ab*fliegen	to depart by airplane
die Ankunft, ¨e	arrival
die Tafel, -n	board (to show announcements)
das Gepäckband, ¨er	baggage conveyor belt, carousel
der Gepäckwagen, -	baggage cart
der Koffer, -	suitcase
die Tasche, -n	bag, handbag, purse
die Sachen	things, belongings
die Ware, -n	merchandise, wares, goods
zollpflichtig	dutiable
der Privatgegenstand, ¨e	personal belongings
das Kleingeld	coins, change
der Bus, -se	bus
die Buslinie, -n	bus line
das Taxi, -s	taxi
die Straße, -n	street
der Pass, ¨e	passport
die Passkontrolle, -n	passport control
der Zoll	customs
aus*laden	to unload
um*buchen	to change reservations
finden	to find
an*zeigen	to show, indicate
kurzfristig	on short notice
einzeln	piece by piece, singly
da oben	up there
dort drüben	over there
Sorgen haben	to be worried, to worry

ÜBUNGEN

A. *Beantworten Sie die Fragen zum Dialog.*

1. *Wie war der Flug?*
2. *Was können Anita und Georg kurzfristig machen?*
3. *Was müssen sie finden?*
4. *Wie kommen Anita und Georg zum Hotel?*

B. *Suchen Sie die richtige deutsche Übersetzung.*

1. Which bus line will we take?
2. Can you help me with the baggage?
3. Our flight was rough.
4. He goes by train but she flies.
5. Our suitcases are brown.
6. Answer with yes or no.

a. *Er fährt mit dem Zug, aber sie fliegt.*
b. *Können Sie mir mit dem Gepäck helfen?*
c. *Antworten Sie mit ja oder nein!*
d. *Unser Flug war stürmisch.*
e. *Unsere Koffer sind braun.*
f. *Welche Buslinie nehmen wir?*

C. *Setzen Sie die "der-Wörter" mit den richtigen Endungen ein.* (Fill in the *der*-words with the correct endings.)

BEISPIEL: _____ *Koffer sind schön. (Such)*
          Solche Koffer sind schön.

1. _____ *Taschen sind hier. (All)*
2. _____ *Koffer gehören mir nicht. (These)*
3. *Wir kennen _____ Stadt in Frankreich. (every)*
4. *Mit _____ Fluglinie fliegen Sie? (which)*
5. _____ *Sommertage waren sehr kühl. (Some)*

116

D. *Verwenden Sie die gegebene Konjunktion und machen Sie aus zwei Sätzen einen.* (Use the given conjunction and combine the two sentences in one.)

BEISPIEL: *Ich habe einen Koffer. Meine Frau hat zwei Taschen. (and)*
Ich habe einen Koffer, und meine Frau hat zwei Taschen.

1. *Wir müssen einen Gepäckträger finden. Wir müssen unsere Koffer einzeln tragen. (or)*
2. *Ich brauche kein Einzelzimmer. Ich brauche ein Doppelzimmer. (but rather)*
3. *Meine Kinder mögen den Süden. Ihnen gefällt auch der Norden. (but)*

E. *Übersetzen Sie.*

1. Do we go by bus or by taxi?
2. Is this hotel good?

KULTURNOTIZ

All German passenger airports offer public transportation into town. Some even offer their own shuttle service. All airports have German Railroad *(Deutsche Bundesbahn,* or *DB)* check-in desks, where baggage can be checked in for any train station within the *DB* network. At Frankfurt airport you can catch a city train *(S-Bahn)* taking you directly to the main train station *(Hauptbahnhof)*. Tickets are available from machines that give change.

Taxi fares consist of a basic flat rate plus a charge per kilometer, and vary from place to place. There may be surcharges for baggage. It is customary to give a tip by rounding off the fare costs, and to add some additional money for baggage if no surcharge has been made.

LÖSUNGEN

A. 1. *Er war ruhig.* 2. *Sie können kurzfristig umbuchen.* 3. *Sie müssen einen Gepäckwagen finden.* 4. *Sie nehmen ein Taxi.*
B. 1.—f 2.—b 3.—d 4.—a 5.—e 6.—c
C. 1. *Alle* 2. *Diese* 3. *jede* 4. *welcher* 5. *Manche*
D. 1. *Wir müssen einen Gepäckträger finden oder unsere Koffer einzeln tragen.* 2. *Ich brauche kein Einzelzimmer, sondern ein Doppelzimmer.*
   3. *Meine Kinder mögen den Süden, aber ihnen gefällt auch der Norden.*
E. 1. *Fahren wir mit dem Bus oder dem Taxi?* 2. *Ist dieses Hotel gut?*

LEKTION 13

A. DIALOG

Auf der Autobahn.

FRAU LANGE: Der Tacho zeigt schon 200 Kilometer. Wohin rasen wir eigentlich? Wir fahren doch ans Meer.

HERR LANGE: Ich habe Hunger. An der ersten Ausfahrt hinter der Grenze fahren wir ab. In dem Städtchen halten wir zum Mittagessen. Da tanken wir auch, denn das Benzin ist billiger, und dann prüfen wir die Reifen.

FRAU LANGE: Was, du hast nicht genug Luft in den Reifen? Das ist doch gefährlich. Bitte fahr auf diese Raststätte hier. Es sind nur 500 Meter. Da gibt's auch eine Tankstelle.

HERR LANGE: Ich kann doch nicht so schnell bremsen, denn sonst fahren die Wagen hinter mir auf uns auf. Wir überholen noch diesen Lastwagen, und dann bleiben wir rechts. Neben dem Verbandskasten liegt eine Tafel Schokolade. Ich möchte gern ein Stück.

FRAU LANGE: Hier, ich lege sie neben dich auf den Vordersitz.

HERR LANGE: Danke schön.

On the Highway.

MRS. LANGE: The speedometer shows 200 kilometers. Where are we going in such a hurry? We're just driving to the ocean.

MR. LANGE: I'm hungry. At the first exit beyond the border we'll turn off. We'll stop for lunch in the little town there. We'll also get gas because it's cheaper, and then we'll check the tires.

MRS. LANGE: What? You don't have enough air in the tires? That's quite dangerous. Please go into this rest stop. It's only 500 meters ahead. There's a gas station, too.

MR. LANGE: I can't brake so quickly, otherwise the cars behind me will drive into us. We'll pass this truck, and then we'll stay on the right. Next to the first-aid kit is a bar of chocolate. I'd like a piece, please.

MRS. LANGE: Here, I'll put it next to you on the front seat.

MR. LANGE: Thanks a lot.

B. GRAMMATIK UND GEBRAUCH

1. *LEGEN* AND *LIEGEN*

To express placing something on something, use *legen* (to put, lay). *Legen* is a transitive verb and can take a direct object.

Ich lege die Schokolade auf den Sitz.
I'll lay (put) the chocolate on the seat.

To express the position of someone or something, use *liegen* (to lie). *Liegen* is an intransitive verb and cannot take a direct object.

Die Schokolade liegt auf dem Sitz.
The chocolate is lying on the seat.

2. *WO* AND *WOHIN*

Wo? means "where?" in the sense of "in what place?"

Wo sind wir?
Where (in what place) are we?

Wohin? means "where?" in the sense of "to what place?"

Wohin fahren wir?
Where (to what place) are we driving?

3. TWO-WAY PREPOSITIONS: *AN, AUF, HINTER, IN, NEBEN*

German has nine so-called two-way (or either-or) prepositions. Nouns or pronouns that follow these prepositions can be either in the dative or in the accusative case. The dative case is used when the preposition indicates a position in space. The accusative case is used when the preposition indicates a change of location. To find out which case to use, ask either *wo?* (where, in what place?) or *wohin?* (to where, to what place?).

POSITION—DATIVE

Wo sind wir?
   Where are we?

Wir sind in der Stadt.
   We are in the city.

DIRECTION—ACCUSATIVE

Wohin fahren wir?
   (To) where are we driving?

Wir fahren in die Stadt.
   We are driving to the city.

Five of the nine two-way prepositions will be introduced in this lesson.

an	at, at the side of; to; on
auf	on, on top of, onto
hinter	in back of, behind
in	in, inside, into
neben	beside, next to

Several two-way prepositions contract with the articles *das* and *dem:*

an dem Meer	→	*am Meer*	at the ocean
an das Meer	→	*ans Meer*	to the ocean
auf das Land	→	*aufs Land*	to the country
in das Büro	→	*ins Büro*	into the office
in dem Büro	→	*im Büro*	in (at) the office

Wo sind wir?
Where are we?

Wir sind am *(an dem)* **Meer. (dative)**
We are at the ocean.

Wohin fahren wir?
Where are we driving to?

Wir fahren ans *(an das)* **Meer. (accusative)**
We are driving to the ocean.

Wo ist die Uhr?
Where is the clock?

Die Uhr ist an der Wand. (dative)
The clock is on the wall.

Wohin hängen wir die Uhr?
Where (on what) do we hang the clock?

Wir hängen die Uhr an die Wand. (accusative)
We hang the clock on the wall.

b. AUF

Wo sind wir?
Where are we?

Wir sind auf der Autobahn. (dative)
We are on the highway.

Wohin fahren wir?
Where are we driving?

Wir fahren auf die Autobahn. (accusative)
We are driving onto the highway.

Wo liegt die Schokolade?
Where is the chocolate lying?

Die Schokolade liegt auf dem Sitz. (dative)
The chocolate is lying on the seat.

Wohin legt er die Schokolade?
Where is he putting (laying) the chocolate?

Er legt die Schokolade auf den Sitz. (accusative)
He's putting (laying) the chocolate on the seat.

C. HINTER

Wo fahren die Autos?
Where are the cars driving?

Die Autos fahren hinter mir. (dative)
The cars are driving behind me.

Wohin läuft er?
Where is he running?

Er läuft hinter das Auto. (accusative)
He runs behind the car.

d. IN

Wo sind wir?
Where are we?

Wir sind in der Stadt. (dative)
We are in the city.

Wohin fahren wir?
Where (into what) are we driving?

Wir fahren in die Stadt. (accusative)
We are driving into the city.

e. NEBEN

Wo liegt der Brief?
Where is the letter lying?

Der Brief liegt neben ihm. (dative)
The letter is lying next to (beside) him.

Wohin legt sie den Brief?
Where is she laying the letter?

Sie legt den Brief neben ihn. (accusative)
She lays the letter next to him.

An and *auf* can both mean "on." Use *an* for vertical surfaces, and *auf* for horizontal surfaces.

4. MEASUREMENTS OF DISTANCE

In German-speaking countries, as in most other European countries, the metric system is used to measure length and distance.

1 *Millimeter (mm)*		= 0.039 inch
100 *Millimeter*	= 1 *Centimeter (cm)*	= 0.394 inch
100 *Centimeter*	= 1 *Meter (m)*	= 1.094 yards
1.000 *Meter*	= 1 *Kilometer (km)*	= 0.621 mile

VOKABELN

auf der Autobahn	on the highway
das Auto, *-s*	car
der Reifen, *-*	tire
der Kilometer, *-*	kilometer (km)
der Tachometer, *-*	speedometer
der Tacho, *-s*	speedometer
der Vordersitz, *-e*	front seat
der Rücksitz, *-e*	back seat
der Verband(s)kasten, ⁚	first-aid kit
tanken	to get gas
die Tankstelle, *-n*	gas station
das Benzin	gasoline
halten	to stop
die Autobahn, *-en*	highway
die Ausfahrt, *-en*	highway exit
die Raststätte, *-n*	rest stop
der Verkehr	traffic
der Lastwagen, *-*	truck
die Bremse, *-n*	brake
die Fahrt, *-en*	trip
bremsen	to brake
rasen	to speed

überholen	to pass, to overtake
die Luft prüfen	to check the air
gefährlich	dangerous
hängen	to hang
legen	to lay
liegen	to lie
billig	cheap
billiger	cheaper
teuer	expensive
die Stadt, ¨e	city
das Städtchen	small city
die Wand, ¨e	wall
die Grenze, -n	border
die Tafel Schokolade	the bar of chocolate
das Stück, -e	the piece
rechts	to the right, on the right
links	to the left, on the left
gern	gladly, readily

ÜBUNGEN

A. *Beantworten Sie die Fragen zum Dialog.*

1. *Was zeigt der Tacho?*
2. *Wo fahren Herr und Frau Lange?*
3. *Wohin soll Herr Lange fahren?*
4. *Warum kann Herr Lange nicht so schnell bremsen?*
5. *Wo liegt die Schokolade?*

B. *Suchen Sie die richtige deutsche Übersetzung.*

1.	to check the air	a.	*die Bremse*
2.	gasoline	b.	*die Tankstelle*
3.	rest stop	c.	*überholen*
4.	speedometer	d.	*das Benzin*
5.	to pass	e.	*die Autobahn*
6.	expressway	f.	*halten*

7. traffic
8. to stop
9. brake
10. gas station

g. *die Luft prüfen*
h. *die Raststätte*
i. *der Verkehr*
j. *der Tacho*

C. *Dativ oder Akkusativ? Setzen Sie die fehlenden Endungen ein.* (Dative or accusative? Supply the missing endings.)

BEISPIEL: Der Verbandskasten liegt auf d__ Rücksitz.
Der Verbandskasten liegt auf dem Rücksitz.

1. *Die Familie wohnt in ein__ Stadt an d__ Grenze.*
2. *Die Mutter kauft in d__ Supermarkt hinter d__ Grenze.*
3. *Neben d__ Supermarkt ist eine Tankstelle.*
4. *Sie tankt an d__ Tankstelle.*
5. *Dann fährt sie auf d__ Autobahn.*

KULTURNOTIZ

There is no speed limit *(Geschwindigkeitsbegrenzung)* on the expressways in Germany unless otherwise indicated. There is only a recommended speed limit of 130 kilometers per hour. On secondary roads outside cities, the speed limit is 100 km per hour. Usually, the speed limit within cities and towns is 50 km per hour, and 30 km per hour in residential areas. In all German-speaking countries it is mandatory for everybody riding in a car to wear a seat belt *(Sicherheitsgurt)*. Children under the age of twelve have to ride in the back. These laws are strictly enforced. It's also mandatory for every car to carry a first-aid kit, which should be displayed, preferably in the rear window. Before driving in German-speaking countries you should be familiar with all traffic signs *(Verkehrsschilder)* and traffic rules *(Verkehrsregeln)*.

LÖSUNGEN

A. 1. *Der Tacho zeigt 200 km.* 2. *Sie fahren auf der Autobahn.* 3. *Er soll auf die Raststätte fahren.* 4. *Die Autos hinter ihm fahren auf ihn auf.* 5. *Sie liegt neben dem Verbandskasten.*

B. 1.—g 2.—d 3.—h 4.—j 5.—c 6.—e 7.—i 8.—f 9.—a 10.—b

C. 1. *einer, d*er 2. *d*em, *d*er 3. *d*em 4. *d*er 5. *d*ie

LEKTION 14

A. DIALOG

In der Autoreparaturwerkstatt.

HERR BAUM: Können Sie heute noch meinen Wagen reparieren?

MECHANIKER: Was fehlt denn?

HERR BAUM: Es ist ein Gebrauchtwagen. Heute bleibt er plötzlich mitten auf der Kreuzung stehen, und direkt hinter mir ist ein Lastwagen. Dann springt er einfach nicht mehr an.

MECHANIKER: Gut. Ich überprüfe den Anlasser und reinige oder ersetze die Zündkerzen. Vielleicht braucht die Batterie auch Wasser oder ist zu alt.

HERR BAUM: Ja. Und das Blinklicht rechts und die Hupe funktionieren nicht. Das Gaspedal klemmt manchmal.

MECHANIKER: Um Himmels Willen! Wo steht er?

HERR BAUM: Vor Tanksäule zwei.

MECHANIKER: Geben Sie mir den Zündschlüssel!

HERR BAUM: Er steckt in der Zündung.

MECHANIKER: Dann stellen Sie das Auto unter das Dach, zwischen den Lieferwagen und das Motorrad.

HERR BAUM: Wann ist das Auto fertig?

MECHANIKER: Zwischen vier und fünf.

HERR BAUM: Gut. Danke.

In the Car Repair Shop.

MR. BAUM: Can you repair my car today?

MECHANIC: What's wrong with it?

MR. BAUM: It's a used car. Today it suddenly stalled in the middle of an intersection, and a truck was directly behind me. Then it simply wouldn't start again.

MECHANIC: All right. I'll check the starter and clean or replace the spark plugs. The battery may be low on water, or may be too old.

MR. BAUM: Yes. And the right turn signal and horn don't work. The gas pedal sometimes jams.

MECHANIC: Good heavens! Where did you park it?

MR. BAUM: In front of pump two.

MECHANIC: Give me the key.

MR. BAUM: It's in the ignition.

MECHANIC: Then put the car under the carport, between the delivery van and the motorcycle.

MR. BAUM: When will the car be ready?

MECHANIC: Between four and five.

MR. BAUM: Very good. Thank you.

B. GRAMMATIK UND GEBRAUCH

1. *SETZEN* AND *STELLEN*; *SITZEN* AND *STEHEN*; *STECKEN*

The transitive verbs *setzen* (to set, to place, to put) and *stellen* (to place, to put) require a direct object and express motion.

Setz das Kind auf den Rücksitz!
Put the child in the backseat.

Ich stelle mein Auto in die Garage.
I put my car in the garage.

The intransitive verbs *sitzen* (to sit) and *stehen* (to stand) cannot have a direct object and express the location of persons and things.

Das Kind sitzt auf dem Rücksitz.
The child sits in the backseat.

Mein Auto steht in der Garage.
My car is in the garage.

The verb *stecken* (to stick, to put) may be transitive or intransitive, expressing motion or location.

a. MOTION

Er steckt den Schlüssel in die Zündung.
He puts the key into the ignition.

The prepositional phrase *in die Zündung* is in the accusative case and answers the question *wohin?*

b. LOCATION

Der Schlüssel steckt in der Zündung.
The key is in the ignition.

The prepositional phrase *in der Zündung* is in the dative case and answers the question *wo?*

2. TWO-WAY PREPOSITIONS: *ÜBER, UNTER, VOR, ZWISCHEN*

Here are four more two-way prepositions in addition to the ones you learned in lesson 13:

über	above, over, across, about
unter	under, beneath, among
vor	in front of, before, ago
zwischen	between

a. ÜBER

Wo hängt die Uhr?
Where is the clock?

Die Uhr hängt über dem Ausgang. (dative)
 The clock is over the exit.

Wohin hängt er die Uhr?
 Where is he putting the clock?

Er hängt die Uhr über den Ausgang. (accusative)
 He is putting the clock over the exit.

b. UNTER

Wo steht das Auto?
 Where is the car (parked)?

Das Auto steht unter einem Dach. (dative)
 The car is (parked) under a carport.

Wohin stellt er das Auto?
 Where is he putting the car?

Er stellt das Auto unter ein Dach. (accusative)
 He's putting the car under a carport.

c. VOR

Wo steht das Gepäck?
 Where is the baggage?

Das Gepäck steht vor dem Eingang. (dative)
 The baggage is in front of the entrance.

Wohin stellen wir das Gepäck?
 Where shall we put the baggage?

Wir stellen das Gepäck vor den Eingang. (accusative)
 We'll put the baggage in front of the entrance.

d. ZWISCHEN

Wo steht mein Motorrad?
 Where is my motorcyle parked?

Mein Motorrad steht zwischen den Autos. (dative)
 My motorcycle is parked between the cars.

Wohin stelle ich mein Motorrad?
 Where will I park my motorcycle?

Ich stelle mein Motorrad zwischen die Autos. (accusative)
  I'll park my motorcycle between the cars.

  Several two-way prepositions contract with the articles *das* and *dem* in spoken German only:

unter das Bett	→	unters Bett	under the bed
unter dem Bett	→	unterm Bett	under the bed
über das Dach	→	übers Dach	over the roof
über dem Dach	→	überm Dach	over the roof
vor das Haus	→	vors Haus	in front of the house
vor dem Haus	→	vorm Haus	in front of the house

3. VERBS WITH PREPOSITIONS

  Prepositions have special meanings when they are combined with specific verbs.

erzählen von (+ dat.)   *Sie erzählt von ihren Eltern.*
  to talk about   She talks about her parents.
fahren mit (+ dat.)   *Ich fahre mit dem Bus.*
  to go (by means of)   I go by bus.
helfen bei (+ dat.)   *Wir helfen bei der Arbeit.*
  to help with   We help with the work.
denken an (+ acc.)   *Er denkt an sie.*
  to think of/about   He thinks of her.
schreiben an (+ acc.)   *Sie schreibt an ihn.*
  to write to   She writes to him.
schreiben über (+ acc.)   *Er schreibt über seine Reise.*
  to write about   He writes about his trip.
sprechen über (+ acc.)   *Sie sprechen über ihren Sohn.*
  to talk about   They talk about their son.
warten auf (+ acc.)   *Er wartet auf den Zug.*
  to wait for   He's waiting for the train.

  For verbs that take a two-way preposition, the case must be learned.

Note that *über* always takes the accusative when it is used figuratively:

Er spricht über seine Reise.
   He's talking about his trip.

VOKABELN

die Autoreparaturwerkstatt, ¨-en	automobile repair shop
der Automechaniker, -	automobile mechanic
reparieren	to repair
der Gebrauchtwagen, -	used car
der Lieferwagen, -	delivery van
das Motorrad, ¨-er	motorcycle
stehen bleiben	to stop, to stall
an*springen	to start
überprüfen	to test, to check
der Anlasser, -	starter
reinigen	to clean
ersetzen	to replace
die Zündkerze, -n	spark plug
die Batterie, -n	battery
Wasser brauchen	to need water, to be low on water
das Blinklicht, -er	turn signal
funktionieren	to function
klemmen	to jam
das Gaspedal, -e	gas pedal
das Bremspedal, -e	brake pedal
die Hupe, -n	horn
der Reifen, -	tire
die Tanksäule, -n	gasoline pump
der Zündschlüssel, -	ignition key
die Zündung, -en	ignition
die Garage, -n	garage
das Dach, ¨-er	roof, carport
die Kreuzung, -en	intersection
mitten auf (+ dat.)	in the middle of
fehlen	to be missing

Was fehlt dir?	What's wrong?
plötzlich	suddenly
manchmal	sometimes
direkt	directly
zu viel	too much
fertig sein	to be ready

ÜBUNGEN

A. *Beantworten Sie die Fragen zum Dialog.*

1. *Wo bleibt das Auto plötzlich stehen?*
2. *Was überprüft der Mechaniker?*
3. *Was braucht die Batterie vielleicht?*
4. *Wohin soll Herr Baum das Auto stellen?*
5. *Wann ist das Auto fertig?*

B. *Suchen Sie die richtige deutsche Übersetzung.*

1. The gas pedal jams.
2. When will the car be ready?
3. The key is in the ignition.
4. What's wrong?
5. Check the tires, too.
6. Does the battery need water?
7. The horn doesn't work.

a. *Der Zündschlüssel steckt in der Zündung.*
b. *Was fehlt dir?*
c. *Die Hupe funktioniert nicht.*
d. *Das Gaspedal klemmt.*
e. *Braucht die Batterie Wasser?*
f. *Wann ist das Auto fertig?*
g. *Überprüfen Sie auch die Reifen!*

C. *Setzen Sie die fehlenden Präpositionen ein.*

1. *Stellen Sie die Koffer _____ das Dach.* (under)
2. *_____ dem Eingang hängt eine Uhr.* (over)

3. *Stell dich _____ mich!* (before)
4. *Ich lege die Handschuhe _____ den Schal und den Pullover.*
   (between)
5. *Wir sprechen _____ den Wetterbericht.* (about)
6. *Er steht _____ dem Schalter.* (in front of)

D. *Übersetzen Sie.*

1. Can you repair my car?
2. When will the car be ready?
3. It's a used car.

KULTURNOTIZ

German-speaking countries have automobile clubs offering assistance to drivers similar to the American Automobile Association (AAA). The highway patrol service of the *ADAC (Allgemeiner Deutscher Automobil Club)* is on duty in Germany along all *Autobahnen* and federal highways. This service is free of charge. Mobile units can be summoned from emergency call boxes placed at regular intervals along the *Autobahnen.* When you need help, ask specifically for *die Straßenwachthilfe* (highway assistance service). In case of special emergencies, motorists traveling in Germany may be contacted by radio announcements through the services of the *ADAC Reiseruf.*

LÖSUNGEN

A. 1. *Es bleibt plötzlich mitten auf der Kreuzung stehen.* 2. *Er überprüft den Anlasser.* 3. *Sie braucht vielleicht Wasser.* 4. *Er soll das Auto unter das Dach, zwischen den Lieferwagen und das Motorrad stellen.* 5. *Es ist zwischen vier und fünf fertig.*
B. 1.—d   2.—f   3.—a   4.—b   5.—g   6.—e   7.—c
C. 1. *unter*   2. *Über*   3. *vor*   4. *zwischen*   5. *über*   6. *vor*
D. 1. *Können Sie mein Auto reparieren?* 2. *Wann ist das Auto fertig?* 3. *Es ist ein Gebrauchtwagen.*

LEKTION 15

BEIM ARZT.   At the Doctor's.

A. DIALOG

Im Wartezimmer.

FRAU BRINK: Warum sind Sie hier?

FRAU KLUGE: Ach, mein Hals tut weh, ich habe Kopf- und Magenschmerzen, mir ist schwindlig, und ich habe 39 Grad Fieber.

FRAU BRINK: Furchtbar. Sie haben sicherlich die Grippe. Die Tochter meiner Nachbarin hat trotz der Grippeimpfung die gleichen Symptome.

FRAU KLUGE: Vielleicht hat sie eine andere Krankheit. Und was fehlt Ihnen?

FRAU BRINK: Ich huste immer während der Nacht.

FRAU KLUGE: Nehmen Sie Hustentropfen?

FRAU BRINK: Sie helfen nicht.

FRAU KLUGE: Haben Sie eine Allergie?

FRAU BRINK: Hoffentlich nicht. Diese Tests und Spritzen halte ich nicht aus. Ein Freund meines Mannes ist seit fünf Monaten wegen seiner Allergie in Behandlung. Statt Ausschlag und Husten hat er jetzt Schwellungen.

FRAU KLUGE: Unglaublich.

Im Sprechzimmer.

ARZT: Sagen Sie Aaaa!

PATIENT: Aaaa!

ARZT: Hmm. Ich verschreibe Ihnen ein Medikament. Nehmen Sie eine dieser Tabletten dreimal täglich. Hier ist das Rezept.

PATIENT: Danke, Herr Doktor.

In the Waiting Room.

MRS. BRINK: Why are you here?

MRS. KLUGE: Oh, my throat hurts, I have a headache and a stomachache, I'm dizzy and have a fever of 102 degrees.

MRS. BRINK: Terrible. I'm sure you have the flu. My neighbor's daughter has the same symptoms, in spite of the flu vaccination.

MRS. KLUGE: Perhaps she has a different illness. And what do you have?

MRS. BRINK: I always cough during the night.

MRS. KLUGE: Are you taking cough drops?

MRS. BRINK: They don't help.

MRS. KLUGE: Do you have an allergy?

MRS. BRINK: I hope not. I can't endure these tests and shots. My husband's friend has been in treatment for an allergy for five months. Instead of rashes and cough, he now has swelling.

MRS. KLUGE: Unbelievable.

In the Consulting Room.

PHYSICIAN: Say aaah!

PATIENT: Aaah!

PHYSICIAN: Hmm. I'll prescribe some medicine for you. Take one of these pills three times a day. Here's the prescription.

PATIENT: Thank you, doctor.

B. GRAMMATIK UND GEBRAUCH

1. THE GENITIVE CASE

German uses the genitive case to show possession or close relationship. The genitive case is used for things as well as for persons. For things and ideas English usually uses a construction with "of."

Masculine and neuter nouns in the singular add -*s* in the genitive case; one-syllable nouns usually add -*es*.

NOM. SING. MASC.	GEN. SING. MASC.
der Vater	*des Vaters*
ein Vater	*eines Vaters*
mein Vater	*meines Vaters*
kein Vater	*keines Vaters*

NOM. SING. FEM.	GEN. SING. FEM.
die Mutter	*der Mutter*
eine Mutter	*einer Mutter*
meine Mutter	*meiner Mutter*
keine Mutter	*keiner Mutter*

NOM. SING. NEUT.	GEN. SING. NEUT.
das Kind	*des Kindes*
ein Kind	*eines Kindes*
mein Kind	*meines Kindes*
kein Kind	*keines Kindes*

NOM. PL. (ALL GENDERS)	GEN. PL. (ALL GENDERS)
die Kinder	*der Kinder*
keine Kinder	*keiner Kinder*
meine Kinder	*meiner Kinder*

Das Buch des Vaters liegt hier.
> The father's book (the book of the father) is here.

Die Tochter meiner Freundin ist krank.
> My girlfriend's daughter (the daughter of my girlfriend) is sick.

Die Suppe des Kindes wird kalt.
  The child's soup (the soup of the child) is getting cold.

Die Grippe der Kinder ist furchtbar.
  The children's flu (the flu of the children) is terrible.

The genitive of proper nouns is designated in German as in English by adding -s to the noun. However, there is no apostrophe in German.

Franks Tabletten	Frank's pills
Frau Brinks Entzündung	Mrs. Brink's inflammation

2. PREPOSITIONS THAT TAKE THE GENITIVE

Nouns following these prepositions are in the genitive case:

(an)statt	instead of
trotz	in spite of
während	during, in the course of
wegen	because of

a. *(AN)STATT*

Anstatt einer Erkältung hat er die Grippe.
  Instead of a cold he has the flu.

Statt seiner Mutter besucht er seine Tante.
  Instead of his mother he visits his aunt.

Note: *Anstatt* is often shortened to *statt*.

b. *TROTZ*

Trotz seines Hustens läuft er Ski.
  In spite of his cough he goes skiing.

Trotz der Impfung ist sie krank.
  In spite of the vaccination she is ill.

c. *WÄHREND*

Während des Abends wird es kalt.
It gets cold during the evening.

Während der Ferien schreibt sie viele Postkarten.
She writes many postcards during vacation.

Ich huste immer während der Nacht.
I always cough during the night.

d. *WEGEN*

Er geht wegen einer Erkältung zum Arzt.
He goes to the physician because of a cold.

Wegen des Verkehrs fährt er nicht auf der Autobahn.
He doesn't take the expressway because of the traffic.

Although it is grammatically incorrect, you will hear *anstatt, trotz,* and *wegen* used with the dative case in colloquial German.

3. THE INTERROGATIVE *WESSEN*

The genitive form of the interrogative *wer* (who) is *wessen* (whose).

Wessen Tochter hat die gleichen Symptome?
Whose daughter has the same symptoms?

Wessen Freund hat eine Allergie?
Whose friend has an allergy?

4. MEASUREMENT OF TEMPERATURE

In German-speaking countries, as in most other European countries, the Celsius scale is used to measure temperature. You can use the following formula to convert Fahrenheit to Celsius.

$$1.8 \times {}^\circ\text{Celsius} + 32 = {}^\circ\text{Fahrenheit}$$

A fever of 39° Celsius equals (1.8 × 39 + 32) 102.2° Fahrenheit.

VOKABELN

die Krankheit, -en	illness, disease
der Schmerz, -en	pain, hurt
schmerzen	to hurt
weh tun	
Es tut weh.	It hurts.
die Halsschmerzen	sore throat
die Kopfschmerzen	headache
die Magenschmerzen	stomachache
die Grippe, -n	flu, influenza
der Husten	cough
husten	to cough
die Erkältung, -en	cold
das Symptom, -e	symptom
die Entzündung, -en	inflammation
der Ausschlag, ¨e	rash, eczema
die Allergie, -n	allergy
die Schwellung, -en	swelling
schwindlig	dizzy
Mir ist schwindlig.	I'm dizzy.
aus*halten	to endure
der Arzt, ¨e	physician (male)
die Ärztin, -nen	physician (female)
der Patient, -en	patient (male)
die Patientin, -nen	patient (female)
das Rezept, -e	prescription, recipe
verschreiben	to prescribe
das Medikament, -e	medication
die Tablette, -n	pill
der Tropfen, -	drop
die Impfung, -en	vaccination
die Spritze, -n	shot, syringe
das Ergebnis, -se	result
furchtbar	terrible
unglaublich	unbelievable
sicherlich	certainly
dreimal täglich	three times a day

A. *Beantworten Sie die Fragen zum Dialog.*

    1. *Warum ist Frau Kluge im Wartezimmer?*
    2. *Wann hustet Frau Brink immer?*
    3. *Warum nimmt Frau Brink keine Hustentropfen?*
    4. *Was verschreibt der Arzt?*

B. *Suchen Sie die richtige deutsche Übersetzung.*

    1. She isn't getting a vaccination.
    2. The family has the flu.
    3. She takes a pill three times a day.
    4. I've got a fever.
    5. She is dizzy.

    a. *Ihr ist schwindlig.*
    b. *Die Familie hat die Grippe.*
    c. *Sie bekommt keine Impfung.*
    d. *Ich habe Fieber.*
    e. *Sie nimmt eine Tablette dreimal täglich.*

C. *Setzen Sie die richtigen Präpositionen ein.*

    1. _____ *des Tages hustet er immer. (During)*
    2. _____ *eines Brötchens isst er jetzt nichts.* (Instead of)
    3. *Er arbeitet* _____ *seiner Schmerzen.* (in spite of)
    4. *Endlich geht er* _____ *seines Hustens zum Arzt.* (because of)

D. *Übersetzen Sie.*

    1. Mrs. Brink's husband
    2. Christa's girlfriend
    3. the tires of the car
    4. my brother's gift
    5. his mother's sister
    6. the bread of the child
    7. Whose sister is ill?

KULTURNOTIZ

The doctor-patient ratio in German-speaking countries is one of the highest in the world. Medical facilities are modern and well equipped. Great emphasis is placed on preventive medicine. Germany has an extensive public healthcare system. Virtually all Germans have health insurance. Doctors handle the insurance claims and the patient usually does not have to lay out any money.

LÖSUNGEN

A. 1. *Ihr Hals tut weh, sie hat Kopf- und Magenschmerzen, ihr ist schwindlig, und sie hat neununddreißig Grad Fieber. 2. Sie hustet immer während der Nacht. 3. Sie helfen nicht. 4. Er verschreibt ein Medikament.*

B. 1.—c 2.—b 3.—e 4.—d 5.—a

C. 1. *Während* 2. *(An)statt* 3. *trotz* 4. *wegen*

D. 1. *Frau Brinks Mann* 2. *Christas Freundin* 3. *die Reifen des Autos* 4. *das Geschenk meines Bruders* 5. *die Schwester seiner Mutter* 6. *das Brot des Kindes* 7. *Wessen Schwester ist krank?*

DRITTE WIEDERHOLUNGSAUFGABE

A. *Setzen Sie die fehlenden Pronomen ein.*

BEISPIEL: _____ *schenkst du nichts? (Whom)*
       Wem schenkst du nichts?

1. *Geben sie* _____ *bitte etwas Kleingeld.* (me)
2. *Was schenkst du* _____? (him)
3. *Er bringt* _____ *immer Blumen.* (us)
4. *Ich glaube* _____. (them)
5. *Wir antworten* _____ *morgen.* (you, pol.)
6. *Wie gefällt* _____ *der Mantel?* (you, fam. sing.)

B. *Setzen Sie die fehlenden Präpositionen ein.*

BEISPIEL: *Liegt der Brief* _____ *der Zeitung? (under)*
      Liegt der Brief unter der Zeitung?

1. *Die Reparaturwerkstatt ist* _____ *der Post. (near)*
2. *Wir fahren* _____ *dem Zug. (by)*
3. _____ *diesem Sommer bleiben wir lange in Amerika. (After)*
4. *Das Geschenk ist* _____ *meiner Freundin. (from)*
5. *Ich nehme ein Taxi* _____ *Flugplatz. (to)*

C. *Verbinden Sie die zwei Sätze mit der gegebenen Konjunktion.* (Combine the two sentences, using the conjunction given.)

BEISPIEL: *Er kommt nicht heute. Er kommt morgen. (rather)*
Er kommt nicht heute, sondern morgen.

1. *Wir fahren nach Italien. Wir fahren nach Spanien. (or)*
2. *Heute bleiben wir im Hotel. Es regnet. (because)*
3. *Ihm gefällt das Meer. Sie mag es nicht.* (but)

D. *Übersetzen Sie.*

1. To whom can we give the keys?
2. It's already getting warm.
3. He thinks about his father.

E. *Setzen Sie die "der-Wörter" mit den richtigen Endungen ein.*

BEISPIEL: _____ *Sommer in Deutschland sind kalt. (Some)*
Manche Sommer in Deutschland sind kalt.

1. *Wohin schicken wir* _____ *Bücher? (these)*
2. _____ *Zimmer haben ein Bad.* (All)
3. _____ *Hotel gefällt Ihnen?* (Which)
4. _____ *Autofahrer muss die Verkehrsregeln kennen.* (Every)

F. *Setzen Sie die fehlenden Wörter ein.*

BEISPIEL: *Legen Sie das Buch in* _____. *(the suitcase)*
Legen Sie das Buch in den Koffer.

1. *Der Brief liegt auf* _____. *(the table)*
2. *Bringen Sie den Koffer in* _____. *(my room)*
3. *Das Paket steht unter* _____. *(the stairs)*
4. *Sprechen wir nicht über* _____. *(them)*

G. *Setzen Sie die fehlenden Wörter ein.*

BEISPIEL: *Die Tochter* _____ *Freundin ist Ärztin. (of my)*
Die Tochter meiner Freundin ist Ärztin.

1. *Während* _____ *Essens lese ich Zeitung. (the)*
2. _____ *Auto ist das? (Whose)*
3. *Trotz* _____ *Krankheit arbeitet er. (his)*
4. *Horst ist der Mann* _____ *Professorin. (of a)*

LÖSUNGEN

A. 1. *mir* 2. *ihm* 3. *uns* 4. *ihnen* 5. *Ihnen* 6. *dir*
B. 1. *bei* 2. *mit* 3. *Nach* 4. *von* 5. *zum*
C. 1. *Wir fahren nach Italien oder nach Spanien.* 2. *Heute bleiben wir im Hotel, denn es regnet.* 3. *Ihm gefällt das Meer, aber sie mag es nicht.*
D. 1. *Wem können wir die Schlüssel geben?* 2. *Es wird schon warm.* 3. *Er denkt an seinen Vater.*
E. 1. *diese* 2. *Alle* 3. *Welches* 4. *Jeder*
F. 1. *dem Tisch* 2. *mein Zimmer* 3. *der Treppe* 4. *sie*
G. 1. *des* 2. *Wessen* 3. *seiner* 4. *einer*

LEKTION 16

AUF DER MESSE.   At a Trade Fair.

A. DIALOG

Streß auf der Messe.

THOMAS: Am Donnerstag bin ich von morgens bis abends auf der Messe. Was machst du dann? Ich weiß nicht, ob die Messe nicht zu anstrengend für dich ist.

RITA: Das sage ich dir, wenn ich die Einzelheiten des Tagesablaufs kenne.

THOMAS: Zuerst besuche ich den Messestand meiner Firma und dann die Ausstellungen der Konkurrenten. Obwohl es Transportmöglichkeiten innerhalb des Messegeländes gibt, muss man viel laufen. Ich hoffe, dass du Sportschuhe dabei hast.

RITA: Ja natürlich.

THOMAS: Wahrscheinlich reicht die Zeit nur für einen Imbiss. Erst habe ich einen Termin mit einem Lieferanten, danach eine Besprechung mit Herren eines Großkonzerns und abends eine Zusammenkunft mit einem Geschäftsführer der Stahlindustrie.

RITA: Wenn ich im Messeprogramm nichts für mich finde, dann fahre ich ins Hotel zurück. Geschäftsbesprechungen sind sehr ermüdend.

Stress at the Trade Fair.

THOMAS: On Thursday, I'll be at the fair from morning to evening. What will you be doing then? I don't know if the fair won't be too strenuous for you.

RITA: I'll tell you that as soon as I know the details of the daily program.

THOMAS: First I'll visit my company's booth and then the competitors' exhibitions. Although there is transportation within the fair grounds, one must walk a lot. I hope that you have athletic shoes.

RITA: Yes, of course.

THOMAS: There probably will only be time for a light lunch. First I have an appointment with a supplier, after that a conference with gentlemen from a very large company, and in the evening, a meeting with a manager in the steel industry.

RITA: If I find nothing for myself in the fair program, I'll go back to the hotel. Business discussions are very tiring.

B. GRAMMATIK UND GEBRAUCH

1. SUBORDINATING CONJUNCTIONS

The subordinating conjunctions include:

dass	that
ob	whether, if
weil	because
wenn	if, when, whenever

Subordinating conjunctions introduce dependent clauses. A dependent clause modifies the main clause, and makes sense only in connection with the main clause.

MAIN CLAUSE	DEPENDENT CLAUSE
I'll tell you that	*as soon as I know the details.*
Das sage ich dir,	*wenn ich die Einzelheiten kenne.*
I hope	**that you have athletic shoes with you.**
Ich hoffe,	*dass du Sportschuhe dabei hast.*

2. WORD ORDER WITH SUBORDINATING CONJUNCTIONS

a. In the subordinate clause, the conjugated verb (that is, the verb that has the ending—also called the finite verb) moves to the end of that clause. The subordinate, or dependent, clause is usually separated from the main clause by a comma.

Ich hoffe, dass du Sportschuhe dabei hast.
I hope that you have athletic shoes with you.

Ich weiß noch nicht, ob wir Zeit zum Essen haben.
I don't know yet whether we'll have time for dinner.

Sie ist blass, weil sie krank war.
She's pale because she was ill.

Wir kaufen kein Benzin, wenn es zu teuer ist.
We won't buy gasoline if it's too expensive.

b. A sentence may begin with the dependent clause. The main clause must then begin with the verb.

Wenn es zu anstrengend wird, gehe ich ins Hotel zurück.
If it gets too strenuous, I'll go back to the hotel.

c. In a dependent clause with a modal auxiliary and a verb in the infinitive, the modal auxiliary moves to the end of the clause.

Er sagt, dass er nicht lange bleiben will.
He says that he doesn't want to stay long.

d. Verbs with separable prefixes do not separate in dependent clauses.

Sie wünschen, dass wir am Sonntag abfahren.
They want us to leave on Sunday.

3. INTERROGATIVES AND ADVERBS AS CONJUNCTIONS

Interrogatives and adverbs can function as subordinate conjunctions.

Sag mir, warum du nicht gern fliegst.
Tell me why you don't like to fly.

Ich arbeite bis ich müde werde.
I'll work until I get tired.

4. FORMS OF MASCULINE *N*-NOUNS

Some masculine nouns, called "*n*-nouns," end in -*en* or -*n* in all cases, singular and plural, except in the nominative singular.

	SINGULAR		PLURAL
Nom.	der Patient		die Patienten
Acc.	den Patienten		die Patienten
Dat.	dem Patienten		den Patienten
Gen.	des Patienten		der Patienten

	SINGULAR		PLURAL
Nom.	der Beamte		die Beamten
Acc.	den Beamten		die Beamten
Dat.	dem Beamten		den Beamten
Gen.	des Beamten		der Beamten

	SINGULAR		PLURAL
Nom.	der Herr		die Herren
Acc.	den Herrn		die Herren
Dat.	dem Herrn		den Herren
Gen.	des Herrn		der Herren

In vocabulary lists as in dictionaries, the genitive singular ending as well as the plural ending of these nouns is indicated as follows:

der Patient, -en, -en

N-nouns ending in *-en* appear in seven identical forms, but their articles and functions will make their meaning clear:

Ich kenne den Lieferanten. (acc. sing.)
I know the supplier.

Schick dem Lieferanten Geld! (dat. sing.)
Send the supplier money.

Wo ist die Adresse des Lieferanten? (gen. sing.)
Where is the supplier's address?

Die Lieferanten waren nicht da. (nom. pl.)
The suppliers weren't there.

Ich kenne die Lieferanten. (acc. pl.)
I know the suppliers.

Wir kaufen von den Lieferanten. (dat. pl.)
We buy from the suppliers.

Die Waren der Lieferanten sind da. (gen. pl.)
The suppliers' merchandise is here.

A small number of *n*-nouns add an *-s* in the genitive singular in addition to the *-n* or *-en* ending.

der Name	the name	*das Herz*	the heart
des Namens	of the name	*des Herzens*	of the heart

Das ist der erste Buchstabe des Namens.
This is the first letter of the name.

5. PRESENT PARTICIPLES

Present participles are formed by adding the ending *-d* to the infinitive:

ermüden	*ermüdend*
to tire	tiring
laufen	*laufend*
to run	running

Die Besuche waren ermüdend.
The visits were tiring.

VOKABELN

die Messe, *-n*	fair, trade show
das Messegelände, *-*	fair exhibition grounds
der Messestand, *˸e*	booth
das Programm, *-e*	program

148

die Ausstellung, -en	exhibition
die Konkurrenz	competition
der Transport, -e	transport, conveyance
die Möglichkeit, -en	possibility
die Transportmöglichkeit, -en	means of conveyance, transportation
die Besprechung, -en	conference
die Zusammenkunft, ̈e	meeting
das Geschäft, -e	business
die Geschäftsbesprechung, -en	business discussion
der Termin, -e	appointment
einen Termin haben	to have an appointment
die Verhandlung, -en	discussion, negotiation
der Konzern, -e	company
der Großkonzern, -e	large company
der Lieferant, -en, -en	supplier, deliverer
der Fabrikant, -en, -en	manufacturer
der Abnehmer, -	buyer
der Geschäftsführer, -	manager
der Präsident, -en, -en	president
der Industrielle, -n	industrialist
die Industrie, -n	industry
der Imbiss, -e	snack
zuerst	at first
danach	afterward
anstrengend	strenuous, taxing
ermüdend	tiring
die Einzelheit, -en	detail
von morgens bis abends	from morning to evening
dass	that
ob	whether, if
weil	because
wenn	if, when, whenever

A. *Beantworten Sie die Fragen zum Dialog.*

1. *Wann ist Thomas auf der Messe?*
2. *Wie lange ist er auf der Messe?*
3. *Was besucht er zuerst?*
4. *Warum hofft er, dass Rita Sportschuhe dabei hat?*
5. *Was ist sehr ermüdend?*

B. *Suchen Sie die richtige deutsche Übersetzung.*

1. I'm visiting the trade show.
2. I'm not going, because it's tiring.
3. I'll visit my competitor's booth.
4. He has a meeting with a supplier.
5. I have an appointment.
6. I know every detail.
7. The competition is strong.
8. The program is interesting.

a. *Die Konkurrenz ist groß.*
b. *Er hat eine Besprechung mit einem Lieferanten.*
c. *Ich habe einen Termin.*
d. *Ich besuche die Messe.*
e. *Ich besuche den Messestand meines Konkurrenten.*
f. *Ich gehe nicht, weil es ermüdend ist.*
g. *Das Programm ist interessant.*
h. *Ich kenne jede Einzelheit.*

C. *Verwenden Sie die gegebene Konjunktion, und machen Sie aus zwei Sätzen einen.* (Use the given conjunction and make one sentence out of the two.)

BEISPIEL: *Ich bin müde. Ich war den ganzen Tag auf der Messe. (because)*
  Ich bin müde, weil ich den ganzen Tag auf der Messe war.

1. *Er fragt. Will sie mitkommen? (whether)*
2. *Man muss viel laufen. Es gibt Transportmöglichkeiten. (although)*
3. *Er sagt. Er kann nur einen Imbiss essen. (that)*
4. *Sie kaufen heute ein. Sie fahren morgen ab. (because)*

D. *Übersetzen Sie.*

1. I would like to visit two suppliers.
2. If I have time, I'll see a competitor.
3. Those days were very strenuous.

E. *Setzen Sie die richtige Form der Nomen ein.* (Fill in the correct form of the *n*-nouns.)

1. *Wir hören den _____ sprechen. (Präsident)*
2. *Der _____ gibt dem _____ den Brief. (Patient, Beamte)*
3. *Ich kenne ihren _____ nicht. (Name)*

KULTURNOTIZ

International trade fairs are held in various German cities throughout the year. Frankfurt is known for its book fair *(Frankfurter Buchmesse)* and other fairs, Offenbach for the leather goods fair *(Internationale Lederwarenmesse)*, Hamburg for the international boat show *(Hanseboot)*, Nürnberg for the toy fair *(Internationale Nürnberger Spielwarenmesse)*, München for the international food industry fair *(IMEGA)*, and Leipzig for the industrial fair *(Leipziger Messe)*, to name just a few.

LÖSUNGEN

A. 1. *Er ist am Donnerstag auf der Messe.* 2. *Er ist von morgens bis abends auf der Messe.* 3. *Er besucht zuerst den Messestand seiner Firma.* 4. *Man muss viel laufen.* 5. *Geschäftsbesprechungen sind sehr ermüdend.*
B. 1.—d 2.—f 3.—e 4.—b 5.—c 6.—h 7.—a 8.—g
C. 1. *Er fragt, ob sie mitkommen will.* 2. *Obwohl es Transportmöglichkeiten gibt, muss man viel laufen.* 3. *Er sagt, dass er nur einen Imbiss essen kann.* 4. *Weil sie morgen abfahren, kaufen sie heute ein.*
D. 1. *Ich möchte zwei Lieferanten besuchen.* 2. *Wenn ich Zeit habe, besuche ich einen Konkurrenten.* 3. *Diese Tage waren sehr anstrengend.*
E. 1. *Präsidenten*   2. *Patient, Beamten*   3. *Namen*

LEKTION 17

AN DER NORDSEE.   At the North Sea.

A. DIALOG

Am Strand.

TOCHTER: Es war toll im Meer, die Wellen waren ganz hoch, aber jetzt habe ich Seetang in den Haaren.

MUTTER: Jetzt zieh' dich schnell um und trockne dich ab. Beeil' dich, sonst erkältest du dich bei dem Wind.

TOCHTER: Das Badetuch ist sandig. Wenn ich das nehme, tut mir mein Sonnenbrand weh.

MUTTER: Zieh' dir meinen Bademantel an. Der liegt im Strandkorb. Und da ist auch noch ein Handtuch. Dann reibe ich dich mit dem Sonnenschutzöl ein und kämme dir die Haare. Aber setz' dich nicht auf meine Sachen, du bist so nass.

TOCHTER: Wo sind Papa und Jan?

MUTTER: Sie schauen sich die Segelboote im Hafen an. Vielleicht mieten wir uns morgen ein Boot, wenn es keine Sturmwarnung gibt und der Wind sich beruhigt.

TOCHTER: Fantastisch. Dann kann ich meinen neuen Segelanzug anziehen.

———————————

At the Beach.

DAUGHTER: It was fabulous in the ocean and the waves were very high, but now I have seaweed in my hair.

MOTHER: Change quickly now and dry yourself. Hurry up, otherwise you'll catch a cold in this wind.

DAUGHTER: The beach towel is sandy. If I use it, my sunburn will hurt.

MOTHER: Put on my bathrobe. It's lying in the beach chair. And there's a towel too. Then I'll rub some suntan oil on you and comb your hair. But don't sit on my things, you're so wet.

DAUGHTER: Where are Daddy and Jan?

MOTHER: They're looking at the sailboats in the harbor. Perhaps we'll rent a boat tomorrow if there is no storm warning and the wind calms down.

DAUGHTER: Fantastic. Then I'll be able to wear my new sailing suit.

B. GRAMMATIK UND GEBRAUCH

1. REFLEXIVE VERBS

Reflexive verbs are verbs that take a reflexive pronoun, that is, one that refers back to the subject of the sentence: "He dries himself." In German, some verbs always have a reflexive pronoun. Often their English equivalents do not require a reflexive construction.

sich abtrocknen	to dry oneself
sich kämmen	to comb one's hair
sich beeilen	to hurry
sich erkälten	to catch a cold

2. REFLEXIVE PRONOUNS

English forms a reflexive pronoun by adding the suffix -self or -selves to the personal pronoun: "myself," "yourself," "themselves." In German, reflexive pronouns are identical to the personal pronouns except in the third person singular and plural and the formal "you."

SINGULAR

Nom.	ich	du	er/sie/es
Acc.	mich	dich	sich
Dat.	mir	dir	sich

PLURAL

Nom.	wir	ihr	sie/Sie
Acc.	uns	euch	sich
Dat.	uns	euch	sich

Note: *Sich* is not capitalized when used with *Sie*.
When the reflexive verb has no direct object other than the reflexive pronoun, the reflexive pronoun is in the accusative case.

Ich kämme mich.
I'm combing my hair.

Du ziehst dich an.
You're getting dressed.

Er schaut sich an.
He's looking at himself.

Wir trocknen uns ab.
We're drying ourselves.

Ihr zieht euch aus.
You're undressing.

Sie sehen sich an.
They're looking at themselves.*
They're looking at each other.

Kämmen Sie sich!
Comb your hair.

When a reflexive verb has a direct object other than the reflexive pronoun, the reflexive pronoun becomes an indirect object and has to be in the dative case.

Ich sehe mich an.
I look at myself.

becomes:

Ich sehe mir den Hafen an.
I look at the harbor.

Du schaust dir das Boot an.
You look at the boat.

* Note the difference in English between reciprocal action (They look at each other) and reflexive action (They look at themselves). In German. however, the reflexive and reciprocal pronouns are identical.

154

Often, the direct object of a reflexive verb is a part of the body or an article of clothing. In German, these nouns are used with a definite article (and not with a possessive adjective, as in English). In this case, the reflexive pronoun is in the dative.

Ich kämme mir die Haare.
  I'm combing my hair.

Du ziehst dir den Mantel an.
  You're putting on your coat.

Wir trocknen uns die Haare ab.
  We're drying our hair.

Ihr zieht euch die Schuhe aus.
  You're taking off your shoes.

Kämmen Sie sich die Haare!
  Comb your hair!

3. WORD ORDER OF REFLEXIVE PRONOUNS

A reflexive pronoun can follow either the verb or the subject. It follows the subject in a sentence with normal word order.

Er beeilt sich.
  He's hurrying.

The reflexive pronoun can follow either the verb or the subject in a yes-no question if the subject is a proper or common noun.

Trocknet sich Jan die Haare?	Is Jan drying his hair?
Trocknet Jan sich die Haare?	Is Jan drying his hair?
Beeilen sich die Männer?	Are the men hurrying?
Beeilen die Männer sich?	Are the men hurrying?

The reflexive pronoun follows the subject:

a. in an imperative statement

Setzen Sie sich!   Sit down.

b. in a yes-no question when the subject is a pronoun

Erkältest du dich?   Are you catching a cold?

c. in a question introduced by a question word

Warum beeilt ihr euch nicht?   Why don't you hurry?

d. if the subject is not the first element in the sentence

Hoffentlich beruhigst du dich.   I hope you'll calm down.

e. in a subordinate clause

Ich weiß nicht, ob er sich   I don't know if he'll hurry.
beeilt.

VOKABELN

der Strand, *⸚e*	beach
der Strandkorb, *⸚e*	large wicker beach chair
das Meer, *-e*	ocean, sea
die Welle, *-n*	wave
der Seetang	seaweed
die Sturmwarnung, *-en*	gale warning
der Sand	sand
sandig	sandy
das Segelboot, *-e*	sailboat
ein Segelboot mieten	to rent a sailboat
der Segelanzug, *⸚e*	sailing suit
das Schiff, *-e*	ship
der Hafen, *⸚*	harbor
das Handtuch, *⸚er*	towel
das Badetuch, *⸚er*	bath towel, beach towel
sich ab*trocknen	to dry oneself
sich um*ziehen	to change one's clothes
sich die Haare trocknen	to dry one's hair
sich an*ziehen	to get dressed

der Bademantel, ̈	bathrobe, beach robe
die Sonnenbräune	suntan
der Sonnenbrand, ̈e	sunburn
das Sonnenschutzöl, -e	suntan oil
sich *(mit etwas)* einreiben	to rub oneself (with something)
toll	great (colloquial)
fantastisch	fantastic
sich erkälten	to catch cold
sich beeilen	to hurry
sich beruhigen	to calm down
sich etwas an*schauen	to look at something

ÜBUNGEN

A. *Beantworten Sie die Fragen zum Dialog.*

1. *Wie waren die Wellen?*
2. *Was soll die Tochter machen?*
3. *Was liegt im Strandkorb?*
4. *Was will die Familie morgen vielleicht machen?*

B. *Suchen Sie die richtige deutsche Übersetzung.*

1. We rent a sailboat.
2. She has a sunburn.
3. Christa, hurry.
4. Mr. Frank, calm down.
5. We are at the beach.
6. The waves are high.

a. *Wir sind am Strand.*
b. *Die Wellen sind hoch.*
c. *Wir mieten ein Segelboot.*
d. *Herr Frank, beruhigen Sie sich!*
e. *Sie hat einen Sonnenbrand.*
f. *Christa, beeil dich!*

C. *Setzen Sie die fehlenden Reflexivpronomen ein.* (Supply the missing reflexive pronouns.)

BEISPIEL: *Ich kämme _____ die Haare.*
   Ich kämme mir die Haare.

1. *Herr Müller, setzen Sie _____!*
2. *Ziehst du _____ den Bademantel an?*
3. *Ich reibe _____ mit Sonnenschutzöl ein.*
4. *Er erkältet _____.*
5. *Wir ziehen _____ um.*

D. *Setzen Sie das fehlende Verb ein.* (Supply the missing verb.)

1. *Frau Schulz _____ sich die Haare. (sich kämmen)*
2. *Nach dem Bad _____ er sich _____. (sich abtrocknen)*
3. *Sie _____ sich die Schuhe _____. (sich anziehen)*
4. *Sie _____ dem Kind den Mantel _____. (anziehen)*
5. *Wir müssen uns _____. (sich beeilen)*
6. *Bitte, _____ Sie sich! (sich beruhigen)*

KULTURNOTIZ

German beaches are located at the North Sea *(Nordsee)* and the Baltic Sea *(Ostsee)*. Both coasts and the small offshore islands are favorite vacation spots. The weather especially off the North Sea coast can be rough, even in summer. People rent large wicker chairs *(Strandkörbe)* to have some protection against the strong wind. The first *Strandkorb* was built in Rostock in 1882 by Wilhelm Bartelmann. To this day his chairs are very popular on German coasts and beaches, as they not only cut down on the wind chill, but also allow some privacy when changing one's clothes. There are often no changing rooms *(Umkleidekabinen)* at the coastal beaches. Not every beach has a life guard *(Rettungsschwimmer)* either.

LÖSUNGEN

A. 1. *Sie waren ganz hoch.* 2. *Sie soll sich umziehen, und sie soll sich abtrocken.* 3. *Der Bademantel und ein Handtuch und die Sachen der Mutter liegen im Strandkorb.* 4. *Morgen will die Familie vielleicht ein Segelboot mieten.*
B. 1.—c   2.—e   3.—f   4.—d   5.—a   6.—b
C. 1. *sich*   2. *dir*   3. *mich*   4. *sich*   5. *uns*
D. 1. *kämmt*   2. *trocknet/ab*   3. *zieht/an*   4. *zieht/an*   5. *beeilen*
   6. *beruhigen*

LEKTION 18

DIE KUR.   The Cure.

A. DIALOG

In einem Kurort.

HERR WIRTH: Herr Kuhn, schön, Sie zu treffen. Erholen Sie sich gut?

HERR KUHN: Ja, danke. Leider müssen wir am Sonntag zurück und wieder einen Tag im Bus sitzen.

HERR WIRTH: Schade! Wie verbringen Sie die Tage hier?

HERR KUHN: Meine Frau macht eine Kur. Jeden Morgen und Abend trinkt sie das Heilquellenwasser. Vormittags schwimmt sie im Mineralbad.

HERR WIRTH: Bekommt sie auch Massagen und Lehmpackungen?

HERR KUHN: Ja, ja. Danach ruht sie sich in der Liegehalle aus. Ich mache während dieser Zeit Gymnastik oder promeniere in der Wandelhalle. Laufen tut mir gut.

HERR WIRTH: Wir hören gern das Kurkonzert und waren auch zweimal wöchentlich im Spielkasino. Aber am Abend und in der Nacht wird es zu kühl, nicht?

HERR KUHN: Ja. Vor zwei Jahren war es hier genauso kalt. Irgendwann einmal fahren wir in einen Kurort weiter südlich.

At a Spa.

MR. WIRTH: Mr. Kuhn, how nice to see you. Are you recuperating?

MR. KUHN: Yes, thanks. Unfortunately, we must return home on Sunday and spend another day on the bus.

MR. WIRTH: Too bad. How are you spending your days here?

MR. KUHN: My wife is taking treatments. She drinks the medicinal spring water every morning and evening. Before noon, she swims in the mineral pool.

159

MR. WIRTH: Does she also get massages and mud packs?

MR. KUHN: Oh yes. After that, she rests in the lounge. I do calisthenics during this time or go for a stroll in the indoor promenade. Walking is good for me.

MR. WIRTH: We like to listen to the concerts and also went to the casino twice a week. But it gets too cool in the evenings and at night, doesn't it?

MR. KUHN: Yes. Two years ago it was just as cold here. Someday we'll go to a health resort farther south.

B. GRAMMATIK UND GEBRAUCH

1. TIME EXPRESSIONS IN THE ACCUSATIVE CASE

In time expressions without a preposition, the accusative case is used.

Jeden Morgen trinkt sie das Wasser.
She drinks the water every morning.

Wir bleiben eine Woche hier.
We're staying here for one week.

Sie fliegt jedes Jahr in den Süden.
She flies south every year.

2. TIME EXPRESSIONS IN THE DATIVE CASE

Time expressions with the preposition *an, in,* and *vor* are in the dative case.

Leider müssen wir am Sonntag zurück.
Unfortunately, we must return home on Sunday.

In der Nacht wird es zu kalt.
It gets too cold at night.

Vor zwei Jahren war es hier genauso kalt.
Two years ago it was just as cold here.

3. TIME EXPRESSIONS IN THE GENITIVE CASE

To express indefinite time, the genitive case is used. Such expressions may refer to the future or the past.

Eines Tages kommt er zu spät.
One day he'll be late.

Eines Morgens war er krank.
One morning he was sick.

4. ADVERBIAL TIME EXPRESSIONS

For repeated, customary actions, adverbial forms and expressions are used. For example:

samstags	on Saturday, Saturdays
vormittags	in the mornings
Montag nachmittags	Monday afternoons
wöchentlich	weekly, once a week

Vormittags schwimmt sie.
She swims in the mornings.

Zweimal wöchentlich waren wir im Spielkasino.
Twice a week we went to the casino.

5. VERBAL NOUNS

English verbal nouns, or gerunds, end in -*ing*. In the example "Walking is good for me," "walking" is a verb used as a noun. In German, a verb can be changed to a noun by capitalizing the infinitive. Verbal nouns are neuter.

Das Laufen tut mir gut.
Walking is good for me.

Das Einkaufen war ermüdend.
Shopping was tiring.

German verbal nouns are frequently used without an article.

Fliegen macht Spaß.
   Flying is fun.

Telefonieren ist teuer.
   Phoning is expensive.

VOKABELN

der Kurort, -e	spa, health resort
sich erholen	to relax, to recuperate
sich aus*ruhen	to relax, to rest
die Kur, -en	cure, treatment
eine Kur machen	to take a cure
die Quelle, -n	spring, well
heilen	to heal
die Heilquelle, -n	medicinal spring
der Lehm, -	mud
die Packung, -en	pack, poultice
die Lehmpackung, -en	mud pack
die Massage, -n	massage
schwimmen	to swim
das Mineralwasserbad, ¨er	a pool with minerals in the water
die Liegehalle, -n	lounge
Gymnastik machen	to do calisthenics
promenieren	to walk back and forth
wandeln	to wander, to walk
Schwimmen tut ihr gut.	Swimming is good for her.
Was tut ihm gut?	What is good for him?
das Konzert, -e	concert
das Kurkonzert, -e	concert at a spa
das Spielkasino, -s	gambling casino
irgendwann	someday
(sich) treffen *(trifft)*	to meet one another, to see one another
verbringen	to pass time
südlich	south of

nördlich	north of
östlich	east of
weiter westlich	farther west
zurück	back
Schade!	Too bad. What a pity.

ÜBUNGEN

A. *Beantworten Sie die Fragen zum Dialog.*

1. *Wen trifft Herr Wirth?*
2. *Wann trinkt Frau Kuhn Heilquellenwasser?*
3. *Wie oft waren Herr und Frau Wirth im Spielkasino?*
4. *Wann wird es zu kühl?*
5. *Was tut Herrn Kuhn gut?*

B. *Suchen Sie die richtige deutsche Übersetzung.*

1. Swimming is good for Mr. and Mrs. Kuhn.
2. We'll meet tomorrow.
3. It's snowing farther north.
4. He's going for a stroll.
5. I'm relaxing.
6. He's recuperating.

a. *Er promeniert.*
b. *Er erholt sich.*
c. *Wir treffen uns morgen.*
d. *Ich ruhe mich aus.*
e. *Weiter nördlich schneit es.*
f. *Schwimmen tut Herrn und Frau Kuhn gut.*

C. *Vervollständigen Sie die Sätze.* (Complete the sentences.)

BEISPIEL: _____ *wird es sehr kalt. (In the evenings)*
          Abends wird es sehr kalt.

1. *Sie müssen _____ zurück. (on Saturday)*
2. *Wir fahren in _____. (a week)*

3. *Wir bleiben _____ immer gern im Hotel.* (at night)

4. *_____ gehen wir ins Kasino.* (Twice a week)

5. *Ich hoffe, dass ich _____ eine Flugreise machen kann.* (one day)

D. *Übersetzen Sie.*

1. How nice to see you.
2. Unfortunately, I must go back in a week.
3. Swimming is good for him.

KULTURNOTIZ

Germany has more than 250 spas *(Kurorte, Badeorte)* that are officially registered and permitted to use the word *Bad* before their name, as, for example, *Bad Tölz.* Some cities derive their names wholly or in part from their mineral or thermal springs: *Wiesbaden, Wildbad, Baden-Baden.* Visitors *(Kurgäste)* have to pay a surcharge *(Kurtaxe)* for an overnight stay. Central Europeans believe in the beneficial value of the spas and make extensive use of these places. Some of the thermal springs have been used since Roman times. Most larger spas, such as *Baden-Baden,* have gambling casinos, and gambling is a favorite pastime of many visitors.

LÖSUNGEN

A. 1. *Er trifft Herrn Kuhn.* 2. *Sie trinkt jeden Morgen und Abend Heilquellenwasser.* 3. *Sie waren zweimal wöchentlich im Spielkasino.* 4. *Am Abend und in der Nacht wird es zu kühl.* 5. *Laufen tut Herrn Kuhn gut.*

B. 1.—f 2.—c 3.—e 4.—a 5.—d 6.—b

C. 1. *am Samstag* 2. *einer Woche* 3. *nachts* 4. *Zweimal wöchentlich* 5. *eines Tages*

D. 1. *Wie schön, Sie zu treffen.* 2. *Leider muss ich in einer Woche zurück.* 3. *Schwimmen tut ihm gut.*

LEKTION 19

DAS HAUS.   The House.

A. DIALOG

Renovierungen.

ILSE: Gestern Abend habe ich Wim und Maria besucht. Sie haben ihr ganzes Haus renoviert.

SYLVIA: Interessant. Erzähl mal.

ILSE: Alle Fenster sind jetzt luftdicht. Alle Fußböden außer in der Küche, den Bädern und dem Keller haben Parkett.

SYLVIA: Haben sie das selber gemacht?

ILSE: Nein. Aber im Wohnzimmer, den Schlafzimmern und Kinderzimmern, im Flur und im Treppenhaus haben Wim und Maria die Wände selbst tapeziert. Die Terrasse haben sie allein umgebaut.

SYLVIA: Wie lange hat das alles gedauert?

ILSE: Sie haben mindestens drei Monate daran gearbeitet.

SYLVIA: Wie haben sie das Ganze denn finanziert?

ILSE: Die Versicherung hat einen Teil bezahlt. Im Winter bei dem Unwetter hat es durchs Dach geregnet. Das Wasser hat die Decken und Böden ruiniert.

SYLVIA: Gut, dass alles wieder in Ordnung ist.

Renovations.

ILSE: Yesterday evening, I visited Wim and Maria. They've renovated their whole house.

SYLVIA: Interesting. Tell me about it.

ILSE: All the windows are airtight now. All the floors except in the kitchen, bathrooms, and cellar have parquet.

SYLVIA: Did they do it themselves?

ILSE: No. But in the living room, bedrooms and children's rooms, hallway, and staircase, Wim and Maria hung the wallpaper themselves. They remodeled the terrace by themselves.

SYLVIA: How long did it take?

ILSE: They worked at least three months on it.

SYLVIA: How did they finance everything?

ILSE: The insurance paid part of it. In winter, during the violent storm, it rained through the roof. The water ruined the ceilings and floors.

SYLVIA: I'm glad everything is all right again.

B. GRAMMATIK UND GEBRAUCH

1. THE PRESENT PERFECT TENSE

German has several past tenses. One is the present perfect tense. The use of the present perfect tense is not exactly parallel in English and German. In German, the present perfect tense is usually used in conversation to describe events in the past. It is often called the conversational past.

The present perfect is a compound tense, consisting of the conjugated form of *haben* + the past participle; *haben* is the helping, or auxiliary, verb.*

ich habe gefragt *du hast gefragt* *er hat gefragt*	*wir haben gefragt* *ihr habt gefragt* *sie haben gefragt* *Sie haben gefragt*

Although the present perfect can be translated into English with either the present perfect or the simple past, the simple past is often more appropriate.

Ich habe Maria gefragt.
I have asked Maria./I asked Maria.

*Certain verbs in German use *sein* (to be) as an auxiliary verb. This is explained in lesson 20.

166

Sie hat das Haus renoviert.
   She has renovated the house./She renovated the house.

2. THE PAST PARTICIPLE

a. REGULAR WEAK VERBS

German verbs are classified according to the way they form their past tense. A regular weak verb does not change its stem in the past participle. The past participle of regular weak verbs is formed thus: *ge-* + stem + *-t*

prüfen	→	*geprüft*	*sagen* →	*gesagt*
to examine		examined	to say	said

The ending *-t* expands to *-et* in verbs whose stem ends in *-d, -t, -n.*

arbeiten	→	*gearbeitet*	*rechnen* →	*gerechnet*
to work		worked	to count	counted
baden	→	*gebadet*	*regnen* →	*geregnet*
to bathe		bathed	to rain	rained

b. VERBS THAT END IN *-IEREN*

Verbs whose infinitive ends in *-ieren* have no *ge-* prefix in the past participle. All verbs that end in *-ieren* are weak verbs.

Das Wasser hat die Decke ruiniert.
   The water ruined the ceiling.

Er hat das Auto repariert.
   He has repaired the car.

Ich habe mein Haus renoviert.
   I renovated my house.

c. INSEPARABLE AND SEPARABLE PREFIX VERBS

Verbs that have inseparable prefixes do not add the *ge-* prefix to the past participle.

besuchen →	besucht	erzählen →	erzählt
to visit	visited	to tell	told

Ich habe meine Freunde besucht.
    I visited my fnends.

Er hat eine Geschichte erzählt.
    He told a story.

The past participle of verbs with separable prefixes is formed by inserting the *ge-* prefix between the separable prefix and the stem.

umbauen →	umgebaut	umbuchen →	umgebucht
to rebuild	rebuilt	to change reservations	changed reservations

Sie haben die Terrasse umgebaut.
    They rebuilt the terrace.

Er hat den Flug umgebucht.
    He changed the flight.

3. WORD ORDER WITH THE PRESENT PERFECT TENSE

In sentences in the present perfect tense, the auxiliary is placed in the verb position. The past participle is in the last position. In a dependent clause the auxiliary is in the last position.

Ich habe nichts gesagt.
    I didn't say anything./I said nothing.

Hast du gefragt?
    Did you ask?/Have you asked?

Wann habt ihr gearbeitet?
    When did you work?/When have you been working?

Er sagt, dass er gearbeitet hat.
    He says that he has been working./He says he worked.

VOKABELN

das Haus, ¨er	house
renovieren	to renovate
das Dach, ¨er	roof
die Treppe, -n	stairs
das Treppenhaus, ¨er	staircase
der Flur, -e	hallway
die Küche, -n	kitchen
das Wohnzimmer, -	living room
das Schlafzimmer, -	bedroom
das Kinderzimmer, -	children's room
die Terrasse, -n	terrace
der Balkon, -e	balcony
der Keller, -	cellar
der Boden, ¨	floor, ground
der Dachboden, ¨	attic
die Decke, -n	ceiling
die Wand, ¨e	wall
die Tapete, -n	wallpaper
tapezieren	to hang wallpaper
die Tür, -en	door
das Fenster, -	window
luftdicht	airtight
der Fußboden, ¨	floor
das Parkett, -s	parquet
um*bauen	to rebuild, remodel
dauern	to last
erzählen	to tell
die Ordnung	order
Alles ist in Ordnung.	Everything is all right.
das Unwetter, -	violent storm
selber, selbst	oneself, myself, themselves, etc.
allein	alone, by oneself
wenigstens	at least
der Teil, -e	part

A. *Beantworten Sie die Fragen zum Dialog.*

1. *Wen hat Ilse gestern Abend besucht?*
2. *Was haben Wim und Maria gemacht?*
3. *Wer hat das Wohnzimmer tapeziert?*
4. *Wann hat es durchs Dach geregnet?*

B. *Suchen Sie die richtige deutsche Übersetzung.*

1. The children's room has no wallpaper.
2. The windows are airtight.
3. The family is sitting in the living room.
4. A clock hangs in the hallway.
5. Everything is all right.

a. *Alles ist in Ordnung.*
b. *Die Familie sitzt im Wohnzimmer.*
c. *Die Fenster sind luftdicht.*
d. *Im Flur hängt eine Uhr.*
e. *Das Kinderzimmer hat keine Tapete.*

C. *Ergänzen Sie die Sätze mit dem Verb, das in Klammern steht, im Perfekt.* (Supplement the sentences with the verb given in parentheses in the present perfect tense.)

1. *Heute _____ es _____. (regnen)*
2. *Wir _____ Radio _____. (hören)*
3. *Dann _____ mein Bruder uns _____. (besuchen)*
4. *Er _____ _____, dass er sein Auto _____ _____.*
   (sagen/reparieren)
5. *Später _____ wir Karten _____. (spielen)*

D. *Setzen Sie die folgende Sätze ins Präsens.*

BEISPIEL: *Heute hat es nicht geregnet.*
          Heute regnet es nicht.

1. *Er hat das ganze Haus renoviert.*
2. *Ich habe meine Mutter besucht.*
3. *Das hat nicht lange gedauert.*
4. *Was haben Sie gesagt?*
5. *Sie hat ihn gesehen.*

E. *Beantworten Sie die folgende Fragen.* (Answer the following questions.)

1. *Hat Herr Schmidt heute gearbeitet? (Ja,...)*
2. *Haben Sie etwas gesagt? (Nein,...)*
3. *Hat es heute geregnet? (Ja,...)*
4. *Haben Sie mit ihm gesprochen oder telefoniert? (telefoniert)*
5. *Was haben Sie sie gefragt? (nichts)*

KULTURNOTIZ

More people in the United States own their houses than in Germany. Germany is one of the most densely populated areas of the world and land is very expensive in urban areas. Most Germans live in apartments. About a third of the apartment dwellers own their own apartments. Seventy percent of all apartments have been built or rebuilt since World War II. Subsidized apartments *(sozialer Wohnungsbau)* for low-income families or individuals are provided by the state.

LÖSUNGEN

A. 1. *Sie hat Wim und Maria besucht.* 2. *Sie haben das ganze Haus renoviert.* 3. *Wim und Maria haben das Wohnzimmer tapeziert.* 4. *Im Winter bei dem Unwetter hat es durchs Dach geregnet.*
B. 1.—e   2.—c   3.—b   4.—d   5.—a
C. 1. *hat—geregnet*   2. *haben—gehört*   3. *hat—besucht*   4. *hat gesagt—repariert hat*   5. *haben—gespielt*
D. 1. *Er renoviert das ganze Haus.* 2. *Ich besuche meine Mutter.* 3. *Das dauert nicht lange.* 4. *Was sagen Sie?* 5. *Sie sieht ihn.*
E. 1. *Ja, er hat heute gearbeitet.* 2. *Nein, ich habe nichts gesagt.* 3. *Ja, es hat heute geregnet.* 4. *Ich habe mit ihm telefoniert.* 5. *Ich habe sie nichts gefragt.*

LEKTION 20

UMZUG.   Moving.

A. DIALOG

Endlich umgezogen.

ARNO: Wo warst du denn? Ich versuche seit Tagen, dich zu erreichen.

KNUT: Ich bin umgezogen.

ARNO: Hat dir deine Wohnung nicht mehr gefallen?

KNUT: Doch. Aber meine Firma hat mir eine Dreizimmerwohnung angeboten. Ich habe zugegriffen.

ARNO: Klar. Hast du deine Möbel mitgenommen?

KNUT: Ja, den Tisch, zwei Stühle, den Sessel und die Bücherregale. Bett und Teppich habe ich zurückgelassen. Die Leselampe ist beim Einladen auf den Boden gefallen und zerbrochen.

ARNO: Schade. Hast du einen Spediteur genommen?

KNUT: Nein. Peter ist mit seinem Anhänger gekommen.

ARNO: Dann schläfst du jetzt auf dem Sofa?

KNUT: Ja, und ich kann jetzt auch kochen. Ein neuer Herd und Kühlschrank sind in der Wohnung.

ARNO: Prima. Wann kann ich zum Essen kommen?

KNUT: Bald, wenn ich mich vom Umzug erholt habe. Am Umzugstag war ich vollkommen erschöpft. Ich bin um elf Uhr schlafen gegangen und erst gegen zehn wieder aufgewacht.

Finally Moved.

ARNO: Where have you been? I've been trying to reach you for days.

KNUT: I've moved.

ARNO: Didn't you like your apartment anymore?

KNUT: Yes. But my company offered me a three-room apartment. I took advantage of it.

ARNO: Of course. Did you take your furniture with you?

KNUT: Yes, the table, two chairs, the easy chair, and the bookshelves. I left the bed and rug behind. During the loading, the reading lamp fell on the floor and broke.

ARNO: What a pity. Did you hire movers?

KNUT: No. Peter came with his trailer.

ARNO: Then you're sleeping on the sofa now?

KNUT: Yes, and I can cook now, too. There's a new stove and refrigerator in the apartment.

ARNO: Great. When can I come to dinner?

KNUT: Soon, once I recover from moving. On the day of the move, I was completely exhausted. I went to bed at eleven o'clock and woke up only around ten.

B. GRAMMATIK UND GEBRAUCH

1. PAST PARTICIPLES OF STRONG VERBS

The past participles of strong verbs have the prefix *ge-* and the ending *-en:*

laufen	→	*gelaufen*
to walk		walked

Most strong verbs show a stem-vowel change:

helfen	→	*geholfen*
to help		helped

Some verbs also have a consonant change:

stehen	→	*gestanden*
to stand		stood

Some, however, do not:

essen →	*gegessen*	*geben* →	*gegeben*
to eat	eaten	to give	given

Since the stem-vowel changes are not predictable, the past participles of strong verbs must be memorized. Here are a few:

a	→	*a:*	*fahren, gefahren*	to drive, driven
au	→	*au:*	*laufen, gelaufen*	to walk, walked
e	→	*e:*	*geben, gegeben*	to give, given
e	→	*o:*	*helfen, geholfen*	to help, helped
ei	→	*ei:*	*heißen, geheißen*	to be named, named
ei	→	*i:*	*streiten, gestritten*	to quarrel, quarreled
ei	→	*ie:*	*schreiben, geschrieben*	to write, written
i	→	*o:*	*schwimmen, geschwommen*	to swim, swum
i	→	*u:*	*finden, gefunden*	to find, found
ie	→	*o:*	*fliegen, geflogen*	to fly, flown
o	→	*o:*	*kommen, gekommen*	to come, come
u	→	*u:*	*rufen, gerufen*	to call, called

Many strong verbs that are irregular in German are also irregular in English:

trinken, getrunken	to drink, drunk
schwimmen, geschwommen	to swim, swum
fliegen, geflogen	to fly, flown

Strong verbs may have separable or inseparable prefixes. Strong verbs with separable prefixes form the past participle by placing the *ge-* between prefixes and verb stem:

auf*stehen →	*aufgestanden*	*sich an*ziehen* →	*angezogen*
to get up	got up	to dress	dressed

Strong verbs with inseparable prefixes do not take the *ge-* in the past participle:

verbinden →	*verbunden*	*zerbrechen* →	*zerbrochen*
to connect	connected	to break	broken

2. VERBS WITH THE AUXILIARY *SEIN*

a. While English uses only forms of "have" as the auxiliary in the present perfect tense, German uses both *haben* and *sein:*

Ich habe drei Monate daran gearbeitet.
    I (have) worked on it for three months.

Ich bin umgezogen.
    I (have) moved.

b. *Sein* is used for verbs that are intransitive and indicate a change of place or condition. A verb is intransitive if it cannot take a direct object, as illustrated in the sentences below:

Die Leselampe ist auf den Boden gefallen.
    The reading lamp fell on the floor.

Peter ist gekommen.
    Peter came.

Most other verbs take *haben* to form the present perfect tense.
    In vocabulary lists as in dictionaries, verbs that take *sein* as an auxiliary are indicated thus:

laufen, ist gelaufen
kommen, ist gekommen

c. Some strong verbs take the auxiliary *sein* even though they do not indicate a change of place or condition.

sein	→	*ist gewesen*	*Wir sind da gewesen.*
			We have been there.
bleiben	→	*ist geblieben*	*Seid ihr lange geblieben?*
			Did you stay long?
werden	→	*ist geworden*	*Es ist warm geworden.*
			It got warm.

d. Although the present perfect tense is commonly used in spoken German, the simple past tense* is preferable with the verb *sein:*

Er war krank.
   He was ill.

Waren Sie in Österreich?
   Were you in Austria?

e. A few verbs may be both intransitive and transitive.

Ich bin in einem Bus gefahren. (intransitive)
   I went in a bus.

Ich habe einen Bus gefahren. (transitive)
   I drove a bus.

f. Here are the past participles of the other strong verbs you have learned so far:

*ab*fahren*	*ist abgefahren*	to depart, departed
*ab*fliegen*	*ist abgeflogen*	to depart by airplane, departed by airplane
*an*kommen*	*ist angekommen*	to arrive, arrived
*an*rufen*	*angerufen*	to call, called
*an*springen*	*ist angesprungen*	to start, started
*aus*halten*	*ausgehalten*	to endure, endured
backen	*gebacken*	to bake, baked
bleiben	*ist geblieben*	to stay, stayed
essen	*gegessen*	to eat, eaten
fliegen	*ist geflogen*	to fly, flown
frieren	*gefroren*	to freeze, frozen
gefallen	*gefallen*	to be pleasing, was pleasing
halten	*gehalten*	to stop, stopped
heißen	*geheißen*	to be named, was named
liegen	*gelegen*	to lie, lain

* Please refer to lesson 27 for more information on the simple past.

nehmen	*genommen*	to take, taken
scheinen	*geschienen*	to shine, shone
schließen	*geschlossen*	to close, closed
sehen	*gesehen*	to see, seen
stehen bleiben	*ist stehen geblieben*	to stop, stopped
trinken	*getrunken*	to drink, drunk
verbinden	*verbunden*	to connect, connected
um*steigen	*ist umgestiegen*	to change trains, changed trains

VOKABELN

der Umzug, ¨e	moving
die Spedition, -en	movers
der Spediteur, -e	mover
um*ziehen, *ist umgezogen*	to move
ein*laden, *eingeladen*	to load
aus*laden, *ausgeladen*	to unload
der Anhänger, -	trailer
die Möbel	furniture
das Bett, -en	bed
der Tisch, -e	table
der Stuhl, ¨e	chair
der Sessel, -	easy chair
das Sofa, -s	sofa
das Regal, -e	shelf
das Bücherregal, -e	bookshelf
die Leselampe, -n	reading lamp
der Teppich, -e	rug, carpet
der Herd, -e	stove
der Kühlschrank, ¨e	refrigerator
der Edelstahl	stainless steel
an*bieten, angeboten	to offer
zu*greifen, zugegriffen	to take the opportunity, take advantage
fallen, *gefallen*	to fall down
zurück*lassen, *zurückgelassen*	to leave behind
Klar!	Certainly! Of course!

Prima!	Great!
zerbrechen, *zerbrochen*	to break
schlafen gehen, *ist schlafen gegangen*	to go to bed
auf*wachen, *ist aufgewacht*	to wake up
erschöpft sein	to be exhausted
sich erholen	to recover

ÜBUNGEN

A. *Beantworten Sie die Fragen zum Dialog.*

1. *Was hat Knut gemacht?*
2. *Wie groß ist Knuts Wohnung?*
3. *Welche Möbel hat Knut mitgenommen?*
4. *Hat Knut einen Spediteur genommen?*
5. *Wann ist Knut schlafen gegangen?*

B. *Verwenden Sie das Wort in Klammern als Subjekt, und verändern Sie die Sätze dementsprechend.* (Use the word in parentheses as subject, and change the sentences accordingly.)

BEISPIEL: *Ich bin früh aufgestanden. (he)*
Er ist früh aufgestanden.

1. *Er ist gestern umgezogen. (we)*
2. *Seid ihr spät schlafen gegangen? (you, pol.)*
3. *Sie ist ans Meer gefahren. (I)*
4. *Ist sie gestern zu Besuch gekommen? (they)*

C. *Suchen Sie die richtige deutsche Übersetzung.*

1. *I need a table and a bed.*
2. I must buy a reading lamp.
3. He always was very quiet.
4. We stayed only one week in Switzerland.
5. I got up very early.

a. *Wir sind nur eine Woche in der Schweiz geblieben.*
b. *Er war immer sehr ruhig.*
c. *Ich bin sehr früh aufgestanden.*
d. *Ich muss eine Leselampe kaufen.*
e. *Ich brauche einen Tisch und ein Bett.*

D. *Übersetzen Sie.*

1. *We were at the ocean yesterday.*
2. The water was already nice and warm.
3. We went into the water twice and drove back again.

KULTURNOTIZ

A three-room apartment in Germany consists of three rooms plus kitchen, bath, usually a hallway *(Flur/Diele),* and often storage space *(Abstellraum).* In multiple-family houses there is usually also space in a laundry room *(Waschküche)* and a storage room in the basement *(Keller).* The first floor is called the *Parterre* or *Erdgeschoss,* the second floor is called the first *(der erste Stock),* the third floor is called the second *(der zweite Stock),* and so forth. Generally, a stove and refrigerator are not provided by the landlord. Many large firms offer housing to their employees, often at rates under market prices.

LÖSUNGEN

A. 1. *Er ist umgezogen. 2. Sie hat drei Zimmer. 3. Er hat den Tisch, zwei Stühle, den Sessel und die Bücherregale mitgenommen. 4. Nein, er hat keinen Spediteur genommen. 5. Er ist um elf Uhr schlafen gegangen.*
B. 1. *Wir sind*   2. *Sind Sie*   3. *Ich bin*   4. *Sind sie*
C. 1.—e   2.—d   3.—b   4.—a   5.—c
D. 1. *Gestern waren wir am Meer. 2. Das Wasser war schon schön warm.*
   3. *Wir sind zweimal ins Wasser gegangen und wieder zurückgefahren.*

VIERTE WIEDERHOLUNGSAUFGABE

A. *Übersetzen Sie.*

1. During the summer we renovated our house.
2. When can I see it?
3. Why doesn't he comb his hair?
4. He doesn't have much hair.
5. Are you (pol.) sick?
6. Yes, my stomach hurts.

B. *Setzen Sie die fehlenden Endungen ein.*

BEISPIEL: Morgen gebe ich mein _____ Freund ein Geschenk.
Morgen gebe ich meinem Freund ein Geschenk.

1. *Vor ein__ Jahr haben wir die Messe besucht.*
2. *Trotz d__ Verhandlungen war es interessant.*
3. *Die Frau mein__ Lieferant__ war sehr nett.*
4. *Jed__ Morgen haben wir einen Imbiss gehabt.*
5. *Wegen d__ Konkurrenz habe ich nicht viel verkauft.*

C. *Verwenden Sie die gegebenen Konjunktionen, und machen Sie aus zwei Sätzen einen Satz.*

BEISPIEL: Ich weiß nicht. Herr Schmidt wohnt in Köln. (whether)
Ich weiß nicht, ob Herr Schmidt in Köln wohnt.

1. *Die Kur war gut. Ich bin ganz gesund. (because)*
2. *Er sagt. Die Ärzte haben ihn viel gefragt. (that)*
3. *Das Wetter ist schön. Wir fahren ans Meer. (if)*
4. *Ich trage einen Pulli. Ich trage eine Bluse. (or)*

D. *Schreiben Sie die Sätze im Perfekt.* (Rewrite the sentences in the present perfect tense.)

BEISPIEL: Ich arbeite zu viel.
Ich habe zu viel gearbeitet.

1. *Ich huste immer während der Nacht.*
2. *Der Arzt sagt, dass ich eine Allergie habe.*
3. *Er fragt mich viel.*
4. *Er schickt mich zur Kur.*
5. *Sie dauert drei Wochen.*

E. *Setzen Sie die fehlenden Reflexivpronomen ein.*

BEISPIEL: *Ich kämme _____.*
       Ich kämme mich.

  1. *Wir erholen _____ gut.*
  2. *Erika, ruh _____ aus!*
  3. *Heute ziehe ich _____ nicht um.*
  4. *Christa und Uwe, was zieht ihr _____ an?*
  5. *Kann er _____ nicht beeilen?*

F. *Nennen Sie das fehlende Partizip.* (Provide the missing past participle.)

BEISPIEL: *Haben Sie heute schon _____? (to eat)*
      Haben Sie heute schon gegessen?

  1. *Gestern ist Richard nach Berlin _____. (to fly)*
  2. *Wann bist du nach Hause _____? (to come)*
  3. *Haben Sie _____? (to call)*
  4. *Vielen Dank, Sie haben mir sehr _____? (to help)*
  5. *Und wann bist du _____? (to get up)*
  6. *Wo haben Sie früher _____? (to work)*

LÖSUNGEN

A. 1. *Während des Sommers haben wir unser Haus renoviert. 2. Wann kann ich es sehen? 3. Warum kämmt er sich nicht die Haare? 4. Er hat nicht viele Haare. 5. Sind Sie krank? 6. Ja, ich habe Magenschmerzen.*
B. 1. *einem* 2. *der* 3. *meines Lieferanten* 4. *Jeden* 5. *der*
C. 1. *Weil die Kur gut war, bin ich ganz gesund. 2. Er sagt, dass die Ärzte ihn viel gefragt haben. 3. Wenn das Wetter schön ist, fahren wir ans Meer. 4. Ich trage einen Pulli oder eine Bluse.*
D. 1. *Ich habe immer während der Nacht gehustet. 2. Der Arzt hat gesagt, dass ich eine Allergie gehabt habe. 3. Er hat mich viel gefragt. 4. Er hat mich zur Kur geschickt. 5. Sie hat drei Wochen gedauert.*
E. 1. *uns* 2. *dich* 3. *mich* 4. *euch* 5. *sich*
F. 1. *geflogen* 2. *gekommen* 3. *gerufen* 4. *geholfen*
   5. *aufgestanden* 6. *gearbeitet*

LESESTÜCK II:
FLOHMÄRKTE[1] IN DEUTSCHLAND

Auch in Deutschland geht man auf den Flohmarkt, denn das Alte und Originelle ist wieder modern. Alles Unmoderne ist in den Jahren des ökonomischen Aufschwungs in den Abfall oder auf den Schutthaufen gewandert.[2] Jetzt kauft man diese Gegenstände[3] von den Flohmarkthändlern wieder zurück.

Bekannte[4] Flohmärkte gibt es in Berlin, München, Frankfurt, Stuttgart und Nürnberg. Sie finden mehrmals im Jahr statt.[5] Aber man findet sie auch in Kleinstädten und auf dem Land.[6]

Wer auf dem Flohmarkt kaufen will, muss handeln können:[7] "Was kostet die Lampe in der Ecke da drüben?[8] Wie viel wollen Sie für den Stuhl hier? Fünfundachtzig Euro? Das ist zu teuer. Ein Fuß und die Polsterung sind doch beschädigt![9] 'Echt Biedermeier',[10] sagen Sie? Leider kenne ich mich in Möbelstilen nicht aus.[11] Aber mir gefällt der Stuhl. Ich biete 40 Euro."[12]

Wenn man eine echte Antiquität erwerben will, braucht man Fachkenntnisse.[13] Antiquitäten sind nicht mehr billig, und bestimmte Artikel sind rar.[14] Und dann braucht man noch Ausdauer, Geduld und Glück, um das Motto "Wer sucht, der findet" in die Realität umzusetzen.[15]

VOKABELN

1. *der Flohmarkt, ¨e*	flea market
2. *unmodern*	old-fashioned
der ökonomische Aufschwung	economic upswing
sind in den Abfall oder auf	were put into the trash
den Schutthaufen	or taken to the dump
gewandert	
3. *der Gegenstand, ¨e*	object
4. *bekannt*	well-known
5. *mehrmals*	several times
statt*finden, stattgefunden	to take place
6. *die Kleinstadt, ¨e*	small town
auf dem Land	in the country
7. *handeln*	to bargain
8. *die Ecke*	corner
9. *der Fuß*	foot
die Polsterung	upholstery
beschädigt sein	to be damaged

10. *echt Biedermeier*	genuine Biedermeier (style)
11. *sich aus*kennen in*	to be versed in
der Möbelstil, -e	furniture style
12. *bieten, geboten*	to offer
13. *die Antiquität, -en*	antique
erwerben	to acquire
die Fachkenntnis, -se	expert knowledge
14. *bestimmte Artikel*	certain articles
rar	rare
15. *die Ausdauer*	perseverance
die Geduld	patience
"Wer sucht, der findet."	"He who searches will find."
in die Realität um*setzen	to implement, realize (an idea)

LEKTION 21

SEHENSWÜRDIGKEITEN.   Sights.

A. DIALOG

In der Altstadt.

LAURA: Wie hübsch die Wandmalereien an den Häusern sind. Und es ist so angenehm, dass es keinen Verkehr gibt.

OLGA: Hast du nicht gewusst, dass viele Stadtzentren Fußgänger-zonen sind? Deshalb haben wir ja auch außerhalb der Stadtmauer geparkt.

LAURA: Ach so. Hast du jetzt Lust, den Marktplatz, das Rathaus, den Dom und das Kloster zu besichtigen?

OLGA: Klar. Sie liegen ja alle nah zusammen. Wir können zuerst auf den Domturm steigen, um einen Überblick über die ganze Stadt zu bekommen. Das empfiehlt auch der Reiseführer. Hast du ihn mitgebracht?

LAURA: Wie dumm von mir, ihn nicht mitzubringen! Wie kommen wir denn jetzt ohne Stadtplan zur Stadtmitte?

OLGA: Wir können fragen oder uns an der Domspitze orientieren. Wir gehen jetzt zuerst geradeaus, später müssen wir dann irgendwo links abbiegen. Und im Dom sind jede halbe Stunde Führungen.

LAURA: Gut.

In the Old Town.

LAURA: How pretty the murals on the houses are. And it's so pleasant that there's no traffic.

OLGA: Didn't you know that many inner cities are pedestrian zones? That's why we parked outside the city walls.

LAURA: Oh, I see. Do you feel like looking at the marketplace, the city hall, the cathedral, and the cloister now?

OLGA: Sure. They're all close together. We can climb the cathedral tower first in order to get an overview of the whole city. The guidebook recommends it also. Did you bring it?

LAURA: How stupid of me not to bring it along! How will we get to the center without the city map?

OLGA: We can ask or orient ourselves by the cathedral tower. First, we'll walk straight ahead, later we'll have to turn to the left. And there are guided tours of the cathedral every half hour.

LAURA: Good.

B. GRAMMATIK UND GEBRAUCH

1. THE PAST PARTICIPLE OF IRREGULAR WEAK VERBS

A few weak verbs have irregular past participles. The past participle ends in -t but the stem vowel changes.

denken	→	*gedacht*	*kennen* →	*gekannt*
to think		thought	to know	known
bringen	→	*gebracht*	*wissen* →	*gewusst*
to bring		brought	to know	known

Das habe ich nicht gewusst.
    I didn't know that.

Hast du den Stadtplan mitgebracht?
    Did you bring the city map along?

2. INFINITIVES WITH *ZU*

In German sentences infinitives are usually preceded by *zu* except when you use a modal.

Hast du Lust, den Dom zu besichtigen?
    Do you feel like visiting the cathedral?

Es dauert lange, durch die Stadt zu fahren.
  It takes a long time to drive through the city.

  If a separable prefix verb is used in the infinitive, *zu* is inserted
  between the separable prefix and the stem.

Wie dumm von mir, es nicht mitzubringen!
  How stupid of me not to bring it along!

Es ist zu früh, sich anzuziehen.
  It's too early to get dressed.

3. THE CONSTRUCTION *UM...ZU* + INFINITIVE

Um...zu plus infinitive is equivalent to the English construction "(in
order) to" plus infinitive.

Wir steigen auf den Domturm, um einen Überblick über die Stadt zu bekommen.
  We'll climb the tower of the cathedral (in order) to get an overview of
  the city.

Um gesund zu bleiben, muss man viel wandern.
  To stay healthy one has to walk a lot.

VOKABELN

die **Besichtigung**, *-en*	sightseeing
besichtigen	to view, to look at
die **Führung**, *-en*	guided tour
der **Reiseführer**, *-*	travel guide, travel guide book
empfehlen, *(empfiehlt), empfohlen*	to recommend
der **Stadtplan**, *̈e*	city map
der **Fußgänger**, *-*	pedestrian
die **Fußgängerzone**, *-n*	pedestrian zone
das **Stadtzentrum**, *Stadtzentren*	city center
die **Stadtmitte**, *-n*	city center
der **Platz**, *̈e*	square, place
der **Markt**, *̈e*	market
die **Stadtmauer**, *-n*	city wall

186

das Rathaus, ¨-er	city hall
die Malerei, -en	painting
die Wandmalerei, -en	mural
der Dom, -e	cathedral
die Kathedrale, -n	cathedral
der Turm, ¨-e	tower
der Überblick, -e	overview
steigen, *ist gestiegen*	to climb
die Spitze, -n	top, tip
das Kloster, ¨-	cloister
zusammen*liegen,	to lay together
zusammengelegen	
nah*(e)*	near, close
sich orientieren	to orient (oneself)
der Weg, -e	the way
nach dem Weg fragen	to ask the way
geradeaus	straight ahead
außerhalb (+ gen.)	outside
innerhalb (+ gen.)	inside
Wie dumm!	How stupid!
mit*bringen, *mitgebracht*	to bring (along)
Lust haben	to feel like
hübsch	pretty
angenehm	pleasant
unangenehm	unpleasant
irgendwo	somewhere

ÜBUNGEN

A. *Beantworten Sie die Fragen zum Dialog.*

1. *Was hat Laura nicht gewusst?*
2. *Was wollen Laura und Olga besichtigen?*
3. *Wohin wollen sie steigen?*
4. *Was hat Laura nicht mitgebracht?*
5. *Wie oft gibt es Führungen im Dom?*

B. *Suchen Sie die richtige deutsche Übersetzung.*

1. The guidebook recommends it.
2. I feel like visiting the cloister.
3. I didn't know it.
4. Go straight ahead.

a. *Ich habe es nicht gewusst.*
b. *Gehen Sie geradeaus.*
c. *Ich habe Lust, das Kloster zu besuchen.*
d. *Der Reiseführer empfiehlt es.*

C. *Ergänzen Sie die Sätze mit dem Verb, das in Klammern steht, im Perfekt.* (Complete the sentences with the verb in parentheses in the present perfect.)

BEISPIEL: *Ich _____ oft an dich _____. (denken)*
Ich habe oft an dich gedacht.

1. *Er _____ die Stadt nicht _____. (kennen)*
2. *Klaus _____ nicht _____, wie sie heißt. (wissen)*
3. *Wir _____ den Stadtplan nicht _____. (bringen)*
4. *_____ du an das Buch _____? (denken)*

D. *Übersetzen Sie.*

1. One has to climb the tower to see the city.
2. How stupid not to bring the city map!

E. *Verbinden Sie die Sätze jeweils mit "um zu".* (Connect each of the two sentences using "um zu.")

BEISPIEL: *Sie gehen ins Restaurant. Sie essen.*
Sie gehen ins Restaurant um zu essen.

1. *Er ruft den Kellner. Er zahlt.*
2. *Wir nehmen die Speisekarte. Wir bestellen.*
3. *Ich spreche mit dem Mann. Ich frage nach dem Weg.*
4. *Sie geht ins Theater. Sie sieht ein Theaterstück.*
5. *Er nimmt das Buch. Er liest.*

F. *Vervollständigen Sie die folgenden Sätze.* (Complete the following sentences.)

1. *Es ist nicht schwer . . . (Deutsch lernen)*

2. *Wir brauchen nicht . . . (die Karte mitnehmen)*
3. *Es dauert nicht lange . . . (das Buch lesen)*
4. *Sie hatten keine Zeit . . . (die Stadt besuchen)*
5. *Es ist sehr nett von dir . . . (mir helfen)*

KULTURNOTIZ

The center of many cities *(Zentrum, Stadtmitte)* in German-speaking countries is often closed to traffic. In most cities these pedestrian zones *(Fußgängerzonen)* are the oldest parts of the town *(Altstadt)*, which are often still surrounded by parts of the original city wall. Very often these pedestrian zones harbor the busiest shops, cafés, and restaurants, and thus are very popular places for townspeople and visitors to meet. In order to preserve the historical nature of these parts of the cities, the local governments subsidize restoration even of private houses, for often it is these private townhouses that are decorated with the most striking geometrical patterns and murals.

LÖSUNGEN

A. 1. *Laura hat nicht gewusst, dass viele Stadtzentren Fußgängerzonen sind. 2. Sie wollen den Marktplatz, das Rathaus, den Dom und das Kloster besichtigen. 3. Sie wollen auf den Domturm steigen. 4. Laura hat den Reiseführer nicht mitgebracht. 5. Es gibt jede halbe Stunde Führungen im Dom.*

B. 1.—d 2.—c 3.—a 4.—b

C. 1. *hat—gekannt* 2. *hat—gewusst* 3. *haben—gebracht* 4. *Hast—gedacht*

D. 1. *Man muss auf den Turm steigen, um die Stadt zu sehen. 2. Wie dumm, den Stadtplan nicht mitzubringen!*

E. 1. *Er ruft den Kellner um zu zahlen. 2. Wir nehmen die Speisekarte um zu bestellen. 3. Ich spreche mit dem Mann, um nach dem Weg zu fragen. 4. Sie geht ins Theater, um ein Theaterstück zu sehen. 5. Er nimmt das Buch um zu lesen.*

F. *Es ist nicht schwer, Deutsch zu lernen. 2. Wir brauchen nicht die Karte mitzunehmen. 3. Es dauert nicht lange, das Buch zu lesen. 4. Sie hatten keine Zeit, die Stadt zu besuchen. 5. Es ist nett von dir, mir zu helfen.*

LEKTION 22

A. DIALOG

Umtausch eines Elektroartikels.

KUNDE: Ich möchte einen Rasierapparat umtauschen.

VERKÄUFER: Ist etwas damit nicht in Ordnung?

KUNDE: Der Apparat ist nur für 220 Volt. Ich will ihn aber auch für 110 Volt benutzen.

VERKÄUFER: Wir haben keine Modelle mit Transformator vorrätig.

KUNDE: Dann gebe ich den Rasierapparat zurück.

VERKÄUFER: Ist er in der Originalverpackung?

KUNDE: Ja, hier ist der Karton. Rechnung, Garantieschein und Gebrauchsanweisung sind auch darin.

VERKÄUFER: Wir machen gern einen Umtausch und zahlen die Differenz zurück. Sie können ein Bügeleisen, einen Haartrockner oder einen Taschenrechner mit Aufladebatterie dafür bekommen. Alle sind für 220 und 110 Volt.

KUNDE: Dafür habe ich keine Verwendung. Wofür brauche ich einen Taschenrechner? Ich bin im Kopfrechnen gut. Rufen Sie bitte den Geschäftsführer.

VERKÄUFER: Er kommt heute erst gegen 11 Uhr.

KUNDE: Dann warte ich auf ihn.

Exchanging an Electrical Appliance.

CUSTOMER: I would like to exchange an electric razor.

SALESMAN: Is something wrong with it?

CUSTOMER: The razor is only for 220 volts. But I want to use it for 110 volts also.

SALESMAN: We have no models with a transformer in stock.

CUSTOMER: Then I'm returning the razor.

SALESMAN: Is it in the original wrapping?

CUSTOMER: Yes, here's the box. Invoice, warranty, and instructions are also inside.

SALESMAN: We'll gladly make an exchange and refund the difference. You can get an iron, a hair dryer, or a pocket calculator with a rechargeable battery for it. All are for 220 and 110 volts.

CUSTOMER: I've no use for them. What do I need a pocket calculator for? I'm good in mental arithmetic. Please call the manager.

SALESMAN: He won't be in until about 11 o'clock today.

CUSTOMER: I'll wait for him.

B. GRAMMATIK UND GEBRAUCH

1. *DA*-COMPOUNDS

In English, one can replace any noun in a prepositional phrase with a pronoun. The noun that we want to replace may refer to a person, thing, or idea.

person: I'll wait for the manager.
            I'll wait for him.

thing: Something is wrong with the razor.
            Something is wrong with it.

idea: We're trying our luck.
            We're trying it.

In German, one can replace the noun in a prepositional phrase with a pronoun only if it refers to a person:

Ich warte auf den Geschäftsführer.
            I'll wait for the manager.

Ich warte auf ihn.
    I'll wait for him.

If the noun in a prepositional phrase refers to a thing or an idea, a *da*-compound is used.

a. *Da*-compounds are formed by joining *da-* to a preposition. Frequently used *da*-compounds are:

dadurch

Ich fahre nicht durch diese Stadt.	I'm not driving through this city.
Ich fahre nicht dadurch.	I'm not driving through it.

damit

Etwas ist mit dem Rasierapparat nicht. in Ordnung.	Something is wrong with the razor.
Etwas ist damit nicht in Ordnung.	Something is wrong with it.

dafür

Du bekommst ein Bücherregal für deine Bücher.	You'll get a bookshelf for your books.
Du bekommst ein Bücherregal dafür.	You'll get a bookshelf for them.

davon

Ich habe nichts von der Sturmwarnung gehört.	I heard nothing about the storm warning.
Ich habe nichts davon gehört.	I heard nothing about it.

dagegen

Ich habe nichts gegen Autos.	I've nothing against cars.
Ich habe nichts dagegen.	I've nothing against them.

As illustrated above in the sentences with *dafür* and *dagegen,* *da*-compounds may replace plural as well as singular nouns in a prepositional phrase.

b. If the preposition begins with a vowel, an *-r-* is inserted between *da* and the preposition.

darin

Die Rechnung ist in dem Karton.	The invoice is in the box.
Die Rechnung ist darin.	The invoice is in it.

darunter

Die Schuhe stehen unter dem Bett.	The shoes are under the bed.
Die Schuhe stehen darunter.	The shoes are under it.

darauf

Die Jungen fahren auf diesen Motorrädern.	The boys ride on these motorcycles.
Die Jungen fahren darauf.	The boys ride on them.

2. WO-COMPOUNDS

a. The interrogative *was* (what) refers to things and ideas. If *was* is preceded by a preposition, it is generally replaced by a *wo*-compound.

Ich fahre mit dem Auto.
I am driving with the car.

Womit (mit was) fahre ich?
With what am I driving?

b. *Wo*-compounds are formed by joining *wo-* to a preposition. Frequently used *wo*-compounds are:

wofür

Wofür brauche ich einen Taschenrechner?	What do I need a pocket calculator for?
Fürs Rechnen.	For arithmetic.

womit

Womit rasiert er sich?	How does he shave himself?
Mit einem Rasierapparat.	With a razor.

wovon

Wovon sprechen sie?	What are they talking about?
Von dem Umtausch.	About the exchange.

c. If the preposition begins with a vowel, an *-r-* is inserted between *wo* and the preposition.

worauf

Worauf warten Sie?	What are you waiting for?
Ich warte auf die Post.	I'm waiting for the mail.

worüber

Worüber habt ihr gesprochen?	What did you talk about?
Wir haben über Elektroartikel gesprochen.	We talked about electrical appliances.

VOKABELN

der Umtausch	exchange
der Verkäufer, -	salesman
der Kunde, *-n*	customer
der Geschäftsführer, -	store manager
umtauschen	to exchange
zurück*geben, *zurückgegeben*	to return
zurück*zahlen, *zurückgezahlt*	to pay back, to reimburse
die Differenz, *-en*	difference
die Originalverpackung, *-en*	factory packaging
der Karton, *-s*	box
die Gebrauchsanweisung, *-en*	directions for use
der Garantieschein, *-e*	warranty

das Modell, *-e*	model
vorrätig sein	to be in stock
Etwas ist nicht in Ordnung.	Something is wrong.
Die Ware ist nicht vorrätig.	The merchandise isn't in stock.
der Elektroartikel, -	electrical appliance
der Strom	electrical current
der Wechselstrom	alternating current (AC)
der Gleichstrom	direct current (DC)
das Volt, -	volt
umschalten	to switch
der Transformator, *-en*	transformer
die Batterie, *-n*	battery
auf*laden, *aufgeladen*	to charge, to load
der Rasierapparat, *-e*	electric razor
sich rasieren	to shave
der Haartrockner, -	hair dryer
das Bügeleisen, -	electric iron
der Taschenrechner, -	pocket calculator
die Verwendung, *-en*	use, utilization
für etwas Verwendung haben	to have a use for something
verwenden	to use
rechnen	to do arithmetic, to count, to calculate
das Kopfrechnen	mental arithmetic

ÜBUNGEN

A. *Beantworten Sie die Fragen zum Dialog.*

1. *Warum will der Kunde den Rasierapparat umtauschen?*
2. *Was kann der Kunde für den Rasierapparat bekommen?*
3. *Wo ist die Rechnung?*
4. *Wen soll der Verkäufer rufen?*
5. *Was will der Kunde machen, weil der Geschäftsführer erst um 11 Uhr kommt?*

B. *Suchen Sie die richtige deutsche Übersetzung.*

1. I would like to exchange something.
2. The manager will come later.
3. I'm returning the razor.
4. What do you shave with?
5. Is something wrong?

a. *Ich gebe den Rasierapparat zurück.*
b. *Womit rasieren Sie sich?*
c. *Ist etwas nicht in Ordnung?*
d. *Ich möchte etwas umtauschen.*
e. *Der Geschäftsführer kommt später.*

C. *Ergänzen Sie die Antworten und benutzen Sie "da"-Zusammensetzungen.*
(Complete the answers, using *da*-compounds.)

BEISPIEL: *Ist mit dem Regal etwas nicht in Ordnung?*
     Doch, alles ist _____ in Ordnung.

    Ist mit dem Regal etwas nicht in Ordnung?
    Doch, alles ist damit in Ordnung.

1. *Hat er dir bei der Arbeit geholfen?*
 Ja, er hat mir _____ geholfen.
2. *Spricht er oft über seine Arbeit?*
 Nein, er spricht nicht oft _____.
3. *Denkt ihr noch an den Tag am Meer?*
 Ja, wir denken noch _____.
4. *Warten Sie auch auf den Bus?*
 Ja, ich warte auch _____.

D. *Ergänzen Sie die Fragen. Benutzen Sie "wo"-Zusammensetzungen.*
(Complete the questions, using *wo*-compounds.)

BEISPIEL: *Die Kleider liegen in ihrem Koffer.*
     Worin liegen die Kleider?

1. *Durch die Kur wird sie gesund.*
 _____ wird sie gesund?
2. *Er wartet auf den Bus.*
 _____ wartet er?
3. *Sie schreibt über ihre Reise.*
 _____ schreibt sie?

196

E. *Übersetzen Sie.*

1. The cathedral is (lies) in the center of the city.
2. Next to it is a hotel.
3. Something is wrong with the hair dryer.
4. I want to exchange it.

F. *Suchen Sie die richtige Übersetzung.*

1. What are you waiting for?
2. Whom are you waiting for?
3. What are they talking about?
4. How does he get to Berlin?
5. With whom is he going to Berlin?

a. *Womit fährt er nach Berlin?*
b. *Worauf warten Sie?*
c. *Auf wen warten Sie?*
d. *Mit wem fährt er nach Berlin?*
e. *Worüber sprechen sie?*

KULTURNOTIZ

The standard voltage of electrical appliances manufactured in Germany is 220 volts. But many appliances are available with dual voltage.

Stores will exchange defective merchandise, usually requiring that it be in the original factory box. Money refund policies differ. You should ask for individual policies before you make larger purchases.

LÖSUNGEN

A. 1. *Er ist nur für 220 Volt. 2. Er kann ein Bügeleisen, einen Haartrockner oder einen Taschenrechner mit Aufladebatterie dafür bekommen. 3. Sie ist in dem Karton. 4. Er soll den Geschäftsführer rufen. 5. Er will warten.*
B. 1.—d   2.—e   3.—a   4.—b   5.—c
C. 1. *dabei*   2. *darüber*   3. *daran*   4. *darauf*
D. 1. *Wodurch*   2. *Worauf*   3. *Worüber*
E. 1. *Der Dom liegt im Stadtzentrum. 2. Daneben ist ein Hotel. 3. Mit dem Haartrockner ist etwas nicht in Ordnung. 4. Ich will ihn umtauschen.*
F. 1.—b   2.—c   3.—e   4.—a   5.—d

LEKTION 23

IM CAFÉ.   In a Café.

A. DIALOG

Ein Cafébesuch.

HEIKE: Du hast wirklich ein nettes, gemütliches Café ausgesucht.

SARAH: Schon als ich klein war, bin ich hierher gekommen.

HEIKE: Was soll ich denn bestellen?

SARAH: Probier' die Sachertorte. Sie backen sie mit herrlicher, bitterer
Schokolade. Sie haben auch unglaublich leckere Schwarzwälder
Kirschtorte. Jeden Tag servieren sie frischen Apfel- und
Kirschstrudel.

HEIKE: Eine schwere Wahl. Eigentlich darf ich gar keine süßen Sachen
essen. Mein besorgter Arzt hat mir das verboten. Zu viele Kalorien.

SARAH: Es gibt auch gesunde Joghurtbecher, natürlich ohne
Schlagsahne, mit frischen, gemischten Früchten. Knuspriges
Nussgebäck haben sie auch, sogar erfrischendes Tofueis.

HEIKE: Ach, heute sündige ich. Aber es gibt keinen freien Tisch.

SARAH: Siehst du die Frau mit einem schwarzen Hut an dem
Fenstertisch? Wir setzen uns zu ihr.

HEIKE: Gut.

A Visit to a Café.

HEIKE: You really picked a nice, cozy café.

SARAH: Even when I was small I always came here.

HEIKE: What should I order?

SARAH: Try the Sachertorte. They bake it with delicious, dark chocolate. They also have incredibly tasty Black Forest cake. Every day they serve fresh apple and cherry strudel.

HEIKE: A difficult choice. Actually I'm not allowed to eat sweets. My worried doctor has forbidden it. Too many calories.

SARAH: There are also healthy yogurt cups with fresh mixed fruit, without whipped cream of course. They also have crunchy nut pastry, even refreshing tofu ice cream.

HEIKE: Oh, well. Today I'm going to sin. But there's no empty table.

SARAH: Do you see the woman with a black hat at the table next to the window? We'll sit with her.

HEIKE: Good.

B. GRAMMATIK UND GEBRAUCH

1. PREDICATE ADJECTIVES

Predicate adjectives are used with *sein* and *werden*. They do not have endings.

Das Mädchen war klein.
  The girl was small.

Die Kuchen sind lecker.
  The cakes are delicious.

Der Kaffee wird kalt.
  The coffee is getting cold.

2. UNPRECEDED ADJECTIVES

Adjectives not preceded by a *der*-word or *ein*-word have the same endings as the *der*-words except in the masculine and neuter genitive singular, which end in -*en*.

	MASCULINE		FEMININE
Nom.	gut*er* Kuchen		gut*e* Torte
Acc.	gut*en* Kuchen		gut*e* Torte
Dat.	gut*em* Kuchen		gut*er* Torte
Gen.	gut*en* Kuchens		gut*er* Torte

	NEUTER		PLURAL
Nom.	gut*es* Brot		gut*e* Torten
Acc.	gut*es* Brot		gut*e* Torten
Dat.	gut*em* Brot		gut*en* Torten
Gen.	gut*en* Brotes		gut*er* Torten

Guter Wein ist teuer.
Good wine is expensive.

Er nimmt grünen Salat.
He takes green salad.

Zu frischem Fisch wählen wir Gemüse.
We choose vegetables with fresh fish.

Statt süßen Weins trinkt er Bier.
Instead of sweet wine he drinks beer.

Bittere Schokolade gibt es in jedem Geschäft.
Bittersweet chocolate can be bought in every store.

Möchtest du heiße Schokolade?
Would you like hot chocolate?

Es gibt keine Getränke außer heißer Schokolade.
There are no beverages except for hot chocolate.

Anstatt knuspriger Torte isst er Gebäck.
Instead of a crisp torte he eats pastry.

Gutes Brot ist gesund.
Good bread is healthy.

Wir bestellen knuspriges Gebäck.
We order crisp pastry.

Er mag Kaffee mit heißer Milch.
   He likes coffee with hot milk.

Leckere Sachertorten sind im Fenster.
   Delicious Sachertortes are in the window.

Es gibt gesunde Joghurtbecher.
   There are healthy yogurt cups.

Wir essen Eis mit gemischten Früchten.
   We eat ice cream with mixed fruit.

Anstatt kalter Torten essen wir Strudel.
   Instead of cold tortes we eat strudel.

3. ADJECTIVES PRECEDED BY *EIN*-WORDS

Adjectives preceded by *ein*-words have the following endings:

MASCULINE

Nom.	ein	gut<u>er</u>	Kuchen
Acc.	einen	gut<u>en</u>	Kuchen
Dat.	einem	gut<u>en</u>	Kuchen
Gen.	eines	gut<u>en</u>	Kuchens

FEMININE

Nom.	keine	gut<u>e</u>	Torte
Acc.	keine	gut<u>e</u>	Torte
Dat.	keiner	gut<u>en</u>	Torte
Gen.	keiner	gut<u>en</u>	Torte

NEUTER

Nom.	ein	gut<u>es</u>	Brot
Acc.	ein	gut<u>es</u>	Brot
Dat.	einem	gut<u>en</u>	Brot
Gen.	eines	gut<u>en</u>	Brotes

PLURAL

Nom.	meine	gut<u>en</u>	Torten
Acc.	meine	gut<u>en</u>	Torten
Dat.	meinen	gut<u>en</u>	Torten
Gen.	meiner	gut<u>en</u>	Torten

Note: The adjective endings for adjectives preceded by *ein*-words are the same in the nominative and accusative singular as for unpreceded adjectives. All adjectives preceded by *ein*-words have the ending *-en* in the plural.

Mein besorgter Arzt hat mir das verboten.
   My worried doctor has forbidden it.

Sie isst seinen leckeren Kuchen.
She's eating his delicious cake.

Nach einem guten Wein wird man müde.
One gets tired after a good wine.

Statt eines frischen Salats serviert sie eine Suppe.
Instead of fresh salad she serves a soup.

Eine leckere Torte kann man schnell backen.
One can bake a delicious cake quickly.

Ich trinke heute keine heiße Schokolade.
I won't drink hot chocolate today.

Sie nimmt viel von meiner süßen Sahne.
She takes a lot of my sweet cream.

Statt einer heißen Schokolade trinken wir Bier.
We drink beer instead of hot chocolate.

Hier ist ein gemütliches Café.
Here is a cozy café.

Wir gehen in ein kleines Café.
We're going to a small café.

Wir sind in einem großen Restaurant.
We are in a big restaurant.

Er geht oft wegen eines erfrischenden Bieres in die Bar.
He often goes to the bar for a refreshing beer.

Unsere süßen Brötchen sind sehr klein.
Our sweet rolls are very small.

Meine Kinder mögen deine gesunden Joghurtbecher.
My children like your healthy yogurt cups.

Wir kaufen Eis zu deinen frischen Früchten.
We buy ice cream to go with your fresh fruit.

Sie essen Sahne statt meiner gesunden Früchtebecher.
They eat cream instead of my healthy fruit cups.

4. ADVERBS

In German, most adverbs have the same form as the predicate adjective.

Er ist schnell.
   He is quick.

Er isst schnell.
   He eats quickly.

Die Geschichte ist schön.
   The story is beautiful.

Der Sänger singt schön.
   The singer sings beautifully.

VOKABELN

das Café, -s	café, coffee shop
die Konditorei, -en	café with bakery and pastry shop
Kaffee trinken	to have coffee
aus*suchen	to pick, to choose
wählen	to choose, select; to vote
bestellen	to order
servieren	to serve
gemütlich	cozy
knusprig	crunchy, crisp
gemischt	mixed
erfrischend	refreshing
herrlich	glorious, delicious
lecker	delicious
unglaublich lecker	unbelievably delicious
süß	sweet
nett	nice
sauer	sour
bitter	bitter, bittersweet
die Wahl, -en	choice, election
der Strudel, -	strudel
die Frucht, ¨e	fruit

die Kirsche, *-n*	cherry
die Schwarzwälder Kirschtorte, *-n*	Black Forest cake
der Apfelstrudel	apple strudel
der Kirschstrudel	cherry strudel
das Gebäck	pastry
die Schokolade	chocolate
der Joghurt	yogurt
die Sahne	cream
die Schlagsahne	whipped cream
der Becher, -	cup, beaker
sogar	even
besorgt	worried
sündigen	to sin
verbieten, *verboten*	to forbid

ÜBUNGEN

A. *Beantworten Sie die Fragen zum Dialog.*

1. *Was hat Sarah ausgesucht?*
2. *Was servieren sie jeden Tag?*
3. *Warum darf Heike keine süßen Sachen essen?*
4. *Was trägt die Frau am Fenstertisch?*

B. *Suchen Sie die richtige deutsche Übersetzung.*

1. What shall I order?
2. Try the mixed fruit.
3. There is crunchy pastry.
4. They've fresh cake.

a. *Es gibt knuspriges Gebäck.*
b. *Probier die gemischten Früchte.*
c. *Was soll ich bestellen?*
d. *Sie haben frischen Kuchen.*

C. *Setzen Sie die fehlenden Endungen ein.*

BEISPIEL: *Jeden Tag gibt es hier frisch___ Sachertorte.*
Jeden Tag gibt es hier frische Sachertorte.

1. *Heute sind wir in ein klein___ Café gegangen.*
2. *Wir haben keinen frei___ Tisch gesehen.*
3. *Wir haben uns zu einer alt___ Frau gesetzt.*
4. *Wir haben gemischt___ Eis und warm___ Apfelstrudel bestellt.*
5. *Meine Freundin hat heiß___ Schokolade getrunken.*
6. *Ich habe Kaffee mit heiß___ Milch getrunken.*
7. *Es hat auch Joghurt mit frisch___ Obst gegeben.*

KULTURNOTIZ

Traditionally, people in German-speaking countries used to eat cake and drink coffee between 3 and 5 P.M. every day. Now, however, among professionals this custom is usually observed only on weekends. In every city and town one can find many coffee houses *(Cafés)* or coffee houses combined with bakeries or pastry shops *(Konditoreien)*. In the summer, people like to sit in sidewalk cafés *(Straßencafés)* or garden cafés *(Gartencafés)*.

It's customary to sit in a café for quite a while without being asked to order more. Frequently people in cafés read local or national newspapers that are supplied by the cafés and are displayed on wooden racks along the wall.

It is common in German-speaking countries to share a table with strangers in a restaurant or café if no free table is available. You should ask, though, whether a seat is available: *Entschuldigung, ist hier noch frei?*

LÖSUNGEN

A. 1. *Sie hat ein wirklich nettes, gemütliches Café ausgesucht. 2. Sie servieren jeden Tag frischen, warmen Apfel- oder Kirschstrudel. 3. Ihr besorgter Arzt hat es verboten. 4. Sie trägt einen schwarzen Hut.*
B. 1.—c 2.—b 3.—a 4.—d
C. 1. *kleines* 2. *freien* 3. *alten* 4. *gemischtes—warmen* 5. *heiße*
   6. *heißer* 7. *frischem*

LEKTION 24

AM RHEIN.   On the Rhine.

A. DIALOG

Eine Fahrt auf dem Rhein.

KURT: Nun fahren wir auf dem berühmten Rhein. Ein imposanter Strom, nicht?

HILDE: Ja, großartig! Das ist meine erste Dampferfahrt. Auf diesem luftigen Aussichtsdeck sitzt man besser als in der ersten Klasse. Das Schöne an so einer Dampferfahrt ist das weite Panorama. Ich genieße den herrlichen Ausblick.

KURT: Mir gefallen die altertümlichen Häuser mit den grauen Schieferdächern. Die grünen Flächen der Weinberge dahinter bilden einen eindrucksvollen Hintergrund. Davon müssen wir eine Aufnahme machen.

HILDE: Der Kontrast zwischen dem schönen und ruhigen Rheintal und den steilen Felsen ist auch bemerkenswert. Schade, dass wir nicht anlegen! Wo bekomme ich Ansichtskarten und Andenken?

KURT: Auf dem Hauptdeck. Aber kauf' sie später, denn jetzt kommen wir an vielen alten Burgen und Ruinen vorbei.

HILDE: Ja, ich möchte doch den Loreleifelsen mit der schönen Lorelei nicht verpassen.

A Trip on the Rhine.

KURT: Now we're on the famous Rhine. An impressive river, isn't it?

HILDE: Yes, magnificent! This is my first steamboat trip. On this breezy observation deck it's better than in first class. The nice thing about such a steamboat trip is the wide panorama. I'm enjoying the glorious view.

KURT: I like the old-fashioned houses with their gray slate roofs. The green areas of the vineyards beyond form a striking background. We must take a picture of it.

HILDE: The contrast between the beautiful and calm Rhine valley and the steep rocks is also remarkable. Too bad that we aren't going to land. Where will I get postcards and souvenirs?

KURT: On the main deck. But buy them later, because now we're going to pass many old castles and ruins.

HILDE: Yes, I wouldn't want to miss the Lorelei rock with the beautiful Lorelei.

B. GRAMMATIK UND GEBRAUCH

1. ADJECTIVES PRECEDED BY DEFINITE ARTICLES OR *DER*-WORDS

Adjectives take the ending -*e* or -*en*, when preceded by a definite article or a *der*-word:

MASCULINE

Nom.	der dieser	} junge	Mann
Acc.	den diesen	} jungen	Mann
Dat.	dem diesem	} jungen	Mann
Gen.	des dieses	} jungen	Mannes

FEMININE

Nom.	die diese	} alte	Stadt
Acc.	die diese	} alte	Stadt
Dat.	der dieser	} alten	Stadt
Gen.	der dieser	} alten	Stadt

	NEUTER			PLURAL		
Nom.	das dieses	grau<u>e</u>	Dach	die diese	gut<u>en</u>	Weine
Acc.	das dieses	grau<u>e</u>	Dach	die diese	gut<u>en</u>	Weine
Dat.	dem diesem	grau<u>en</u>	Dach	den diesen	gut<u>en</u>	Weinen
Gen.	des dieses	grau<u>en</u>	Daches	der dieser	gut<u>en</u>	Weine

Dieser steile Felsen ist sehr imposant.
    That steep rock is very impressive.

Wir wollen den guten Rheinwein versuchen.
    We want to taste the good Rhine wine.

Die schöne Lorelei soll auf diesem steilen Felsen sitzen.
    The beautiful Lorelei is supposed to sit on this steep rock.

Das ist ein Bild des steilen Felsens.
    This is a picture of the steep rock.

Wo ist die schöne Lorelei?
    Where is the beautiful Lorelei?

Diese herrliche Fahrt mache ich noch einmal.
    I'll take this glorious trip again.

Auf der alten Burg ist ein Restaurant.
    There's a restaurant in the old castle.

Wir haben Aufnahmen dieser alten Burg.
    We have photographs of this old castle.

Das luftige Aussichtsdeck ist sehr angenehm.
    The breezy observation deck is very pleasant.

Ich kenne das schöne Rheintal.
    I know the beautiful Rhine valley.

Wir trinken in dem kleinen Café ein Glas Wein.
    We'll have a glass of wine in the small café.

Die Städte dieses lieblichen Tals sind sehr alt.
　The cities of this lovely valley are very old.

Die grünen Flächen bilden einen bemerkenswerten Hintergrund.
　The green areas form a remarkable background.

Ich mag diese alten Städte.
　I like these old cities.

Hinter den alten Städten liegen die Weinberge.
　Beyond the old cities lie the vineyards.

Die Dächer der altertümlichen Häuser sind aus Schiefer.
　The roofs of the old-fashioned houses are of slate.

2. ADJECTIVAL NOUNS

Adjectives used as nouns take the same endings as adjectives that precede nouns; however, they are capitalized like nouns.

a. If adjectival nouns refer to things, they are neuter, and mostly singular:

das Schöne
　the beautiful (thing)

das Gute
　the good (thing)

Das Gute daran ist, dass er wieder arbeiten kann.
　The good thing about it is that he can work again.

b. If adjectival nouns refer to people, they are masculine or feminine, singular or plural:

der Kranke	the sick man; the sick one
die Kranke	the sick woman; the sick one
die Kranken	the sick people; the sick

Der Neue soll aus München sein.
　The new man is supposed to be from Munich.

Wir kennen den Neuen noch nicht.
We don't know the new man yet.

Ich will der Neuen helfen.
I want to help the new woman.

Die Familie des Neuen wohnt noch nicht hier.
The new man's family doesn't live here yet.

Die Arme hat keine Wohnung.
The poor woman has no home.

Die Reichen sind nicht immer glücklich.
The rich are not always happy.

3. ORDINAL NUMBERS

The numbers you have learned are the cardinal numbers (one, two, three . . .), which are used in counting. There are also ordinal numbers (first, second, third . . .), which indicate position in a series.

In German, the ordinal numbers are formed by adding -t to the cardinal numbers from 2 to 19 *(der zweite Stock,* the second floor), and -st to the cardinal numbers from 20 to 100 *(der dreiundzwanzigste Stock).* Four German ordinal numbers are irregular: first, third, seventh, and eighth.

eins	**erster,** *-e, -es*	*dreizehn*	**dreizehnter,** *-e, -es*
zwei	**zweiter,** *-e, -es*	*sechzehn*	**sechzehnter,** *-e, -es*
drei	**dritter,** *-e, -es*	*siebzehn*	**siebzehnter,** *-e, -es*
vier	**vierter,** *-e, -es*	*achtzehn*	**achtzehnter,** *-e, -es*
fünf	**fünfter,** *-e, -es*	*zwanzig*	**zwanzigster,** *-e, -es*
sechs	**sechster,** *-e, -es*	*einundzwanzig*	**einundzwanzigster,** *-e, -es*
sieben	**siebter,** *-e, -es*	*dreißig*	**dreißigster,** *-e, -es*
acht	**achter,** *-e, -es*	*vierzig*	**vierzigster,** *-e, -es*
neun	**neunter,** *-e, -es*	*einhundert*	**einhundertster,** *-e, -es*
zehn	**zehnter,** *-e, -es*	*hunderteins*	**hunderterster,** *-e, -es*
elf	**elfter,** *-e, -es*	*hundertzwei*	**hundertzweiter,** *-e, -es*
zwölf	**zwölfter,** *-e, -es*	*eintausend*	**eintausendster,** *-e, -es*

Ordinal numbers take adjective endings:

der achte April
    the eighth of April

die erste Klasse
    the first class

das dritte Kind
    the third child

die ersten Blumen
    the first flowers

Das ist ihre erste Reise auf einem Dampfer.
    That is her first trip on a steamboat.

Auf dem Aussichtsdeck ist es genau so gut wie in der ersten Klasse.
    On the observation deck it is as good as in first class.

VOKABELN

die Rheintour	the Rhine tour
der Tourist, *-en, -en*	tourist (m.)
die Dampferfahrt, *-en*	steamboat trip
die erste Klasse	first class
das Aussichtsdeck, *-s*	observation deck
das Panorama, *-s*	panorama
der Ausblick, *-e*	view
der Hintergrund, *⸚e*	background
das Tal, *⸚er*	valley
das Dorf, *⸚er*	village
der Strom, *⸚e*	river
die Burg, *-en*	castle
die Ruine, *-n*	ruin
der Felsen, *-*	rock
der Berg, *-e*	hill, mountain
der Weinberg, *-e*	vineyard
die Fläche, *-n*	area, surface

der Kontrast, -e	contrast
die Ansichtskarte, -n	postcard
das Andenken, -	souvenir
die Aufnahme, -n	photo
der Photoapparat, -e	camera
auf*nehmen *(nimmt auf)*, *aufgenommen*	to take a picture
an*legen	to land (a boat)
vorbei*fahren *(fährt vorbei)*, *ist* *vorbeigefahren*	to pass by
genießen, *genossen*	to enjoy, to savor
verpassen	to miss
berühmt	famous
imposant	impressive
großartig	magnificent
bemerkenswert	remarkable
eindrucksvoll	striking
altertümlich	old-fashioned
ruhig	calm, quiet
luftig	breezy
weit	wide, far
dahinter	behind, beyond

ÜBUNGEN

A. *Beantworten Sie die Fragen zum Dialog.*

1. *Auf welchem Strom machen Hilde und Kurt eine Dampferfahrt?*
2. *Was gefällt Kurt?*
3. *Was ist das Schöne an so einer Dampferfahrt?*
4. *Wo bekommt man Ansichtskarten und Andenken?*
5. *Was möchte Hilde nicht verpassen?*

B. *Suchen Sie die richtige deutsche Übersetzung.*

1. This is my first trip on a steamboat.
2. He's enjoying the glorious view.

3. The houses have gray roofs.
4. I want to take a picture of that.

a. *Die Häuser haben graue Dächer.*
b. *Davon will ich eine Aufnahme machen.*
c. *Das ist meine erste Dampferfahrt.*
d. *Er genießt den herrlichen Ausblick.*

C. *Setzen Sie die fehlenden Endungen ein.*

BEISPIEL: *In diesem neu___ Haus ist ein schönes Café.*
   In diesem neuen Haus ist ein schönes Café.

1. *Morgen machen wir die erst___ Dampferfahrt.*
2. *Wir fahren auf dem berühmt___ Rhein.*
3. *Die Fahrt geht an alt___ Burgen vorbei.*
4. *Wir wollen Plätze auf dem schön___ Aussichtsdeck.*
5. *Wir freuen uns auf die frisch___ Luft und den herrlich___ Ausblick.*
6. *Wir hoffen, dass wir an dem steil___ Loreleifelsen vorbeifahren.*
7. *Wir möchten auch den gut___ Rheinwein probieren.*

D. *Vervollständigen Sie die Sätze.* (Fill in the missing words.)

1. *Wir wohnen im _____ Stock.* (second)
2. *Heute ist der _____ Juli.* (fifth)
3. *Am _____ Juli fliegen wir nach Frankfurt.* (fifth)
4. *Der letzte Tag im Jahr ist der _____ Dezember.* (31st)
5. *Das ist mein _____ Auto.* (third)

E. *Bringen Sie die Sätze ins Plural.* (Change the sentences to plural.)

1. *Die rote Rose ist sehr schön.*
2. *Ich habe einen guten Stadtplan.*
3. *Die bemerkenswerte Burg ist am Rhein.*
4. *Wir essen viel grünen Salat.*
5. *Sehen Sie das große Haus?*

KULTURNOTIZ

The Rhine *(der Rhein)* is the most important German waterway. It has its source in Switzerland, traverses Germany, and flows through the Netherlands into the North Sea. Along the banks of the Rhine small, romantic cities with a rich history are located. *Vater Rhein,* as the Germans call the river in poetry and song, and the wine of the region have shaped the people's life there. Numerous restaurants, hotels, and outdoor cafés cater to tourists. Although excursion boats on the Rhine now have diesel engines, they are still called *Dampfer (dampfen,* to steam). But along the Rhine's banks one also finds ports where large cargo ships load and unload.

The Lorelei rock *(Loreleifelsen)* is a steep rock on the Rhine's right bank just below the city of Kaub. Folklore has it that the water nymph Lorelei used to sit on the rock and entice the passing boatmen with her singing and golden hair, so that their boats were wrecked and they drowned. The Lorelei has been immortalized by several poets; the best-known poem is *Die Lorelei* by Heinrich Heine. Its text, *"Ich weiß nicht, was soll es bedeuten,"* was set to music by Friedrich Silcher.

LÖSUNGEN

A. 1. *Sie machen auf dem Rhein eine Dampferfahrt.* 2. *Ihm gefallen die altertümlichen Häuser mit den grauen Schieferdächern.* 3. *Das weite Panorama ist das Schöne an so einer Dampferfahrt.* 4. *Auf dem Hauptdeck bekommt man Ansichtskarten und Andenken.* 5. *Sie möchte den Loreleifelsen mit der schönen Lorelei nicht verpassen.*

B. 1.—c   2.—d   3.—a   4.—b

C. 1. *erste*   2. *berühmten*   3. *alten*   4. *schönen*   5. *frische—herrlichen*   6. *steilen*   7. *guten*

D. 1. *ersten* (the second floor is called the first in Europe)   2. *fünfte*   3. *fünften*   4. *einunddreißigste*   5. *drittes*

E. 1. *Die roten Rosen sind sehr schön.* 2. *Ich habe gute Stadtpläne.* 3. *Die bemerkenswerten Burgen sind am Rhein.* 4. *Wir essen viele grüne Salate.* 5. *Sehen Sie die großen Häuser?*

LEKTION 25

SPORT. Sports.

A. DIALOG

König Fußball und andere Sportarten.

DIETER: Tooor!

HILDE: Warum schreist du so laut?

DIETER: Unsere Mannschaft hat gerade die beste in der Liga kurz vor der Halbzeit geschlagen. Unsere Stürmer sind am schnellsten gelaufen. Und der Torwart, Spitze! Wir werden immer besser.

HILDE: Schaust du die zweite Halbzeit an?

DIETER: Natürlich. Ich muss doch den erstaunlichsten Sieg der Saison sehen.

HILDE: In zehn Minuten übertragen sie ein Tennismatch. Unsere jüngste Spielerin kämpft gegen die erste und älteste auf der Weltrangliste.

DIETER: Das Spiel verlieren wir sowieso. Außerdem ist Tennis gar nicht so spannend wie Fußball.

HILDE: Ich sehe es aber lieber.

DIETER: Hmm. Heute Abend bringen sie Höhepunkte vom Tennisspiel, der Leichtathletik und den Boxkämpfen. Dann kannst du die stärksten Männer bewundern.

HILDE: Hör auf mich zu ärgern. Ich treibe lieber Sport und fahre Rad. Gesünder als Fernsehen.

DIETER: Tschüs.

King Soccer and Other Sports.

DIETER: Goal!

HILDE: Why are you screaming so loudly?

DIETER: Our team just beat the best team in the league shortly before halftime. Our forwards ran fastest. And the goalie, first rate! We're getting better and better.

HILDE: Are you going to watch the second half?

DIETER: Of course. I've got to watch the most amazing victory of the season.

HILDE: In ten minutes, they're going to broadcast a live tennis match. Our youngest player is going to play the first and oldest on the world-class list.

DIETER: We're going to lose the game anyhow. Besides, tennis isn't as exciting as soccer.

HILDE: But I prefer it.

DIETER: Hmm. This evening, they're going to show highlights from the tennis matches, the track and field meets, and the boxing matches. Then you can admire the strongest men of the world.

HILDE: Stop teasing me. I prefer to play sports and ride my bicycle. Healthier than watching TV.

DIETER: Bye.

B. GRAMMATIK UND GEBRAUCH

1. THE POSITIVE OF ADJECTIVES AND ADVERBS

a. There are three degrees of comparison:

POSITIVE	COMPARATIVE	SUPERLATIVE
big	bigger	the biggest
gently	more gently	the most gently

In the positive form an adjective or adverb simply describes a noun or verb.

Warum schreist du so laut?
  Why are you screaming so loudly?

Fußball ist spannend.
Soccer is exciting.

Die neue Saison fängt an.
The new season is starting.

Note that in German, unlike in English, adjectives and adverbs usually have the same form.

Unsere Mannschaft ist gut.
Our team is good.

Sie spielt gut.
It (the team) plays well.

b. The construction *so...wie* compares similar persons and things with one another and is equivalent to the English *as...as*.

Tennis ist so spannend wie Fußball.
Tennis is as exciting as soccer.

2. THE COMPARATIVE OF ADJECTIVES AND ADVERBS

A comparative adjective or adverb compares persons or things that are not alike.

Fußball ist spannender als Tennis.
Soccer is more exciting than tennis.

a. The comparative of an adjective or adverb is formed by adding *-er* to the positive form.

POSITIVE		COMPARATIVE	
laut	loud	*lauter*	louder
schnell	fast	*schneller*	faster
gesund	healthy	*gesünder*	healthier

Many one-syllable adjectives and adverbs with stem vowels of *a, o,* or *u* add an umlaut in the comparative form. Some frequently used adjectives and adverbs with this pattern are:

POSITIVE		COMPARATIVE
stark	→	*stärker*
kalt	→	*kälter*
warm	→	*wärmer*
groß	→	*größer*
jung	→	*jünger*
alt	→	*älter*
lang	→	*länger*
kurz	→	*kürzer*

b. When you compare people and things, the word *als,* equivalent to the English "than," is used.

Radfahren ist gesünder als Fernsehen.
Cycling is healthier than TV.

Mein Auto fährt schneller als dein Motorrad.
My car goes faster than your motorcycle.

c. A comparative adjective that precedes its noun takes the appropriate adjective ending.

Der Porsche ist ein schnelleres Auto als der Mercedes.
The Porsche is a faster car than the Mercedes.

Beim Fußball braucht man eine größere Mannschaft als beim Handball.
You need a bigger team for soccer than for handball.

d. Note the use of *immer* + comparative:

Es wird immer kälter.
It's getting colder and colder. (It's getting ever colder.)

Die Tage werden immer kürzer.
The days are getting shorter and shorter. (The days are getting ever shorter.)

3. THE SUPERLATIVE OF ADJECTIVES AND ADVERBS

A superlative adjective or adverb describes a person, thing, or action that cannot be surpassed.

Das ist der erstaunlichste Sieg der Saison.
It's the most amazing victory of the season.

a. The superlative of adjectives is formed by adding the ending *-st-* to the positive.

POSITIVE		SUPERLATIVE
schnell	→	*schnellst-*
klein	→	*kleinst-*

One-syllable adjectives add an umlaut as in the comparative:

POSITIVE		SUPERLATIVE
jung	→	*jüngst-*
warm	→	*wärmst-*

If the basic form of the adjective or adverb ends in a *-d, -t, -s, -ß,* or *-z,* an *e* is usually added to the stem. *Groß* is an exception:

POSITIVE		SUPERLATIVE	POSITIVE		SUPERLATIVE
alt	→	*ältest-*	*groß*	→	*größt-*
gesund	→	*gesündest-*	*naß*	→	*näßest-*

b. If the superlative form of the adjective precedes the noun, the appropriate endings have to be added.

Ich muss den erstaunlichsten Sieg der Saison sehen.
I must watch the most amazing victory of the season.

Die jüngste Spielerin kämpft gegen die älteste.
The youngest player is playing against the oldest.

Du kannst die stärksten Männer bewundern.
You can admire the strongest men.

c. The superlative of adverbs and predicate adjectives* is formed by inserting *am* before the word and adding the suffix *-en* to it.

Diese Mannschaft läuft am schnellsten.
This team runs fastest.

Diese Frau ist am jüngsten.
This woman is the youngest.

You can also express the last sentence by saying:

Diese Frau ist die jüngste.

4. IRREGULAR FORMS OF THE COMPARATIVE AND SUPERLATIVE

As in English, there are irregular forms of the comparative and superlative in German. The most frequently used are:

positive:	*gut*	*hoch*	*gern*	*viel*
comparative:	*besser*	*höher*	*lieber*	*mehr*
superlative:	*best-*	*höchst-*	*liebst-*	*meist-*

Er ist ein guter Spieler.
He's a good player.

Sein Vater ist ein besserer Spieler.
His father is a better player.

Sein Bruder ist der beste Spieler.
His brother is the best player.

Er spielt gut.
He plays well.

Sein Vater spielt besser.
His father plays better.

Sein Bruder spielt am besten.
His brother plays best.

---

* A predicate adjective is one that follows the verb "to be" and certain other verbs: *Sie ist jung.* (She is young.) *Wir werden stark.* (We are becoming strong.)

Hier steht ein hohes Haus.
Here is a high house.

Der Turm ist höher als das Haus.
The tower is higher than the house.

Der Berg ist am höchsten./Der Berg ist der höchste.
The mountain is highest.

Ich sehe gern Tennis.
I like to watch tennis.

Ich sehe lieber Fußball.
I prefer to watch soccer.

Ich sehe am liebsten Leichtathletik.
I like to watch track and field best of all.

Leichtathletik ist mein liebster Sport.
Track and field is my favorite sport.

Note: *Gern* and *lieber* can only be used as adverbs.

Ein Tisch kostet viel.
A table costs a lot.

Ein Auto kostet mehr als ein Tisch.
A car costs more than a table.

Ein Haus kostet am meisten.
A house costs the most.

Die Schweiz hat viele Städte.
Switzerland has many cities.

Österreich hat mehr Städte als die Schweiz.
Austria has more cities than Switzerland.

Deutschland hat die meisten Städte.
Germany has the most cities.

Note: If *viel* precedes a noun it takes adjective endings only in the plural. *Mehr* never takes adjective endings.

VOKABELN

der Sport	sport
Sport treiben *(getrieben)*	to engage in, pursue sports
die Liga, -*s*	league
die Mannschaft, -*en*	team
der Fußball	soccer
König Fußball	King soccer
das Fußballspiel, -*e*	soccer match
das Spiel, -*e*	game
der Spieler, -	male player
die Spielerin, -*nen*	female player
die Halbzeit, -*en*	halftime
das Turnen	gymnastics
turnen	to do gymnastics
der Radsport	cycling
das Rad, ⁻*er*	bicycle
Rad fahren, *ist Rad gefahren*	to bicycle
die Leichtathletik	track and field
das Boxen	boxing
der Boxkampf, ⁻*e*	boxing match
schwimmen, *ist geschwommen*	to go swimming
der Sieg, -*e*	victory
die Niederlage, -*n*	defeat
kämpfen	to fight
schlagen *(schlägt),* geschlagen	to beat
siegen	to win
verlieren, *verloren*	to lose
schreien, *geschrie(e)n*	to scream, to yell
beobachten	to watch, observe
bewundern	to admire
übertragen	to broadcast
erstaunlich	amazing
spannend	exciting, thrilling
langweilig	boring
stark	strong
schwach	weak
sowieso	in any case, anyhow

ÜBUNGEN

A. *Beantworten Sie die Fragen zum Dialog.*

1. *Wen hat Dieters Mannschaft geschlagen?*
2. *Wie wird Dieters Mannschaft?*
3. *Wen kann Hilde bei den Boxkämpfen anschauen?*
4. *Was will Hilde machen?*

B. *Suchen Sie die richtige deutsche Übersetzung.*

1. In ten minutes they're going to broadcast a soccer match.
2. Tennis is as exciting as soccer.
3. We're going to lose anyhow.
4. Most of all I like to play sports.
5. That's the most amazing victory of the season.

a. *Tennis ist so spannend wie Fußball.*
b. *Das ist der erstaunlichste Sieg der Saison.*
c. *Ich treibe am liebsten Sport.*
d. *In zehn Minuten übertragen sie ein Fußballspiel.*
e. *Wir verlieren sowieso.*

C. *Übersetzen Sie.*

1. He runs fastest.
2. She is the smallest.
3. Erik is the tallest man.
4. I'm better than you.
5. We're getting older and older.
6. He's as weak as we are.

D. *Setzen Sie die fehlenden Endungen ein.*

BEISPIEL: *Sie fährt ein größer__ Auto als ich.*
               Sie fährt ein größeres Auto als ich.

1. *Er sieht das best__ Fußballspiel.*
2. *Er hat eine kleiner__ Wohnung als sein Bruder.*
3. *Unsere Mannschaft kämpft am best__.*
4. *Man überträgt das langweiligst__ Spiel.*
5. *Ein spannender__ Spiel gibt es nicht.*

KULTURNOTIZ

Soccer *(Fußball)* is the most popular spectator as well as participatory sport in German-speaking countries. That's why its nickname is *König Fußball.* Germans of all ages engage in sports. A third of the population belongs to a sports club *(Sportverein).* After soccer, gymnastics is the most popular sport. Other sports many people engage in are tennis, track and field, handball, skiing, and swimming.

LÖSUNGEN

A. 1. *Sie hat die beste Mannschaft in der Liga geschlagen.* 2. *Sie wird immer besser.* 3. *Sie kann die stärksten Männer anschauen.* 4. *Sie will Sport treiben und Rad fahren.*

B. 1.—d 2.—a 3.—e 4.—c 5.—b

C. 1. *Er läuft am schnellsten.* 2. *Sie ist die Kleinste/am kleinsten.* 3. *Erik ist der größte Mann.* 4. *Ich bin besser als du.* 5. *Wir werden immer älter.* 6. *Er ist so schwach wie wir.*

D. 1. *beste* 2. *kleinere* 3. *besten* 4. *langweiligste* 5. *spannenderes*

FÜNFTE WIEDERHOLUNGSAUFGABE

A. *Setzen Sie die fehlenden Endungen ein.*

BEISPIEL: Frau Sommer hat ein__ neu__ Wohnung.
   Frau Sommer hat eine neue Wohnung.

1. *Ich bin in die hübsch__, klein__ Wohnung unter dem Dach eingezogen.*
2. *Dort habe ich einen weit__ Ausblick auf den grün__ Park.*
3. *Meine alt__ Möbel habe ich nicht mitgebracht.*
4. *Nur der groß__, bequem__ Sessel fehlt mir.*
5. *Ich habe auch schon meine erst__ Party gegeben.*
6. *Leider sind die Kinder der jung__ Leute im Nachbarhaus sehr laut.*

B. *Übersetzen Sie.*

1. the fifth review lesson
2. the first day

3. the second street to the right
4. the twentieth year
5. the third hot summer
6. We're living in our second house.
7. He has his fiftieth birthday today.

C. *Übersetzen Sie.*

1. Do you want to know what we did yesterday? (fam.)
2. We took a ride on a new steamship on the old Rhine river.
3. We enjoyed the grand panorama, and drank a good glass of wine.
4. We took the first tour at 9:30.
5. One must be there early in order to get a good seat.
6. Unfortunately, there were no empty seats on the observation deck.

D. *Ersetzen Sie die unterstrichenen Wörter mit einer "Da"-Zusammensetzung.* (Replace the underlined word with a *da*-compound.)

BEISPIEL: *Das weite Panorama ist das Schöne an dieser Dampferfahrt.*
Das weite Panorama ist das Schöne daran.

1. *Wir fahren mit diesem Dampfer.*
2. *Fahren wir an dem Felsen vorbei?*
3. *Sollen wir eine Ansichtskarte von dem Felsen schicken?*

E. *Bilden Sie Fragen zu den unterstrichenen Wörtern. Benutzen Sie eine "Wo-" Zusammensetzung.* (Form questions asking for the underlined words. Use a *wo*-compound.)

BEISPIEL: *Wir kommen jetzt an vielen alten Burgen und Schlössern vorbei.*
Woran kommen wir jetzt vorbei?

1. *Die schöne Lorelei soll auf dem Felsen sitzen.*
2. *Er will eine Aufnahme von dem großartigen Panorama machen.*
3. *Wir fahren mit einem Dampfer.*

F. *Beenden Sie die Sätze.* (Finish the sentences.)

BEISPIEL: *Stuttgart ist groß, aber München ist _____.*
Stuttgart ist groß, aber München ist größer.

1. *Werner ist 14 Jahre alt, Klaus ist _____.*
2. *Im Herbst ist es kalt, im Winter _____.*
3. *Ich bin stark. Du bist _____.*

LÖSUNGEN

A. 1. *hübsche—kleine*   2. *weiten—grünen*   3. *alten*   4. *große—bequeme*   5. *erste*   6. *jungen*

B. 1. *die fünfte Wiederholungsaufgabe*   2. *der erste Tag*   3. *die zweite Straße rechts*   4. *das zwanzigste Jahr*   5. *der dritte heiße Sommer*   6. *Wir wohnen in unserem zweiten Haus.*   7. *Er hat heute seinen fünfzigsten Geburtstag.*

C. 1. *Willst du wissen, was wir gestern gemacht haben?* 2. *Wir sind mit einem neuen Dampfer auf dem alten Rhein gefahren.* 3. *Wir haben das großartige Panorama genossen und ein Glas guten Wein getrunken.* 4. *Wir haben die erste Tour um 9.30 Uhr genommen.* 5. *Man muss früh da sein, um einen guten Platz zu bekommen.* 6. *Leider waren auf dem Aussichtsdeck keine freien Plätze.*

D. 1. *Wir fahren damit.* 2. *Fahren wir daran vorbei?* 3. *Sollen wir eine Ansichtskarte davon schicken?*

E. 1. *Worauf soll die schöne Lorelei sitzen?* 2. *Wovon will er eine Aufnahme machen?* 3. *Womit fahren wir?*

F. 1. *älter*   2. *kälter*   3. *stärker*

LEKTION 26

IM GEBIRGE.   In the Mountains.

A. DIALOG

Am Gipfel.

HEINER: Die Sicht auf die Gletscher ist fabelhaft. Schade, dass wir absteigen müssen.

VOLKER: Ja, ich werde auch unruhig. Die schwarze Wolke am Himmel ist bedrohlich, und wenn es dunkel wird, müssen wir auf der Hütte sein.

HEINER: Also los. Nehmen wir wieder unsere Rucksäcke.

VOLKER: Warte, wir haben uns nicht ins Gipfelbuch eingetragen.

HEINER: Guck mal! Interessant. Vor uns war eine Gruppe Pfadfinder da. Die machen auch eine Gipfelwanderung.

VOLKER: Ach, denen gehört sicher der Schlafsack hier im Gras neben den Bergblumen. Sollen wir den für die mitschleppen?

HEINER: Besser nicht. Der Pfad geht jetzt erst über einen engen Grat. Später ist der steile Abstieg über die spitzen Steine bis zum Wald endlos.

VOLKER: Na, dann können die Gemsen heute nacht weich schlafen.

On the Summit.

HEINER: The view of the glaciers is fabulous. Too bad we've got to go down.

VOLKER: Yes, I'm getting worried too. The black clouds in the sky are threatening, and when it gets dark we have to be at the shelter.

HEINER: Let's go. Let's put on our backpacks again.

VOLKER: Wait, we didn't sign the summit book.

HEINER: Look, how interesting. A group of Boy Scouts came before us. They're also taking a hike along the summit.

227

VOLKER: Oh, the sleeping bag here in the grass next to the mountain flowers probably belongs to them. Should we take it along for them?

HEINER: Better not. First the trail leads along a narrow ridge. Later the steep descent over the sharp rocks to the forest is endless.

VOLKER: Well then, the mountain goats can sleep comfortably tonight.

B. GRAMMATIK UND GEBRAUCH

1. THE DEMONSTRATIVE PRONOUNS

Demonstrative adjectives and pronouns point to something. In English, "this," "that," "there," and "those" are demonstratives. You already know the German demonstrative adjective *dieser.*

Diese Sicht ist fabelhaft.
This view is fabulous.

German also has the demonstrative pronouns *der, die, das.*

	MASCULINE		FEMININE
Nom.	der		die
Acc.	den		die
Dat.	dem		der
Gen.	dessen		deren

	NEUTER		PLURAL
Nom.	das		die
Acc.	das		die
Dat.	dem		denen
Gen.	dessen		deren

These forms are identical with the definite article except in the dative plural. They are often used instead of the personal pronouns, especially when the pronoun is emphasized.

Ist der Berg hoch? Ja, der ist wirklich hoch.
Is the mountain high? Yes, it's really high.

Sollen wir den Schlafsack mitschleppen? Nein, den schleppen wir nicht mit.
Should we take along the sleeping bag? No, we won't take it along.

Hilfst du dem Pfadfinder? Nein, dem helfe ich nicht.
Are you going to help the Boy Scout? No, I'm not going to help him.

Ist die Wiese schön? Ja, die ist wirklich schön.
Is the meadow beautiful? Yes, it's very beautiful.

Siehst du die Hütte? Ja, die sehe ich.
Do you see the shelter? Yes, I see it.

Nimmst du die Blume? Nein, die nehme ich nicht.
Are you taking the flower? No, I'm not taking it.

Ist er in der Hütte? Nein, in der ist er nicht.
Is he in the shelter? No, he isn't in it.

Das Gipfelbuch ist interessant, nicht? Ja, das ist sehr interessant.
The summit book is interesting, isn't it? Yes, it's very interesting.

Siehst du das Gebirge? Ja, das sehe ich.
Do you see the mountains? Yes, I see them.

Sprichst du mit dem Wanderer? Ja, mit dem spreche ich.
Are you talking with the hiker? Yes, I'm talking with him.

Die Pfade sind sehr steil, nicht? Ja, die sind sehr steil.
The trails are very steep, aren't they? Yes, they are very steep.

Siehst du die Wolken? Ja, die sehe ich.
Do you see the clouds? Yes, I see them.

Gehören die Schlafsäcke den Pfadfindern? Ja, denen gehören sie.
Do the sleeping bags belong to the Boy Scouts? Yes, they belong to them.

2. WORD FORMATION

a. THE PREFIX *UN-*

As in English, the prefix *un-* gives a word a negative or opposite meaning.

ruhig	→	**unruhig**	**klar**	→	**unklar**
calm		restless	clear		unclear

interessant	→	**uninteressant**	**angenehm**	→	**unangenehm**
interesting		uninteresting	pleasant		unpleasant

Ich werde unruhig. I'm getting restless.

b. THE SUFFIX *-LOS*

The suffix *-los* is used to form adjectives and adverbs from nouns. It is often equivalent to the English suffix *-less*.

das Ende	→	**endlos**	**der Zahn**	→	**zahnlos**
the end		endless	the tooth		toothless

der Kopf	→	**kopflos**
the head		headless

Der Abstieg ist endlos. The descent is endless.

c. THE SUFFIX *-HAFT*

The suffix *-haft* is used to form adjectives from nouns and other adjectives so as to designate related qualities.

die Fabel	→	**fabelhaft**	**das kind**	→	**kindhaft**
the fable		fabulous	the child		childlike

krank	→	**krankhaft**
sick		pathological

230

Die Sicht ist fabelhaft. The view is fabulous.

    d. THE SUFFIX *-UNG*

The suffix *-ung* may be added to the stem of a verb to form a noun. All nouns ending in *-ung* are feminine. The plural ending is *-en*.

wandern to hike	*wander-* + *ung*	→	**die Wanderung** the hike
führen to lead	*führ-* + *ung*	→	**die Führung** the guided tour
wohnen to live	*wohn-* + *ung*	→	**die Wohnung** the apartment
sitzen to sit	*sitz* + *ung*	→	**die Sitzung** the meeting

Die machen auch eine Gipfelwanderung. They're also doing a summit hike.

VOKABELN

das Gebirge, *-e*	mountains, mountain range
der Berg, *-e*	mountain
der Gletscher, *-*	glacier
der Gipfel, *-*	summit, peak
die Sicht	view
der Himmel, *-*	sky, heaven
die Wolke, *-n*	cloud
der Stein, *-e*	rock
der Wald, *̈er*	forest, woods
die Wiese, *-n*	meadow
die Blume, *-n*	flower
das Gras, *̈er*	grass
der Pfad, *-e*	path, trail
auf*steigen, *ist aufgestiegen*	to ascend, climb

ab*steigen, *ist abgestiegen*	to descend, go down
der Aufstieg, *-e*	ascent
der Abstieg, *-e*	descent
steil	steep
eng	narrow
wandern	to hike
die Wanderung, *-en*	hike
der Pfadfinder, *-*	Boy Scout
der Rucksack, *¨e*	backpack
schleppen	to lug, haul
der Schlafsack, *¨e*	sleeping bag
die Hütte, *-n*	shelter, hut
weich	soft
hart	hard
unruhig	restless
sich ein*tragen *(trägt ein),* *eingetragen*	to register
bedrohlich	threatening
fabelhaft	fabulous

ÜBUNGEN

A. *Beantworten Sie die Fragen zum Dialog.*

1. *Wie ist die Sicht?*
2. *Was ist am Himmel?*
3. *Wer war vor Heiner und Volker auf dem Gipfel?*
4. *Wem gehört sicher der Schlafsack?*

B. *Suchen Sie die richtige deutsche Übersetzung.*

1. The view is fabulous.
2. A black cloud is in the sky.
3. It's cool in the forest.
4. The sleeping bag is lying in the grass.
5. The trail is steep and narrow.
6. The descent is endless.

a. *Der Pfad ist eng und steil.*
b. *Die Sicht ist fabelhaft.*
c. *Der Abstieg ist endlos.*
d. *Eine schwarze Wolke ist am Himmel.*
e. *Der Schlafsack liegt im Gras.*
f. *Es ist kühl im Wald.*

C. *Ersetzen Sie die unterstrichenen Substantive im ersten Satz durch ein Demonstrativpronomen im zweiten Satz.* (Replace the underlined items in the first sentence by a demonstrative pronoun in the second sentence.)

BEISPIEL: *Kennen Sie das Restaurant hier? _____ kenne ich.*
    Das kenne ich.

1. *Wie findest du den Pfad?*
   _____ finde ich sehr steil.
2. *Siehst du die Hütte?*
   Ja, _____ sehe ich.
3. *Möchtest du mit den Pfadfindern sprechen?*
   Ja, mit _____ möchte ich sprechen.
4. *Hast du das Essen mitgebracht?*
   Ja, _____ habe ich mitgebracht.

D. *Nennen Sie das Hauptwort.* (Provide the noun.)

BEISPIEL: *zahnlos*
    der Zahn

1. *sitzen*
2. *wohnen*
3. *kindhaft*
4. *kopflos*
5. *fabelhaft*

E. *Übersetzen Sie.*

1. The trail is endless.
2. Yesterday we descended from the summit.
3. The grass in the meadow was very soft.
4. Then we came to the forest.

F. *Ergänzen Sie das Gegenteil des Adjektivs mit Hilfe der Vorsilbe –un.*
   (Supply the missing opposite adjective using the prefix -un.)

   1. *Grammatik ist nicht immer sehr klar. Sie ist manchmal . . .*
   2. *Das Wetter ist heute nicht schön. Es ist . . .*
   3. *Die Temperatur ist nicht angenehm. Sie ist . . .*
   4. *Zigaretten sind nicht gesund. Sie sind . . .*
   5. *Dieses Buch ist nicht interessant. Es ist . . .*

KULTURNOTIZ

There are numerous hiking trails in the Alpine regions *(Alpen)* of Germany, Austria, and Switzerland. They are maintained by Alpine hiking and climbing clubs *(Gebirgsvereine)* which also maintain some of the shelters *(Hütten)*. The shelters range from primitive lean-tos to comfortable accommodations.

Cattle and goats graze on mountain pastures *(Almen)* during the short summer months. The animals are herded by local boys *(Hirtenjungen)*. In some mountain meadows one can also find restaurants and overnight accommodations.

Some mountain meadows and peaks are accessible to all by mountain railways *(Bergbahnen)* or chair lifts *(Sesselbahnen)*. On almost all higher mountain peaks, crosses *(Gipfelkreuze)* have been erected. Attached to the crosses you often find a book *(Gipfelbuch)* where you can sign your name. There are no registries at trailheads. It's not advisable to hike alone in the higher Alpine regions. One should never cross glaciers *(Gletscher)* alone.

LÖSUNGEN

A. 1. *Sie/die ist fabelhaft. 2. Eine schwarze Wolke ist am Himmel. 3. Eine Gruppe Pfadfinder war auf dem Gipfel. 4. Der/er gehört sicher den Pfadfindern.*
B. 1.—b   2.—d   3.—f   4.—e   5.—a   6.—c
C. 1. *Den*   2. *die*   3. *denen*   4. *das*
D. 1. *die Sitzung*   2. *die Wohnung*   3. *das Kind*   4. *der Kopf*   5. *die Fabel*
E. 1. *Der Pfad ist endlos. 2. Gestern sind wir vom Gipfel abgestiegen. 3. Das Gras auf den Wiesen war sehr weich. 4. Dann sind wir zum Wald gekommen.*
F. 1. *unklar*   2. *unschön*   3. *unangenehm*   4. *ungesund* 5. *uninteressant*

LEKTION 27

STUDIUM UND BERUFE.   Studies and Professions.

A. DIALOG

Alte Freunde treffen sich.

AXEL: Lisa, seit zehn Jahren haben wir uns nicht gesehen!

LISA: Ja, wir flirteten miteinander, machten das Abitur zusammen, feierten toll und trennten uns.

AXEL: Ich hörte, dass du Juristin geworden bist.

LISA: Stimmt. Erst studierte ich Sozialwissenschaft, dann wechselte ich in das Jurastudium über.

AXEL: Alle Achtung! Hast du dein eigenes Büro?

LISA: Nein, ich wollte in den Staatsdienst, und darauf musste ich eine Weile warten. Ich arbeitete zuerst als Aushilfe bei einem Rechtsanwalt. Aber wie ist es dir gegangen?

AXEL: Ich konnte damals keinen Studienplatz für Zahnmedizin bekommen. Mein Notendurchschnitt war nicht gut genug. Da machte ich eine Lehre als Zahntechniker.

LISA: Gut! Du hattest schon immer handwerkliches Geschick.

AXEL: Aber jetzt mache ich doch noch das Studium als Zahnarzt. In einem Jahr bin ich fertig.

LISA: Das freut mich. Die Berufsaussichten sind glänzend.

Old Friends Meet.

AXEL: Lisa, it's been ten years since we last saw each other.

LISA: Yes, we used to flirt, then we graduated together from high school, we celebrated wildly, and we separated.

AXEL: I heard you became a lawyer.

LISA: That's right. At first I studied social science, then I switched to law.

AXEL: Congratulations. Do you have your own office?

LISA: No, I wanted a government job and had to wait awhile for it. I worked at first as a temporary for a lawyer. But how have you made out?

AXEL: I couldn't get into dental school at the time. My grade-point average wasn't high enough. So I trained as a dental technician.

LISA: That's good. You were always quite skilled with your hands.

AXEL: But now I'm studying dentistry after all. I'll be finished in a year.

LISA: I'm glad. The prospects for that profession are splendid.

B. GRAMMATIK UND GEBRAUCH

1. THE SIMPLE PAST TENSE OF REGULAR WEAK VERBS

The simple past tense, like the present perfect tense, expresses past actions and events. Whereas the present perfect tense is used primarily in conversation, the simple past is used to narrate connected past actions or events, and in writing:

Lotte telefonierte mit ihrer Freundin.
Lotte was talking on the telephone to her girlfriend.

Es läutete.
The doorbell rang.

Sie öffnete die Tür.
She opened the door.

a. Weak verbs add the past tense marker -t- and personal endings to the stem of the infinitive.

$$\text{stem} + t + \text{ending}$$

fragen	*ich frag + t + e*	I asked, was asking
	du frag + t + est	you asked, were asking
	er frag + t + e	he asked, was asking
	wir frag + t + en	we asked, were asking
	ihr frag + t + et	you asked, were asking
	sie frag + t + en	they asked, were asking
	Sie frag + t + en	you asked, were asking

Das Kind war krank. Es fragte nach seiner Mutter.
The child was ill. He asked for his mother.

As with the German present perfect tense, the German simple past may be rendered in English by the progressive form of the past tense, if the context requires it.

Lotte telefonierte.
Lotte was talking on the telephone.

b. If the stem ends in *-d* or *-t* or in a consonant cluster as in *atmen* (to breathe), *regnen* (to rain), or *öffnen* (to open), an *e* is inserted between the stem and the past tense marker *-t*.

reden	*er redete*	he talked, was talking
arbeiten	*er arbeitete*	he worked, was working
atmen	*er atmete*	he breathed, was breathing
regnen	*es regnete*	it rained, was raining

Es war ein heißer Tag, und es regnete.
It was a hot day, and it was raining.

Note that simple past tense forms in the second person singular and plural are generally replaced by the present perfect tense:

Hast du Zahnmedizin studiert?
Did you study dentistry?

Ihr habt gestern nicht gearbeitet.
You didn't work yesterday.

237

c. Weak verbs with separable prefixes also separate in the simple past.

Ich machte die Tür auf.
I opened the door.

Ursula lachte Rainer aus.
Ursula laughed about Rainer.

abschicken   *Ich schickte das Paket gestern ab.*
                                I mailed the package yesterday.

2. THE SIMPLE PAST TENSE OF *HABEN*

ich hatte	I had	*wir hatten*	we had
du hattest	you had	*ihr hattet*	you had
er hatte	he had	*sie hatten*	they had
		Sie hatten	you had

Er hatte schon immer handwerkliches Geschick.
He was always quite skilled with his hands.

The present tense stem consonant *b* of *haben* changes to *t*, followed by the past tense marker -*t* and the past tense endings of weak verbs.

3. THE SIMPLE PAST TENSE OF MODAL AUXILIARIES

Modal auxiliaries form their past tense by adding -*te* plus an ending for the second person singular and the plural to the infinitive stem. *Dürfen*, *können*, and *müssen* also drop the umlaut of the infinitive.

wollen	→	*wollte*	*dürfen*	→	*durfte*
sollen	→	*sollte*	*können*	→	*konnte*
müssen	→	*mußte*	*mögen*	→	*mochte*

WOLLEN

ich wollte	I wanted to
du wolltest	you wanted to
er wollte	he wanted to
wir wollten	we wanted to
ihr wolltet	you wanted to
sie wollten	they wanted to
Sie wollten	you wanted to

DÜRFEN

ich durfte	I was allowed to
du durftest	you were allowed to
er durfte	he was allowed to
wir durften	we were allowed to
ihr durftet	you were allowed to
sie durften	they were allowed to
Sie durften	you were allowed to

Mögen drops the umlaut and changes *g* to *ch*:

MÖGEN

ich mochte	I liked to
du mochtest	you liked to
er mochte	he liked to
wir mochten	we liked to
ihr mochtet	you liked to
sie mochten	they liked to
Sie mochten	you liked to

As in the present tense, the past tense modal auxiliary takes the position of the conjugated verb. The main verb is in the infinitive form and has to be at the end of the sentence. The main verb can be omitted, if it is clearly implied.

Sie wollte eine Staatsstellung *(haben).*
She wanted (to have) a government job.

Sie musste darauf warten.
She had to wait for it.

Er konnte keinen Studienplatz bekommen.
He couldn't get into a university.

Durfte er schon wieder schwimmen?
Was he already allowed to swim again?

Der Zug sollte eine Stunde früher ankommen.
The train was supposed to arrive an hour earlier.

Wir mochten das Essen nicht.
We didn't like the food.

VOKABELN

die Schule, *-n*	school
die Universität, *-en*	university, college
Abitur machen	to take the exam for the diploma
das Studium, *Studien*	studies
der Student, *-en, -en*	student
studieren	to study, to go to college
die Note, *-n*	grade
der Durchschnitt	average
der Beruf, *-e*	profession
der Jurist, *-en, -en*	lawyer
der Rechtsanwalt, *¨e*	lawyer
Er studiert Jura.	He is studying law.
die Zahnmedizin	dentistry
der Wissenschaftler, -	scientist
die Sozialwissenschaft, *-en*	social science
der Fotograf, *-en, -en*	photographer
der Lehrer, -	teacher
die Lehre, *-n**	apprenticeship
lehren	to teach
lernen	to learn
die Berufsaussichten	prospects (for a profession)
das Handwerk	handicraft, trade
handwerkliches Geschick	manual dexterity, skill
das Büro, *-s*	office
der Dienst, *-e*	service
die Aushilfearbeit	temporary employment
flirten	to flirt
feiern	to celebrate
sich trennen	to part, to separate
über*wechseln	to change, to transfer
die Weile	while, short time

*Another term for "apprenticeship" is *die Ausbildung.*

der Staat, *-en*	state
Alle Achtung!	Congratulations!
glänzend	splendid

ÜBUNGEN

A. *Beantworten Sie die Fragen zum Dialog.*

1. *Wie lange haben sich Lisa und Axel nicht gesehen?*
2. *Was hörte Axel?*
3. *Warum hat Lisa kein eigenes Büro?*
4. *Was hatte Axel schon immer?*
5. *Wie war damals Axels Notendurchschnitt?*

B. *Suchen Sie die richtige deutsche Übersetzung.*

1. He studied dentistry.
2. He wanted to learn a trade.
3. He trained as a dental technician.
4. They haven't seen each other for a long time.
5. She worked at first as a temporary.

a. *Sie haben sich lange nicht gesehen.*
b. *Sie arbeitete zuerst als Aushilfe.*
c. *Er wollte ein Handwerk lernen.*
d. *Er studierte Zahnmedizin.*
e. *Er machte eine Lehre als Zahntechniker.*

C. *Schreiben Sie die folgenden Sätze in der einfachen Vergangenheit.*
(Rewrite the following sentences in the simple past tense.)

BEISPIEL: *Sie studiert Jura.*
       Sie studierte Jura.

1. *Sie macht jede Arbeit gern.*
2. *Er hat keine guten Noten.*
3. *Was mögen Sie nicht?*
4. *Ich will ein Handwerk lernen.*
5. *Wir müssen lange fahren.*
6. *Ich probiere den neuen Wein.*

7. *Die Jüngste spielt gegen die Älteste.*
8. *Er schickt das Paket ab.*

D. *Übersetzen Sie.*

1. I wanted to go to college.
2. But I didn't have my high school diploma yet.
3. I also needed money.
4. So I worked for a year.
5. I had to work as a temporary in an office.
6. Then I could go to college.

E. *Fügen Sie das Modalverb in der einfachen Vergangenheit ein.* (Add the modal verb in the simple past.)

BEISPIEL: *Er arbeitete heute nicht. (können)*
               Er konnte heute nicht arbeiten.

1. *Wir fragten nach dem Weg. (müssen)*
2. *Es regnete den ganzen Tag. (sollen)*
3. *Er öffnete das Fenster nicht. (wollen)*
4. *Wir redeten mit ihm. (können)*
5. *Sie rauchte nicht im Haus. (dürfen)*

F. *Bringen Sie die folgende Sätze in die einfache Vergangenheit.* (Change the following sentences to simple past.)

1. *Ich habe keine Zeit.*
2. *Müssen Sie heute arbeiten?*
3. *Wir haben kein eigenes Büro.*
4. *Willst du nach Deutschland fliegen?*
5. *Es regnet oft in Berlin.*

KULTURNOTIZ

The German school system is rather different from that of the United States. Germany has three different kinds of schools in place of the American high school: *Hauptschule, Realschule,* and *Gymnasium.*

The *Hauptschule* (fifth to ninth grade) prepares students for apprenticeships in the crafts. The *Realschule* goes up to tenth grade, preparing students for administrative careers. The *Gymnasium* (fifth to thirteenth grades) is the traditional high school in Germany. Its diploma (the *Abitur)* allows one to attend the university *(Hochschule).* There are three types of *Gymnasien:* the *Gymnasium* for modern languages, the *Gymnasium* for classical languages, and the one for sciences. Schools for the fine arts, economics, technical subjects, and so on, also exist, as well as numerous special schools *(Sonderschulen)* for students with physical and psychological problems. It is always possible to change from one kind of school to another.

Since 1965 the number of high school graduates *(Abiturienten)* has increased so much that the universities cannot accommodate all applicants. Thus, certain admission requirements have been established. The "closed numbers" system *(Numerus Clausus)* admits students to overcrowded disciplines only on the basis of their grade average *(Notendurchschnitt).* If their grade average is not high enough, some students may be placed on a waiting list. Some students, however, decide to study a discipline that is not quite as popular instead. It is also possible to complete one's education or train for a new occupation in night schools *(Abendgymnasien)* in the socalled second educational track *(zweiter Bildungsweg).* All education in Germany is free.

LÖSUNGEN

A. 1. *Sie haben sich seit zehn Jahren nicht gesehen. 2. Er hörte, dass Lisa Juristin geworden ist. 3. Sie wollte in den Staatsdienst. 4. Axel hatte schon immer handwerkliches Geschick. 5. Axels Notendurchschnitt war damals nicht gut genug.*

B. 1.—d   2.—c   3.—e   4.—a   5.—b

C. 1. *machte*   2. *hatte*   3. *mochten*   4. *wollte*   5. *mussten*   6. *probierte*
7. *spielte*   8. *schickte*

D. 1. *Ich wollte studieren. 2. Aber ich hatte noch kein Abitur. 3. Ich brauchte auch Geld. 4. Deshalb arbeitete ich ein Jahr. 5. Ich musste als Aushilfe in einem Büro arbeiten. 6. Dann konnte ich studieren.*

E. 1. *Wir mussten nach dem Weg fragen. 2. Es sollte den ganzen Tag regnen.*
3. *Er wollte das Fenster nicht öffnen. 4. Wir konnten mit ihm reden. 5. Sie durfte im Haus nicht rauchen.*

F. 1. *Ich hatte kein Zeit. 2. Mussten Sie heute arbeiten? 3. Wir hatten kein eigenes Büro. 4. Wolltest du nach Deutschland fliegen? 5. Es regnete oft in Berlin.*

LEKTION 28
TAGESROUTINE.   Daily Routine.

A. DIALOG

Ein schlechter Tag.

LOTTE: Tag, Judith. Ich rief dich gestern an, bekam aber keine Antwort.

JUDITH: Ich verschlief und stand erst um neun auf.

LOTTE: Hast du keinen Wecker?

JUDITH: Doch, aber er hat nicht geläutet.

LOTTE: Wo warst du denn später?

JUDITH: Ich sollte um zehn zur Fußpflegerin. Ich traf auch pünktlich ein.

LOTTE: Du bist flink.

JUDITH: Hör erst mal, wie es ausging! Ich dusche mich ja abends, brauchte mir also nur das Gesicht und die Hände zu waschen, mich zu kämmen und mir die Zähne zu putzen.

LOTTE: Du hast nicht mal gefrühstückt?

JUDITH: Ich trank nur einen Saft, zog mich an und rannte los. Als ich bei der Fußpflege ankam, hing an der Tür ein Schild: "Montags geschlossen."

LOTTE: Was?

JUDITH: Und ich dachte, es ist Dienstag!

———————

A Bad Day.

LOTTE: Hello, Judith. I called you yesterday, but got no answer.

JUDITH: I overslept and didn't get up until nine.

LOTTE: Don't you have an alarm clock?

244

JUDITH: Yes, but it didn't ring.

LOTTE: Where were you later?

JUDITH: I was supposed to go to the pedicurist at ten. I arrived on time, too.

LOTTE: You're quick.

JUDITH: First hear how it ended! I shower in the evening, so I needed only to wash my face and hands, comb my hair, and brush my teeth.

LOTTE: You didn't even have breakfast?

JUDITH: I drank only a glass of juice, dressed, and dashed off. When I arrived at the pedicurist's there was a sign on the door: "Closed on Mondays."

LOTTE: What?

JUDITH: And I thought it was Tuesday!

B. GRAMMATIK UND GEBRAUCH

1. THE SIMPLE PAST TENSE OF STRONG VERBS

a. Strong verbs have a stem-vowel change in their simple past tense forms, and personal endings are added to the past tense stem.

TRINKEN **TO DRINK**   **PAST TENSE:** *TRANK*

ich trank	I drank	*wir tranken*	we drank
du trankst	you drank	*ihr trankt*	you drank
sie trank	she drank	*sie tranken*	they drank
		Sie tranken	you drank

Note that the first and third person singular take no ending.

b. If the past tense of a strong verb ends in *-d* or *-t*, an *e* is inserted in the ending of the *du-* and *ihr*-forms. For verbs whose past tense stem ends in an *s* sound *(s, ss, ß, z)*, only the *du*-form inserts *e*.

Du fandest das auch zu teuer, nicht?
You also found that too expensive, didn't you?

Fandet ihr die Fahrt anstrengend?
  Did you find the trip strenuous?

Du hieltest das Buch doch in der Hand!
  You were holding the book in your hand!

Was hieltet ihr von der Mannschaft?
  What did you think of the team?

Warum aßest du das Gemüse nicht?
  Why didn't you eat the vegetables?

In spoken German the past tense forms for *du* and *ihr* are usually replaced by the present perfect tense.

c. Strong verbs with separable prefixes also separate in the simple past.

Wir standen früh auf.
  We got up early.

Sie zogen sich schnell an.
  They dressed quickly.

d. Since the past tense forms of strong verbs are not predictable, they must be memorized. From this lesson on, strong verbs will be listed in the vocabularies with the third person singular past tense form, the past participle, and the third person singular form of the auxiliary *sein,* if it applies:

gehen, ging, ist gegangen
  to go

auf*stehen, stand auf, ist aufgestanden
  to get up

Here are the strong verbs whose present and present perfect you have learned:

ab*fahren	*fuhr ab*	*ist abgefahren*
ab*fliegen	*flog ab*	*ist abgeflogen*
ab*steigen	*stieg ab*	*ist abgestiegen*
an*bieten	*bot an*	*angeboten*

an*kommen	kam an	ist angekommen
an*rufen	rief an	angerufen
an*sehen	sah an	angesehen
an*ziehen	zog an	angezogen
aus*laden	lud aus	ausgeladen
aus*ziehen	zog aus	ausgezogen
backen	backte	gebacken
bleiben	blieb	ist geblieben
ein*laden	lud ein	eingeladen
ein*tragen	trug ein	eingetragen
essen	aß	gegessen
fahren	fuhr	ist gefahren
fallen	fiel	ist gefallen
finden	fand	gefunden
fliegen	flog	ist geflogen
frieren	fror	gefroren
gehen	ging	ist gegangen
genießen	genoss	genossen
heißen	hieß	geheißen
helfen	half	geholfen
kommen	kam	ist gekommen
laden	lud	geladen
lassen	ließ	gelassen
laufen	lief	ist gelaufen
nehmen	nahm	genommen
scheinen	schien	geschienen
schlafen	schlief	geschlafen
schlagen	schlug	geschlagen
schließen	schloss	geschlossen
schreiben	schrieb	geschrieben
schwimmen	schwamm	ist geschwommen
sehen	sah	gesehen
stehen	stand	gestanden
steigen	stieg	ist gestiegen
treffen	traf	getroffen
trinken	trank	getrunken
tun	tat	getan

übertragen	*übertrug*	*übertragen*
verbieten	*verbot*	*verboten*
verbinden	*verband*	*verbunden*
vergessen	*vergaß*	*vergessen*
verlieren	*verlor*	*verloren*
verschreiben	*verschrieb*	*verschrieben*
vorbei*fahren	*fuhr vorbei*	*ist vorbeigefahren*
wachsen	*wuchs*	*gewachsen*
waschen	*wusch*	*gewaschen*
werden	*wurde*	*ist geworden*
zerbrechen	*zerbrach*	*zerbrochen*
zu*greifen	*griff zu*	*zugegriffen*

2. THE SIMPLE PAST TENSE OF IRREGULAR WEAK VERBS

Irregular weak verbs have the same past tense endings as weak verbs, but like strong verbs have a stem-vowel change.

DENKEN **TO THINK**   **PAST TENSE:** *DACH-*

ich dach<u>te</u>	I thought		*wir dach<u>ten</u>*	we thought
du dach<u>test</u>	you thought		*ihr dach<u>tet</u>*	you thought
er dach<u>te</u>	he thought		*sie dach<u>ten</u>*	they thought
			Sie dach<u>ten</u>	you thought

There are only a few other irregular weak verbs:

bringen	→	*brachte*	to bring, take
kennen	→	*kannte*	to know, to be acquainted with
nennen	→	*nannte*	to name
rennen	→	*rannte*	to run
senden	→	*sandte*	to send
verbringen	→	*verbrachte*	to spend (time)
wissen	→	*wusste*	to know

Sie wusste, dass die Fußpflege montags geschlossen ist.
She knew that the pedicurist is closed on Mondays.

248

Aber sie dachte nicht daran.
    But she didn't think of it.

Er kannte viele berühmte Leute.
    He knew many famous people.

Sie rannte zum Bus.
    She dashed to the bus.

Sie brachte Blumen mit.
    She brought flowers.

Wir verbrachten zwei Wochen in der Schweiz.
    We spent two weeks in Switzerland.

VOKABELN

die Tagesroutine	daily routine
die Routine	routine
verschlafen *(verschläft), verschlief, verschlafen*	to oversleep
auf*stehen, *stand auf, ist aufgestanden*	to get up
der Wecker, -	alarm clock
läuten	to ring
sich duschen	to take a shower
sich waschen	to wash (oneself)
sich die Zähne putzen	to brush one's teeth
sich die Haare kämmen	to comb one's hair
frühstücken	to have breakfast
zu Abend essen	to have dinner
los*rennen, *rannte los, ist losgerannt*	to dash off
ein*treffen *(trifft ein), traf ein, ist eingetroffen*	to arrive
die Körperpflege	personal hygiene
der Körper, -	body
die Fußpflege	pedicure
der Fußpfleger, -	male pedicurist
die Fußpflegerin, -nen	female pedicurist

der Fuß, ⸚*e*	foot
die Zehe, *-n (or der Zeh)*	toe
der Fußnagel, ⸚	toenail
das Bein, *-e*	leg
denken, *dachte, gedacht*	to think
der Gedanke, *-n*	the thought
aus*gehen, *ging aus, ist* ausgegangen	to end
schließen, *schloss, geschlossen*	to close
das Schild, *-er*	sign
flink	quick

ÜBUNGEN

A. *Beantworten Sie die Fragen zum Dialog.*

1. *Warum verschlief Judith?*
2. *Wohin sollte Judith um zehn?*
3. *Was hatte Judith zum Frühstück?*
4. *Wann ist die Fußpflege geschlossen?*

B. *Suchen Sie die richtige deutsche Übersetzung.*

1. He took a shower.
2. The alarm clock didn't ring.
3. We overslept yesterday.
4. My big toe hurt.
5. She always washed her face only with water.

a. *Meine große Zehe schmerzte.*
b. *Sie wusch ihr Gesicht immer nur mit Wasser.*
c. *Er duschte sich.*
d. *Der Wecker hat nicht geläutet.*
e. *Wir verschliefen gestern.*

C. *Schreiben Sie die folgenden Sätze in der einfachen Vergangenheit.*
(Rewrite the following sentences in the simple past.)

BEISPIEL: *Mein Vater hat keine Zeit.*
Mein Vater hatte keine Zeit.

1. *Mein Sohn steht spät auf.*
2. *Dann wäscht er sich Gesicht und Hände.*
3. *Er vergisst natürlich, sich die Zähne zu putzen.*
4. *Aber er kämmt sich.*
5. *Es ist heiß.*
6. *Er zieht sich kurze Hosen an.*
7. *Dann fährt er an den Strand.*

D. *Übersetzen Sie.*

1. I thought that the restaurant was open today.
2. But there was a sign on the door, "Closed on Mondays."
3. I didn't know the baker moved.
4. He baked the best bread in town.

KULTURNOTIZ

In Germany, one out of two women between the ages of fifteen and sixty-five work. In 1976, women were granted full equality with men. The law stating that women were responsible for the household, and could have a job only if it didn't interfere with their marital responsibilities, was repealed.

LÖSUNGEN

A. 1. *Der Wecker läutete nicht.* 2. *Sie sollte zur Fußpflegerin.* 3. *Sie trank einen Saft.* 4. *Die Fußpflege ist montags geschlossen.*
B. 1.—c 2.—d 3.—e 4.—a 5.—b
C. 1. *stand* 2. *wusch* 3. *vergaß* 4. *kämmte* 5. *war* 6. *zog*
7. *fuhr*
D. 1. *Ich dachte, dass das Restaurant heute geöffnet ist.* 2. *Aber da hing ein Schild an der Tür, "Montags geschlossen".* 3. *Ich wusste nicht, dass der Bäcker umgezogen ist.* 4. *Er backte das beste Brot in der Stadt.*

LEKTION 29

A. DIALOG

Beim Zahnarzt.

ZAHNARZT: Ihre Zähne sind schlecht; Zahnbelag, Zahnfleischschwund. Bürsten Sie regelmäßig?

PATIENT: Immer.

ZAHNARZT: Sie haben Karies.

PATIENT: Ja, das ist eine Krankheit, an der meine ganze Familie leidet.

ZAHNARZT: Heute ist die oft heilbar. Ich reinige jetzt Ihre Zähne, und dann schicke ich Sie zu einem Spezialisten, der Zahnfleisch behandelt.

PATIENT: Aber ich habe schreckliche Zahnschmerzen. Sehen Sie kein Loch auf dem Röntgenbild? Es muss der Backenzahn hier links sein, der mich die ganze Nacht wach gehalten hat, und dessen Füllung schon einmal herausgebrochen ist.

ZAHNARZT: Aha. Die Zahnwurzel ist entzündet. Sie brauchen eine Wurzelbehandlung.

PATIENT: Mein Gott! Können Sie nicht etwas anderes machen? Hilft eine Krone vielleicht?

ZAHNARZT: Ich kann ziehen.

PATIENT: Nein! Das ist noch schlimmer.

ZAHNARZT: Ich setze Ihnen eine Spritze, die Sie örtlich betäubt.

PATIENT: Hoffentlich.

At the Dentist's.

DENTIST: Your teeth are bad; you have plaque and receding gums. Do you brush regularly?

PATIENT: Always.

DENTIST: You have caries.

PATIENT: Yes, that's a disease my whole family suffers from.

DENTIST: Today it's often curable. I'll clean your teeth now, and then I'll send you to a specialist who treats gums.

PATIENT: But I've a horrible toothache. Can't you see a cavity on the X-ray? It has to be the molar here on the left; it kept me awake the whole night, and the filling fell out once before.

DENTIST: I see. The root is infected. You'll need a root canal.

PATIENT: My God! Can't you do something else? Would a crown help?

DENTIST: I can pull it out.

PATIENT: No! That's even worse.

DENTIST: I'll give you a shot that will numb you locally.

PATIENT: I hope so.

B. GRAMMATIK UND GEBRAUCH

1. RELATIVE PRONOUNS

A relative pronoun introduces a clause (called a "relative clause") that gives information about a noun in the sentence. The relative pronoun "relates" back to the noun, its antecedent. Consider this sentence:

> He is a specialist who treats gums.

The relative clause is "who treats gums." The relative pronoun "who" refers back to "specialist," its antecedent.

In German the following relative pronouns are used:

	MASCULINE	FEMININE	NEUTER	PLURAL
Nom.	der	die	das	die
Acc.	den	die	das	die
Dat.	dem	der	dem	denen
Gen.	dessen	deren	dessen	deren

Note: The forms of the relative pronouns are the same as the forms of the definite article, except for the dative plural and all genitive forms.

2. RELATIVE CLAUSES

a. A relative clause is a dependent clause. The finite verb has to be in the last position.

Ich setze eine Spritze, die Sie betäubt.
I'll give you a shot that will numb you.

b. In German, the relative pronoun always has to be stated. In English, it sometimes can be left out.

Das ist eine Krankheit, an der meine ganze Familie leidet.
That's a disease (that) my whole family suffers from.

c. The gender of the relative pronoun depends on the gender of the noun it describes (the antecedent). Whether a relative pronoun is singular or plural also depends on the antecedent.

Das ist der Zahn, der schmerzt.
That's the tooth that hurts.

Das sind die Zähne, die schmerzen.
Those are the teeth that hurt.

d. The case of the relative pronoun depends on its function within the relative clause.

Das ist der Zahn, den Sie ziehen müssen. (acc.)
That's the tooth (that) you have to pull.

254

The antecedent is *der Zahn*. *Zahn* is masculine singular. While in the main clause, *Zahn* is the subject, within the relative clause *Zahn* is the direct object, and therefore it has to be in the accusative case. The relative pronoun in the masculine singular accusative is *den*.

Das ist der Zahn, der eine Füllung braucht. (nom.)
That is the tooth that needs a filling.

Ich gehe zu einem Zahnarzt, den ich gut kenne. (acc.)
I visit a dentist (whom) I know well.

Das ist der Patient, dem das Zahnfleisch weh tut. (dat.)
That's the patient whose gums hurt.

Das ist der Backenzahn, dessen Wurzel schmerzt. (gen.)
That's the molar whose root hurts.

Hier ist die Patientin, die gestern kam. (nom.)
Here is the patient who came yesterday.

Hier ist die Krone, die kaputt ist. (nom.)
Here is the crown that is broken.

Fragen Sie die Patientin, der der Zahnarzt geholfen hat. (dat.)
Ask the patient whom the dentist helped.

Das ist die Frau, deren Backenzahn ein Loch hat. (gen.)
That's the woman whose molar has a cavity.

Wo ist das Röntgenbild, das hier war? (nom.)
Where is the X-ray that was here?

Hier ist das Röntgenbild, das Sie gestern gemacht haben. (acc.)
Here is the X-ray (that) you made yesterday.

Sehen Sie das Röntgenbild, dem der Name fehlt? (dat.)
Do you see the X-ray which is missing a name?

Hier ist das Röntgenbild, dessen Bild nicht scharf ist. (gen.)
Here is the X-ray whose image isn't sharp.

Hier sind die Füllungen, die herausgebrochen sind. (nom.)
Here are the fillings that fell out.

Ich frage die Zahnärzte, die ich kenne. (acc.)
I ask the dentists whom I know.

Hier sind die Patienten, denen man die Zähne reinigen muss. (dat.)
Here are the patients whose teeth have to be cleaned.

Hier sind die Röntgenbilder der Patienten, deren Zähne schlecht sind. (gen.)
   Here are the X-rays of the patients whose teeth are bad.

   e. A preposition followed by a relative pronoun can introduce a relative
   clause. The case of the relative pronoun is then determined by the
   preposition. *Leiden an,* for example, takes dative.

Das ist eine Krankheit, an der meine ganze Familie leidet.
   That's a disease from which my whole family suffers.

Ich sehe die Spritze, mit der der Zahnarzt mich betäubt.
   I see the shot with which the dentist will numb me.

VOKABELN

der Zahnarzt, ¨*e*	male dentist
die Zahnärztin, *-nen*	female dentist
der Zahn, ¨*e*	tooth
der Vorderzahn, ¨*e*	front tooth
der Backenzahn, ¨*e*	molar
der Weisheitszahn, ¨*e*	wisdom tooth
das Gebiss, *-sse*	the bite, teeth
die Zahnschmerzen (pl.)	tooth ache
schrecklich	horrible
leiden, *litt, gelitten*	to suffer
leiden an (+ dative)	to suffer from
wach halten *(hält wach), hielt wach, wach gehalten*	to keep awake
behandeln	to treat
das Loch, ¨*er*	hole, cavity
das Röntgenbild, *-er*	X-ray
die Röntgenaufnahme, *-n*	X-ray
betäuben	to numb
die Betäubung	anesthesia, numbing
die örtliche Betäubung	local anesthesia
eine Spritze setzen	to give a shot
bohren	to drill
füllen	to fill

die Füllung, *-en*	filling
die Krone, *-n*	crown
heraus*brechen *(bricht heraus),* *brach heraus, ist* *herausgebrochen*	to break off, to fall out
das Zahnfleisch	gum
der Zahnbelag	plaque
reinigen	to clean
Karies	caries, tooth decay
heilen	to cure, to heal
heilbar	curable
die Wurzel, *-n*	root
die Wurzelbehandlung, *-en*	root canal

ÜBUNGEN

A. *Beantworten Sie die Fragen zum Dialog.*

1. *Wo ist der Patient?*
2. *Wie heißt die Krankheit, an der die ganze Familie leidet?*
3. *Warum ist der patient beim Zahnarzt?*
4. *Was ist entzündet?*

B. *Suchen Sie die richtige deutsche Übersetzung.*

1. The filling fell out.
2. My molar hurts.
3. Our family suffers from caries.
4. The shot numbs.
5. The X-ray shows a cavity in your front tooth.
6. The dentist gives a shot.

a. *Mein Backenzahn schmerzt.*
b. *Das Röntgenbild zeigt ein Loch in Ihrem Vorderzahn.*
c. *Der Zahnarzt setzt eine Spritze.*
d. *Unsere Familie leidet an Karies.*
e. *Die Füllung ist herausgebrochen.*
f. *Die Spritze betäubt.*

C. *Setzen Sie die fehlenden Relativpronomen ein.* (Fill in the missing relative pronouns.)

BEISPIEL: *Der Zahn, _____ gestern schon schmerzte, tut mir wieder weh.*
Der Zahn, der gestern schon schmerzte, tut mir wieder weh.

1. *Ich gehe zu einem Zahnarzt, _____ sehr bekannt ist.*
2. *Er behandelt mein Zahnfleisch, _____ schlecht aussieht.*
3. *Zuerst reinigt er meine Zähne, _____ Zahnbelag haben.*
4. *Morgen muss er zwei Kronen, mit _____ er nicht zufrieden ist, herausbrechen.*
5. *Bestimmt gibt er mir dann eine Spritze, _____ mich betäubt.*

D. *Verbinden Sie die folgenden Sätze mittels Relativpronomen.* (Connect the following sentences using the relative pronoun.)

BEISPIEL: *Das ist der Zahn. Er tut mir weh.*
Das ist der Zahn, der mir weh tut.

1. *Ich hatte ein Auto. Es war blau.*
2. *Das ist der Zahnarzt. Ich war bei ihm.*
3. *Hier ist das Haus. Er ist in dem Haus.*
4. *Heidelberg ist die Stadt. Wir besuchen die Stadt.*

KULTURNOTIZ

Germany's extensive health-care system also covers most dental work. Cosmetic dental work and tooth replacements such as crowns, bridges, implants, and dentures are mostly paid for by the patient. Dental tools and machinery are a major German export item.

LÖSUNGEN

A. 1. *Er ist beim Zahnarzt.* 2. *Die Krankheit, an der die ganze Familie leidet, heißt Karies.* 3. *Er hat schreckliche Zahnschmerzen.* 4. *Die Zahnwurzel ist entzündet.*
B. 1.—e   2.—a   3.—d   4.—f   5.—b   6.—c
C. 1. *der*   2. *das*   3. *die*   4. *denen*   5. *die*
D. 1. *Ich hatte ein Auto, das blau war.* 2. *Das ist der Zahnarzt, bei dem ich war.* 3. *Hier ist das Haus, in dem er ist.* 4. *Heidelberg ist die Stadt, die wir besuchen.*

LEKTION 30

IM FRISEURSALON.   At the Hairdresser's.

A. DIALOG

Im Herrensalon.

KUNDE: Waschen und schneiden bitte! Aber nicht zu kurz. Ich habe leider nicht mehr viele Haare. Wenn Sie zu viel schneiden, bleibt gar nichts mehr.

FRISEUR: Nun, Glatze ist wieder modern. Soll ich alles abrasieren?

KUNDE: Nein! Sie können mir den Nacken ausrasieren und, wenn Sie wollen, den Bart stutzen. Meine Haare wachsen noch sehr gut. Nur nicht da, wo ich will.

FRISEUR: Wie wär's mit einem der neuen Haarwuchsmittel?

KUNDE: Glauben Sie an Märchen?

Im Damensalon.

KUNDIN: Eine neue Dauerwelle bitte!

FRISEUSE: Soll ich auch färben?

KUNDIN: Nein, ich möchte wieder einmal meine natürliche Haarfarbe sehen.

FRISEUSE: Wann haben Sie mit dem Färben angefangen?

KUNDIN: Als ich sechzehn war. Davor hatte ich immer glatte, blonde Haare gehabt, denn meine Mutter hatte mir das Färben und Kräuseln verboten.

FRISEUSE: Wie Sie wollen. Hier ist ein Kittel.

At the Men's Hairdresser's.

CUSTOMER: Wash and cut please. But not too short. Unfortunately, I don't have much hair left. If you cut too much, not much will remain.

HAIRDRESSER: Well, baldness is back in fashion. Shall I shave off everything?

CUSTOMER: No! You can shave my neck and, if you want to, trim my beard. My hair is still growing quite well. Only not where I want it.

HAIRDRESSER: How about one of the new hair-growth products?

CUSTOMER: Do you believe in fairy tales?

At the Women's Hairdresser's.

CUSTOMER: A new perm, please.

HAIRDRESSER: Should I dye your hair, too?

CUSTOMER: No, I would like to see my natural hair color again.

HAIRDRESSER: When did you start to dye your hair?

CUSTOMER: When I was sixteen. Before then I had always had straight blond hair because my mother had forbidden me to dye and curl it.

HAIRDRESSER: As you wish. Here's a gown.

B. GRAMMATIK UND GEBRAUCH

1. THE FORMATION OF THE PAST PERFECT TENSE

In German, as in English, the past perfect tense parallels the present perfect tense, except that the past tense of *haben* and *sein* is used.

a. The past perfect with the auxiliary *haben*.

PRESENT PERFECT	PAST PERFECT
ich habe geschnitten I have cut	*ich hatte geschnitten* I had cut
du hast geschnitten you have cut	*du hattest geschnitten* you had cut

er hat geschnitten	*er hatte geschnitten*
he has cut	he had cut
wir haben geschnitten	*wir hatten geschnitten*
we have cut	we had cut
ihr habt geschnitten	*ihr hattet geschnitten*
you have cut	you had cut
sie haben geschnitten	*sie hatten geschnitten*
they have cut	they had cut

Ich hatte blonde Haare gehabt.
   I had (had) blond hair.

b. The past perfect with the auxiliary *sein.*

SINGULAR	PLURAL
ich war gewachsen	*wir waren gewachsen*
I had grown	we had grown
du warst gewachsen	*ihr wart gewachsen*
you had grown	you had grown
er war gewachsen	*sie waren gewachsen*
he had grown	they had grown

Ich war zum Friseur gegangen.
   I had gone to the hairdresser.

2. THE USE OF THE PAST PERFECT TENSE

The past perfect tense is rarely used in isolation. It is used when an event or events are reported in the past and a more distant past then has to be described.

Gestern bin ich zum Friseurgegangen. Davor hatte ich eingekauft.
   Yesterday I went to the hairdresser. Before that I had been shopping.

Bevor ich meine Haare färbte, hatte ich schwarze Haare gehabt.
   Before I dyed my hair, I had had black hair.

3. *ALS, WENN,* AND *WANN*

Als, wenn, and *wann* are equivalent to the English *when,* but they are not interchangeable.

Als refers to a specific action or state in the past.

Als ich ein Kind war, hatte ich blonde Haare.
   When I was a child, I had blond hair.

Wenn expresses events or possibilities in the past, present, or future.

Wenn meine Haare lang sind, gehe ich zum Friseur.
   When (if, whenever) my hair is long, I go to the barber.

Immer wenn der Friseur meine Haare schnitt, war ich traurig.
   When (if, whenever) the barber cut my hair, I was sad.

Wann introduces direct or indirect questions concerned with specific time.

Wann gehst du heute zum Friseur?
   When (at what time) are you going to the hairdresser?

Er fragt, wann der Salon offen ist.
   He's asking when (at what time) the shop is open.

VOKABELN

der Friseursalon, *-s*	barbershop, hairdresser's salon, beauty parlor
der Friseur, *-e*	male hairdresser, barbershop, beauty parlor
die Friseuse, *-n*	female hairdresser
der Herrenfriseursalon, *-s*	barbershop
der Damenfriseursalon, *-s*	hairdresser's (shop)

frisieren	to do someone's hair
der Kittel, -	gown, apron
schneiden, *schnitt, geschnitten*	to cut
der Haarschnitt, *-e*	haircut
die Schere, *-n*	scissors
die Locke, *-n*	curl
die Glatze, *-n*	bald head
kraus	frizzy
lockig	curly
glatt	straight, smooth
der Bart, *¨e*	beard
der Schnurrbart, *¨e*	mustache
stutzen	to trim
der Nacken, -	neck
aus*rasieren	to shave (neck)
ab*rasieren	to shave off
die Dauerwelle, *-n*	permanent
wachsen, *wuchs, ist gewachsen*	to grow
färben	to dye
das Färben	coloring, dying
die Haarfarbe, *-n*	hair color
blond	blond, fair
rötlich	reddish
brünett	brunette
das Haarwuchsmittel, -	hair-growth product
bevor	before (conj.)
davor	before (adv.)
als	when
verbieten, *verbot, verboten*	to forbid
Wie Sie wollen.	As you wish.

A. *Beantworten Sie die Fragen zum Dialog.*

1. *Was soll der Friseur für den Kunden machen?*
2. *Was möchte die Kundin?*
3. *Soll die Friseuse die Haare färben?*
4. *Welche Farbe hatten die Haare der Kundin gehabt, als sie ein Kind war?*

B. *Suchen Sie die richtige deutsche Übersetzung.*

1. Please cut my hair.
2. My beard is too long.
3. I would like a permanent.
4. I don't like the color of my hair.
5. I'll take the new hair-growth product.
6. This beauty parlor is too expensive.

a. *Mein Bart ist zu lang.*
b. *Ich nehme das neue Haarwuchsmittel.*
c. *Dieser Friseursalon ist zu teuer.*
d. *Schneiden Sie mir bitte die Haare.*
e. *Meine Haarfarbe gefällt mir nicht.*
f. *Ich möchte eine Dauerwelle.*

C. *Setzen Sie "wann," "wenn," oder "als" ein.* (Fill in *wann, wenn,* or *als.*)

BEISPIEL: _____ *ich ein Kind war, hatte ich lange Haare.*
   Als ich ein Kind war, hatte ich lange Haare.

1. _____ *meine Haare zu lang sind, gehe ich zum Friseur.*
2. _____ *ich heute zum Friseursalon kam, war er geschlossen.*
3. *Ich fragte einen Nachbarn des Friseurs,* _____ *der Laden offen ist.*
4. *Er sagte,* _____ *der Friseur keine Kunden hat, schließt er den Laden.*

D. *Schreiben Sie die fehlenden Verbformen im Plusquamperfekt. Benutzen Sie die Verben in Klammern.* (Write the missing verb forms in the past perfect. Use the verbs given in parentheses.)

BEISPIEL: *Früher _____ meine Mutter ihre Haare selbst _____. (schneiden)*
Früher hatte meine Mutter ihre Haare selbst geschnitten.

1. *Er _____ immer lange Haare _____. (haben)*
2. *Dann _____ er zum Friseur _____. (gehen)*
3. *Der Friseur _____ ihm auch den Nacken _____. (ausrasieren)*
4. *Dann _____ er dem Friseur ein Trinkgeld _____. (geben)*

E. *Übersetzen Sie.*

1. Where can I find a hairdresser?
2. I would like to have curls.

KULTURNOTIZ

In German-speaking countries barbers and hairdressers have to complete an apprenticeship; in addition, they have to attend a trade school to get their license. It is fairly expensive to visit a hairdresser or barber. Small services such as hair spraying *(Haarsprühen)* carry an extra charge. Tips are expected.

LÖSUNGEN

A. 1. *Er soll die Haare waschen und schneiden und den Nacken ausrasieren. 2. Sie möchte eine neue Dauerwelle. 3. Nein, sie soll nicht die Haare färben. 4. Als die Kundin ein Kind war, hatte sie blonde Haare gehabt.*
B. 1.—d 2.—a 3.—f 4.—e 5.—b 6.—c
C. 1. *Wenn* 2. *Als* 3. *wann* 4. *wenn*
D. 1. *hatte . . . gehabt* 2. *war . . . gegangen* 3. *hatte . . . ausrasiert* 4. *hatte . . . gegeben*
E. 1. *Wo kann ich einen Friseur finden? 2. Ich möchte gerne Locken haben.*

SECHSTE WIEDERHOLUNGSAUFGABE

A. *Setzen Sie die fehlenden Wörter ein.*

BEISPIEL: Horst ist _____ alt _____ ich.
Horst ist so alt wie ich.

1. *Tennis ist _____ spannend _____ Handball.*
2. *Radfahren ist gesünder _____ Fernsehen.*
3. *Dieses Restaurant ist nicht _____ teuer _____ dieses.*

B. *Übersetzen Sie.*

1. It's getting warmer and warmer.
2. In June it's hottest.
3. My father swims well.
4. My brother swims better, but I swim best of all.
5. Then we like to eat.
6. My brother prefers to eat cake.
7. I like to eat ice cream best of all.

C. *Ersetzen Sie das unterstrichene Wort durch ein Demonstrativpronomen.*
(Replace the underlined word with a demonstrative pronoun.)

BEISPIEL: Der Mann ist wirklich nett.
Der ist wirklich nett.

1. *Der Berg ist sehr hoch.*
2. *Die Blumen sind sehr schön.*
3. *Ich helfe dem Wanderer.*
4. *Der Schlafsack gehört den Pfadfindern.*

D. *Übersetzen Sie und gebrauchen Sie die einfache Vergangenheit.*
(Translate using the simple past.)

1. We celebrated.
2. Then we separated.
3. I studied social sciences.
4. Later I wanted to become a lawyer.
5. I called you yesterday. (fam., sing.)
6. The telephone didn't ring.

7. I came to your house.
8. Where were you? (fam., sing.)
9. I wanted to bring you flowers.
10. They were supposed to be fabulous.

E. *Setzen Sie die Relativpronomen ein.* (Fill in the relative pronouns.)

BEISPIEL: *Siehst du das Haus, neben _____ wir stehen?*
Siehst du das Haus, neben dem wir stehen?

1. *Hier wohnt der Zahnarzt, _____ ich gut kenne.*
2. *Er ist ein Mann, _____ schnell arbeitet.*
3. *Ein Loch, _____ ich im Vorderzahn hatte, hat er gefüllt.*
4. *Er benutzte eine Betäubung, _____ ich gut fand.*
5. *Er hat Patienten, mit _____ ich gerne rede.*

F. *Setzen Sie die Sätze ins Plusquamperfekt.* (Rewrite the sentences in the past perfect.)

BEISPIEL: *Ich bin neun Jahre alt gewesen.*
Ich war neun Jahre alt gewesen.

1. *Ich bin zum Friseur gegangen.*
2. *Als Kind habe ich auch lange Haare gehabt.*
3. *Ich habe mich damals noch nicht rasiert.*

LÖSUNGEN

A. 1. *so, wie*   2. *als*   3. *so, wie*
B. 1. *Es wird immer wärmer.* 2. *Im Juni ist es am heißesten.* 3. *Mein Vater schwimmt gut.* 4. *Mein Bruder schwimmt besser, aber ich schwimme am besten.* 5. *Dann möchten wir essen.* 6. *Mein Bruder isst lieber Kuchen.* 7. *Ich esse am liebsten Eis.*
C. 1. *Der*   2. *Die*   3. *dem*   4. *denen*
D. 1. *Wir feierten.* 2. *Dann trennten wir uns.* 3. *Ich studierte Sozialwissenschaften.* 4. *Später wollte ich Rechtsanwalt werden.* 5. *Ich rief dich gestern an.* 6. *Das Telefon läutete nicht.* 7. *Ich kam zu deinem Haus.* 3. *Wo warst du?* 9. *Ich wollte dir Blumen bringen.* 10. *Sie sollten fabelhaft sein.*
E. 1. *den*   2. *der*   3. *das*   4. *die*   5. *denen*
F. 1. *Ich war zum Friseur gegangen.* 2. *Als Kind hatte ich auch lange Haare gehabt.* 3. *Ich hatte mich damals noch nicht rasiert.*

LESESTÜCK III

BERLIN

"Berlin ist eine Reise wert."[1] Diesen Werbespruch[2] der Bundesbahn[3] konnte man viele Jahre auf den Bahnhöfen in Deutschland lesen. Seit 1989 hat sich der Wert[4] einer Reise nach Berlin verdoppelt.[5] Heute kann ein Besucher der neuen Hauptstadt Deutschlands nicht nur[6] den Kurfürstendamm, die elegante Straße im Westen Berlins, sondern auch—ohne Schwierigkeit[7]—Unter den Linden, die historische Prachtstraße[8] im ehemaligen[9] Ost-Berlin, bewundern.[10] 1989 fiel die Mauer, die die beiden Teile der Stadt 28 Jahre lang trennte. Ein kleines Stück dieser Mauer soll in der Bernauerstraße zur Erinnerung[11] an diese Zeit erhalten bleiben.[12] Berlin bietet[13] alles, was man von einer kulturellen Metropole erwartet:[14] berühmte Theater, Museen, Opernhäuser, Symphonieorchester, internationale Festivals für Film, Jazz- und Rockkonzerte, historische und moderne Gebäude und Künstlerviertel.[15] Berlin hat elegante Kaufhäuser, wie das Ka-De-We oder Kaufhaus des Westens, zahllose[16] Boutiquen, und Restaurants, Cafés und Hotels in jeder Preislage.[17] 3,4 Millionen Einwohner, bekannt wegen[18] Schlagfertigkeit[19] und Mutterwitz,[20] leben in dieser aufregenden,[21] lebendigen Metropole, die schnell wieder zu einer vereinten Stadt zusammenwächst.[22]

VOKABELN

1. *wert sein*	to be worth
2. *der Werbespruch, ¨e*	advertising slogan
3. *die Bundesbahn*	National Railroad
4. *der Wert, -e*	value
5. *sich verdoppeln*	to double
6. *nicht nur . . . sondern auch*	not only . . . but also
7. *die Schwierigkeit, -en*	trouble
8. *die Pracht*	splendor, pomp, display
9. *ehemalig*	former
10. *bewundern*	to admire
11. *zur Erinnerung an*	in memory of
12. *erhalten bleiben*	to remain preserved

13. *bieten, bat, geboten*	to offer
14. *erwarten*	to expect
15. *das Künstlerviertel*	district of a town where artists live
16. *zahllos*	numerous
17. *die Preislage, -n*	price range
18. *bekannt wegen*	known for
19. *die Schlagfertigkeit*	ready wit
20. *der Mutterwitz*	common sense
21. *aufregend*	exciting
22. *zusammenwachsen*	to grow together

LEKTION 31

A. DIALOG I

In der Apotheke.

KUNDIN: Ist das Rezept für Ott fertig?

APOTHEKER: Ott? Ja, aber wir mussten ein Präparat bestellen: das Mittel gegen Sehnenzerrung.

KUNDIN: Was für ein Medikament ist es, und wann werden Sie es bekommen?

APOTHEKER: Es ist ein Öl zum Einreiben. Es wird sicher mit der Morgenlieferung eintreffen. Kommen Sie nach zwölf vorbei.

KUNDIN: Das wird wohl nicht möglich sein.

APOTHEKER: Dann werden wir das Medikament mit einem Boten schicken.

KUNDIN: Wie oft soll die Patientin die Tabletten gegen die Allergie einnehmen?

APOTHEKER: Nach dem Abendessen, mit einem Glas Wasser. Es steht auf der Packung.

At the Pharmacy.

CUSTOMER: Is the prescription for Ott ready?

PHARMACIST: Ott? Yes, but we had to order one item—the medication for the torn tendon.

CUSTOMER: What kind of medicine is it, and when will you get it?

PHARMACIST: It's a rubbing oil. It'll probably arrive with the morning delivery. Come by after twelve.

CUSTOMER: That probably won't be possible.

PHARMACIST: Then we'll send the medication by messenger.

CUSTOMER: How should the patient take the allergy pills?

PHARMACIST: After supper, with a glass of water. It says this on the box.

B. DIALOG II

In der Drogerie.

HERR MAI: Können Sie mir helfen, die Artikel auf diesem Zettel zu finden? Ich bin in Eile.

DROGISTIN: Mal sehen: Sonnenschutzcreme, Bademütze, Körperpuder, Deodorant, Seife, Mundwasser, eine weiche Zahnbürste, Zahnpasta und Rasiercreme. Es wird ein paar Minuten dauern.

HERR MAI: Gut. Ich hole alles später ab.

———————————

At the Drugstore.

MR. MAI: Can you help me find the articles on this slip of paper? I'm in a hurry.

DRUGSTORE EMPLOYEE: Let's see: sunscreen lotion, bathing cap, dusting powder, deodorant, soap, mouthwash, a soft toothbrush, toothpaste, and shaving cream. It'll take a few minutes.

MR. MAI: All right. I'll pick up everything later.

C. GRAMMATIK UND GEBRAUCH

1. THE FUTURE TENSE

a. Compare the English and German future tenses:

English: shall/will + verb
German: *werden* + infinitive

Ich werde das Medikament schicken.
   I will send the medication.

Du wirst das Medikament schicken.
   You will send the medication.

Er wird das Medikament schicken.
   He will send the medication.

Wir werden das Medikament schicken.
   We will send the medication.

Ihr werdet das Medikament schicken.
   You will send the medication.

Sie werden das Medikament schicken.
   They will send the medication.

Sie werden das Medikament schicken.
   You (pol.) will send the medication.

b. The conjugated form of *werden* takes the place of the verb, and the infinitive of the main verb moves to the end of the clause:

Ich werde das Medikament mit einem Boten schicken.
   I'll send the medication by messenger.

Es wird ein paar Minuten dauern.
   It'll take a few minutes.

c. In a dependent clause the conjugated form of *werden* moves to the end of the clause:

Er hofft, dass das Rezept fertig sein wird.
   He hopes that the prescription will be ready.

Weißt du, ob sie das Medikament schicken werden?
   Do you know whether they will send the medication?

2. THE FUTURE TENSE OF MODAL AUXILIARIES

a. If a modal auxiliary is used in a future tense, a double infinitive construction results. The infinitive of the modal auxiliary follows the infinitive of the main verb:

Wir werden die Sonnenschutzcreme bestellen müssen.
   We'll have to order the sunscreen lotion.

Werden wir das teurere Präparat kaufen können?
Will we be able to buy the more expensive medication?

b. In a dependent clause the conjugated form of *werden* can also be placed before the double infinitive:

Sie sagt, dass sie mit den Tabletten keinen Alkohol wird trinken dürfen.
She says that she won't be allowed to drink alcohol with the pills.

3. THE USES OF THE FUTURE TENSE

a. Generally, German uses the present tense whenever the context clearly implies future actions or events, particularly when the sentence contains an adverb indicating future time:

Ich hole alles später ab.
I'll pick up everything later.

b. However, if the time of the action is not clear, the future tense may be used:

Wir werden das Medikament mit einem Boten schicken.
We'll send the medication by messenger.

Ich werde weniger essen.
I'm going to eat less.

Was wirst du tun?
What will you do?

c. The future tense is also used with adverbs such as *wohl*, *wahrscheinlich*, and *sicher* to express probability or supposition.

Das Präparat wird sicher mit der Morgenlieferung kommen.
The preparation will probably arrive with the morning delivery.

Das wird wohl nicht möglich sein.
That probably won't be possible.

Er wird wohl recht haben.
He's probably right.

d. The future tense can also express determination:

Ich werde nicht länger warten.
    I'm not going to wait any longer.

Ich werde die Tabletten einnehmen müssen.
    I'll have to take the pills.

VOKABELN

die Apotheke, *-n*	pharmacy
der Apotheker, *-*	pharmacist
das Rezept, *-e*	prescription
das Präparat, *-e*	preparation (medical or chemical), medication
das Mittel, *-*	medicine
die Tablette, *-n*	pill
das Aspirin, *-*	aspirin
die Allergie, *-n*	allergy
die Salbe, *-n*	salve
die elastische Binde, *-n*	elastic bandage
der Verbandstoff	bandages, dressing
das Öl, *-e*	oil, ointment
die Sehne, *-n*	tendon
die Zerrung, *-en*	sprain
zerren	to tear, to sprain
der Bote, *-n*	messenger
die Lieferung, *-en*	delivery
die Packung, *-en*	box
Es steht auf der Packung.	It's (written) on the box.
ein*nehmen, *nahm ein, eingenommen*	to take, to swallow
ein*reiben, *rieb ein, eingerieben*	to rub in
die Drogerie, *-n*	drugstore
der Drogist, *-en, -en*	druggist
die Zahnbürste, *-n*	toothbrush
die Zahnpasta, *Zahnpasten*	toothpaste
das Mundwasser, *-*	mouthwash

das Deodorant, -s	deodorant
der Körperpuder, -	dusting powder
die Seife, -n	soap
die Sonnenschutzcreme, -n	sunscreen lotion
die Bademütze, -n	bathing cap
die Rasiercreme, -n	shaving cream
der Artikel, -	article
der Zettel, -	slip of paper
wahrscheinlich ⎱ wohl ⎰	probably

ÜBUNGEN

A. *Beantworten Sie die Fragen zum Dialog.*

Dialog I
1. *Was hat der Apotheker gemacht, da das Öl nicht vorrätig war?*
2. *Was wird der Apotheker machen, da die Kundin das Präparat nicht abholen kann?*
3. *Wie soll die Patientin die Tabletten gegen die Allergie einnehmen?*

Dialog II
4. *Was fragt Herr Mai?*
5. *Warum fragt er das?*

B. *Suchen Sie die richtige deutsche Übersetzung.*

1. It'll probably take awhile.
2. It's written on the box.
3. Where can I find a pharmacy?
4. How should I take the medication?
5. Take two pills with a glass of water.

a. *Wie soll ich das Medikament einnehmen?*
b. *Wo kann ich eine Apotheke finden?*
c. *Es wird wahrscheinlich eine Weile dauern.*
d. *Nehmen Sie zwei Tabletten mit einem Glas Wasser.*
e. *Es steht auf der Packung.*

C. *Setzen Sie die Sätze ins Futur.* (Rewrite the sentences in the future tense.)

BEISPIEL: *Wir nehmen ein Taxi.*
          Wir werden ein Taxi nehmen.

1. *Ich rufe dich an.*
2. *Wie lange dauert das?*
3. *Die Kinder kommen.*
4. *Laufen Sie viel?*
5. *Seid ihr am Strand?*

D. *Antworten Sie in der Zukunft, und benutzen Sie das gegebene Modalverb.* (Answer in the future tense, using the modal auxiliary given.)

BEISPIEL: *Warum trinkt er keinen Wein? (dürfen)*
          Er wird keinen Wein trinken dürfen.

1. *Warum antwortet er nicht? (wollen)*
2. *Warum geht er nicht in die Sonne? (dürfen)*
3. *Warum bezahlt er die Rechnung nicht? (können)*

E. *Übersetzen Sie.*

1. When will the prescription be ready?
2. It's probably going to take thirty minutes.

F. *Beantworten Sie die folgende Fragen in der Zukunft.* (Answer the following questions using the future tense.)

1. *Regnet es heute? (Nein, morgen . . .)*
2. *Geht Frau Schulz ins Theater? (Am Sonntag . . .)*
3. *Ist das Rezept fertig? (In ein paar Minuten . . .)*
4. *Haben Sie Zeit für mich? (Nein, heute . . .)*
5. *Kaufen Sie ein neues Auto? (Im Februar . . .)*

G. *Schreiben Sie die folgenden Sätze in der Zukunft.*

1. *Ich muss am Samstag nicht arbeiten.*
2. *Wir können euch im Dezember besuchen.*
3. *Er darf nach der Krankheit nicht mehr rauchen.*

4. *Sie will ihre Medizin nicht nehmen.*

5. *Es mag heute regnen.*

KULTURNOTIZ

A pharmacy *(Apotheke)* sells prescription and nonprescription drugs. It may also carry cosmetic articles, usually those of well-known manufacturers. A drugstore *(Drogerie)* sells any kind of toiletry, but it does not sell drugs. In many cities, one can also find cheaper self-service drugstores *(Drogeriemärkte)* that sell nonprescription drugs. A druggist *(Drogist)* must undergo a three-year apprenticeship and attend a trade school. A pharmacist *(Apotheker)*, on the other hand, has to attend university and study pharmacy.

The German health-care system also provides for medication. Germans pay only a token amount for each prescription, which is unrelated to the actual cost of the medication.

LÖSUNGEN

A. *Dialog I*
   1. *Er hat es bestellt.* 2. *Er wird das Medikament mit einem Boten schicken.* 3. *Sie soll die Tabletten gegen die Allergie nach dem Abendessen mit einem Glas Wasser einnehmen.*
   Dialog II
   4. *Er fragt, ob die Drogistin ihm helfen kann, die Artikel auf dem Zettel zu finden.* 5. *Er ist in Eile.*

B. 1.—c   2.—e   3.—b   4.—a   5.—d

C. 1. *Ich werde dich anrufen.* 2. *Wie lange wird das dauern?* 3. *Die Kinder werden kommen.* 4. *Werden Sie viel laufen?* 5. *Werdet ihr am Strand sein?*

D. 1. *Er wird nicht antworten wollen.* 2. *Er wird nicht in die Sonne gehen dürfen.* 3. *Er wird die Rechnung nicht bezahlen können.*

E. 1. *Wann wird das Rezept fertig sein?* 2. *Es wird wohl dreißig Minuten dauern.*

F. 1. *Nein, morgen wird es regnen.* 2. *Am Sonntag wird Frau Schulz ins Theater gehen.* 3. *In ein paar Minuten wird das Rezept fertig sein.*
   4. *Nein, heute werde ich keine Zeit für Sie haben.* 5. *Im Februar werde ich ein neues Auto kaufen.*

G. 1. *Ich werde am Samstag nicht arbeiten müssen.* 2. *Wir werden euch im Dezember besuchen können.* 3. *Er wird nach der Krankheit nicht mehr rauchen dürfen.* 4. *Sie wird ihre Medizin nicht nehmen wollen.* 5. *Es wird heute regnen mögen.*

LEKTION 32

A. DIALOG

Auf dem Fundbüro.

TOURIST: Ist hier eine braune Reisetasche abgegeben worden?

BEAMTER: Bitte beschreiben Sie die Tasche näher!

TOURIST: Es ist eine Umhängetasche. Sie ist aus Leder, hat ein Kombinationsschloss und ein Außenfach mit Reißverschluss. Auf der rechten Seite sind die Initialen "H.G.".

BEAMTER: Wann haben Sie die Reisetasche verloren?

TOURIST: Heute Nachmittag, kurz nach zwei. Ich habe sie wohl im Kaufhaus gelassen. Vielleicht ist sie auch gestohlen worden.

BEAMTER: Ja, Diebe gibt es heutzutage überall. Beschreiben Sie bitte den Inhalt der Tasche!

TOURIST: Eine Kreditkarte, eine Geldbörse mit Kleingeld, ein Notizbuch und die Tageszeitung. Ach, mein Reisepass ist auch darin!

BEAMTER: Es wurde keine Reisetasche abgegeben. Aber vielleicht wird sie noch gefunden.

TOURIST: Bitte benachrichtigen Sie mich. Ich kann im Hotel telefonisch erreicht werden.

BEAMTER: Sie gehen am besten sofort zum amerikanischen Konsulat. Dort kann ein neuer Pass ausgestellt werden.

At the Lost and Found.

TOURIST: Has a brown travel bag been handed in?

CLERK: Please describe the bag in more detail.

TOURIST: It's a shoulder bag. It's made of leather, and it has a combination lock and an outside compartment with a zipper. On the right side are the initials "H.G."

CLERK: When did you lose the travel bag?

TOURIST: This afternoon, shortly after two. I probably left it in the department store. Perhaps it was stolen.

CLERK: Yes, thieves are everywhere nowadays. Please describe the contents of the bag.

TOURIST: A credit card, a purse for coins, a notebook, and the newspaper. Oh, my passport is in it, too!

CLERK: No travel bag was handed in. But perhaps it'll still be found.

TOURIST: Please notify me. I can be reached by telephone in the hotel.

CLERK: You should immediately go to the American consulate. A new passport can be issued there.

B. GRAMMATIK UND GEBRAUCH

1. THE FORMATION OF THE PASSIVE VOICE

a. All sentences up to now have been in the active voice: the subject of the sentence acts, i.e., does what the verb expresses.

Peter stellte das Auto in die Garage.
Peter put the car in the garage.

In the passive voice the subject is acted upon, i.e., the subject is passive.

Das Auto wurde von Peter in die Garage gestellt.
The car was put in the garage by Peter.

In the preceding sentence *das Auto* is the subject, but the action is performed by an agent, Peter.

Compare the English and German passive voices:

English: to be   +   past participle
German: *werden*   +   past participle

Ich werde heute geprüft.
    I am being tested today.

b. The passive voice can be formed for all tenses. The auxiliary *werden* changes to form the tense, but the past participle remains invariable:

PRESENT
Die Medizin wird bestellt.
    The medicine is being ordered.

PAST
Die Medizin wurde bestellt.
    The medicine was ordered.

PRESENT PERFECT
Die Medizin ist bestellt worden.
    The medicine has been ordered.

PAST PERFECT
Die Medizin war bestellt worden.
    The medicine had been ordered.

FUTURE
Die Medizin wird bestellt werden.
    The medicine will be ordered.

Note that the past participle *geworden* is shortened to *worden* in the passive voice.

2. THE USES OF THE PASSIVE VOICE

a. In a dependent clause, the conjugated form of *werden* (that is, the form that corresponds to the subject of the dependent clause) takes the place of the verb and follows the past participle:

Er weiß nicht, ob die Möbel heute geliefert werden.
    He doesn't know whether the furniture will be delivered today.

Sie sagte, dass das Haus verkauft wird.
    She said that the house is being sold.

b. In a passive sentence the performer of the action (the agent) may or may not be named:

Er wird heute geprüft. (no agent)
He's being tested today.

Er wird heute von dem Professor geprüft. **(agent** = *der Professor)*
He's being tested today by the professor.

Wir hoffen, dass die Nachbarn nicht geweckt werden. **(no agent)**
We hope that the neighbors won't be woken up.

Wir hoffen, dass die Nachbarn durch den Lärm nicht geweckt werden.
(agent = *der Lärm)*
We hope that the neighbors won't be woken up by the noise.

Note how the agent is generally expressed:

if a person:	*von*	+	dat.
if a thing:	*durch*	+	acc.

c. In German, a dative object in an active sentence remains unchanged in the corresponding passive sentence.*

Die Mutter hilft den Kindern.
The mother helps the children.

Den Kindern wird von der Mutter geholfen.
The children are being helped by the mother.

Ein Fremder gibt ihm Geld.
A stranger is giving him money.

Ihm wird von einem Fremden Geld gegeben.
He is being given money by a stranger.

Note that passive sentences with a dative verb do not have a grammatical subject. The impersonal subject *es* is understood, but not necessarily expressed. There is no direct English equivalent.

---

* For verbs that take the dative. see lesson 10.

Es wird den Kindern von der Mutter geholfen.
Den Kindern wird von der Mutter geholfen.
>   The children are being helped by the mother.

Es wird ihr nicht geglaubt.
Ihr wird nicht geglaubt.
>   One doesn't believe her.
>   (She isn't believed.)

3. THE PASSIVE VOICE WITH MODAL AUXILIARIES

All tenses can be formed with modal auxiliaries in the passive voice. The modal auxiliary forms the tense, and the passive consists of the past participle of the verb plus *werden*. However, only three tenses are generally used:

PRESENT
Die Reisetasche kann noch gefunden werden.
>   The travel bag may yet be found.

PAST
Das Medikament konnte geliefert werden.
>   They were able to send the medication.
>   (The medication could be sent.)

FUTURE
Der Zahn wird gerettet werden können.
>   The tooth can probably be saved.

Die Tropfen werden bestellt werden müssen.
>   The drops will probably have to be ordered.

Note that the future tense construction with a modal auxiliary generally expresses probability or supposition.

VOKABELN

das Fundbüro	the lost and found
verlieren, *verlor, verloren*	to lose
finden, *fand, gefunden*	to find
lassen, *ließ, gelassen*	to let, to leave
ab*geben *(gibt ab), gab ab, abgegeben*	to hand in
beschreiben, *beschrieb, beschrieben*	to describe
benachrichtigen	to notify
stehlen *(stiehlt), stahl, gestohlen*	to steal
der Dieb, *-e*	male thief
die Diebin, *-nen*	female thief
der Diebstahl, *:-e*	theft
persönliche Gegenstände	personal items
die Reisetasche, *-n*	travel bag
die Umhängetasche, *-n*	shoulder bag
das Außenfach, *:-er*	outside compartment
das Innenfach, *:-er*	inside compartment
das Kombinationsschloss, *:-er*	combination lock
der Reißverschluss, *:-e*	zipper
der Inhalt, *-e*	contents
die Initiale, *-n*	initial
das Leder, *-*	leather
aus Leder	(made) of leather
die Kreditkarte, *-n*	credit card
die Geldbörse, *-n*	purse
das Kleingeld	coins, small change
der Reisepass, *:-e*	passport
das Notizbuch, *:-er*	notebook, address book
das Konsulat, *-e*	consulate
der Konsul	consul
aus*stellen	to issue
telefonisch erreichen	to reach by telephone
heutzutage	nowadays
überall	everywhere

A. *Beantworten Sie die Fragen zum Dialog.*

1. *Was fragt der Tourist auf dem Fundbüro?*
2. *Wo hat der Tourist die Reisetasche wahrscheinlich gelassen?*
3. *Was ist der Inhalt der Reisetasche?*
4. *Was empfiehlt der Beamte dem Touristen?*

B. *Suchen Sie die richtige deutsche Übersetzung.*

1. The travel bag will perhaps be found.
2. I can describe the contents.
3. No credit card was handed in.
4. The bag is made of leather.
5. I lost my passport.

a. *Die Tasche ist aus Leder.*
b. *Es wurde keine Kreditkarte abgegeben.*
c. *Ich habe meinen Reisepass verloren.*
d. *Ich kann den Inhalt beschreiben.*
e. *Die Reisetasche wird vielleicht gefunden werden.*

C. *Übersetzen Sie.*

1. *Das Medikament muss bestellt werden.*
2. *Er sagt, dass der Zahn gezogen werden muss.*
3. *Im amerikanischen Konsulat kann ein neuer Paß ausgestellt werden.*
4. *Meine Haare wurden gestern gewaschen und geschnitten.*
5. *Sein Auto kann morgen repariert werden.*
6. *Ihm wird nichts mehr gegeben.*
7. *Das Haus ist zum zweiten Mal renoviert worden.*
8. *Den Kindern muss geholfen werden.*

D. *Übersetzen Sie.*

1. Can you please help me?
2. My travel bag was stolen.
3. I need a new passport quickly.
4. How do I get to the consulate?

KULTURNOTIZ

Lost and found offices *(Fundbüros)* are usually located at city hall and at local police stations. Railroad stations in larger cities and big private enterprises may also have such services. Always inquire first at the place where the loss occurred.

There are American consulates in several of the large German cities. In German-speaking countries as elsewhere, American consuls help American tourists and residents who have lost their passports or money, been involved in an accident, need a lawyer, or require information on trade. They also witness (but do not perform) marriages; authenticate documents such as birth, marriage, and death certificates; take depositions from witnesses for use in American courts; distribute Social Security checks; trace missing compatriots; and even arrange funerals.

LÖSUNGEN

A. 1. *Der Tourist fragt, ob eine braune Reisetasche abgegeben worden ist. 2. Er hat sie wahrscheinlich im Kaufhaus gelassen. 3. In der Reisetasche sind eine Kreditkarte, eine Geldbörse mit Kleingeld, ein Notizbuch, eine Tageszeitung und ein Reisepass. 4. Der Beamte empfiehlt dem Touristen, sofort zum amerikanischen Konsulat zu gehen.*

B. 1.—e   2.—d   3.—b   4.—a   5.—c

C. 1. The medicine must be ordered. 2. He says that the tooth will have to be pulled. 3. A new passport can be issued at the American consulate. 4. My hair was washed and cut yesterday. 5. His car can be repaired tomorrow. 6. He isn't given anything anymore. 7. The house was renovated for the second time. 8. The children must be helped.

D. 1. *Können Sie mir bitte helfen?* 2. *Meine Reisetasche ist gestohlen worden (wurde gestohlen).* 3. *Ich brauche schnell einen neuen Pass.* 4. *Wie komme ich zum Konsulat?*

LEKTION 33

A. DIALOG

Ein neuer Computer.

Gudrun und Andreas haben sich einen neuen Computer gekauft.

ANDREAS: Und was kann man mit diesem Computer besser machen?

GUDRUN: Mit dem neuen Modem kann man sehr viel schneller das Internet surfen und mit dem allerneuesten Browser lassen sich alle Internetseiten anzeigen. Selbst Webseiten mit beweglichen Grafiken oder Video kann man problemlos herunterladen.

ANDREAS: Lässt sich denn auch E-Mail schneller schicken?

GUDRUN: Nicht schneller! E-Mail kann doch ohnehin schon superschnell geschickt werden, aber man kann sie jetzt auch noch einfacher schicken, selbst wenn man Fotos, Tonaufnahmen oder andere Dateien beifügt. Zudem können wir jetzt automatisch benachrichtigt werden, ob wir E-Mail haben, sobald wir den Computer hochfahren.

ANDREAS: Das ist ja toll. Auch unsere E-Mail-Adresse ist einfach zu merken.

GUDRUN: Und in allen Programmen sind wir nur ein Mausklick vom weltweiten Netz entfernt.

ANDREAS: Na dann lass uns mal 'ne Runden surfen.

A new computer.

Gudrun and Andreas have bought a new computer.

ANDREAS: And what can be done better with this new computer?

GUDRUN: With the new modem one can surf the Internet a lot faster, and with the brand-new browser all Web sites can be fully displayed. Even the pages with moving graphics or video can be downloaded without a problem.

ANDREAS: Can e-mail be sent faster, as well?

GUDRUN: Not faster! E-mail can be sent extremely fast anyway, but now it is also much easier, even if photos, audio recordings, or other data files are attached. Besides that, now we can be notified automatically of new e-mail as soon as we boot up the computer.

ANDREAS: That is really terrific. Our e-mail address is easy to remember, as well.

GUDRUN: And within every program, we are only a click of the mouse away from the World Wide Web.

ANDREAS: Well, then, let's surf the Net for a while.

B. GRAMMATIK UND GEBRAUCH

1. SUBSTITUTE CONSTRUCTIONS FOR THE PASSIVE VOICE

In German, other constructions may be used in place of the passive voice.

a. *MAN* + ACTIVE VERB

Man is often used if no particular agent is expressed. *Man* (one, you, we, they, people) constitutes the subject; the sentence is in the active voice.

Die E-Mail wird heute geschickt.
The e-mail is being sent today.

→ **Man schickt die E-Mail heute.**
They are (one is) sending the e-mail today.

Ein Foto wird beigefügt.
A photo is (being) attached.

→ **Man fügte ein Foto bei.**
They (one) attached a photo.

Die Datei wurde gefunden.
The file was found.

→ **Man fand die Datei.**
They (one) found the file.

h. *MAN* + MODAL + INFINITIVE

This is frequently used with *müssen* or *können:*

Das Foto kann heruntergeladen werden.	→	**Man kann das Foto herunterladen.**
The photo can be downloaded.		One can download the photo.
Der Computer muss hochgefahren werden.	→	**Man muss den Computer hochfahren.**
The computer must be booted up.		One must boot up the computer.

c. *SEIN* + *ZU* + INFINITIVE

This may be used with *können* or *müssen* in order to express the possibility or necessity of an action.

Das kann schnell gemacht werden.	→	**Das ist schnell zu machen.**
That can be done quickly.		That is quickly done.
Was musste noch beigefügt werden?	→	**Was war noch beizufügen?**
What still had to be attached?		What was still to be attached?

d. *SICH LASSEN* + INFINITIVE

This can replace *können* and a passive infinitive.

E-Mail kann schnell geschickt werden.	→	**E-Mail lässt sich schnell schicken.**
E-mail can be sent quickly.		E-mail can be sent quickly.
Das kann gemacht werden.	→	**Das lässt sich machen.**
That can be done.		That can be done.

VOKABELN

der Computer, -	computer
das Modem, -s	modem
das Internet	Internet
allerneuest-	brand-new
der Browser, -	Web browser
die Internetseite, -n	Web page
(often means all pages of a site)	
das Web-Site, -s	Web site
an*zeigen	to display
selbst	even, self
beweglich	animated, moving, movable
die Grafik, -en	graphic
das Video, -s	video
problemlos	uncomplicated(ly)
die E-Mail	e-mail
ohnehin	anyway, nevertheless
superschnell	superfast
herunterladen, *lud herunter,* *heruntergeladen*	to download
einfach	simple, simply, easily
die Tonaufnahme, -n	audio recording
Datei, -en	file
bei*fügen	to attach, to add
zudem	besides, in addition to that
automatisch	automatically
benachrichtigen	to notify
sobald	as soon as
hochfahren	to boot up
toll	terrific
das Mausklick	mouse click
weltweit	worldwide
das Netz	Net
entfernt	away (from)
die Runde	round, a little while
surfen	to surf

A. *Beantworten Sie die Fragen zum Dialog.*

1. *Was kann man schneller mit dem neuen Modem machen?*
2. *Kann man mit dem neuen Computer schneller eine E-Mail schicken?*
3. *Was können Gudrun und Andreas der E-Mail beifügen?*
4. *Wann werden Gudrun und Andreas benachrichtigt, ob sie E-Mail haben?*

B. *Suchen Sie die richtige deutsche Übersetzung.*

1. Can you send e-mail with this computer?
2. Where can I (one) find the information?
3. One can send e-mail much easier now.
4. You are notified automatically.
5. We can download all Web pages.

a. *Sie werden automatisch benachrichtigt.*
b. *Kann man mit diesem Computer E-Mail schicken?*
c. *Man kann jetzt E-Mail viel einfacher schicken.*
d. *Wo kann man diese Informationen finden?*
e. *Wir können alle Webseiten herunterladen.*

C. *Setzen Sie die passiven Sätze ins Aktiv mit "man".* (Rewrite the passive sentences as active sentences using *man.*)

BEISPIEL: *Die E-Mail kann schnell geschickt werden.*
Man kann die E-Mail schnell schicken.

1. *Der Computer muss hochgefahren werden.*
2. *Mein Brief wurde gelesen.*
3. *Es wird über das Internet gesprochen.*
4. *Der neue Schreibtisch wird heute gebracht.*
5. *Es wird gesagt, dass moderne Technologie viel Zeit spart.*

D. *Antworten Sie mit "ja" oder "nein", wie in Klammern angezeigt, und benutzen Sie "sich lassen" und den Infinitiv des Verbs.* (Answer with *ja* or *nein*, as indicated in parentheses, and use *sich lassen* and the infinitive of the verb.)

BEISPIEL: *Kann der Computer repariert werden? (ja)*
Ja, der Computer lässt sich reparieren.

1. *Kann der Brief noch heute geschrieben werden? (nein)*
2. *Kann ein 5 Jahre alter Computer noch verkauft werden? (nein)*

3. *Können die Informationen an alle Angestellten gegeben werden? (ja)*
4. *Kann dieses Video per E-Mail geschickt werden? (ja)*

E. *Übersetzen Sie.*

1. Shall these photos be sent by e-mail?
2. Yes, but the long file must be sent by mail.
3. I thought all files can be sent by e-mail.
4. That's possible, but some can't be downloaded easily.

KULTURNOTIZ

Most data lines in Germany are currently provided by German Telecom. Even though they are the same as the regular telephone lines, data lines have different standards and connectors and have to be specially installed. This gave T-Online (Telecom's Internet provider) an advantage in the past. However, deregulation has brought many more ISPs to the market. The largest in Germany today is AOL. It is expected that there will be no more on-line charges in the near future, since many companies with a commercial interest will provide free, unlimited Internet access.

LÖSUNGEN

A. 1. *Man kann schneller das Internet surfen. 2. Nein, nicht schneller (aber einfacher). 3. Sie können Fotos, Tonaufnahmen und andere Dateien beifügen. 4. Sie werden benachrichtigt, sobald sie den Computer hochfahren.*
B. 1.—b 2.—d 3.—c 4.—a 5.—e
C. 1. *Man muss den Computer hochfahren. 2. Man hat meinen Brief gelesen. (Man las meinen Brief.) 3. Man spricht über das Internet. 4. Man bringt den neuen Schreibtisch heute. 5. Man sagt, dass moderne Technologie viel Zeit spart.*
D. 1. *Nein, der Brief lässt sich heute nicht mehr schreiben. 2. Nein, ein 5 Jahre alter Computer lässt sich nicht mehr verkaufen. 3. Ja, die Informationen lassen sich an alle Angestellten geben. 4. Ja, dieses Video lässt sich per E-Mail schicken.*
E. 1. *Sollen diese Fotos per (mit) E-Mail geschickt werden? 2. Ja, aber die große Datei muss per Post geschickt werden. 3. Ich dachte, man kann alle Dateien per E-Mail schicken./Ich dachte, alle Dateien lassen sich per E-Mail schicken./Ich dachte, alle Dateien können per E-Mail geschickt werden. 4. Das ist möglich, aber manche lassen sich nicht einfach herunterladen./. . . aber manche können nicht einfach heruntergeladen werden./. . . aber manche sind nicht einfach herunterzuladen.*

LEKTION 34

AUF DER BANK.   At the Bank.

A. DIALOG I

Die Kontoeröffnung

KUNDIN: Ich möchte ein neues Konto eröffnen. Ich habe schon ein Girokonto bei Ihnen. Hier ist meine Karte.

BANKANGESTELLTE: Moment bitte, ich werde in der Kartei nachsehen. Gut, Frau Buse, ich nehme an, Sie möchten ein Sparkonto einrichten.

KUNDIN: Richtig. Der Zinssatz wird ja augenblicklich immer höher. Es lohnt sich.

BANKANGESTELLTE: Ja, Sparen ist eine gute Anlage. Füllen Sie nun dieses Einzahlungsformular aus, und schreiben Sie hier auf, wer als Nutznießer eingesetzt wird.

KUNDIN: So, jetzt ist alles ausgefüllt.

BANKANGESTELLTE: Hier ist Ihr Sparbuch.

KUNDIN: Keine Bearbeitungsgebühr?

BANKANGESTELLTE: Nein, Sie leihen uns ja Geld.

Opening an Account.

FEMALE CUSTOMER: I would like to open a new account. I already have a checking account with you. Here is my card.

BANK EMPLOYEE: One moment please, I'll look in the files. Fine, Mrs. Buse, I assume you want to open a savings account.

FEMALE CUSTOMER: That's right. Just now the interest rate is getting higher and higher. It's worthwhile.

BANK EMPLOYEE: Yes, saving is a good investment. Now please fill out this deposit slip and write down here who is being named beneficiary.

FEMALE CUSTOMER: Okay. Now everything is filled out.

BANK EMPLOYEE: Here is your passbook.

FEMALE CUSTOMER: No service charge?

BANK EMPLOYEE: No, you are lending us money.

B. DIALOG II

Geldwechsel.

KUNDE: Bitte, wechseln Sie tausend Dollar.

BANKANGESTELLTE: Sie bekommen achthundertelf Euro. Wie soll ich das Geld auszahlen?

KUNDE: Geben Sie mir acht Hunderteuroscheine, einen Zehneurochein, und den Rest in Kleingeld. Der Kurs ist heute niedrig.

ANGESTELLTE: Leider.

———————

Foreign Exchange.

MALE CUSTOMER: Please change 1,000 dollars.

BANK EMPLOYEE: You'll receive 811 euros. How shall I pay out the money?

MALE CUSTOMER: Give me eight 100-euro bills, one 10-euro bill, and the rest in change. The exchange rate is low today.

BANK EMPLOYEE: Unfortunately.

C. GRAMMATIK UND GEBRAUCH

1. THE STATIVE PASSIVE

The passive voice always shows a process: something is, will, or has been done to the subject.

> The account is being opened.

The stative passive describes the result of the action performed on the subject. It shows a condition or a state of being.

> Now it is opened.

The stative passive is not a real passive construction; it is also called an "apparent passive."
   To form the stative passive, German uses *sein* + past participle.

Jetzt ist alles ausgefüllt.
   Now everything is filled out.

The stative passive is generally used only in the present and simple past tenses.

PASSIVE VOICE	STATIVE PASSIVE

Das Konto wird eröffnet.
   The account is being opened.
	Das Konto ist eröffnet.
	   The account is (already) open(ed).

Das Restaurant wird geöffnet.
   The restaurant is being opened.
	Das Restaurant ist geöffnet.
	   The restaurant is (already) open(ed).

Das Geld wurde ausgezahlt.
   The money was paid out.
	Das Geld ist ausgezahlt.
	   The money has been paid out.

Das Formular wird ausgefüllt.
   The form is being filled out.
	Das Formular ist ausgefüllt.
	   The form is (already) filled out.

2. DIFFERENT USES OF THE VERB *WERDEN*

a. *Werden* can be used as the main verb with the meaning "to become," "to get." Then it is followed either by a predicate adjective or a predicate noun.

Der Zinssatz wird immer höher.
The interest rate is getting higher and higher.

Er wurde Bankpräsident.
He became the bank president.

b. *Werden* can be used as an auxiliary to form the future tense. Then the main verb is in the infinitive.

Ich werde in der Kartei nachsehen.
I'll look in the files.

Die Bearbeitungsgebühren werden sicher hoch sein.
The service charges are certainly going to be high.

c. *Werden* can be used as an auxiliary to form the passive voice. Then the main verb is a past participle.

Wer wird als Nutznießer eingesetzt?
Who is being named beneficiary?

Das Geld wird heute gewechselt.
The money is being changed today.

VOKABELN

die Bank, *-en*	bank
der Bankangestellte, *-n*	male bank clerk, teller
die Bankangestellte, *-n*	female bank clerk, teller
das Konto, *Konten*	account
ein Konto eröffnen	to open an account
ein Konto einrichten	to open an account
ein Konto schließen	to close an account
der Kontoauszug, *-̈e*	bank statement

überweisen, überwies, überwiesen	to transfer money
das Girokonto	checking account
das Sparkonto	savings account
sparen	to save
das Sparbuch	passbook
das Bargeld	cash
der Scheck	check
einen Scheck einlösen	to cash a check
aus*zahlen	to pay out
das Auszahlungsformular, -e	withdrawal slip
ein*zahlen	to deposit
das Einzahlungsformular, -e	deposit slip
der Schein, -e	bill (money)
der Zehneuroschein, -e	ten-euro bill
wechseln	to change
der Wechselkurs, -e	exchange rate
der Kurs, -e	exchange rate
Der Kurs ist niedrig.	The exchange rate is low.
Der Kurs ist hoch.	The exchange rate is high.
leihen, lieh, geliehen	to lend, to borrow
die Anlage, -n	investment
die Zinsen (pl.)	interest
der Zinssatz, ̈e	interest rate
der Nutznießer, -	beneficiary
einen Nutznießer einsetzen	to name someone beneficiary
die Bearbeitungsgebühr, -en	service charge
augenblicklich	current, currently, just now
Es lohnt sich.	It's worthwhile.

ÜBUNGEN

A. *Beantworten Sie die Fragen zum Dialog.*

1. *Was möchte die Kundin machen?*
2. *Was für ein Konto hat die Kundin schon bei der Bank?*
3. *Was nennt die Bankangestellte Sparen?*
4. *Was muss die Kundin ausfüllen?*
5. *Wie viel Dollar möchte der Kunde wechseln?*

B. *Suchen Sie die richtige deutsche Übersetzung.*

1. I would like to open an account.
2. The interest rate is getting higher and higher.
3. Please, fill out the deposit slip.
4. I have changed 500 dollars.
5. He needs ten 100-euro bills.
6. He has a savings account at the bank.
7. The exchange rate is low.
8. There is no service charge.

a. *Der Wechselkurs ist niedrig.*
b. *Der Zinssatz wird immer höher.*
c. *Ich möchte ein Konto eröffnen.*
d. *Er braucht zehn Hunderteuroscheine.*
e. *Ich habe fünfhundert Dollar gewechselt.*
f. *Er hat ein Sparkonto bei der Bank.*
g. *Es gibt keine Bearbeitungsgebühr.*
h. *Bitte füllen Sie das Einzahlungsformular aus.*

C. *Übersetzen Sie.*

1. The account is opened.
2. The bank is closed.
3. The money was changed.

D. *Zeigen Sie an, ob "werden" als Hauptverb (a), als Hilfsverb für das Futur (b) oder als Hilfsverb für das Passiv (c) benutzt wird.* [Indicate whether *werden* is used as the main verb (a), as an auxiliary for the future (b), or as an auxiliary for the passive voice (c).]

1. *Der Kunde wird nach seiner Karte gefragt.*
2. *Er wird ein Konto bei der Bank eröffnen.*
3. *Es wird eine gute Anlage sein.*
4. *Der Zinssatz wird immer höher.*

KULTURNOTIZ

The banking systems in the United States and Germany are quite similar, though there are some differences. In Germany it's possible to do common bank transactions at the post office, where you can have a checking and savings account *(Postscheckkonto, Postsparkonto)*. Regular monthly payments such as rent, gas, or electricity are not usually paid by check but directly from a *Girokonto*. Salaries are automatically transferred to this account and regular monthly payments are made from it by the bank. There is a charge *(Bankgebühr)* for this service. Bank statements *(Kontoauszüge)* come every three months. Business people and self-employed people might have a checking account *(Scheckkonto)*.

In German-speaking countries money can be changed at every bank, at the post office, and at special places called *Wechselstuben* that are found at border crossings, train stations, and airports. Automatic money-changing machines *(Geldwechselautomaten)* are often found in front of banks at some of the major resorts and tourist spots.

The euro is the official form of payment throughout the European Union, including Germany.

LÖSUNGEN

A. 1. *Sie möchte ein Konto eröffnen.* 2. *Die Kundin hat schon ein Girokonto.* 3. *Sie nennt Sparen eine gute Anlage.* 4. *Sie muss ein Einzahlungsformular ausfüllen.* 5. *Er möchte tausend Dollar wechseln.*
B. 1.—c 2.—b 3.—h 4.—e 5.—d 6.—f 7.—a 8.—g
C. 1. *Das Konto ist eröffnet.* 2. *Die Bank ist geschlossen.* 3. *Das Geld wurde gewechselt.*
D. 1.—c 2.—b 3.—b 4.—a

LEKTION 35
DAS THEATER.   The Theater.

A. DIALOG

An der Theaterkasse.

THEATERBESUCHER: Hätten Sie noch zwei Karten für die Vorstellung heute Abend?

KASSIERER: Wir haben Plätze im Parkett und im ersten Rang.

THEATERBESUCHER: Könnten Sie mir bitte die Plätze auf dem Sitzplan zeigen?

KASSIERER: Hier, Parkett, dritte Reihe, rechts, fünf und sechs.

THEATERBESUCHER: Wir säßen lieber links von der Bühne und in der Nähe des Notausganges.

KASSIERER: Da hätte ich nur zwei hintereinander liegende Plätze.

THEATERBESUCHER: Gut. Die nehme ich. Gäbe es auch noch Karten für die Matinée am nächsten Samstag?

KASSIERER: Wir sind ausverkauft, aber es könnten einige Karten zurückgegeben werden.

THEATERBESUCHER: Meine Frau sähe das Theaterstück gern. Sie würde sich sehr freuen.

KASSIERER: Dann wäre es am besten, wenn Sie am Montag noch einmal nachfragten oder vorbeikämen.

At the Theater Box Office.

THEATERGOER: Would you still have two tickets for the performance tonight?

CASHIER: We still have seats in the orchestra and in the dress circle.

THEATERGOER: Could you please show me the seats on the seating plan?

CASHIER: Here, orchestra, third row, on the right side, five and six.

THEATERGOER: We would prefer to sit to the left of the stage and near the emergency exit.

CASHIER: There I would have only two seats, one behind the other.

THEATERGOER: All right, I'll take them. Would you also still have tickets for the matinee next Saturday?

CASHIER: We're sold out, but some tickets might be returned.

THEATERGOER: My wife would like to see the play. She would enjoy it very much.

CASHIER: In that case, it would be best if you inquired or came by again on Monday.

B. GRAMMATIK UND GEBRAUCH

1. THE SUBJUNCTIVE MOOD

Most verbs used up to now have been in the indicative or imperative mood. The indicative mood states a fact or what the speaker considers to be a fact. The imperative is the mood of requests and commands. The subjunctive mood expresses hypothetical conditions, wishful thinking, doubt, and polite requests. Compare these sentences in English:

I am going to the theater.	a fact: indicative
Go to the theater.	a command: imperative
If only I were going to the theater!	wishful thinking: subjunctive

In German, the subjunctive is much more common than in English. German has a general subjunctive (Konjunktiv II) and a special subjunctive (Konjunktiv I). Each of the two subjunctives has four tenses—present, past, future and perfect.

This chapter will treat the general subjunctive for present time.

2. THE FORMATION OF THE PRESENT-TIME GENERAL SUBJUNCTIVE

The forms of the general subjunctive* are derived from the past-tense indicative. For example: *wir kauften* (we bought), *wir fuhren* (we traveled).

Kaufte er nur ein besseres Auto.
If only he would buy a better car.

Führe er nur ein besseres Auto.
If only he would drive a better car.

There is one set of endings for all subjunctive forms:

-e	*-en*
-est	*-et*
-e	*-en*

These endings are attached to the stem of the past tense indicative.

a. WEAK VERBS

The present-time general subjunctive of weak verbs is identical with the simple past indicative. Context, however, should reveal the meaning.

ich kaufte	I would buy	*wir kauften*	we would buy
du kauftest	you would buy	*ihr kauftet*	you would buy
sie kaufte	she would buy	*sie kauften*	they would buy
		Sie kauften	you would buy

Wenn Theaterkarten nur nicht so viel kosteten!
If only theater tickets didn't cost so much!

Fragtest du das wirklich?
Would you really ask that?

---

* Many texts, including the advanced level of this series, use the term *Konjunktiv II*. For descriptive purposes, you will see the term "general subjunctive" in this course.

The verbs *haben*, *denken*, and *bringen* take an umlaut in the simple past to form the present-time general subjunctive:

INFINITIVE	PAST TENSE	GENERAL SUBJUNCTIVE	
haben	*wir hatten*	*wir hätten*	we had
			we would have
denken	*wir dachten*	*wir dächten*	we thought
			we would think
bringen	wir brachten	*wir brächten*	we brought
			we would bring

Hätten wir nur mehr Zeit!
    If only we had more time.

Wüßte ich nur seine Adresse!
    If only I knew his address.

The verbs *rennen*, *kennen*, *nennen*, and *brennen* (to burn) retain their present-tense vowel plus the past tense indicator -*t*- to form the present-time general subjunctive:

rennen	*wir rannten*	*wir rennten*	we ran
kennen	*wir kannten*	*wir kennten*	we knew
nennen	*wir nannten*	*wir nennten*	we named
brennen	*wir brannten*	*wir brennten*	we burned

Renntest du wirklich so weit?
    Would you really run that far?

Nennten Sie mir nur Ihren Preis!
    If only you would name your price!

c. STRONG VERBS

In forming the present-time general subjunctive of strong verbs, an umlaut is added to the simple past of verbs with the stem vowel *a*, *o*, or *u*.

ich käme		wir kämen	
du kämest		ihr kämet	
er käme		Sie kämen	

Käme er nur immer pünktlich!
If only he were always on time.

ich wäre		wir waren	
du wärest		ihr wäret	
es wäre		Sie wären	

Wärest du bitte so nett?
Would you please be so kind?

ich würde		wir würden	
du würdest		ihr würdet	
es würde		Sie würden	

Er würde morgen zwanzig Jahre alt, wenn er noch hier wäre.
Tomorrow he would turn twenty years old, if he were still here.

ich riefe an		wir riefen an	
du riefest an		ihr rieft an	
er riefe an		Sie riefen an	

Es wäre am besten, wenn Sie vorbeikämen oder anriefen.
It would be best, if you came by or called.

In the general subjunctive of strong verbs that do not take an umlaut on the vowel, the forms of the first- and third-person plural, and of the second-person formal, are identical with the simple past indicative.

PRESENT-TIME
GENERAL SUBJECTIVE

ich schriebe
du schriebest
sie schriebe

SIMPLE PAST INDICATIVE

wir schrieben
ihr schriebet
Sie schrieben

d. MODAL AUXILIARIES AND THE VERB *WISSEN*

The modal auxiliaries and *wissen* follow the pattern of the weak verbs. *Sollen* and *wollen* have general subjective forms identical to the past tense forms. *Müssen, können, dürfen,* and *mögen* take an umlaut.

INFINITIVE	PAST TENSE	GENERAL SUBJUNCTIVE	
sollen	wir sollten	wir sollten	we should
wollen	wir wollten	wir wollten	we wanted (would want)
müssen	wir mussten	wir müssten	we should
können	wir konnten	wir könnten	we could
dürfen	wir durften	wir dürften	we might
mögen	wir mochten	wir möchten	we would like to
wissen	wir wussten	wir wüssten	we would know

Könnten Sie mir bitte helfen?
Could you help me, please?

Wüsste sein Vater vielleicht die neue Telefonnummer?
Would his father know the new phone number?

e. THE PASSIVE VOICE

The present-time general subjunctive for the passive voice is formed by using the general subjunctive form of the appropriate auxiliary:

INDICATIVE
Die Karten werden zurückgegeben.
The tickets are being returned.

SUBJUNCTIVE
Die Karten würden zurückgegeben.
The tickets would be returned.

INDICATIVE WITH A MODAL AUXILIARY
Die Karten können zurückgegeben werden.
   The tickets can be returned.

SUBJUNCTIVE WITH A MODAL AUXILIARY
Die Karten könnten zurückgegeben werden.
   The tickets could (might) be returned.

3. THE USE OF THE PRESENT-TIME GENERAL SUBJUNCTIVE

The present-time general subjunctive is used for the following purposes:

a. TO EXPRESS HYPOTHETICAL CONDITIONS

Hypothetical conditions are those that are presumed or supposed, rather than factual:

Es wäre am besten, wenn Sie noch einmal vorbeikämen.
   It would be best if you came by again.

Es könnten einige Karten zurückgegeben werden.
   Some tickets might be returned.

b. TO EXPRESS WISHFUL THINKING

Ich wünschte, wir bekämen Plätze im Parkett.
   I wish we'd get seats in the orchestra.

c. TO EXPRESS POLITE REQUESTS

Könnten Sie mir bitte die Plätze auf dem Sitzplan zeigen?
   Could you please show me the seats on the seating plan?

4. THE FORMATION OF THE *WÜRDE* + INFINITIVE CONSTRUCTION

This construction is formed by using the subjunctive form of the auxiliary verb *werden* plus the infinitive of the main verb. As with the future tense, in main clauses the conjugated verb is in second position, and the infinitive is placed at the end of the clause:

Wir würden lieber links von der Bühne sitzen.
We would prefer to sit to the left of the stage.

In subordinate clauses the conjugated verb moves to the end of the clause:

Er fragt, ob sie lieber links sitzen würden.
He asks if they would prefer to sit on the left.

5. THE USE OF THE *WÜRDE* + INFINITIVE CONSTRUCTION

In colloquial speech, this construction is used more and more frequently as an alternate form for the present-time general subjunctive.

ich führe	or	*ich würde fahren*	I would drive
du fielest	or	*du würdest fallen*	you would fall
ihr brächtet	or	*ihr würdet bringen*	you would bring

It is especially used to avoid ambiguity when the forms of the simple past indicative and the present-time general subjunctive are identical. As was pointed out above, these identical forms occur with strong verbs that do not take an umlaut in the past tense form, and with all weak verbs as well.

wir liefen	*wir würden laufen*	we would walk
wir gingen	*wir würden gehen*	we would go
wir arbeiteten	*wir würden arbeiten*	we would work

Note, however, that the *würde* + infinitive construction is not used with *haben, sein,* or the modal auxiliaries.

VOKABELN

das Theater, -	theater
die Theaterkasse, *-n*	theater box office

die Theaterkarte, -n	theater ticket
das Theaterstück, -e	play
die Vorstellung, -en	performance
die Matinée, -s	matinee
der Intendant, -en	director
der Dirigent, -en	conductor
der Autor, -en	author
der Dramatiker, -	playwright
der Schauspieler, -	actor
der Musiker, -	musician
der Sänger, -	singer
der Kassierer, -	cashier
der Theaterbesucher, -	theatergoer
das Publikum	audience
der Platzanweiser, -	usher
die Bühne, -n	stage
der Sitzplan, ⸚e	seating plan
das Parkett	orchestra
der Rang, ⸚	dress circle
der Platz, ⸚e	seat
der Logensitz, -e	box seat
der Mittelgang, ⸚e	middle aisle
der Eingang, ⸚e	entrance
der Ausgang, ⸚e	exit
der Notausgang, ⸚e	emergency exit
das Programm, -e	program
der Akt, -e	act
der Aufzug, ⸚e	act
die Szene, -n	scene
die Pause, -n	intermission
die Rolle, -n	role
nach*fragen	inquire
vorbei*kommen	to come by
hintereinander	one behind the other
ausverkauft	sold out
pünktlich	on time

ÜBUNGEN

A. *Beantworten Sie die Fragen zum Dialog.*

1. *Wieviele Karten möchte der Theaterbesucher?*
2. *Wo säßen er und seine Frau lieber?*
3. *Was würde die Frau sehr freuen?*
4. *Was wäre am besten?*

B. *Suchen Sie die richtige deutsche Übersetzung.*

1. It would be best if you came by again.
2. Would you still have tickets for tonight?
3. Could you tell us where the theater is?
4. We would prefer to sit to the left of the stage.

a. *Wir möchten lieber links von der Bühne sitzen.*
b. *Könnten Sie uns sagen, wo das Theater liegt?*
c. *Hätten Sie noch Plätze für heute Abend?*
d. *Es wäre am besten, wenn Sie noch einmal vorbeikämen.*

C. *Schreiben Sie die Sätze im Konjunktiv II; gebrauchen Sie "würde" +
Infinitiv, wo nötig.* (Form the present-time general subjunctive; use the
würde + infinitive construction, where necessary.)

BEISPIEL: *Können Sie mir den Sitzplan zeigen?*
Könnten Sie mir den Sitzplan zeigen?

Fragen Sie noch einmal nach.
Würden Sie noch einmal nachfragen.

1. *Gibt es noch Plätze im ersten Rang?*
2. *Leider nein, aber wir haben noch etwas im Parkett.*
3. *In welcher Reihe ist das?*
4. *Sind die Parkettplätze viel teurer als der erste Rang?*
5. *Sie kosten nicht mehr, wenn Sie Plätze im zweiten Parkett nehmen.*

D. *Übersetzen Sie.*

1. Could you buy theater tickets for Saturday evening?
2. I would like to see a play again, and you would find it interesting
too.

308

3. You would have to go to the box office before four o'clock.
4. Would you try to get orchestra seats?

KULTURNOTIZ

The German theater has a long tradition dating back to the court theaters *(Hoftheater)* of the many German states in the seventeenth and eighteenth centuries. Germany has many excellent theaters in the larger cities, and Germans are avid theatergoers. A large number of theater enthusiasts have seasonal subscriptions. Germany has several hundred federal theaters *(Staatstheater)*, state theaters *(Landestheater)*, and municipal theaters *(Stadttheater)*, and a smaller number of private theaters. The federal, state, and city theaters are repertory theaters: in every season *(Spielzeit)* they perform a number of plays that alternate daily. Many theaters are heavily subsidized by municipal funds, since the admission charges cover only a minimal part of the costs. Freedom for experimentation exists, since commercial considerations do not play a primary role. There are, however, more and more theaters in recent years that have primarily a commercial interest. These theaters arrange their programs mainly according to public interest, and they are not subsidized at all.

Austrian theater has always been known for its high standards. Vienna's *Burgtheater* is one of Europe's leading theaters. In Austria there are federal theaters, such as the *Burgtheater* and the *Akademietheater* in Vienna, private theaters, and provincial theaters run by provincial or local authorities such as the *Landestheater Salzburg,* or the *Tiroler Landestheater* in Innsbruck.

LÖSUNGEN

A. 1. *Er möchte zwei Karten.* 2. *Sie säßen lieber links von der Bühne und in der Nähe des Notausganges.* 3. *Es würde sie sehr freuen, wenn sie das Theaterstück sehen könnte.* 4. *Es wäre am besten, wenn er am Montag noch einmal nachfragte oder vorbeikäme.*
B. 1.—d   2.—c   3.—b   4.—a
C. 1. *Gäbe*   2. *hätten*   3. *wäre*   4. *Wären*   5. *Sie würden nicht mehr kosten, wenn Sie Plätze im zweiten Parkett nähmen.*
D. 1. *Könntest du Theaterkarten für Samstag Abend kaufen?* 2. *Ich sähe gern einmal wieder ein Theaterstück, und du fändest es auch interessant.* 3. *Du müsstest vor vier Uhr zur Theaterkasse gehen.* 4. *Würdest du versuchen, Parkettplätze zu bekommen?*

SIEBTE WIEDERHOLUNGSAUFGABE

A. *Setzen Sie "als", "wenn", oder "wann" ein. (Fill in* als, wenn, *or* wann.*)*

  1. _____ seine Haare zu lang wurden, ging er zum Friseur.
  2. *Der Friseur fragte,* _____ *er seine Haare das letzte Mal geschnitten hat.*
  3. *Der Mann sagte: Ich weiß es nicht.* _____ *meine Haare zu lang werden, komme ich zu Ihnen.*
  4. *Aber* _____ *ich das letzte Mal bei Ihnen war, war ein Haarschnitt billiger.*

B. *Übersetzen Sie.*

  1. Before he came to New York, he had lived in Zürich.
  2. In Zürich he had had a big house.
  3. In the summer, he had hiked in the mountains.
  4. In the winter, he had read a lot.

C. *Übersetzen Sie. Gebrauchen Sie das Futur.* (Translate. Use the future tense.)

  1. The messenger will bring the medication.
  2. He will probably come in the morning.
  3. Unfortunately, you (pol.) will have to wait.

D. *Schreiben Sie den folgenden Satz (1) in der einfachen Vergangenheit, (2) im Perfekt, (3) im Plusquamperfekt, (4) im Futur. Dann übersetzen Sie die Sätze ins Englische.* [Rewrite the following sentence (1) in the simple past, (2) in the present perfect, (3) in the past perfect, (4) in the future tense. Then translate the sentence into English.]

  Eine Reisetasche wird abgegeben.

E. *Schreiben Sie die Sätze vom Passiv ins Aktiv um und gebrauchen Sie "man". (Change the sentences from the passive voice into the active voice. Use man.)*

BEISPIEL: *Die Arbeit kann pünktlich gemacht werden.*
          Die Arbeit kann man pünktlich machen.

  1. *Die Nummer wird hier eingegeben.*
  2. *Auch Fotos können per E-Mail geschickt werden.*

310

3. *Jedes Dokument im Internet kann gespeichert oder ausgedruckt werden.*

4. *Monatlich muss eine Gebühr bezahlt werden.*

F. *Übersetzen Sie.*

1. *Das Konto ist eröffnet.*
2. *Das Einzahlungsformular ist ausgefüllt.*
3. *Das Geld ist gewechselt.*

G. *Zeigen Sie an, ob "werden" als Hauptverb (a), als Hilfsverb für das Futur (b) oder als Hilfsverb für das Passiv (c) benutzt wird. Dann übersetzen Sie die Sätze ins Englische.* [Show whether *werden* is used as main verb (a), as auxiliary for the future tense (b), or as auxiliary for the passive voice (c). Then translate the sentence into English.]

1. *Ein Medikament wird vom Arzt verschrieben.*
2. *Der Patient wird zur Apotheke gehen.*
3. *Leider werden die Preise augenblicklich immer höher.*
4. *Die Salbe wird eingerieben.*
5. *Die Tabletten werden rot sein.*

H. *Schreiben Sie die Sätze im Konjunktiv II. Benutzen Sie "würde" + Infinitiv, wenn nötig.* (Form the present-time general subjunctive. Use *würde* + infinitive if necessary.)

BEISPIELE: *Können Sie mir helfen?*
        Könnten Sie mir helfen?

        Geben Sie mir das.
        Würden Sie mir das bitte geben.

1. *Wir sitzen lieber links von der Bühne.*
2. *Können wir die Karten zurückgeben?*
3. *Weiß sein Vater vielleicht, wo er wohnt?*
4. *Sollen wir das Haus lieber nicht kaufen?*

LÖSUNGEN

A. 1. *Als* 2. *wann* 3. *Wenn* 4. *als*
B. 1. *Bevor er nach New York kam, hatte er in Zürich gelebt.* 2. *In Zürich hatte er ein großes Haus gehabt.* 3. *Im Sommer war er in den Bergen gewandert.* 4. *Im Winter hatte er viel gelesen.*

C. 1. *Der Bote wird die Medizin bringen.* 2. *Er wird wahrscheinlich am Morgen kommen.* 3. *Leider werden Sie warten müssen.*

D. 1. *Eine Reisetasche wurde abgegeben.* A travel bag was handed in. 2. *Eine Reisetasche ist abgegeben worden.* A travel bag has been handed in. 3. *Eine Reisetasche war abgegeben worden.* A travel bag had been handed in. 4. *Eine Reisetasche wird abgegeben werden.* A travel bag will be handed in.

E. 1. *Die Nummer kann man hier eingeben.* 2. *Auch Fotos kann man per E-Mail schicken.* 3. *Man kann jedes Dokument im Internet speichern oder ausdrucken.* 4. *Man muss monatlich eine Gebühr bezahlen.*

F. 1. The account is opened. 2. The deposit slip is filled out. 3. The money has been changed.

G. 1.—c: A medication is being prescribed by the doctor. 2.—b: The patient will go to the pharmacy. 3.—a: Unfortunately, prices are getting higher and higher right now. 4.—c: The salve is rubbed in. 5.—b: The pills will be red.

H. 1. *Wir würden lieber links von der Bühne sitzen.* 2. *Könnten wir die Karten zurückgeben?* 3. *Wüsste sein Vater vielleicht, wo er wohnt?* 4. *Sollten wir das Haus lieber nicht kaufen?*

LEKTION 36

A. DIALOG

Wählen gehen—ja oder nein?

HERR BRIGGE: Es soll schon wieder eine Steuererhöhung geben.

FRAU BRIGGE: Warum beklagst du dich? Nur wenn du in den letzten Wahlen zur Urne gegangen wärest, hättest du jetzt ein Recht, dich zu beschweren.

HERR BRIGGE: Unsinn. Als ob meine Stimme einen Unterschied gemacht hätte.

FRAU BRIGGE: Wenn alle Wähler so dächten, gäbe es keine Demokratie mehr.

HERR BRIGGE: Für welche Partei hätte ich denn meine Stimme abgeben sollen? Im Wahlkampf versprechen alle Politiker Steuersenkung, Rentenerhöhung, Beseitigung der Arbeitslosigkeit, soziale Gerechtigkeit und das Blaue vom Himmel.

FRAU BRIGGE: Aber du kennst doch die unterschiedlichen Ziele der CDU, SPD, FDP, der Grünen und der Splitterparteien.

HERR BRIGGE: Und du stimmst doch wohl mit mir überein, dass keine meine Interessen ganz vertritt.

FRAU BRIGGE: Klar. Aber du hättest für die Partei wählen können, die unsere Interessen am besten vertritt.

Voting—Yes or No?

MR. BRIGGE: There is supposedly going to be another tax increase.

MRS. BRIGGE: Why do you complain? Only if you had voted in the last election would you now have a right to complain.

MR. BRIGGE: Nonsense. As if my vote would have made a difference.

MRS. BRIGGE: If all voters thought like that, there would be no more democracy.

MR. BRIGGE: And for which party should I have cast my vote? In the campaign all politicians promise a tax decrease, a pension increase, the elimination of unemployment, social justice, and the moon.

MRS. BRIGGE: But you know the different goals of the Christian Democratic Union, the Social Democratic Party of Germany, the Free Democratic Party, the Green Party, and the splinter parties.

MR. BRIGGE: And you agree with me that none of them really represents my interests fully.

MRS. BRIGGE: Of course. But you could have voted for the party that best represents our interests.

B. GRAMMATIK UND GEBRAUCH

1. THE PAST-TIME GENERAL SUBJUNCTIVE

The past-time general subjunctive expresses wishes, hypothetical conclusions, and contrary-to-fact conditions in the past. There is only one past tense for the general subjunctive. It is formed by using the subjunctive of *haben* or *sein* + past participle.

Es hätte keinen Unterschied gemacht.
It wouldn't have made any difference.

Er wäre zur Urne gegangen.
He would have voted.

Ich hätte gewählt.
I would have voted.

Du hättest übereingestimmt.
You would have agreed.

Er hätte uns vertreten.
He would have represented us.

Wir hätten keine Steuererhöhung gehabt.
We wouldn't have had a tax increase.

Ihr hättet euch beschwert.
    You would have complained.

Sie hätten sich nicht beklagt.
    They/You would not have complained.

Ich wäre zur Urne gegangen.
    I would have voted.

Du wärest glücklich gewesen.
    You would have been happy.

Er wäre Sieger geworden.
    He would have been the winner.

Wir wären nach Berlin gefahren.
    We would have traveled to Berlin.

Ihr wäret zu uns gekommen.
    You would have come to us.

Sie wären zu Hause geblieben.
    They/You would have stayed home.

2. THE PAST-TIME GENERAL SUBJUNCTIVE OF MODALS

Modals may be used with or without a dependent infinitive.

a. The past-time general subjunctive of models without a dependent infinitive is formed by using a subjunctive form of *haben* + the past participle of the modal.

Ich hätte das nicht gedurft.
    I would not have been allowed to do that.

Er hätte es nicht gekonnt.
    He couldn't have done that.

Wir hätten es nicht gesollt.
    We weren't supposed to do it.

Ihr hättet es nicht gewollt.
    You wouldn't have wanted it.

Sie hätten es nicht gemocht.
    They/You would not have liked it.

b. The past-time general subjunctive of models with a dependent infinitive is formed by using a subjunctive form of *haben* + the infinitive of the dependent verb + the infinitive of the modal.

Ich hätte für ihn wählen sollen.
    I should have voted for him.

Du hättest mit mir übereinstimmen können.
    You could have agreed with me.

Er hätte uns vertreten müssen.
    He should have represented us.

Wir hätten mit ihm sprechen dürfen.
    We should have been allowed to speak with him.

Ihr hättet ihn vielleicht sehen mögen.
    Perhaps you would have liked to see him.

Sie hätten sich beklagen können.
    They/You could have complained.

3. THE CONDITIONAL

In English a conditional sentence consists of an if-clause and a conclusion:

if-clause   conclusion
If all voters thought like that,   (then) there would be no democracy.

In German too, a conditional sentence consists of a *wenn* (if)-clause and a conclusion. The *wenn*-clause is a dependent clause, so the conjugated, or finite, verb has to be in the last position. The main clause or conclusion, if it follows the if-clause, starts with the finite verb.

if-clause   conclusion
Wenn alle Wähler so dächten,   *(dann) gäbe es keine Demokratie.*
If all voters thought like that,   (then) there would be no democracy.

A condition may or may not be contrary to fact.

Not contrary to fact: If people vote, democracy exists. (The speaker considers this a fact.)

316

Contrary to fact: If I were president, I would change everything. (The speaker knows that she/he is not president.)

a. If a condition is stated that is not contrary to fact, the indicative is used.

Wenn alle Wähler so denken, (dann) gibt es keine Demokratie.
If all voters think like that, (then) there will be no democracy.

Wenn er wählt, (dann) ist er zufrieden.
If he votes, he will be content.

Wenn die Steuern niedrig sind, (dann) beklagt er sich nicht.
If taxes are low, (then) he won't complain.

b. If a condition is stated that is contrary to fact, the subjunctive is used. If the contrary to fact condition is stated in the present, the present-time subjunctive is used.

Wenn alle Wähler so dächten, (dann) gäbe es keine Demokratie/(dann) würde es keine Demokratie geben.
If all voters thought like that, (then) there would be no democracy.

Wenn er wählte, (dann) ginge er jetzt zur Urne/(dann) würde er jetzt zur Urne gehen.
If he were to vote, (then) he would go to the polls now.

Wenn die Steuern niedrig wären, (dann) beklagte er sich nicht/(dann) würde er sich nicht beklagen.
If taxes were low, (then) he wouldn't complain.

Note: The *würde* + infinitive construction is usually not used in the *wenn-* clause.

c. If a contrary-to-fact condition is stated in the past, the past-time subjunctive is used.

Wenn alle Wähler so gedacht hätten, (dann) hätte es keine Demokratie gegeben.
If all voters had thought like that, (then) there would not have been any democracy.

Wenn er gestern gewählt hätte, (dann) wäre er zufriedener gewesen.
If he had voted yesterday, (then) he would have been more content.

Wenn die Steuern letztes Jahr niedrig gewesen wären, (dann) hätte er sich nicht beklagt.

If taxes had been low last year, (then) he wouldn't have complained.

Note: The *würde* + infinitive construction is not used in the past-time subjunctive.

d. Sometimes the *wenn*-clause follows the conclusion. Then the word order in the main clause changes: the finite verb has to be in the second position.

PRESENT-TIME GENERAL SUBJUNCTIVE

Er würde sich nicht beklagen, wenn die Steuern jetzt niedrig wären.

He wouldn't complain if taxes were low now.

PAST-TIME GENERAL SUBJUNCTIVE

Er hätte sich nicht beklagt, wenn die Steuern niedrig gewesen wären.

He wouldn't have complained, if taxes had been low.

4. THE CONJUNCTIONS *ALS WENN* AND *ALS OB*

The conjunctions *als wenn* and *als ob* are interchangeable; both mean "as if," "as though." Both introduce a dependent clause, so the finite verb has to be in the last position. In addition, both introduce statements that require the subjunctive. The present-time subjunctive is used if the statement refers to the present.

Als ob das jetzt einen Unterschied machte.

As if that would make a difference now.

Als wenn er das wüsste.

As if he knew it.

The past-time subjunctive is used in statements that refer to the past.

Als wenn das einen Unterschied gemacht hätte.

As if that would have made a difference.

Als ob er das gewusst hätte.

As if he had known that.

VOKABELN

die Wahl, *-en*	election
die Bundestagswahl, *-en*	federal election
die Landtagswahl, *-en*	state election
die Kommunalwahl, *-en*	local election
der Wahlkampf, *¨e*	political campaign
das Wahlergebnis, *-se*	election result
der Wähler, *-*	male voter
die Wählerin, *-nen*	female voter
wählen	to vote
die Stimme, *-n*	vote, voice
seine Stimme abgeben	to cast one's vote, to vote
zur Urne gehen	to go to the polls, to cast one's vote
überein*stimmen	to agree
nicht überein*stimmen	to disagree
sich beschweren	to complain
sich beklagen	to complain
das Recht, *-e*	right, law
ein Recht haben	to have a right
vertreten, *vertrat, vertreten*	to represent
die Demokratie, *-n*	democracy
die Politik	politics
der Politiker, *-*	male politician
die Politikerin, *-nen*	female politician
versprechen, *versprach, versprochen*	to promise
das Blaue vom Himmel versprechen	to promise the moon
die Steuererhöhung, *-en*	tax increase
die Steuersenkung, *-en*	tax decrease
die Arbeitslosigkeit	unemployment
die Vollbeschäftigung	full employment
die Wiedervereinigung	reunification
die Gerechtigkeit	justice
die Partei, *-en*	party (political)
die Splitterpartei, *-en*	splinter party
die Christlich-Demokratische Union (CDU)	the Christian Democratic Union

die Sozialdemokratische Partei Deutschlands (SPD)	the Social Democratic Party of Germany
die Freie Demokratische Partei (FDP)	the Free Democratic Party
die Grünen	the Green Party

ÜBUNGEN

A. *Beantworten Sie die Fragen zum Dialog.*

1. *Worüber beklagt sich Herr Brigge?*
2. *Warum hat Herr Brigge kein Recht sich zu beschweren?*
3. *Wie heißen die vier größten Parteien in Deutschland?*
4. *Für welche Partei hätte Herr Brigge wählen sollen?*

B. *Suchen Sie die richtige deutsche Übersetzung.*

1. He votes in every election.
2. She promises social justice.
3. He complains about the low pensions.
4. The party represents the interests of the voters.
5. As if it would have made a difference.
6. The campaign could have been longer.

a. *Sie verspricht soziale Gerechtigkeit.*
b. *Der Wahlkampf hätte länger sein können.*
c. *Er beschwert sich über die niedrige Pension.*
d. *Die Partei vertritt die Interessen der Wähler.*
e. *Als ob das einen Unterschied gemacht hätte.*
f. *Er wählt in jeder Wahl.*

C. *Schreiben Sie die Sätze in der Vergangenheit im Konjunktiv II, falls nicht anders angezeigt. Dann übersetzen Sie die neuen Sätze.* (Rewrite the sentences in the past-time of the general subjunctive, unless indicated otherwise. Then translate the new sentences.)

BEISPIEL: *Als ob meine Stimme einen Unterschied machen würde.*
Als ob meine Stimme einen Unterschied gemacht hätte.
As if my vote would have made a difference.

1. *Er tut, als ob er nicht an die Demokratie glauben würde. (Change tun to the simple past, indicative.)*
2. *Wenn er wählte, würde seine Stimme zählen.*
3. *Er sollte das machen.*
4. *Seine Frau würde mit ihm übereinstimmen.*
5. *Dann könnte er sich jetzt beklagen.*

KULTURNOTIZ

Germany is a federal republic *(Bundesrepublik)* with a parliamentary form of democracy. Elections for the house of representatives *(Bundestag)* are held every four years. All German citizens eighteen and older have the right to vote *(Wahlrecht)*. German citizens have two votes, a first vote *(Erststimme)* and a second vote *(Zweitstimme)*. Citizens cast their first vote for a particular candidate *(Kandidat)* and their second vote for a particular party. The candidate one votes for does not have to be a member of the party one votes for. Voter turnout *(Wahlbeteiligung)* is fairly high, in most elections between 80 percent and 90 percent.

If a party wants to be represented in parliament, it has to have at least 5 percent of the vote. Parties on the extreme right or left usually do not overcome the 5 percent barrier. The three major parties—the Christian Democratic Union *(CDU,* also called the Christian Social Union, or *CSU,* in Bavaria), the Social Democratic Party *(SPD),* and the Free Democratic Party *(FDP)*— have left and right wings, as does the smaller Green Party *(die Grünen).*

LÖSUNGEN

A. 1. *Er beklagt sich über die Steuererhöhung.* 2. *Er ist in den letzten Wahlen nicht zur Urne gegangen.* 3. *Die vier größten Parteien heißen CDU, SPD, FDP und die Grünen.* 4. *Er hätte für die Partei wählen sollen, die am besten seine Interessen vertritt.*
B. 1.—f 2.—a 3.—c 4.—d 5.—e 6.—b
C. 1. *Er tat, als ob er nicht an die Demokratie geglaubt hätte.* He acted as if he didn't believe in democracy. 2. *Wenn er gewählt hätte, hätte seine Stimme gezählt.* If he had voted, his vote would have counted. 3. *Er hätte das machen sollen.* He should have done it. 4. *Seine Frau hätte mit ihm übereingestimmt.* His wife would have agreed with him. 5. *Dann hätte er sich beklagen können.* Then he could have complained.

LEKTION 37

A. DIALOG I

Karneval/Fasching.

MARION: Erika hat mir gesagt, dass sie mir ihre Karten für den Maskenball am Rosenmontag schenke. Sie brauche sie nicht, weil sie nach Köln zum Umzug fahre. Hättest du Lust mitzumachen?

SABINE: Natürlich. Das ist hier das beste und verrückteste Fest. Aber wie verkleiden wir uns?

MARION: Erika meinte, ich solle als Katze gehen.

SABINE: Dann trage ich mein altes Hundekostüm. Niemand wird uns erkennen.

MARION: Großartig. Die Feste hören gar nicht mehr auf.

SABINE: Genieß die schöne Zeit! Am Aschermittwoch beginnt die Fastenzeit.

Carnival.

MARION: Erika told me that she's going to give me her tickets for the costume ball on Rose Monday. She doesn't need them because she is going to Cologne for the parade. Would you like to join me?

SABINE: Of course. Around here that's the best and craziest celebration. But how are we going to dress up?

MARION: Erika thought I should go as a cat.

SABINE: Then I'll wear my old dog costume. Nobody will recognize us.

MARION: Great. The parties never stop.

SABINE: Enjoy the good times. On Ash Wednesday, Lent will start.

B. DIALOG II

Kirchweih.

TOURIST: Ich habe gelesen, dass heute hier im Dorf ein großer Feiertag sei.

EINHEIMISCHER: Ja, heute ist Kirchweih. Deshalb hängen hier doch überall die Fahnen und Girlanden. In einer Viertelstunde ziehen die Trachtengruppen mit der Kapelle auf.

TOURIST: Danke. Ich hole schnell meinen Photoapparat.

A Parish Fair.

TOURIST: I read that there was going to be a big holiday here.

LOCAL CITIZEN: Yes, today is a parish fair. That's why flags and garlands are hung everywhere. In a quarter of an hour, the costumed groups are going to march in with the band.

TOURIST: Thanks. I'll fetch my camera at once.

C. GRAMMATIK UND GEBRAUCH

1. THE FORMS OF THE PRESENT-TIME SPECIAL SUBJUNCTIVE

Besides the general subjunctive, German also has a special subjunctive* or subjunctive I *(Konjunktiv I)*. The present-time special subjunctive is formed by adding the subjunctive endings to the infinitive stem of the verb.

*Many texts, including the advanced level of this series, use the term *Konjunktiv I*. For descriptive purposes, you will see the term "special subjunctive" in this course.

ich schenke
du schenkest
er schenke

wir schenken
ihr schenket
sie schenken
Sie schenken

The present-time special subjunctive of the verb *sein* is slightly irregular.

ich sei
du seiest
es sei

wir seien
ihr seiet
sie seien
Sie seien

Since most of the forms of the special subjunctive are close or identical to the indicative, only the forms of *sein* and the second- and third-person singular of most other verbs are frequently used.

2. THE USE OF THE SPECIAL SUBJUNCTIVE: INDIRECT DISCOURSE

The special subjunctive is mostly used in indirect discourse. In indirect discourse one person reports what another person has said without quoting him or her directly.

DIRECT DISCOURSE
Erika sagt: "Ich schenke dir meine Karten."
Erika says: "I'm giving you my tickets."

INDIRECT DISCOURSE
Erika sagt, sie schenkt mir ihre Karten.
Erika sagt, sie schenke mir ihre Karten.
Erika says she's giving me her tickets.

or:

Erika sagt, dass sie mir ihre Karten schenkt.
Erika sagt, dass sie mir ihre Karten schenke.
Erika says that she's giving me her tickets.

Note that in indirect discourse the personal pronoun and the possessive adjective shift to the perspective of the speaker.

In German the subjunctive is frequently used in indirect discourse, especially in lengthy indirect quotes. In newspaper writing and formal writing the subjunctive is always used. In colloquial German, it may or may not be used. In indirect discourse the special and general subjunctive can be used interchangeably, but the general subjunctive often indicates a higher degree of doubt.

Sie sagt, sie komme.	*Sie sagt, sie käme.*
She says she's coming.	She says she's coming. (But maybe she won't.)

Usually the form of the subjunctive that is most clearly different from the indicative will be used. This eliminates almost all forms of the special subjunctive except for the second- and third-person singular and the verb *sein*.

Er sagt, hier sei ein Fest.
He says there'll be a festival here.

Frequently people will also say:

Er sagt, hier wäre ein Fest.
He says there'll be a festival here.

In German, if the direct quote is in the present tense, the indirect quote will be in the present tense indicative or the present-time subjunctive. The tense of the introductory statement does not matter.

Present:	*Sie sagt, sie trage ihr Kostüm.*
Simple Past:	*Sie sagte, sie trage ihr Kostüm.*
Present Perfect:	*Sie hat gesagt, sie trage ihr Kostüm.*
Past Perfect:	*Sie hatte gesagt, sie trage ihr Kostüm.*

VOKABELN

das Fest, -e	party, celebration, festival
die Feier, -n	celebration, ceremony
der Festtag, -e	holiday
die Kirchweih(e)	parish festival, church fair
der Feiertag, -e	holiday, day of rest
der Nationalfeiertag, -e	national holiday
der kirchliche Feiertag, -e	religious holiday
feiern	to celebrate
Neujahr	New Year
der Karneval	carnival (period before Lent)
der Fasching	carnival
der Rosenmontag	Rose Monday, the Monday before Lent
die Fastenzeit	Lent
der Aschermittwoch	Ash Wednesday
der Karfreitag	Good Friday
Ostern	Easter
Pfingsten	Pentecost, Whitsuntide
Himmelfahrt	Ascension Day
Weihnachten	Christmas
der Umzug, ¨e	parade
die Kapelle, -n	band
die Fahne, -n	flag
die Girlande, -n	garland
auf*ziehen, zog auf, aufgezogen	to parade, to march up
mit*machen	to participate
der Ball, ¨e	ball
der Maskenball	costume ball
erkennen, erkannte, erkannt	to recognize
genießen, genoß, genossen	to enjoy
die Tracht, -en	local costume
das Dorf, ¨er	the village
der Einheimische, -n	local resident

ÜBUNGEN

A. *Beantworten Sie die Fragen zum Dialog.*

1. *Was für Karten will Erika Marion schenken?*
2. *Was sagt Sabine über den Maskenball?*
3. *Wie will Sabine sich verkleiden?*
4. *Wann beginnt die Fastenzeit?*
5. *Was für ein Fest ist im Dorf?*

B. *Suchen Sie die richtige deutsche Übersetzung.*

1. I'm dressing up as a cat.
2. I'm wearing my costume.
3. I'm going (driving) to the parade.
4. The parties never stop.
5. Today is Ash Wednesday.
6. People say that the carnival is craziest in Cologne.
7. Soon the costumed groups will march in.
8. Flags and garlands are hung everywhere.

a. *Ich fahre zum Umzug.*
b. *Überall hängen Fahnen und Girlanden.*
c. *Bald ziehen die Trachtengruppen auf.*
d. *Ich verkleide mich als Katze.*
e. *Ich trage mein Kostüm.*
f. *Heute ist Aschermittwoch.*
g. *Man sagt, dass der Karneval in Köln am verrücktesten sei.*
h. *Die Feste hören gar nicht auf.*

C. *Ändern Sie die indirekte Rede zur direkten Rede.* (Change the indirect discourse to direct.)

BEISPIEL: *Sie sagt, dass das Fest schön sei.*
            Sie sagt: "Das Fest ist schön."

1. *Sie sagt, dass heute ein Feiertag sei.*
2. *Sie sagt, dass viele Kapellen kämen.*
3. *Sie meint, sie trage ihr Kostüm.*

D. *Übersetzen Sie.*

    1. *Man sagt, dass es in Deutschland viele Feste gäbe.*
    2. *Das schönste Fest sei vielleicht Weihnachten.*

KULTURNOTIZ

The period before Lent, called *Karneval* in the Rhine region and *Fasching* in southern Germany, is celebrated in all parts of Germany where Catholics are in the majority. Usually the celebrations culminate on the Monday before Lent *(Rosenmontag)* with a parade *(Umzug)* of floats and of local citizens dressed as fools. The most famous parade takes place in Cologne *(Köln)*.

Kirchweih—also called *Kirmes, Kirchtag,* or *Jahrmarkt* in different regions of Germany—is usually celebrated on the day the local church was consecrated. In larger communities, an annual market and an amusement fair are commonly part of the festival. In small rural communities in southern Germany, Austria, and Switzerland, people wear their local costumes *(Trachten),* and local bands *(Kapellen)* play regional tunes. Often people from surrounding villages will get together and have dances and parties.

LÖSUNGEN

A. 1. *Sie will ihr ihre Karten für den Maskenball am Rosenmontag schenken. 2. Sie sagt, dass es das beste und verrückteste Fest sei. 3. Sabine will ihr Hundekostüm tragen. 4. Am Aschermittwoch beginnt die Fastenzeit. 5. Im Dorf ist heute Kirchweih.*
B. 1.—d   2.—e   3.—a   4.—h   5.—f   6.—g   7.—c   8.—b
C. 1. *Sie sagt: "Heute ist ein Feiertag." 2. Sie sagt: "Viele Kapellen kommen." 3. Sie meint: "Ich trage mein Kostüm."*
D. 1. People say (that) there are lots of festivals in Germany. 2. Perhaps the nicest holiday is Christmas.

LEKTION 38

DIE MEDIEN.   The Media.

A. DIALOG

Information ist alles.

INTERVIEWLEITER: Wie haben sich Ihre Telefon-Interview-Teilnehmer in den letzten Wochen über Aktuelles informiert?

INTERVIEWER: Der Erste erklärte, dass er die Nachrichten meistens im Radio gehört habe.

INTERVIEWLEITER: Das mache ich auch.

INTERVIEWER: Der Zweite sagte, er informiere sich durch die Tagesschau im Fernsehen. Er habe meistens das Dritte Programm eingeschaltet. Außerdem habe er eine Tageszeitung gelesen.

INTERVIEWLEITER: Haben Sie auch eine Frau interviewt?

INTERVIEWER: Ja, eine Film-Enthusiastin. Sie werde sich in Zukunft durch Zeitschriften auf dem Laufenden halten.

INTERVIEWLEITER: Haben alle Befragten kooperiert?

INTERVIEWER: Nein, einer wurde wütend. Er habe noch nicht einmal seinen Mantel ablegen können, da habe er schon das Telefon beantworten müssen.

INTERVIEWLEITER: Er habe das gemusst, sagte er? Das finde ich witzig. Wir haben ihn ja wohl kaum dazu gezwungen.

Information Is Everything.

INTERVIEW DIRECTOR: Through which media have your telephone interview participants informed themselves about current events over the past few weeks?

INTERVIEWER: The first one explained that he had mostly listened to the news on the radio.

INTERVIEW DIRECTOR: I do that, too.

INTERVIEWER: The second one said he was staying informed through the news on television. He had mostly tuned in to Channel Three. In addition, he had read a daily newspaper.

INTERVIEW DIRECTOR: Did you also interview a woman?

INTERVIEWER: Yes, a movie fan. In the future she'll keep abreast of the news through magazines.

INTERVIEW DIRECTOR: Did all of the people questioned cooperate?

INTERVIEWER: No, one was furious. He said he hadn't even been able to take off his coat yet when he had to answer the telephone.

INTERVIEW DIRECTOR: He had to do it, he said? I find that funny. We hardly forced him to.

B. GRAMMATIK UND GEBRAUCH

1. THE PAST-TIME SPECIAL SUBJUNCTIVE

The past-time special subjunctive is composed of the special subjunctive forms of the auxiliaries *haben* or *sein* plus the past participle of the verb:

Er sagte, er habe meistens das Dritte Programm eingeschaltet.
He said he had mostly tuned in to Channel Three.

Die Film-Enthusiastin sagte, sie sei jede Woche in ein Kino gegangen.
The movie fan said she had gone to a theater every week.

2. THE PAST-TIME SPECIAL SUBJUNCTIVE OF MODALS

a. The past-time special subjunctive of models without a dependent infinitive is composed of the special subjunctive of *haben* plus the past participle of the modal:

Er sagte, er habe das gemusst.   He said he had to do it.

b. The past-time special subjunctive of modals with a dependent infinitive is composed of the special subjunctive of *haben* plus the infinitive of the dependent verb plus the infinitive of the modal:

Er habe noch nicht seinen Mantel abnehmen können, da habe er schon das Telefon beantworten müssen.
He hadn't been able to take off his coat yet when he had to answer the telephone.

3. THE FUTURE-TIME SPECIAL SUBJUNCTIVE

The future-time special subjunctive is composed of the special subjunctive of the auxiliary *werden* plus the infinitive of the verb:

Sie werde sich in Zukunft durch Zeitschriften auf dem Laufenden halten.
In the future she'll keep abreast of the news through magazines.

The special subjunctive forms of *werden* are:

ich werde	*wir werden*
du werdest	*ihr werdet*
er werde	*sie werden*
	Sie werden

Only the second- and third-person singular of the special subjunctive of *werden* differ from the indicative. When the special subjunctive and indicative forms are the same, the general subjunctive must be used:

Sie antworten, sie würden (werden) sich besser informieren.
They answered that they would inform themselves better.

VOKABELN

die **Massenmedien** (pl.)	mass media
der **Fernseher**, -	television set

fern*sehen	to watch TV
im Fernsehen	on TV
im Radio	on the radio
das Zweite Programm	Channel Two
der Sender, -	station
die Nachricht, *-en*	news
die Nachrichten (pl.)	news broadcast
einschalten	to tune in, to turn on
der Film, *-e*	film, movie
der Film-Enthusiast,	male movie fan
-en, -en	
die Film-Enthusiastin, *-nen*	female movie fan
die Presse	press
die Zeitung, *-en*	newspaper
die Zeitschrift, *-en*	magazine
das Videogerät, *-e*	VCR
aktuell	current, topical
das Aktuelle	current events
die Tagesschau, *-en*	daily newsreel
das Interview, *-s*	interview
der Interviewleiter, -	interview director
interviewen	to interview
der Befragte, *-n*	male interviewee
die Befragte, *-n*	female interviewee
der Teilnehmer, -	participant
sich informieren über (+ acc.)	to inform oneself about, to stay informed
sich orientieren	to orient oneself
sich auf dem Laufenden halten	to keep abreast of the news, to stay informed
kooperieren	to cooperate
beantworten	to answer
wütend sein	to be furious
witzig	witty, funny
zwingen, *zwang, gezwungen*	to force

ÜBUNGEN

A. *Beantworten Sie die Fragen zum Dialog.*

1. *Was erklärte der erste Interview-Teilnehmer?*
2. *Was sagte der Zweite?*
3. *Was tat der Zweite außerdem?*
4. *Warum war einer wütend?*

B. *Suchen Sie die richtige deutsche Übersetzung.*

1. How do you stay informed?
2. Did all of the people questioned cooperate?
3. In the future she'll keep abreast of the news through magazines.
4. He said he had mostly tuned in to Channel Three.
5. Now she's bought a video system.

a. *Er sagte, er habe meistens das Dritte Programm eingeschaltet.*
b. *Wie informieren Sie sich?*
c. *Sie habe (hat) jetzt ein Videogerät gekauft.*
d. *Sie werde (wird) sich in Zukunft durch Zeitschriften auf dem Laufenden halten.*
e. *Haben alle Befragten kooperiert?*

C. *Verwandeln Sie die direkten Aussage-Sätze in indirekte Aussagen unter Verwendung von Konjunktiv I.* (Change the direct to indirect discourse using the special subjunctive.)

BEISPIEL: *Er sagte: "Ich hatte noch nicht meinen Mantel abgelegt, da läutete schon das Telefon."*
Er sagte, er habe noch nicht seinen Mantel abgelegt, da habe schon das Telefon geläutet.

1. *Der Erste bemerkte: "Ich hörte die Nachrichten im Radio."*
2. *Olaf sagte: "Das mache ich auch."*
3. *Der Zweite sagte: "Ich informiere mich durch die Tagesschau im Fernsehen. Ich habe meistens das Dritte Programm eingeschaltet. Außerdem habe ich eine Tageszeitung gelesen."*
4. *Die Frau informierte mich: "Ich bin jede Woche in ein Kino gegangen, das eine Wochenschau zeigt."*
5. *Sie sagte auch: "Ich werde mich in Zukunft durch Zeitschriften auf dem Laufenden halten."*

D. *Setzen Sie die folgenden Sätze in die Vergangenheit des Konjunktiv I.*
   (Put the following sentences in the past-time special subjunctive.)

BEISPIEL: *Er sagte, er lese eine Tageszeitung.*
   Er sagte, er habe eine Tageszeitung gelesen.
   Er sagte, dass er eine Tageszeitung gelesen habe.

1. *Er sagte, er sehe fern.*
2. *Das Programm sei interessant.*
3. *Es informiere ihn über Aktuelles.*
4. *Er schalte das Erste Programm ein.*

E. *Übersetzen Sie.*

1. He asked if she had seen the daily newsreel on TV.
2. She answered that she had stayed informed through newspapers and magazines.
3. He also said that his friend prefers to listen to the news on the radio.

KULTURNOTIZ

In Germany, Austria, and Switzerland, almost everyone has access to both radio and TV. Germans, Austrians, and the Swiss are avid readers of newspapers as well. The German constitution guarantees the freedom of the press. There is no censorship.

Germany has two national public TV networks, the *ARD (Allgemeine Deutsche Rundfunkanstalten)*, colloquially called the first program *(das Erste Programm)* and the *ZDF (Zweites Deutsches Fernsehen)*, colloquially called the second program *(das Zweite Programm)*. The third program *(das Dritte Programm)*, featuring regional broadcasts, is produced by affiliated stations of the *ARD* throughout Germany. There are also many cable programs *(Kabelprogramme)*, which are run privately.

The radio stations broadcast entertainment, music, politics, sports, regional news, plays, operas, and literary and science series. Special programs for foreign workers *(Gastarbeiter)* are offered in various languages.

Public TV and radio programs are not interrupted by advertising. Commercials are shown in clusters in the early evening. Public TV and radio are financed primarily by fees from the viewers and listeners for each television owned. As in the United States, cable TV is financed through a monthly charge and advertising.

In Germany, Austria, and Switzerland, every city or region has its own local newspaper, which is read by local residents. In addition to these local newspapers, there are several widely read national newspapers such as the *Süddeutsche Zeitung*, published in Munich, the *Frankfurter Allgemeine Zeitung* (colloquially just called the *FAZ)*, published in Frankfurt, and *Die Zeit*, published in Hamburg. The most widely read German newspaper is the *Bild-Zeitung*, which is published in Hamburg and caters to a tabloid audience. The most widely read newspaper in the German-speaking part of Switzerland is the *Neue Zürcher Zeitung*, and in Austria many people read the *Kronenzeitung*, published in Vienna, or the *Wiener Kurier* and *Der Standard*.

LÖSUNGEN

A. 1. *Er erklärte, dass er im Radio die Nachrichten gehört habe.* 2. *Er sagte, er informiere sich durch die Tagesschau im Fernsehen.* 3. *Er sagte, außerdem habe er eine Tageszeitung gelesen.* 4. *Er sagte, er habe noch nicht seinen Mantel ablegen können, da habe er schon das Telefon beantworten müssen.*

B. 1.—b   2.—e   3.—d   4.—a   5.—c

C. 1. *Er bemerkte, er habe die Nachrichten im Radio gehört.* 2. *Olaf sagte, er mache das auch.* 3. *Der Zweite sagte, er informiere sich durch die Tagesschau im Fernsehen. Er habe meistens das Dritte Programm eingeschaltet. Außerdem habe er eine Tageszeitung gelesen.* 4. *Die Frau informierte mich, sie sei jede Woche in ein Kino gegangen, das eine Wochenschau zeige.* 5. *Sie sagte auch, dass sie sich in Zukunft durch Zeitschriften auf dem Laufenden halten werde.*

D. 1. *Er sagte, dass er ferngesehen habe.* 2. *Das Programm sei interessant gewesen.* 3. *Es habe ihn über Aktuelles informiert.* 4. *Er habe das Erste Programm eingeschaltet.*

E. 1. *Er fragte, ob sie die Tagesschau im Fernsehen gesehen habe.* 2. *Sie antwortete, dass sie sich durch Zeitungen und Zeitschriften informiert habe.* 3. *Er sagte auch, sein Freund höre lieber die Nachrichten im Radio.*

LEKTION 39

MUSEEN. Museums.

A. DIALOG

Im Museum.

KARIN: Wie gefällt dir diese Ausstellung?

SARAH: Die meisten Gemälde und Plastiken finde ich ein bisschen seltsam. Ich kann damit nichts anfangen.

KARIN: Möchtest du noch einen Raum anschauen, oder sollen wir ein anderes Mal wiederkommen?

SARAH: Vielleicht könnten wir eine andere Periode wählen.

KARIN: Wie wär's mit der Malerei des Mittelalters oder der Gemäldegalerie des achtzehnten Jahrhunderts?

SARAH: Ich würde sehr gern die orientalische Abteilung ansehen.

KARIN: Heute ist die leider nicht auf. Was hast du denn noch gern?

SARAH: Ich mag Kunstgewerbe. Gibt es nicht eine Sonderausstellung über moderne Töpferei und Glas?

KARIN: Ja, und die ist nur noch drei Tage geöffnet. Dein Vorschlag gefällt mir gut. Ich sehe besonders gern Keramikstücke. Dann stelle ich mir vor, wie die bei mir aussehen würden.

At the Museum.

KARIN: How do you like this exhibition?

SARAH: I find most of the pictures and sculptures a bit strange. I can't relate to them.

KARIN: Would you like to look at another room, or shall we come again at another time?

SARAH: Perhaps we could choose another period.

KARIN: How about medieval paintings, or the picture gallery of the eighteenth century?

SARAH: I would very much like to see the Oriental collection.

KARIN: Unfortunately, it's closed today. What else do you like?

SARAH: I like arts and crafts. Isn't there a special exhibit of modern pottery and glass?

KARIN: Yes, and it's only going to be there for another three days. I like your suggestion very much. I especially like to see ceramics. Then I always imagine how they would look in my place.

B. GRAMMATIK UND GEBRAUCH

1. GERMAN EQUIVALENTS OF "TO LIKE"

a. *Gern* + verb expresses that one likes to do something. *Gern* means "gladly, willingly, with pleasure."

Ich sehe Keramikstücke gern.
I like to see ceramics.

Er besucht das Museum gern.
He likes to visit the museum.

To say that you like to do something very much, use *sehr* + *gern*.

Ich sehe Plastiken sehr gern.
I very much like to see sculptures.

b. *Haben* + *gern* expresses that you like someone or something.

Was hast du gern?
What do you like?

Er hat Dürer gern.
He likes Dürer.

c. *Gefallen* expresses pleasure or displeasure about something or someone in a neutral way, usually referring to visual appearance.

Wie gefällt dir die Ausstellung?

How do you like the exhibition? (How does the exhibition please you?)

Sie gefällt mir nicht.

I don't like it. (It doesn't please me.)

Note: The subject of *gefallen* is the person or thing that is liked or disliked. The person who "does the liking" is a dative object.

d. *Mögen* expresses a stronger like or dislike than *gefallen*.

Ich mag Kunstgewerbe.

I like arts and crafts.

Wir mögen den Museumsdirektor nicht.

We don't like the museum director.

Mögen is most frequently used to express likes and dislikes about food.

Magst du Bohnen?

Do you like beans?

Nein, die mag ich nicht.

No, I don't like them.

e. *Sympathisch* indicates that you find people likable.

Der Maler ist mir sympathisch.

I like the painter.

2. THE POSITION OF *GERN*

a. *Gern* often follows adverbs of time.

Ich sehe samstags gern Ausstellungen.

I like to see exhibits on Saturdays.

b. *Gern* follows personal pronouns.

Ich sehe ihn gern.

I like to see him.

c. *Gern* usually precedes prepositional phrases.

Ich gehe gern mit dir in die Ausstellung.
I'll gladly go with you to the exhibit.

    d. *Gern* follows or precedes accusative objects.

Sie sieht Keramikstücke gern./Sie sieht gern Keramikstücke.
She likes to see ceramics.

Note: If you use *gern + haben*, *gern* is in the last position, unless the sentence uses a compound verb or includes a dependent clause.

Ich habe den Künstler gern.
I like the artist.

Ich habe den Künstler immer gern gehabt.
I have always liked the artist.

Sie sagt, dass sie den Künstler gern hat.
She says that she likes the artist.

3. THE GERMAN EQUIVALENT OF "ANOTHER"

Ein/eine ander- and *noch ein* both mean "another" in English, but they cannot be used interchangeably in German.

    a. *Ein/eine ander-* means "a different one."

Vielleicht könnten wir eine andere Periode wählen.
Perhaps we could choose another (a different) period.

Sollen wir ein anderes Mal wiederkommen?
Shall we come again at another (a different) time?

Note: *Ander-* takes the adjective endings for adjectives preceded by *ein* words.

    b. *Noch ein* means "one more."

Möchtest du noch einen Raum anschauen?
Would you like to look at another (one more) room?

Er kauft noch ein Gemälde.
He buys another (one more) painting.

VOKABELN

das Museum, *Museen*	museum
das Kunstmuseum	art museum
die Kunst, ¨e	art
der Künstler, -	artist
das Kunstgewerbe, -	arts and crafts
das Kunstwerk, *-e*	work of art
die Ausstellung, *-en*	exhibition
die Sonderausstellung, *-en*	special exhibition
das Gemälde, -	painting
die Malerei	painting
der Maler, -	painter
malen	to paint
die Plastik, *-en*	sculpture
die Skulptur, *-en*	sculpture
die Bildhauerei	sculpture
der Bildhauer, -	sculptor
die Zeichnung, *-en*	drawing
zeichnen	to draw
die Töpferei	pottery
die Keramik	ceramics
der Töpfer, -	potter
die Weberei	weaving
der Weber, -	weaver
weben	to weave
der Glasbläser, -	glassblower
blasen, *blies, geblasen*	to blow
der Raum, ¨e	room
die Halle, *-en*	hall
die Abteilung, *-en*	department, collection
sympathisch sein	to be likeable
Er ist mir sympathisch.	I like him. (He is likeable to me.)
seltsam	strange, odd
der Vorschlag, ¨e	suggestion
sich vor*stellen	to imagine
gern	gladly, willingly, with pleasure

ÜBUNGEN

A. *Beantworten Sie die Fragen zum Dialog.*

1. *Wie gefällt Sarah die Ausstellung?*
2. *Welche Abteilung möchte Sarah besonders gern sehen?*
3. *Was mag Sarah?*
4. *Warum sieht Sarah gern Keramik?*

B. *Suchen Sie die richtige deutsche Übersetzung.*

1. We can only see the paintings for another three days.
2. I'm fond of drawings.
3. How do you like this exhibition?
4. I like sculptures.
5. Perhaps we could choose another period.
6. The Oriental collection isn't open.
7. I like your suggestion.

a. *Die orientalische Abteilung ist nicht auf.*
b. *Wie gefällt dir diese Ausstellung?*
c. *Wir können die Gemälde nur noch drei Tage sehen.*
d. *Dein Vorschlag gefällt mir.*
e. *Ich mag Plastiken.*
f. *Ich habe Zeichnungen gern.*
g. *Vielleicht könnten wir eine andere Periode wählen.*

C. *Übersetzen Sie.*

1. Would you (fam.) like to see another exhibit?
2. Another room would be too much.
3. How about another period?
4. Perhaps at another time.
5. How do you (fam.) like this room? (use *gefallen*)
6. I'm very fond of arts and crafts.
7. Does he like to go to special exhibits on Sunday? (use *gern*)
8. No. He doesn't like art. (use *mögen*)

KULTURNOTIZ

There are numerous art museums *(Kunstmuseen)* and galleries *(Galerien)* as well as other types of museums in German-speaking countries. In Germany, the tradition of museums and exhibitions goes back to the beginning of the nineteenth century, when city and state museums were established alongside princely collections that already had existed for a long time. Most museums receive public funding, but there are a few private museums also.

Most major German cities have internationally famous museums. Among the many museums in Berlin the Dahlem Gallery (for classical painting) and the National Gallery (for modern art) are perhaps best known. The famous *Alte Pinakothek* in Munich shows art of the Bavarian State Collection. The German Museum *(das Deutsche Museum)*, also located in Munich, is the largest European museum for natural sciences and technology. The number of visitors to all types of exhibitions has greatly increased in recent years.

The most famous international contemporary art show in Germany is the *Dokumenta,* which has been held at irregular intervals since 1955 in Kassel. This exhibition is viewed all over the world as setting new trends in art.

LÖSUNGEN

A. 1. *Sarah findet die meisten Gemälde und Plastiken ein bisschen seltsam.*
2. *Sie möchte gern die orientalische Abteilung sehen. 3. Sie mag Kunstgewerbe. 4. Sie stellt sich vor, wie die bei ihr aussehen würden.*
B. 1.—c 2.—f 3.—b 4.—e 5.—g 6.—a 7.—d
C. 1. *Möchtest du noch eine andere Ausstellung sehen? 2. Noch ein Raum wäre zu viel. 3. Wie wär's mit einer anderen Periode? 4. Vielleicht ein anderes Mal. 5. Wie gefällt dir dieser Raum? 6. Ich habe Kunstgewerbe sehr gern. 7. Geht er sonntags gern in Sonderausstellungen? 8. Nein, er mag keine Kunst.*

LEKTION 40

A. TEXT

Ein Exzerpt aus Johann Wolfgang von Goethe's "Faust."

FAUST: Habe nun, ach! Philosophie,
Juristerei[1] und Medizin
Und leider auch Theologie
durchaus studiert, mit heißem Bemühn.
Da steh' ich nun, ich armer Tor!
Und bin so klug als wie zuvor;
Heiße Magister, heiße Doktor gar,
Und ziehe schon an die zehen[2] Jahr
Herauf, herab und quer und krumm
Meine Schüler an der Nase herum—
Und sehe, dass wir nichts wissen können!
Das will mir schier das Herz verbrennen.
Zwar bin ich gescheiter als alle die Laffen[3]
Doktoren, Magister, Schreiber und Pfaffen;[4]
Mich plagen keine Skrupel noch Zweifel,
Fürchte mich weder vor Hölle noch Teufel—
Dafür ist mir auch alle Freud' entrissen
Bilde mir nicht ein was Rechts zu wissen,
Bilde mir nicht ein ich könnte was lehren,
Die Menschen zu bessern und zu bekehren.
Auch hab' ich weder Gut[5] noch Geld,
Noch Ehr' und Herrlichkeit der Welt;
Es möcht' kein Hund so länger leben!

---

1. *die Juristerei* = an old expression for *Jura* (the study of law)
2. *zehen* = *zehn*
3. *der Laffe, -n* = arrogant person
4. *der Pfaffe, -n* = a derogatory expression for priest
5. *das Gut* = possession

---

*An Excerpt from Johann Wolfgang von Goethe's Faust.**

FAUST: Alas, I've studied philosophy, jurisprudence and medicine, regrettably, theology, too, all with hot fervor. Now I, poor fool, stand here no wiser than before. I'm a magister, I'm even a doctor, and for ten long years left and right, crossways and straight, I led my students by the nose, and see that there is nothing we can know! That almost consumes my heart. True, I am cleverer than all the fops, doctors, magisters, clerks and priests, I'm not plagued by any scruples nor doubts, not afraid of hell nor devil—for this, all my joy is gone, I don't flatter myself to know anything worthwhile, I don't flatter myself I could teach something to my students to better and to convert men. Also, I have neither possessions nor money, nor any worldly honor and glory; no dog would want to live like that.

B. GRAMMATIK UND GEBRAUCH

1. VARIOUS USES OF *ES*

a. THE IMPERSONAL *ES*

Besides replacing a neuter noun† as a personal pronoun, *es* can also be used as an impersonal pronoun. Verbs used impersonally take *es* as the subject.

Es regnet.	It's raining.
Es schneit.	It's snowing.
Es brennt.	It's burning.
Es ist mir egal.	It's all the same to me.

b. THE INTRODUCTORY *ES*

Sometimes an introductory *es* is used for emphasis and stylistic reasons. The true subject follows the verb.

---

* This is a literal translation. For poetic translations, please refer to: *Goethe's "Faust,"* translated by Barker Fairley, University of Toronto Press, 1970. *Faust,* bilingual, rev. ed., translated by Peter Salm, Bantam Classics, 1985.
† Please refer to lesson 1, Subject Pronouns.

Es möchte kein Hund so länger leben.	No dog wants to live like that any longer.
Es spricht der Kandidat Herr Meier.	The candidate Mr. Meier is giving a speech.
Es kommen heute drei Juristen.	Three lawyers are coming today.
Es ist niemand zu Hause.	No one is at home.

C. THE ANTICIPATORY *ES*

Es can be used to anticipate a dependent clause or an infinitive phrase.

Ich kann es nicht glauben, dass er sich vor nichts fürchtet.
I can't believe that he isn't afraid of anything.

Er hasst es, nichts davon zu wissen.
He hates not knowing anything about it.

2. A FEW IDIOMS

German, like English, has many idiomatic expressions. Goethe's drama *Faust* is a source of many idioms. One of them is:

Er führt seine Schüler an der Nase herum.
He misleads his students. (He leads his students around by the nose.)

Some other common German expressions and idiomatic phrases are:

Sie ist mit ihrem Urteil immer sehr schnell bei der Hand.
She makes her judgments rather quickly. (She is quick at hand with her judgments.)

Alles ist in Butter.
Everything is fine (running smoothly). (Everything is in butter.)

Ich hoffe, wir bleiben dabei nicht auf der Strecke.
I hope we will not lose in this fight. (I hope we won't be left on the road.)

Ich will noch nicht zum alten Eisen gehören.
I do not yet want to be considered old. (I don't want to be part of old iron yet.)

Er geht mit dem Kopf durch die Wand.
He does as he pleases. (He goes with his head through the wall.)

Sie ist sehr betucht.

> She is well heeled. (She is well clothed.)

Idiomatic expressions are usually very difficult to transfer from culture to culture. You will learn them gradually in conversations with native speakers.

VOKABELN

die Philosophie, *-n*	philosophy
Jura	law studies
die Medizin	medicine
das Bemühen	effort
die Theologie	theology
der Tor, *-en, -en*	fool
töricht	foolish
klug	intelligent
zuvor	before
(so)gar	even
ziehen, *zog, gezogen*	to pull
quer	crosswise
krumm	crooked
schier	almost
das Herz, *-en*	heart
brennen, *brannte, gebrannt*	to burn
verbrennen	to burn
plagen	to trouble
gescheit	intelligent
die Skrupel (pl.)	scruples
der Zweifel, -	doubt
die Hölle	hell
der Teufel, -	devil
die Freude, *-n*	joy
entreißen, *entriss, entrissen*	to tear away
sich einbilden	to imagine
lehren	to teach
der Mensch, *-en, -en*	human, people, man

bessern	to improve
bekehren	to convert
die Ehre, *-n*	honor
die Welt, *-en*	world
der Hund, *-e*	dog

ÜBUNGEN

A. *Beantworten Sie die Fragen zum Text.*

1. *Was hat Faust studiert?*
2. *Wen führt Faust an der Nase herum?*
3. *Kann Faust die Menschen bessern?*
4. *Hat Faust Geld?*

B. *Suchen Sie die richtige deutsche Übersetzung.*

1. It's snowing.
2. He doesn't know that he is a fool.
3. It's burning.
4. It's the same to him.
5. No one is here.
6. She does as she pleases.

a. *Es ist niemand hier.*
b. *Es schneit.*
c. *Er weiß nicht, dass er ein Tor ist.*
d. *Es ist ihm egal.*
e. *Sie geht mit dem Kopf durch die Wand.*
f. *Es brennt.*

C. *Schreiben Sie das unterstrichene Verb im Präsens.* (Rewrite the underlined verb in the present tense.)

1. *Faust studierte Philosophie.*
2. *Er hieß Doktor.*
3. *Er fürchtete sich nicht vor der Hölle.*
4. *Ihn plagten keine Zweifel.*
5. *Er bildete sich ein, ein Tor zu sein.*

D. *Streichen Sie das Wort aus, das nicht passt.* (Cross out the word that doesn't fit.)

1. *Medizin, Theologie, Schüler, Jura*
2. *Hölle, zuvor, verbrennen, Teufel*
3. *klug, intelligent, krumm, gescheit*

KULTURNOTIZ

Johann Wolfgang von Goethe (born 1749 in Frankfurt am Main, died 1832 in Weimar) is one of the most famous German poets. He studied law and was employed by the duke of Saxe-Weimar as chief minister of state. Goethe worked on his drama *Faust* all his life. The work is based on a historical figure who lived in the middle of the sixteenth century. Goethe's Faust consists of two parts, *Faust I* and *Faust II*. In the play, Goethe shows man's struggle to define himself.

LÖSUNGEN

A. 1. *Faust hat Philosophie, Jura (Juristerei), Medizin und Theologie studiert. 2. Er führt seine Schüler an der Nase herum. 3. Nein, er kann die Menschen nicht bessern. 4. Nein, er hat kein Geld.*
B. 1.—b   2.—c   3.—f   4.—d   5.—a   6.—e
C. 1. *studiert*   2. *heißt*   3. *fürchtet*   4. *plagen*   5. *bildet*
D. 1. *Schüler*   2. *zuvor*   3. *krumm*

ACHTE WIEDERHOLUNGSAUFGABE

A. *Schreiben Sie die Sätze im Konjunktiv II. Benutzen Sie "würde" + Infinitiv, wo nötig.*

BEISPIEL: *Haben Sie heute Zeit für mich?*
       Hätten Sie heute Zeit für mich?

1. *Haben Sie noch Karten für heute Abend?*
2. *Können Sie die Plätze für mich reservieren?*

3. *Kostet es weniger, wenn ich die Karten kurz vor Anfang der Vorstellung kaufe?*
4. *Man sagte mir, einige Karten werden vielleicht zurückgegeben.*

B. *Ändern Sie die Sätze in der Gegenwart im Konjunktiv II zur Vergangenheit im Konjunktiv II.* (Change the sentences from the present-time general subjunctive to the past-time general subjunctive.)

BEISPIEL: *Wenn ich nur reich wäre!*
Wenn ich nur reich gewesen wäre!

1. *Wenn es nur bessere Kandidaten gäbe!*
2. *Könnten wir uns nicht beklagen?*
3. *Ich würde mit einer Steuererhöhung nicht übereinstimmen.*

C. *Ändern Sie die direkte Rede zur indirekten Rede. Gebrauchen Sie Konjunktiv I.* (Change the direct discourse to indirect, using subjunctive I.)

BEISPIEL: *Sie schrieb: "Wir werden uns bald einen neuen Fernseher kaufen."*
Sie schrieb, sie würden sich bald einen neuen Fernseher kaufen.

1. *Sie fragte: "Gibt es in Amerika auch so viele Maskenbälle?"*
2. *Er meinte: "Der Karneval in Rio de Janeiro ist am bekanntesten."*
3. *Sie sagte: "Die Feiertage in Deutschland hören gar nicht auf."*
4. *Er antwortete: "Ich habe meistens eine Tageszeitung gelesen."*
5. *Sie erzählte: "Ich habe mir eine Wochenzeitschrift bestellt."*
6. *Er hoffte: "Peter wird sich bald besser informieren."*

D. *Übersetzen Sie.*

1. *Ich mag moderne Kunst.*
2. *Die Künstler sind mir sympathisch.*
3. *Aber mir gefallen auch die Gemälde des achtzehnten Jahrhunderts.*
4. *Die Skulpturen dieser Zeit habe ich besonders gern.*
5. *Leider hat meine Freundin ein anderes Hobby.*
6. *Sie hat Kunstgewerbe gern.*
7. *An Winterabenden zeichnet sie gern.*
8. *An allen Wänden hängen Zeichnungen.*
9. *Aber sie macht immer noch eine.*

E. *Übersetzen Sie.*

1. Could you tell me where the theater is?
2. I wish I had a city map.
3. It would be better to take a taxi.
4. They say it is difficult to get a taxi on Friday evening.

LÖSUNGEN

A. 1. *Hätten Sie noch Karten für heute Abend? 2. Könnten Sie die Plätze für mich reservieren? 3. Würde es weniger kosten, wenn ich die Karten kurz vor Anfang der Vorstellung kaufen würde? 4. Man sagte mir, einige Karten würden vielleicht zurückgegeben.*
B. 1. *Wenn es nur bessere Kandidaten gegeben hätte! 2. Hätten wir uns nicht beklagen können? 3. Ich hätte mit einer Steuererhöhung nicht übereingestimmt.*
C. 1. *Sie fragte, ob es in Amerika auch so viele Maskenbälle gebe. 2. Er meinte, der Karneval in Rio de Janeiro sei am bekanntesten. 3. Sie sagte, die Feiertage in Deutschland würden gar nicht aufhören. 4. Er antwortete, er habe meistens eine Tageszeitung gelesen. 5. Sie erzählte, sie habe sich eine Wochenzeitschrift bestellt. 6. Er hoffte, Peter werde sich bald besser informieren.*
D. 1. I like modern art. 2. I like the artists. 3. But I also like the paintings of the eighteenth century. 4. I especially like the sculptures of that time. 5. Unfortunately, my girlfriend has a different hobby. 6. She likes arts and crafts. 7. She likes to draw on winter evenings. 8. There are drawings on all the walls. 9. But she'll still make another.
E. 1. *Könnten Sie mir sagen, wo das Theater liegt? 2. Ich wünschte, ich hätte einen Stadtplan. 3. Es wäre besser, ein Taxi zu nehmen. 4. Man sagt, es wäre (sei) schwierig, Freitag abends ein Taxi zu bekommen.*

LESESTÜCK IV

UMWELTPROBLEME[1]

In Deutschland, Österreich und der Schweiz gibt es, wie in den meisten Ländern, viele Umweltprobleme. Wie versuchen die Leute in den deutschsprachigen Ländern die Probleme zu reduzieren? In allen drei Ländern wird schon seit mehreren Jahren recycelt. Jetzt findet man auch in vielen Supermärkten in Deutschland Kisten,[2] in die man sofort die überflüssige[3] Verpackung[4] der Lebensmittel werfen kann. Und natürlich bekommen Kunden in den Lebensmittelgeschäften und Supermärkten keine Plastiktüten[5] für ihre Einkäufe. Man muss seine eigene Tasche mitbringen oder eine Tüte kaufen.

Und was macht man außerdem noch für eine saubere Umwelt? Hier sind noch einige Beispiele.[6] In allen drei Ländern kaufen viele Leute auf dem Markt, wo es regionale und oft auch organisch angebaute[7] Produkte wie Obst, Gemüse, Eier und Fleisch gibt. Immer mehr Leute fahren jetzt mit dem Fahrrad zur Arbeit, oder sie benutzen öffentliche[8] Verkehrsmittel. In allen Städten und auf dem Land gibt es gute Fahrradwege und das Netz[9] der Fahrradwege wird ständig[10] erweitert.[11] In Österreich wird im Winter auf die verschneiten oder vereisten Straßen kein Salz sondern Sand gestreut.[12] Sand schadet[13] der Umwelt weniger als Salz.

Noch viel muss getan werden, damit Luft und Wasser wieder sauberer werden. Aber ein Anfang ist gemacht. Und am wichtigsten ist es vielleicht, dass sich immer mehr Menschen der Umweltprobleme bewusst werden.[14] Deshalb können auch Lösungen gefunden werden.

VOKABELN

1.	*die Umwelt*	environment
2.	*die Kiste, -n*	box, container
3.	*überflüssig*	superfluous, unnecessary
4.	*die Verpackung, -en*	wrapping, packaging
5.	*die Tüte, -n*	bag
6.	*das Beispiel, -e*	example
7.	*angebaut*	grown
8.	*öffentlich*	public
9.	*das Netz, -e*	net, network
10.	*ständig*	constantly, continuously
11.	*erweitern*	to increase
12.	*streuen*	to sprinkle
13.	*schaden*	to hurt
14.	*sich bewusst werden*	to become aware of

Herzlichen Glückwunsch!
Congratulations!

Now that you have completed the course, you'll be able to use this manual as a reference book for expressions and grammar. The appendix that follows provides even more information for additional study. We also recommend that you review the material, looking carefully at sections that seemed difficult. Both sets of recordings will be of further use as you study and review at home, in your car, or while jogging. . . . Keep up the good work!

APPENDIXES

A. CONTINENTS, COUNTRIES, AND LANGUAGES

1. GERMAN-ENGLISH

KONTINENTE

Afrika	Africa
Antarktik	Antarctica
Asien	Asia
Australien	Australia
Europa	Europe
Nordamerika	North America
Südamerika	South America

LÄNDER

Argentinien	Argentina
Belgien	Belgium
Bosnien	Bosnia
Brasilien	Brazil
Bulgarien	Bulgaria
China	China
Dänemark	Denmark
Deutschland	Germany
England	England
Finnland	Finland
Frankreich	France
Gemeinschaft Unabhängiger Staaten (G.U.S.)	Commonwealth of Independent States (C.I.S.)
Griechenland	Greece
Großbritannien	Great Britain

Herzegowina	Herzegovina
Holland/die Niederlande	Holland/the Netherlands
Indien	India
der Irak	Iraq
der Iran	Iran
Irland	Ireland
Israel	Israel
Italien	Italy
Japan	Japan
Jugoslawien	Yugoslavia
Kanada	Canada
Korea	Korea
Kroatien	Croatia
der Libanon	Lebanon
Liechtenstein	Liechtenstein
Luxemburg	Luxembourg
Marokko	Morocco
Mexiko	Mexico
Neuseeland	New Zealand
Norwegen	Norway
Österreich	Austria
Polen	Poland
Portugal	Portugal
Rumänien	Romania
Russland	Russia
Schottland	Scotland
Schweden	Sweden
die Schweiz	Switzerland
die Slowakei	Slovakia
Spanien	Spain
Südafrika	South Africa
die Tschechische Republik	Czech Republic
die Türkei	Turkey
Ukraine	Ukraine
Ungarn	Hungary
die Vereinigten Staaten von Amerika (die U.S.A.)	United States of America

SPRACHEN

Arabisch	Arabic
Chinesisch	Chinese
Deutsch	German
Englisch	English
Finnisch	Finnish
Französisch	French
Griechisch	Greek
Hebräisch	Hebrew
Italienisch	Italian
Japanisch	Japanese
Koreanisch	Korean
Polnisch	Polish
Portugiesisch	Portuguese
Russisch	Russian
Schwedisch	Swedish
Spanisch	Spanish
Türkisch	Turkish

2. ENGLISH-GERMAN

CONTINENTS

Africa	Afrika
Antarctica	Antarktik
Asia	Asien
Australia	Australien
Europe	Europa
North America	Nordamerika
South America	Südamerika

COUNTRIES

Argentina	*Argentinien*
Austria	*Österreich*
Belgium	*Belgien*
Bosnia	*Bosnien*
Brazil	*Brasilien*
Bulgaria	*Bulgarien*
Canada	*Kanada*
China	*China*
Commonwealth of Independent States (C.I.S.)	*Gemeinschaft Unabhängiger Staaten (G.U.S.)*
Croatia	*Kroatien*
Czech Republic	*die Tschechische Republik*
Denmark	*Dänemark*
England	*England*
Finland	*Finnland*
France	*Frankreich*
Germany	*Deutschland*
Great Britain	*Großbritannien*
Greece	*Griechenland*
Herzegovina	*Herzegowina*
Holland/the Netherlands	*Holland/die Niederlande*
Hungary	*Ungarn*
India	*Indien*
Iran	*der Iran*
Iraq	*der Irak*
Ireland	*Irland*
Israel	*Israel*
Italy	*Italien*
Japan	*Japan*
Korea	*Korea*
Lebanon	*der Libanon*
Liechtenstein	*Liechtenstein*
Luxembourg	*Luxemburg*
Mexico	*Mexiko*
Morocco	*Marokko*
New Zealand	*Neuseeland*

Norway	*Norwegen*
Poland	*Polen*
Portugal	*Portugal*
Romania	*Rumänien*
Russia	*Russland*
Scotland	*Schottland*
Slovakia	*die Slowakei*
South Africa	*Südafrika*
Spain	*Spanien*
Sweden	*Schweden*
Switzerland	*die Schweiz*
Turkey	*die Türkei*
Ukraine	*die Ukraine*
United States of America	*die Vereinigten Staaten von Amerika (die U.S.A.)*
Yugoslavia	*Jugoslawien*

LANGUAGES

Arabic	*Arabisch*
Chinese	*Chinesisch*
English	*Englisch*
Finnish	*Finnisch*
French	*Französisch*
Greek	*Griechisch*
German	*Deutsch*
Hebrew	*Hebräisch*
Italian	*Italienisch*
Japanese	*Japanisch*
Korean	*Koreanisch*
Polish	*Polnisch*
Portuguese	*Portugiesisch*
Russian	*Russisch*
Spanish	*Spanisch*
Swedish	*Schwedisch*
Turkish	*Türkisch*

B. GRAMMAR AND VERB CHARTS

1. THE DEFINITE ARTICLE

	MASCULINE	FEMININE	NEUTER	PLURAL
Nom.	der	die	das	die
Acc.	den	die	das	die
Dat.	dem	der	dem	den
Gen.	des	der	des	der

2. DER-WORDS: DIESER, JENER, WELCHER, JEDER, ALLE, MANCHE, SOLCHE

	MASCULINE	FEMININE	NEUTER	PLURAL
Nom.	dieser	diese	dieses	diese
Acc.	diesen	diese	dieses	diese
Dat.	diesem	dieser	diesem	diesen
Gen.	dieses	dieser	dieses	dieser

3. THE INDEFINITE ARTICLE

	MASCULINE	FEMININE	NEUTER
Nom.	ein	eine	ein
Acc.	einen	eine	ein
Dat.	einem	einer	einem
Gen.	eines	einer	eines

4. EIN-WORDS: KEIN, MEIN, DEIN, SEIN, IHR, UNSER, EUER, IHR, IHR

	MASCULINE	FEMININE	NEUTER	PLURAL
Nom.	*mein*	*meine*	*mein*	*meine*
Acc.	*meinen*	*meine*	*mein*	*meine*
Dat.	*meinem*	*meiner*	*meinem*	*meinen*
Gen.	*meines*	*meiner*	*meines*	*meiner*

5. MASCULINE N-NOUNS

	SINGULAR	PLURAL
Nom.	*der Patient*	*die Patienten*
Acc.	*den Patienten*	*die Patienten*
Dat.	*dem Patienten*	*den Patienten*
Gen.	*des Patienten*	*der Patienten*

6. PRECEDED ADJECTIVES

	MASCULINE	FEMININE	NEUTER
Nom.	*der junge Mann*	*die alte Stadt*	*das graue Dach*
	ein junger Mann	*eine alte Stadt*	*ein graues Dach*

PLURAL
die guten Weine
keine guten Weine

| Acc. | den jungen Mann | die alte Stadt | das graue Dach |
| | einen jungen Mann | eine alte Stadt | ein graues Dach |

PLURAL

die guten Weine
keine guten Weine

| Dat. | dem jungen Mann | der alten Stadt | dem grauen Dach |
| | einem jungen Mann | einer alten Stadt | einem grauen Dach |

PLURAL

den guten Weinen
keinen guten Weinen

| Gen. | des jungen Mannes | der alten Stadt | des grauen Daches |
| | eines jungen Mannes | einer alten Stadt | eines grauen Daches |

PLURAL

der guten Weine
keiner guten Weine

7. UNPRECEDED ADJECTIVES

	MASCULINE	FEMININE	NEUTER	PLURAL
Nom.	guter Kuchen	gute Torte	gutes Brot	gute Torten
Acc.	guten Kuchen	gute Torte	gutes Brot	gute Torten
Dat.	gutem Kuchen	guter Torte	gutem Brot	guten Torten
Gen.	guten Kuchens	guter Torte	guten Brotes	guter Torten

8. PERSONAL PRONOUNS

SINGULAR

Nom.	ich	du	er	sie	es
Acc.	mich	dich	ihn	sie	es
Dat.	mir	dir	ihm	ihr	ihm

PLURAL

Nom.	wir	ihr	sie	Sie
Acc.	uns	euch	sie	Sie
Dat.	uns	euch	ihnen	Ihnen

9. INTERROGATIVE PRONOUNS

	MASC./FEM.	NEUTER
Nom.	wer	was
Acc.	wen	was
Dat.	wem	-
Gen.	wessen	wessen

10. THE DEMONSTRATIVE PRONOUNS

	MASCULINE	FEMININE	NEUTER	PLURAL
Nom.	der	die	das	die
Acc.	den	die	das	die
Dat.	dem	der	dem	denen

11. RELATIVE PRONOUNS

	MASCULINE	FEMININE	NEUTER	PLURAL
Nom.	der	die	das	die
Acc.	den	die	das	die
Dat.	dem	der	dem	denen
Gen.	dessen	deren	dessen	deren

12. VERBS IN THE INDICATIVE

PRESENT

I ask, I am asking, I do ask

ich	frage	wir	fragen
du	fragst	ihr	fragt
er/sie/es	fragt	sie	fragen
		Sie	fragen

PRESENT PERFECT

I have asked, I asked, I did ask

ich	habe gefragt		wir	haben gefragt
du	hast gefragt		ihr	habt gefragt
er/sie/es	hat gefragt		sie	haben gefragt
			Sie	haben gefragt

I have come, I came, I did come

ich	bin gekommen		wir	sind gekommen
du	bist gekommen		ihr	seid gekommen
er/sie/es	ist gekommen		sie	sind gekommen
			Sie	sind gekommen

SIMPLE PAST

I asked, I was asking

ich	fragte		wir	fragten
du	fragtest		ihr	fragtet
er/sie/es	fragte		sie	fragten
			Sie	fragten

I came, I was coming

ich	kam		wir	kamen
du	kamst		ihr	kamt
er/sie/es	kam		sie	kamen
			Sie	kamen

363

PAST PERFECT

I had asked

ich	hatte gefragt
du	hattest gefragt
er/sie/es	hatte gefragt

wir	hatten gefragt
ihr	hattet gefragt
sie	hatten gefragt
Sie	hatten gefragt

I had come

ich	war gekommen
du	warst gekommen
er/sie/es	war gekommen

wir	waren gekommen
ihr	wart gekommen
sie	waren gekommen
Sie	waren gekommen

FUTURE

I will ask

ich	werde fragen
du	wirst fragen
er/sie/es	wird fragen

wir	werden fragen
ihr	werdet fragen
sie	werden fragen
Sie	werden fragen

13. VERBS IN THE SUBJUNCTIVE

PRESENT-TIME GENERAL SUBJUNCTIVE (SUBJUNCTIVE II)

I would ask

ich	*fragte*		*wir*	*fragten*
du	*fragtest*		*ihr*	*fragtet*
er/sie/es	*fragte*		*sie*	*fragten*
			Sie	*fragten*

I would come

ich	*käme*		*wir*	*kämen*
du	*kämest*		*ihr*	*kämet*
er/sie/es	*käme*		*sie*	*kämen*
			Sie	*kämen*

PAST-TIME GENERAL SUBJUNCTIVE (SUBJUNCTIVE II)

I would have asked

ich	*hätte gefragt*		*wir*	*hätten gefragt*
du	*hättest gefragt*		*ihr*	*hättet gefragt*
er/sie/es	*hätte gefragt*		*sie*	*hätten gefragt*
			Sie	*hätten gefragt*

I would have come

ich	*wäre gekommen*	wir	*wären gekommen*
du	*wärest gekommen*	ihr	*wäret gekommen*
er/sie/es	*wäre gekommen*	sie	*wären gekommen*
		Sie	*wären gekommen*

PRESENT-TIME SPECIAL SUBJUNCTIVE (SUBJUNCTIVE I)

I would ask

ich	*frage*	wir	*fragen*
du	*fragest*	ihr	*fraget*
er/sie/es	*frage*	sie	*fragen*
		Sie	*fragen*

I would come

ich	*komme*	wir	*kommen*
du	*kommest*	ihr	*kommet*
er/sie/es	*komme*	sie	*kommen*
		Sie	*kommen*

PAST-TIME SPECIAL SUBJUNCTIVE (SUBJUNCTIVE I)

I asked (indirect speech)

ich	*habe gefragt*	wir	*haben gefragt*
du	*habest gefragt*	ihr	*habet gefragt*
er/sie/es	*habe gefragt*	sie	*haben gefragt*
		Sie	*haben gefragt*

I came (indirect speech)

ich	sei gekommen	wir	seien gekommen
du	seiest gekommen	ihr	seiet gekommen
er/sie/es	sei gekommen	sie	seien gekommen
		Sie	seien gekommen

FUTURE-TIME SPECIAL SUBJUNCTIVE (SUBJUNCTIVE I)

I will ask (indirect speech)

ich	werde fragen	wir	werden fragen
du	werdest fragen	ihr	werdet fragen
er/sie/es	werde fragen	sie	werden fragen
		Sie	werden fragen

14. PASSIVE VOICE

PRESENT

I am asked

ich	werde gefragt	wir	werden gefragt
du	wirst gefragt	ihr	werdet gefragt
er/sie/es	wird gefragt	sie	werden gefragt
		Sie	werden gefragt

SIMPLE PAST

I was asked, I have been asked

ich	wurde gefragt	wir	wurden gefragt
du	wurdest gefragt	ihr	wurdet gefragt
er/sie/es	wurde gefragt	sie	wurden gefragt
		Sie	wurden gefragt

PRESENT PERFECT

I was asked, I have been asked

ich	bin gefragt worden	wir	sind gefragt worden
du	bist gefragt worden	ihr	seid gefragt worden
er/sie/es	ist gefragt worden	sie	sind gefragt worden
		Sie	sind gefragt worden

PAST PERFECT

I had been asked

ich	war gefragt worden	wir	waren gefragt worden
du	warst gefragt worden	ihr	wart gefragt worden
er/sie/es	war gefragt worden	sie	waren gefragt worden

15. PRINCIPAL PARTS OF STRONG VERBS, IRREGULAR WEAK VERBS, AND MODALS

INFINITIVE	PRESENT	SIMPLE PAST	PAST PARTICIPLE
anfangen to begin	*fängt an*	*fing an*	*angefangen*
backen to bake	*backt*	*backte*	*gebacken*
beginnen to begin		*begann*	*begonnen*
bekommen to receive		*bekam*	*bekommen*
beweisen to prove		*bewies*	*bewiesen*
bieten to offer		*bot*	*geboten*
bleiben to remain		*blieb*	*ist geblieben*
brechen to break	*bricht*	*brach*	*gebrochen*
bringen to bring		*brachte*	*gebracht*
denken to think		*dachte*	*gedacht*
dürfen to be allowed to	*darf*	*durfte*	*gedurft*

INFINITIVE	PRESENT	SIMPLE PAST	PAST PARTICIPLE
einladen to invite	lädt ein	lud ein	eingeladen
empfehlen to recommend	empfiehlt	empfahl	empfohlen
essen to eat	isst	aß	gegessen
fahren to drive	fährt	fuhr	ist gefahren
fallen to fall	fällt	fiel	ist gefallen
finden to find		fand	gefunden
fliegen to fly		flog	ist geflogen
frieren to freeze		fror	gefroren
geben to give	gibt	gab	gegeben
gefallen to please	gefällt	gefiel	gefallen
gehen to go		ging	ist gegangen
genießen to enjoy		genoss	genossen

INFINITIVE	PRESENT	SIMPLE PAST	PAST PARTICIPLE
gewinnen to win		*gewann*	*gewonnen*
greifen to seize		*griff*	*gegriffen*
haben to have	*hat*	*hatte*	*gehabt*
halten to hold; to stop	*hält*	*hielt*	*gehalten*
hängen to hang, be hanging		*hing* *hängte*	*gehangen* (intransitive) *gehängt* (transitive)
heißen to be called, named		*hieß*	*geheißen*
helfen to help	*hilft*	*half*	*geholfen*
kennen to know		*kannte*	*gekannt*
kommen to come		*kam*	*ist gekommen*
können to be able to, can	*kann*	*konnte*	*gekonnt*
lassen to let, leave behind	*lässt*	*ließ*	*gelassen*

INFINITIVE	PRESENT	SIMPLE PAST	PAST PARTICIPLE
laufen to run, walk	*läuft*	*lief*	*ist gelaufen*
leiden to suffer		*litt*	*gelitten*
leihen to lend, to borrow		*lieh*	*geliehen*
lesen to read	*liest*	*las*	*gelesen*
liegen to lie (down)		*lag*	*gelegen*
mögen to like (to)	*mag*	*mochte*	*gemocht*
müssen to have to, must	*muss*	*musste*	*gemusst*
nehmen to take	*nimmt*	*nahm*	*genommen*
nennen to name, call		*nannte*	*genannt*
reiben to rub		*rieb*	*gerieben*
rennen to run		*rannte*	*ist gerannt*

INFINITIVE	PRESENT	SIMPLE PAST	PAST PARTICIPLE
rufen to call		*rief*	*gerufen*
scheinen to shine, seem		*schien*	*geschienen*
schlafen to sleep	*schläft*	*schlief*	*geschlafen*
schlagen to hit	*schlägt*	*schlug*	*geschlagen*
schließen to close		*schloss*	*geschlossen*
schneiden to cut		*schnitt*	*geschnitten*
schreiben to write		*schrieb*	*geschrieben*
schreien to scream		*schrie*	*geschrie(e)n*
schwimmen to swim		*schwamm*	*ist geschwommen*
sehen to see	*sieht*	*sah*	*gesehen*
sein to be	*ist*	*war*	*ist gewesen*
sitzen to sit		*saß*	*gesessen*

INFINITIVE	PRESENT	SIMPLE PAST	PAST PARTICIPLE
sollen should, to be supposed to	*soll*	*sollte*	*gesollt*
sprechen to speak	*spricht*	*sprach*	*gesprochen*
springen to jump		*sprang*	*ist gesprungen*
stehen to stand		*stand*	*gestanden*
steigen to climb		*stieg*	*ist gestiegen*
streiten to fight		*stritt*	*gestritten*
tragen to carry; to wear	*trägt*	*trug*	*getragen*
treffen to meet	*trifft*	*traf*	*getroffen*
treten to tread, kick	*tritt*	*trat*	*getreten*
trinken to drink		*trank*	*getrunken*
tun to do		*tat*	*getan*

INFINITIVE	PRESENT	SIMPLE PAST	PAST PARTICIPLE
verbieten to forbid		*verbot*	*verboten*
verbinden to connect		*verband*	*verbunden*
verlieren to lose		*verlor*	*verloren*
wachsen to grow	*wächst*	*wuchs*	*ist gewachsen*
waschen to wash	*wäscht*	*wusch*	*gewaschen*
werden to become; to get	*wird*	*wurde*	*ist geworden*
wissen to know	*weiß*	*wusste*	*gewusst*
wollen to want, wish, intend to	*will*	*wollte*	*gewollt*
ziehen to pull		*zog*	*gezogen*

C. LETTER WRITING

1. THANK-YOU NOTES

1.4.2004

Sehr geehrte Frau Wendler,

Recht herzlichen Dank für das interessante Buch über München. Es hat mir sehr gut gefallen, und ich hoffe, die Stadt München bald zu besuchen.

Mit freundlichen Grüßen
Käthe Wüst

April 1, 2004

Dear Mrs. Wendler,

Thank you very much for the interesting book about Munich. I like it very much, and hope to visit Munich soon.

Sincerely,
Käthe Wüst

2. BUSINESS LETTERS

Karl Holl   *5.4.2004*
Schuhmannstraße 8
22083 Hamburg

Verlag Max Wöller
Postfach 20
80805 München

Sehr geehrte Herren,

Anbei übersende ich Ihnen einen Scheck über €21,00 für ein Exemplar Ihres Reiseführers und sehe einer baldigen Lieferung entgegen.

Hochachtungsvoll
Karl Holl

Anlage

Schuhmannstraße 8
22083 Hamburg
April 5, 2004

Max Wöller Publishers
P.O. Box 20
80805 München

Dear Sirs:

    Enclosed please find a check for €21.00 for the guidebook. I look forward to delivery at your earliest convenience.

                             Truly yours,
                             Karl Holl

Enclosure

Joseph Becker   *28.3.2004*
Sürther Straße 32
50996 Köln

Fa. Ludwig Horn
Postfach 24
45127 Essen

Auftragsbestätigung

Sehr geehrte Damen und Herren,

Herzlichen Dank für Ihre Bestellung vom 25.3.96. Ihr Auftrag wird Ende dieser Woche ausgeliefert.

Mit freundlichen Grüßen
Joseph Becker

Sürther Straße 32
50996 Köln
March 28, 2004

Ludwig Horn Co.
P.O. Box 24
45127 Essen

Acknowledgment of order

Dear Sirs:

   Thank you for your order of March 25, 1996. Delivery will be made by the end of this week.

Sincerely,
Joseph Becker

3. INFORMAL LETTERS

8. April 2004

Lieber Christian!

Herzlichen Dank für deinen letzten Brief. Stell dir vor, ich komme vom 5. bis 10. Mai zu einem Kongreß nach Berlin. Ich freue mich jetzt schon, dich und deine Familie wiederzusehen. Dieses Mal kommt Sylvia auch mit. Sie möchte euch endlich kennenlernen. Ich hoffe, wir können viel zusammen unternehmen.

Zur Zeit geht mein Geschäft sehr gut. Und wie steht's mit dir? Ich bin gespannt, mehr über deine letzten Forschungsarbeiten zu hören.

Wir haben ein Zimmer im Hotel Maier in der Nähe des Kurfürstendamms bestellt. Das ist ja nicht weit von euch.

Bis bald. Liebe Grüße, auch an Elke,

dein Thomas

April 8, 2004

Dear Christian,

Thank you for your last letter. Just think, I'm coming to Berlin from May 10 to 15 to attend a congress. I'm looking forward to seeing you and your family again. This time Sylvia will come along too. She is anxious to meet you all. I hope we'll be able to do a lot together.

My business is doing well at the moment. How is everything with you? I'm anxious to hear more about your latest research.

We've booked a room at the Hotel Maier near the Kurfürstendamm. That's not far from you.

See you soon. Say hello to Elke for me.

Love,
Thomas

4. SALUTATIONS AND COMPLIMENTARY CLOSINGS

FORMAL SALUTATIONS

Sehr geehrter Herr Holl,	Dear Mr. Holl:
Sehr geehrte Frau Holl,	Dear Mrs. Holl:
Sehr geehrte Damen und Herren,	Dear Madames and Sirs:
Sehr geehrter Herr Doktor,	Dear Doctor:
Sehr geehrter Herr Dr. Kuhn,	Dear Dr. Kuhn,
Sehr geehrte Frau Doktor,	Dear Doctor:
Sehr geehrte Frau Dr. Merz,	Dear Dr. Merz:
Sehr geehrter Herr Professor,	Dear Professor:
Sehr geehrter Herr Professor Mai,	Dear Professor Mai:
Sehr geehrter Herr Bürgermeister,	Dear Mayor:

INFORMAL SALUTATIONS

Lieber Karl,	Dear Karl,
Liebe Else,	Dear Else,
Lieber Karl, liebe Else,	Dear Karl and Else,
Mein lieber Karl,	My dear Karl,
Meine liebe Else,	My dear Else,
Meine Lieben,	My dears,
Mein Liebling,	My Darling, (m. and f.)
Mein Liebster,	My Darling, (m.)
Meine Liebste,	My Darling, (f.)

FORMAL COMPLIMENTARY CLOSINGS

1. *Mit freundlichen Grüßen*	Sincerely,
("With friendly greetings")	
2. *Hochachtungsvoll*	Truly yours,
("Full of high respect")	

INFORMAL COMPLIMENTARY CLOSINGS

1. *Mit herzlichem Gruß,*   Love, Kind regards,
   ("With hearty greeting")
2. *Mit herzlichen Grüßen,*   Love,
3. *Mit besten Grüßen,*   Best regards,
4. *Grüße und Küsse,*   Love and kisses,
   ("Greetings and kisses")
5. *Liebe Grüße,*   Love,

Note:

The academic titles *Professor* and *Doktor* are considered part of the name and are written before the name; degrees and vocational and occupational job titles are used in the written address, but not in the salutation:

ADDRESS	SALUTATION
Herrn* Professor *Dr. Erich Weimer*	*Sehr geehrter Herr Professor,* *Sehr geehrter Herr Professor Weimer,*

Herrn Rechtsanwalt
   Dr. Friedrich Baum
 (Mr. Friedrich Baum, attorney
   at law)
	Sehr geehrter Herr Dr. Baum,

Herrn Dipl. Ing Helmut Kern (Mr. Helmut Kern, licensed engineer)	*Sehr geehrter Herr Kern,*
Frau Direktor Ilse Rau	*Sehr geehrte Frau Rau,*
Herrn Bürgermeister Kirchner (Mayor Kirchner)	*Sehr geehrter Herr Kirchner,*

* *Herrn,* the accusative of *Herr,* is used in the written address, because the preposition *an* as part of the full address *an Herrn,* while deleted, is always assumed.

5. FORM OF THE ENVELOPE

Martin Bauer
Bahnhofstraße 5
59380 Siegen

                        Herrn Arno Wenz
                        Am Grauberg 18
                        89780 Immenstadt

Or:

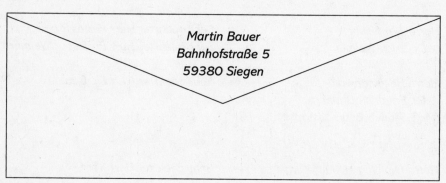

Martin Bauer
Bahnhofstraße 5
59380 Siegen

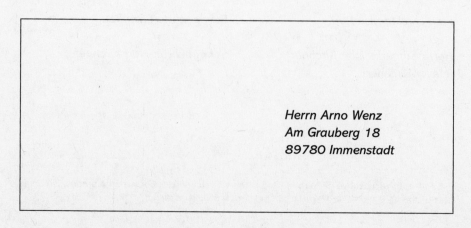

Herrn Arno Wenz
Am Grauberg 18
89780 Immenstadt

GLOSSARY

Abbreviations

accusative	*acc.*	literal	*lit.*
adjective	*adj.*	masculine	*m.*
adverb	*adv.*	neuter	*neu.*
article	*art.*	noun	*n.*
conjunction	*conj.*	object	*obj.*
dative	*dat.*	plural	*pl.*
colloquial	*coll.*	polite	*pol.*
definite	*def.*	preposition	*prep.*
direct	*dir.*	pronoun	*pron.*
familiar	*fam.*	possessive	*poss.*
feminine	*f.*	singular	*sing.*
genitive	*gen.*		

An asterisk (*) indicates separable prefix verbs.

DEUTSCH–ENGLISCH

A

der Abend, -e *evening*
  Abend *evening, hello (fam.)*
  guten Abend *good evening (pol.)*
  Heiligabend *Christmas Eve*
  zu Abend essen *to have supper*
das Abendessen, - *supper*
  zum Abendessen *for supper*
das Abendgymnasium *night school*
  abends *evenings, in the evening*
  aber *but, however*
  ab*fahren, fuhr ab, ist abgefahren *to depart*
  ab*fliegen, flog ab, ist abgeflogen *to depart by airplane*
der Abflug, ⁈e *departure (by plane)*
  ab*geben, gab ab, abgegeben *to hand in*

das Abitur, -s *high school examination, diploma*
  Abitur machen *to take the exam for the diploma*
der Abiturient, -en, -en *high school graduate*
der Abnehmer, - *buyer*
  ab*rasieren *to shave off*
  ab*schicken *to send off*
der Absender, - *return address; sender of mail*
  ab*steigen, stieg ab, ist abgestiegen *to descend, go down*
der Abstellraum, ⁈e *storage space, storage room*
der Abstieg, -e *descent*
das Abteil, -e *compartment*
die Abteilung, -en *department (section of a museum)*

ab*trocknen *to dry dishes*
    sich ab*trocknen *to dry oneself*
acht *eight*
die **Achtung** *attention; respect*
    Alle Achtung! *I compliment you.*
achtzehn *eighteen*
achtzig *eighty*
die **Adresse, -n** *address*
    Ade *(Swiss) good-bye*
der **Akt, -e** *act*
aktuell *current, topical*
das **Aktuelle** *current events*
das **Album, -s** *album*
  alle *all*
  allein *alone*
die **Allergie, -n** *allergy*
  alles *everything*
die **Alm, -en** *Alpine pasture*
die **Alpen** *the Alps*
das **Alphabet** *alphabet*
  als *when*
  alt *old*
  altertümlich *old-fashioned*
die **Altstadt, ⁼e** *old town, city*
  Amerika *America*
  an *at, at the side of; to; on*
  an*bauen *to grow, to produce*
  an*bieten, bot an, angeboten *to offer*
das **Andenken, -** *souvenir*
  andere *others*
  angenehm *pleasant*
  Angenehm. *Pleased to meet you.*
der/die **Angestellte, -n, -n** *clerk, employee*
der **Anhänger, -** *trailer*
  an*kommen, kam an, ist angekommen *to arrive*
die **Ankunft, ⁼e** *arrival*
die **Anlage, -n** *investment*
der **Anlasser, -** *starter*
  an*legen *to land (a boat)*
das **Anmeldeformular, -e** *registration form*
der **Anruf, -e** *telephone call*
  an*rufen, rief an, angerufen *to call, to telephone*
  an*schauen *to look at, view*
    sich etwas an*schauen *to look at something*
der **Anschluss, ⁼sse** *connection*
die **Anschrift, -en** *address*
  an*sehen (sieht an), sah an, angesehen *to look at*
    sich an*sehen *to look at oneself*

die **Ansichtskarte, -n** *postcard*
  an*springen, sprang an, ist angesprungen *to start*
  (an)statt *instead of*
  anstrengend *strenuous*
die **Antiquität, -en** *antique object*
  antworten *to answer*
  an*zeigen *to show; to display*
  an*ziehen, zog an, angezogen *to put on, dress*
    sich an*ziehen *to get dressed*
der **Anzug, ⁼e** *suit (man's)*
der **Apfel, ⁼** *apple*
die **Apfelsine, -n** *orange*
der **Apfelstrudel** *apple strudel*
die **Apotheke, -n** *pharmacy*
  in der Apotheke *at the pharmacy*
der **Apotheker, -** *pharmacist*
der **Apparat, -e** *machine*
  Wer ist am Apparat? *Who is on the phone?*
der **April** *April*
die **Arbeit, -en** *work*
  arbeiten *to work*
die **Arbeitslosigkeit** *unemployment*
  arrangieren *to arrange*
der **Artikel, -** *object, article*
der **Arzt, ⁼e** *physician (m.)*
  beim Arzt *at the physician's*
die **Ärztin, -nen** *physician (f.)*
der **Aschermittwoch** *Ash Wednesday*
das **Aspirin, -** *aspirin*
  auf *on, on top of, onto*
der **Aufenthalt, -e** *stay*
  Ich wünsche einen angenehmen Aufenthalt. *Have a pleasant stay.*
die **Aufgabe, -n** *task; homework*
  auf*laden, lud auf, aufgeladen *to load*
  auf*legen *to hang up*
die **Aufnahme, -n** *photo*
  auf*nehmen, nahm auf, aufgenommen *to take a picture*
  aufregend *exciting*
der **Aufschlag, ⁼e** *surcharge*
  einen Aufschlag berechnen *to charge extra*
der **Aufschnitt** *cold cuts*
  auf*stehen, stand auf, ist aufgestanden *to get up*
  auf*steigen, stieg auf, ist aufgestiegen *to ascend, climb*
der **Aufstieg, -e** *ascent*

auf*wachen *to wake up*

auf*ziehen *to parade, to march*

der Aufzug, ⁻e *elevator; act (in a play)*

der Augenblick, -e *moment*

augenblicklich *current, currently, just now*

der August *August*

aus *out of, from (is a native of)*

der Ausblick *view*

die Ausdauer *perseverance*

aus*drucken *to print out*

die Ausfahrt, -en *exit (on the highway)*

der Ausgang, ⁻e *exit*

ausgebucht *booked, sold out*

aus*gehen, ging aus, ist ausgegangen *to go out, to run out*

ausgezeichnet *excellent*

der Ausguss, ⁻sse *sink*

aus*halten, hielt aus, ausgehalten *to endure*

die Aushilfearbeit *temporary employment*

aus*kennen: sich aus*kennen in, kannte aus, ausgekannt *to be well versed in*

aus*laden, lud aus, ausgeladen *to unload*

aus*rasieren *to shave (neck)*

aus*ruhen: sich aus*ruhen *to relax, to rest*

der Ausschlag *rash*

das Außenfach, ⁻er *outside compartment*

außer *except (for), besides*

außerhalb *(+ gen.) outside of*

das Aussichtsdeck *observation deck*

aus*stellen *to issue, to exhibit*

die Ausstellung, -en *exhibition*

aus*suchen *to pick, to choose*

der Ausverkauf, ⁻e *sale*

ausverkauft *sold out*

aus*zahlen *to pay out*

das Auszahlungsformular, -e *withdrawal slip*

aus*ziehen, zog aus, ausgezogen *to undress, to take off*

sich aus*ziehen *to get undressed*

das Auto, -s *automobile, car*

die Autobahn, -en *highway, expressway*

auf der Autobahn *on the highway*

automatisch *automatically*

der Automechaniker, - *automobile mechanic*

der Autor, -en *author*

die Autoreparaturwerkstatt, ⁻en *automobile repair shop*

in der Autoreparaturwerkstatt *at the automobile repair shop*

B

backen, backte, gebacken *to bake*

der Backenzahn, ⁻e *molar*

das Bad, ⁻er *bathroom; bath*

der Bademantel, ⁻ *bathrobe, beach robe*

die Bademütze, -n *bathing cap*

baden *to bathe*

der Badeort, -e *spa, health resort*

das Badetuch, ⁻er *bath towel, beach towel*

das Badezimmer, - *bathroom*

die Bahn, -en *train*

die Deutsche Bundesbahn (DB) *German National Railway*

der Bahnhof, ⁻e *train station*

am Bahnhof *at the train station*

der Bahnsteig, -e *platform*

bald *soon*

der Balkon, -e *balcony*

der Ball, ⁻e *ball*

die Bank, -en *bank*

auf der Bank *at the bank*

der/die Bankangestellte, -n, -n *bank clerk, teller*

die Bankgebühr, -en *charge, fee*

die Banküberweisung, -en *bank transfer*

das Bargeld *cash*

der Bart, ⁻e *beard*

die Batterie, -n *battery*

der Beamte, -n, -n *official, civil servant*

beantworten *to answer*

die Bearbeitungsgebühr, -en *service charge*

der Becher, - *cup, beaker*

bedrohlich *threatening*

beeilen: sich beeilen *to hurry*

der/die Befragte, -n, -n *participant*

die Begrüßung, -en *greeting*

behandeln *to treat*

bei *with, at the home of; at a place of business; near; during, at*

bei*fügen *to attach*

das Bein, -e *leg*

das Beispiel, -e *example*

zum Beispiel *for example*

bekannt *well known*

beklagen *to lament*

sich beklagen *to complain*

bekommen, bekam, bekommen *to get*

beliebt *well-liked, popular*
bemerkenswert *remarkable*
benachrichtigen *to notify*
das Benzin *gasoline*
beobachten *to watch*
berechnen *to calculate, to charge*
der Berg, -e *hill, mountain*
die Bergbahn, -en *mountain railway*
der Beruf, -e *profession*
die Berufsaussicht, -en *prospects for a profession*
beruhigen *to quiet, to calm*
  sich beruhigen *to calm down*
berühmt *famous*
beschädigt *damaged, injured*
beschreiben, beschrieb, beschrieben *to describe*
beschweren *to burden*
  sich beschweren *to complain*
besetzt *busy, occupied*
besichtigen *to view, to look at*
die Besichtigung, -en *sightseeing; inspection*
besorgt *worried*
die Besprechung, -en *conference*
bestellen *to order*
bestimmt *certain*
der Besuch, -e *visit*
  zu Besuch kommen *to come for a visit*
besuchen *to visit*
betäuben *to numb*
die Betäubung *anesthesia*
  die örtliche Betäubung *local anesthesia*
das Bett, -en *bed*
bevor *before (conj.)*
beweglich *animated, moving, movable*
bewundern *to admire*
bewusst *aware*
bezahlen *to pay*
das Bier, -e *beer*
bieten, bot, geboten *to offer*
das Bild, -er *picture*
der Bildhauer *sculptor*
die Bildhauerei *sculpture*
der Bildungsweg, -e *educational track*
billig *cheap*
die Binde, -n *bandage*
  die elastische Binde *elastic bandage*
bis *until*
  bis bald. *See you soon.*
  bis Montag *until Monday*

bis morgen *until tomorrow, see you tomorrow*
bitter *bitter*
blasen, blies, geblasen *to blow*
blass *pale*
blau *blue*
bleiben, blieb, ist geblieben *to stay*
  Bleiben Sie am Apparat. *Stay on the line.*
  Wie lange bleiben Sie? *How long will you stay?*
blond *blond*
die Blume, -n *flower*
das Blumengeschäft, -e *flower shop*
die Bluse, -n *blouse*
der Boden, ⁻ *ground; floor*
die Bohne, -n *bean*
bohren *to drill*
der Bote, -n *messenger (m.)*
die Botin, -nen *messenger (f.)*
das Boxen *boxing*
der Boxkampf, ⁻e *boxing match*
brauchen *to need*
braun *brown*
die Bräune *suntan*
die Bremse, -n *brake*
bremsen *to brake*
das Bremspedal, -en *brake pedal*
brennen, brannte, gebrannt *to burn*
der Brief, -e *letter*
der Briefkasten, - *mailbox*
die Briefmarke, -n *stamp*
die Brille, -n *eyeglasses*
bringen, brachte, gebracht *to bring; to take*
das Brot, -e *bread*
  belegtes Brot *sandwich*
das Brötchen, - *roll*
der Browser, - *Web browser*
der Bruder, ⁻ *brother*
brünett *brunette*
das Buch, ⁻er *book*
das Bücherregal, -e *bookshelf*
das Bügeleisen, - *electric iron*
die Bühne, -n *stage*
die Bundesbahn *national railway*
die Bundesrepublik *Federal Republic*
der Bundestag *House of Representatives*
die Bundestagswahl, -en *federal election*
die Burg, -en *castle*
das Büro, -s *office*
der Bus, -se *bus*
die Buslinie, -n *bus line*

die **Butter** butter
 das **Butterbrot**, -e slice of bread and butter

C

das **Café**, -s café, coffee shop
 im Café in a café
die **Christlich-Demokratische Union (CDU)** the Christian Democratic Union
der **Computer**, - computer

D

 da there, here
  da oben up there
das **Dach**, ⸚er roof, carport
der **Dachboden**, ⸚ attic
 dahinter behind, beyond
der **Damenfriseur**, -e lady's hairdresser
der **Damenfriseursalon**, -s lady's hairdresser's
 dampfen to steam
der **Dampfer**, - steamboat
die **Dampferfahrt**, -en steamboat trip
 danach afterward
der **Dank** thanks; gratitude
  Recht herzlichen Dank für... Thank you very much for...
 danke thank you
 danken to thank
 dann then
 das the (neu.)
 dass that (conj.)
 Datei, -en file
 dauern to last
die **Dauerwelle**, -n permanent wave
 davor before
die **Decke**, -n ceiling
 dein your (fam. sing)
die **Demokratie**, -n democracy
 denken, dachte, gedacht to think
 denken an (+ acc.) to think of
 denn because
das **Deodorant**, -s deodorant
 der the (m.)
 Deutschland Germany
der **Dezember** December
der **Dialog**, -e dialogue
 die the (f.)
der **Dieb**, -e male thief

der **Diebstahl**, ⸚e theft
die **Diele**, -n hallway
der **Dienst**, -e service
der **Dienstag** Tuesday
 dieser this
die **Differenz**, -en difference
 direkt directly
der **Dirigent**, -en conductor
der **Dom**, -e cathedral
der **Donnerstag** Thursday
das **Doppelzimmer**, - double room
das **Dorf**, ⸚er village
 dort there
  dort drüben over there
der **Dramatiker**, - playwright
 drei three
 dreißig thirty
 dreizehn thirteen
die **Drogerie**, -n drugstore
  in der Drogerie at the drugstore
der **Drogeriemarkt**, ⸚e self-service drugstore
der **Drogist**, -en, -en drugstore employee
 du you (fam.)
 dumm stupid, silly
  Wie dumm! How silly!
 durch through
der **Durchschnitt** average
 dürfen to be allowed to, may (permission)
die **Dusche**, -n shower
 duschen to shower
  sich duschen to take a shower

E

die **Ecke**, -n corner
der **Edelstahl** stainless steel
 ehemalig former
das **Ei**, -er egg
 eigen own
 eigentlich actually
der **Eilbrief**, -e express letter
die **Eile** hurry
  Ich bin in Eile. I'm in a hurry.
 eindrucksvoll striking
 einfach simple, simply, easily
der **Eingang**, ⸚e entrance
der/die **Einheimische**, -n local resident
der **Einkauf**, ⸚e purchase
  Einkäufe machen shopping
 einkaufen to shop

die Einkaufsliste, -n *shopping list*
ein*laden, lud ein, eingeladen *to load; to invite*
einmal *once*
  noch einmal *once more*
ein*nehmen, nahm ein, eingenommen *to take, to swallow*
ein*reiben, rieb ein, eingerieben *to rub*
  sich ein*reiben *to rub oneself*
eins *one*
ein*schalten *to turn on*
das Einschreiben, - *registered letter*
ein*tragen, trug ein, eingetragen *to register*
  sich ein*tragen *to register oneself*
ein*treffen, traf ein, ist eingetroffen *to arrive*
ein*zahlen *to deposit*
das Einzahlungsformular, -e *deposit slip*
die Einzelheit, -en *detail*
einzeln *piece by piece, singly*
das Einzelzimmer, - *single room*
das Eis *ice; ice cream*
eisig *icy*
das Elektrogerät, -e *electrical appliance*
elf *eleven*
die Eltern *parents*
die E-Mail *e-mail*
der Empfänger, - *receiver of mail*
der Empfangschef, -s *reception clerk*
empfehlen (empfiehlt), empfahl, empfohlen *to recommend*
das Ende *end*
endlich *finally*
endlos *endless*
eng *narrow*
England *England*
der Enkel, - *grandson*
die Enkelin, -nen *granddaughter*
entfernt *away (from)*
entschuldigen *to excuse*
  sich entschuldigen *to apologize*
  Entschuldigen Sie. *Excuse me.*
die Entschuldigung, -en *excuse*
die Entzündung, -en *inflammation*
er *he/it*
die Erbse, -n *pea*
die Erdbeermarmelade, -n *strawberry jam*
das Erdgeschoss *first floor*
erfrischend *refreshing*
das Ergebnis, -se *result*

erhalten, erhielt, erhalten *to preserve; to receive*
erholen: sich erholen *to relax, to recuperate*
erinnern: sich erinnern *to remember, to remind*
die Erinnerung, -en *memory*
  zur Erinnerung *in memory of*
erkälten: sich erkälten *to catch cold*
die Erkältung, -en *cold*
erkennen, erkannte, erkannt *to recognize*
ermüdend *tiring*
erschöpft *exhausted*
ersetzen *to replace*
erstaunlich *amazing*
die Erststimme *first vote*
erwarten *to expect*
erweitern *to increase, to broaden*
erwerben *to acquire*
erzählen *to tell, to narrate*
  erzählen von *(+ dat.) to tell about*
es *it*
essen (isst), aß, gegessen *to eat*
euer *your (fam. pl.)*

F

die Fabel, -n *fable*
fabelhaft *fabulous*
der Fabrikant, -en, -en *manufacturer (m.)*
das Fach, ̈er *compartment; subject*
die Fachkenntnis, -se *knowledge in a particular field*
die Fahne, -n *flag*
fahren, fuhr, ist gefahren *to drive*
  fahren mit *(+ dat.) to go by means of*
die Fahrkarte, -n *ticket*
fallen, fiel, ist gefallen *to fall*
die Familie, -n *family*
fangen (fängt), fing, gefangen *to catch*
fantastisch *fantastic*
die Farbe, -n *color*
färben *to dye*
das Färben *coloring, dyeing*
der Fasching *carnival*
die Fastenzeit *Lent*
der Februar *February*
fehlen *to be missing*
  Was fehlt? *What's missing?*

Was fehlt denn? *What is wrong?*
Was fehlt dir? *What's wrong with you?*
die Feier, -n *celebration, ceremony*
  feiern *to celebrate*
der Feiertag, -e *holiday, day of rest*
  der kirchliche Feiertag, -e *religious holiday*
der Felsen, - *rock*
das Fenster, - *window*
die Feriensaison *vacation season*
das Ferngespräch, -e *long-distance call*
  fern*sehen, sah fern, ferngesehen *to watch TV*
das Fernsehen, - *television*
  im Fernsehen *on TV*
der Fernseher, - *television set*
das Fest, -e *party, celebration, festival*
der Festtag, -e *holiday, festivity*
der Film, -e *film, movie*
der Film-Enthusiast, -en, -en *movie fan*
  finden, fand, gefunden *to find*
der Fisch, -e *fish*
die Fläche, -n *plane, surface*
die Flasche, -n *bottle*
das Fleisch *meat*
  fliegen, flog, ist geflogen *to fly*
  flink *quick*
  flirten *to flirt*
der Flohmarkt, -e *flea market*
der Flug, ⁻e *flight*
der Fluggast, ⁻e *airplane passenger*
der Flughafen, ⁻ *airport*
  auf dem Flughafen *at the airport*
das Flugzeug, -e *airplane*
der Flur, -en *hallway*
das Formular, -e *form*
der Fotograf, -en, -en *photographer*
die Frage, -n *question*
  Frankreich *France*
die Frau, -en *woman, wife; Ms. (used as a form of address)*
das Fräulein, - *Miss (old-fashioned form of address for young, unmarried women)*
die Freie Demokratische Partei (FDP) *the Free Democratic Party*
der Freitag *Friday*
  freuen: sich freuen *to be glad*
der Freund, -e *male friend, boyfriend*
die Freundin, -nen *female friend, girlfriend*

frieren, fror, gefroren *to freeze*
  Es friert. *It's freezing.*
frisch *fresh*
der Friseursalon, -s *barbershop, hairdresser's salon, beauty parlor*
  im Friseursalon *at the barbershop/hairdresser's*
der Friseur, -e *male hairdresser*
die Friseuse, -n *female hairdresser*
  frisieren *to do someone's hair*
die Frucht, ⁻e *fruit*
der Frühling *spring*
das Frühstück *breakfast*
  inklusive Frühstück *including breakfast*
  zum Frühstück *for breakfast*
  frühstücken *to have breakfast*
  führen *to lead*
die Führung, -en *guided tour*
  füllen *to fill*
die Füllung, -en *filling*
das Fundbüro, -s *lost and found*
  auf dem Fundbüro *at the lost and found*
  fünf *five*
  fünfzehn *fifteen*
  fünfzig *fifty*
  funktionieren *to function*
  für *for*
  furchtbar *terrible*
der Fuß, ⁻sse *foot*
der Fußball *soccer*
das Fußballspiel, -e *soccer match*
der Fußboden, ⁻ *floor*
der Fußgänger, - *pedestrian*
die Fußgängerzone, -n *pedestrian zone*
der Fußnagel, ⁻ *toenail*
die Fußpflege *pedicure*
der Fußpfleger, - *male pedicurist*
die Fußpflegerin, -nen *female pedicurist*

G

die Galerie, -n *gallery*
der Gang, ⁻e *aisle, hallway, corridor*
die Garage, -n *garage*
der Garantieschein, -e *warranty*
das Gartencafé, -s *garden café*
das Gaspedal, -e *gasoline pedal*
der Gastarbeiter, - *foreign worker*
das Gebäck *pastry*
  geben (gibt), gab, gegeben *to give*

das Gebirge, - *mountains, mountain*
    im Gebirge *in the mountains*
der Gebirgsverein, -e *hiking and climbing club*
das Gebiss, -sse *set of teeth*
der Gebrauch *usage*
die Gebrauchsanweisung, -en *directions for use*
der Gebrauchtwagen, - *used car*
der Gedanke, -n *thought*
die Geduld *patience*
gefallen (gefällt), gefiel, gefallen *to please*
gegen *against; around*
    gegen zehn Uhr *around ten o'clock*
der Gegenstand, ⸚e *object*
    persönliche Gegenstände *personal items*
gehen, ging, ist gegangen *to go, to leave*
    Wie geht es Ihnen? *How are you? (pol.)*
    Wie geht's? *How are you? (fam.)*
    Mir geht's nicht so gut. *I'm not feeling so well.*
gehören *to belong to*
gelb *yellow*
das Geld, -er *money*
die Geldbörse, -n *purse*
der Geldwechselautomat, -en *automatic money changing machine*
das Gemälde, - *painting*
gemischt *mixed*
das Gemüse *vegetable(s)*
gemütlich *cozy*
genießen, genoss, genossen *to enjoy*
geöffnet *open*
das Gepäck *luggage*
das Gepäckband *baggage conveyor belt*
der Gepäckwagen, - *baggage cart*
gerade *straight*
geradeaus *straight ahead*
die Gerechtigkeit *justice*
gern *gladly, willingly*
das Geschäft, -e *store, business*
die Geschäftsbesprechung, -en *business discussion*
der Geschäftsführer, - *manager*
das Geschenk, -e *gift*
der Geschenkeinkauf, -e *gift purchase*
geschlossen *closed*
die Geschwindigkeitsbegrenzung *speed limit*

das Gespräch, -e *conversation, talk*
gestatten *to allow, to permit*
    Gestatten Sie. *Permit me. May I introduce myself?*
gestern *yesterday*
gesund *healthy*
das Getränk, -e *beverage*
die Gewerkschaft, -en *union*
der Gipfel, - *summit, mountain top*
die Girlande, -n *garland*
das Girokonto *checking account*
glänzend *splendid*
das Glas, ⸚er *glass*
der Glasbläser, - *glassblower*
glatt *smooth*
die Glatze, -n *bald head*
glauben *to believe*
der Gleichstrom *direct current (DC)*
der Gletscher, - *glacier*
das Gold *gold*
die Goldfüllung, -en *gold filling*
die Goldkrone, -n *gold crown*
die Grafik, -en *graphic*
das Gramm, - *gram*
die Grammatik *grammar*
das Gras, ⸚er *grass*
grau *gray*
die Grenze, -n *border*
Griechenland *Greece*
die Grippe, -n *flu*
groß *big*
großartig *magnificent*
die Größe, -n *size*
der Großkonzern, -e *large concern, company*
die Großmutter, ⸚ *grandmother*
der Großvater, ⸚ *grandfather*
Grüetzi *hello (Swiss)*
grün *green*
die Grünen *the Green Party*
die Gruppentour, -en *group tour*
der Gruß, ⸚e *greeting*
    Mit freundlichen Grüßen *Sincerely*
grüßen *to greet*
    Grüß Gott! *Hello! (So. German)*
gucken *to look*
    Guck mal! *Look!*
der Gürtel, - *belt*
gut *good, well*
das Gymnasium, Gymnasien *high school*
die Gymnastik *gymnastics, calisthenics*
    Gymnastik machen *to do calisthenics*

H

das Haar, -e *hair*
die Haarfarbe, -n *hair color*
der Haarschnitt *haircut*
der Haartrockner, - *hair dryer*
das Haarwuchsmittel, - *hair growth product*
haben, hatte, gehabt *to have*
der Hafen, ∴ *harbor*
die Halbzeit, -en *half time*
die Halle, -n *hall*
hallo *hello*
der Hals, ∵e *throat*
die Halsschmerzen *(pl.) sore throat*
halten *to stop*
    sich auf dem Laufenden halten *to keep abreast of the news, to stay informed*
handeln *to bargain*
der Handschuh, -e *glove*
das Handtuch, ∵er *towel*
das Handwerk *handicraft; trade*
handwerklich *manual*
    handwerkliches Geschick *manual dexterity; skilled hands*
hängen *to hang*
hart *hard*
die Hauptpost *main post office*
das Haus, ∵er *house*
heilbar *curable*
heilen *to heal*
die Heilquelle, -n *medicinal spring*
das Heimatland *homeland*
    Mein Heimatland ist... *My homeland is...*
heiß *hot*
heißen, hieß, geheißen *to be called*
helfen (hilft), half, geholfen *to help*
    helfen bei *(+ dat.) to help with*
das Hemd, -en *shirt*
heraus*brechen (bricht), brach heraus, ist herausgebrochen *to break off; to fall out*
der Herbst *autumn*
der Herd, -e *stove*
der Herr, -en, -en *gentleman, mister (usually used only in address)*
der Herrenfriseur *barber, barbershop*
der Herrenfriseursalon, -s *barbershop*
herrlich *glorious, wonderful*
herunter*laden, lud herunter, heruntergeladen *to download*
heute *today*

heutzutage *nowadays*
der Himmel, - *sky, heaven*
Himmelfahrt *Ascension Day*
hin *(to) there*
    hin und zurück *round-trip*
hinter *behind*
hintereinander *one behind the other*
der Hintergrund, ∵e *background*
der Hirtenjunge, -n, -n *shepherd boy*
hoch *high*
das Hochdeutsch *High German, Standard German*
hoch*fahren *to boot up*
die Hochschule *university, academy*
hoffentlich *hopefully*
das Hoftheater, - *court theater*
hören *to hear, to listen*
    auf Wiederhören *good-bye (on the telephone)*
der Hörer *receiver*
die Hose, -n *pants, slacks*
das Hotel, -s *hotel*
    im Hotel *in the hotel*
der Hotelpage, -n *bellhop*
hübsch *pretty*
das Huhn, ∵er *chicken*
hundert *hundred*
    hunderteins *one hundred one*
    zweihundert *two hundred*
der Hunger *hunger*
die Hupe, -n *horn*
husten *to cough*
der Husten *cough*
der Hut, ∵e *hat*
die Hütte, -n *shelter, hut*

I

ich *I*
die Idee, -n *idea*
ihr *you (fam. pl.): her; their*
Ihr *your (pol.)*
immer *always*
die Impfung, -en *vaccination*
imposant *impressive*
in *in, inside, into*
individuell *individual*
die Industrie, -n *industry*
der Industrielle, -n *industrialist*
informieren *to inform*
    sich informieren über *(+ acc.) to inform oneself about, to stay informed*
der Inhalt, -e *contents*

die Initiale, -n *initial*
das Innenfach, ⁔er *inside compartment*
   innerhalb *(+ gen.) inside*
der Intendant, -en *director*
   interessant *interesting*
das Internet *Internet*
die Internetseite, -n *Web page*
das Interview, -s *interview*
   interviewen *to interview*
der Interviewleiter *interview director*
   irgendwann *sometime, someday*
   irgendwo *somewhere*
   Italien *Italy*

J

die Jacht, -en *yacht*
die Jacke, -n *jacket*
die Jahreszeit, -en *season*
der Januar *January*
   jeder *each, every*
   jener *that*
   jetzt *now*
der/das Joghurt *yogurt*
der Juli *July*
   jung *young*
der Juni *June*
der Jurist, -en, -en *lawyer*
   Er studiert Jura. *He is studying law.*

K

das Kabelfernsehprogramm, -e *cable
     program*
der Kaffee, -s *coffee*
   Kaffee trinken *to have coffee*
das Kalbfleisch *veal*
   kalt *cold*
   kämmen *to comb*
     sich (die Haare) kämmen *to comb
      one's hair*
   kämpfen *to fight*
   Kanada *Canada*
der Kandidat, -en *candidate*
die Kapelle, -n *band*
   kaputt *broken; tired*
     Ich bin kaputt. *I'm exhausted.*
der Karfreitag *Good Fnday*
die Karies *periodontal disease, cavity,
     caries*
der Karneval *carnival (period before Lent)*
die Kartoffel, -n *potato*

der Karton, -s *box*
der Käse *cheese*
der Kassierer, - *cashier*
die Kathedrale, -n *cathedral*
   kaufen *to buy*
das Kaufhaus, ⁔er *department store*
   im Kaufhaus *in the department
     store*
der Keller, - *cellar, basement*
   kennen, kannte, gekannt *to know
     (people, places, or things)*
die Keramik *ceramics*
   das Keramikstück *ceramic piece*
das Kilo, -s *kilo*
der Kilometer, - *kilometer (km)*
das Kind, -er *child*
das Kinderzimmer, - *child's room*
   kindhaft *childlike*
der Kiosk, -s *kiosk, newsstand*
die Kirsche, -n *cherry*
der Kirschstrudel *cherry strudel*
die Kiste, -n *box, container*
der Kittel, - *gown, apron*
   klar *clear*
     Klar! *Certainly! Of course!*
die Klasse, -n *class*
die erste Klasse *the first class*
   erster Klasse *first class*
das Kleid, -er *dress*
die Kleidung *clothing*
   klein *small*
das Kleingeld *coins, change*
die Kleinstadt, ⁔e *small town*
   klemmen *to jam*
das Kloster, ⁔ *cloister*
   knusprig *crunchy, crispy*
   kochen *to cook*
der Koffer, - *suitcase*
das Kombinationsschloss, ⁔sser
     combination lock
   kommen, kam, ist gekommen *to
     come*
     kommen aus *(+ dat.) to come from
     (with locations)*
     Ich komme aus . . . *I come from . . .*
die Kommunalwahl, -en *local election*
die Konditorei, -en *confectionery, café with
     baker and pastry shop*
die Konferenz, -en *conference, meeting*
die Konkurrenz *competition*
   können *to be able to, can (ability)*
der Konsul, -n *consul*
das Konsulat, -e *consulate*
das Konto, Konten *account*

ein Konto einrichten *to open an account*

ein Konto eröffnen *to open an account*

der Kontoauszug, ⁀e *bank statement*

der Kontrast, -e *contrast*

der Konzern, -e *company, corporation*

das Konzert, -e *concert*

kooperieren *to cooperate*

das Kopfrechnen *mental arithmetic*

der Kopf, ⁀e *head*

kopflos *headless*

die Koptschmerzen *(pl.) headache*

das Kopfweh *headache*

der Körper, - *body*

die Körperpflege *personal hygiene*

der Körperpuder, - *dusting powder*

kosten *to cost*

Was kostet das? *How much does it cost?*

krank *ill, sick*

Ich bin krank. *I'm sick.*

krankhaft *pathological*

die Krankheit, -en *illness, disease*

kraus *frizzy*

die Kreditkarte, -n *credit card*

das Kreuz, -e *cross*

die Kreuzung, -en *intersection*

die Krone, -n *crown*

die Küche, -n *kitchen*

der Kuchen, - *cake*

der Kühlschrank, ⁀e *refrigerator*

die Kultur, -en *culture*

die Kulturnotiz, -en *cultural note*

der Kunde, -n *customer*

die Kunst, ⁀e *art*

der Kunstler, - *artist*

das Kunstlerviertel, - *artists' district, district inhabited by artists*

das Kunstmuseum, Kunstmuseen *art museum*

das Kunstwerk, -e *work of art*

die Kur, -en *cure, treatment*

eine Kur machen *to take a cure*

der Kurgast, ⁀e *spa visitor*

das Kurkonzert, -e *concert at a spa*

der Kurort, -e *spa, health resort*

in einem Kurort *in a spa*

der Kurs, -e *exchange rate*

Der Kurs ist niedrig/hoch. *The exchange rate is low/high.*

der Kurswagen, - *through coach (on a train)*

die Kurtaxe, -n *spa surcharge*

kurz *short*

kurzfristig *on short notice*

die Kusine, -n *cousin (f.)*

L

laden, lud, geladen *to load*

die Lampe, -n *lamp*

das Land, ⁀er *country*

auf dem Land *in the country*

die Landtagswahl, -en *state election*

lang *long (adj.)*

lange *long (adv.)*

Es dauert lange. *It takes a long time.*

langweilig *boring*

lassen, ließ, gelassen *to leave, to let*

der Lastwagen, - *truck*

laufen, lief, ist gelaufen *to run, to walk*

laut *loud*

läuten *to ring*

leben *to live, to be alive*

die Lebensmittel *(pl.) groceries*

der Lebensretter, - *life-saver*

lecker *delicious*

Die Kuchen sind lecker. *The cakes are delicious.*

das Leder *leather*

aus Leder *made of leather*

leer *empty*

legen *to lay, to put*

der Lehm *mud*

die Lehmpackung, -en *mud pack*

die Lehre, -n *apprenticeship*

lehren *to teach*

der Lehrer, - *teacher*

der Lehrling, -e *apprentice*

leisten: sich leisten *to afford*

lernen *to learn*

die Leichtathletik *track and field*

Leid: Es tut mir Leid. *I'm sorry.*

leiden, litt, gelitten *to suffer*

leiden an *(+ dat.) to suffer from*

leihen, lieh, geliehen *to lend, to borrow*

die Leitung, -en *line*

Die Leitung ist besetzt. *The line is busy.*

Die Leitung ist gestört. *The line is temporarily out of order.*

die Leselampe, -n *reading lamp*

die Leute *people (always pl.)*

der Lieferant, -en, -en *supplier, deliverer*

die Lieferung, -en *delivery*

393

der Lieferwagen, - *delivery van*
die Liegehalle, -n *lounge*
   liegen, lag, gelegen *to lie*
der Liegewagen, - *couchette (on a train)*
die Liga, -s *league*
   links *to the left, on the left*
der Liter, - *liter*
das Loch, ⸚er *hole*
      das Loch im Zahn *cavity*
die Locke, -n *curl*
   lockig *curly*
der Logensitz, -e *box seat*
   lohnen *to reward*
      Es lohnt sich. *It's worthwhile.*
   los: Was ist los? *What's the matter?*
   losrennen, rannte los, ist losgerannt
      to dash off
die Lösung, -en *answer, solution*
   luftdicht *airtight*
   luftig *breezy*
die Luftpost *air mail*
      mit Luftpost *by airmail*
die Lust, ⸚e *pleasure, delight*
      Lust haben *to feel like*

M

   machen *to make, to do*
      (Es) macht nichts. *(It) doesn't matter.*
      Das macht 125 Euro. *That'll be 125
         euros.*
die Magenschmerzen *(pl.) stomachache*
der Mai *May*
   malen *to paint*
der Maler, - *painter*
die Malerei, -en *painting*
   manche *some (usually pl.)*
   manchmal *sometimes*
der Mann, ⸚er *man, husband*
die Mannschaft, -en *team*
der Markt, ⸚e *market*
der März *March*
der Maskenball, ⸚e *costume ball*
die Massage, -n *massage*
die Massenmedien *mass media*
die Matinée, -s *matinee*
das Mausklick *mouse click*
das Medikament, -e *medication*
das Meer, -e *ocean, sea*
die Meeresküste, -n *coast, shore*
das Mehl *flour*
   mehr *more*
   mehrmals *several times*
   mein *my*

die Menge *a lot*
die Messe, -n *trade fair, exhibition*
      auf der Messe *at the trade fair*
das Messegelände, - *exhibition grounds*
der Messestand, ⸚e *booth*
das Metall, -e *metal*
der Metallfaden, ⸚ *metal thread*
   mieten *to rent*
      ein Segelboot mieten *to rent a
         sailboat*
die Million, -en *million*
das Mineralwasserbad, ⸚er *bath or pool
         with mineral water*
die Minute, -n *minute*
   mit *with; by means of (transportation)*
   mitbringen, brachte mit, mitgebracht
      to bring along
   mitmachen *to participate*
der Mittag, -e *noon*
das Mittagessen, - *lunch (main meal)*
      zum Mittagessen *for lunch*
die Mitte, -n *middle*
das Mittel, - *medicine*
der Mittelgang, ⸚e *middle aisle*
das Mittelmeer *Mediterranean Sea*
die Mittelmeerinsel, -n *Mediterranean
         island*
   mitten: mitten auf *(+ dat.) in the
         middle of*
die Mitternacht, ⸚e *midnight*
der Mittwoch *Wednesday*
die Möbel *(pl.) furniture*
der Möbelstil, -e *furniture style*
das Modell, -e *model*
das Modem, -s *modem*
   mögen *to like to (inclination); may
         (possibility)*
die Möglichkeit, -en *possibility*
die Möhre, -n *carrot*
der Moment, -e *moment*
der Monat, -e *month*
der Montag *Monday*
   morgen *tomorrow*
      morgen früh *tomorrow morning*
der Morgen *morning*
      guten Morgen *good morning (pol.)*
      Morgen *morning, hello (fam.)*
   morgens *mornings, in the morning*
das Motorrad, ⸚er *motorcycle*
   müde *tired*
      Ich bin müde. *I'm tired.*
das Mundwasser, - *mouthwash*
der Münzenfernsprecher, - *coin-operated
         telephone*

das Museum, Museen *museum*
    im Museum *at the museum*
der Musiker, - *musician*
das Müsli, -s *muesli*
    müssen *to have to, must (necessity)*
die Mutter, ∺ *mother*
die Mütze, -n *cap*

N

    nach *after; toward, to (used with cities and masculine and neuter countries)*
    nach*fragen *inquire*
die Nachricht, -en *news item*
    eine Nachricht hinterlassen *to leave a message*
die Nachrichten *news broadcast*
die Nacht, ∺e *night*
    gute Nacht *good night*
der Nachtisch, -e *dessert*
    nachts *night, at night*
der Nacken, - *neck*
    nah(e) *near, close*
der Nahverkehrszug, ∺e *short-distance train*
der Name, -n *name*
    nass *wet*
der Nationalfeiertag, -e *national holiday*
    neb(e)lig *foggy*
    neben *beside, next to*
der Neffe, -n, -n *nephew*
    nehmen (nimmt), nahm, genommen *to take*
    Ich nehme die Bluse in gelb. *I'll take the blouse in yellow.*
    nein *no*
    nennen, nannte, genannt *to name*
    nett *nice*
das Netz, -e *net, network*
    neu *new*
das Neujahr *New Year*
    neun *nine*
    neunzehn *nineteen*
    neunzig *ninety*
    nicht *not*
die Nichte, -n *niece*
das Nichtraucherabteil, -e *no smoking compartment*
    nichts *nothing*
die Niederlage, -n *defeat*
    noch *still; yet*
    noch nicht *not yet*
    nördlich *northerly*

die Nordsee *North Sea*
der Notausgang, ∺e *emergency exit*
die Note, -n *grade*
die Notiz, -en *note*
    das Notizbuch, ∺er *notebook*
der Notruf, -e *emergency call*
der November *November*
der Numerus Clausus *"closed numbers" system limiting university admissions*
die Nummer, -n *number*
der Nutznießer, - *beneficiary*
    einen Nutznießer einsetzen *to name a beneficiary*

O

    ob *whether, if*
das Obst *fruit*
    oder *or*
    öffentlich *public, open*
    ohne *without*
    ohnehin *anyway, nevertheless*
der Oktober *October*
das Öl, -e *oil, ointment*
der Omnibus, -se *bus*
der Onkel, - *uncle*
die Ordnung, -en *order*
    Alles ist in Ordnung. *Everything is all right.*
    Etwas ist nicht in Ordnung. *Something is wrong.*
    orientieren *to inform, to instruct*
    sich orientieren *to orient oneself*
die Originalverpackung, -en *factory box/wrapping*
    Ostern *Easter*
    Österreich *Austria*
    östlich *easterly*
die Ostsee *Baltic*

P

das Paar, -e *pair*
    ein paar *a few*
die Packung, -en *box*
    Es steht auf der Packung. *It's written on the box.*
das Paket, -e *package*
das Panorama *panorama*
das Parkett, -s *parquet; orchestra*
die Partei, -en *political party*
das Parterre *first floor*
der Pass, ∺sse *passport*

die Passkontrolle, -n *passport control*
passen *to fit*
    Der Mantel paßt mir. *The coat fits me.*
der Patient, -en *patient (m.)*
die Patientin, -nen *patient (f.)*
die Pause, -n *intermission*
der Personenzug, ⁻e *passenger train*
der Pfad, -e *path, trail*
der Pfadfinder, - *Boy Scout*
der Pfennig, -e *penny (outdated)*
Pfingsten *Pentecost, Whitsuntide*
das Pfund, -e *pound; half a kilo*
die Pizzeria, -s *pizza shop*
das Photo, -s *photo (also: Foto)*
der Photoapparat, -e *camera*
der Plan, ⁻e *plan*
planen *to plan*
die Plastik, -en *sculpture*
der Platz, ⁻e *seat; square, place*
der Platzanweiser, - *usher*
plötzlich *suddenly*
die Politik *politics*
der Politiker, - *politician*
die Polsterung *upholstery*
die Post *post office; mail*
    auf der Post *at the post office*
das Postamt, ⁻er *post office*
die Postkarte, -n *postcard*
die Postleitzahl, -en *zip code*
das Postscheckkonto *postal checking account*
das Postsparkonto *postal savings account*
die Pracht *splendor, pomp*
prachtvoll *splendid*
das Präparat, -e *medical or chemical preparation, medication*
der Präsident, -en, -en *president*
preisgünstig *reasonable*
die Presse *press*
der Privatgegenstand, ⁻e *personal belonging*
problemlos *uncomplicated(ly)*
das Programm, -e *program*
das Zweite Programm *Channel Two*
promenieren *to stroll about, to promenade*
prüfen *to check, to examine*
    die Luft prüfen *to check the air*
das Publikum *audience*
der Pullover, - *sweater*
pünktlich *on time, punctual*

putzen *to clean*
    sich die Zähne putzen *to brush one's teeth*

Q

die Quelle, -n *spring, well*
die Quittung, -en *receipt*

R

das Rad, ⁻er *bicycle*
Rad*fahren, fuhr Rad, ist Rad gefahren *to bicycle*
das Radio, -s *radio*
    im Radio *on the radio*
der Radsport *cycling*
der Rand, ⁻er *edge, border*
der Rang, ⁻e *dress circle*
rar *rare*
rasen *to speed*
der Rasierapparat, -e *electric razor*
die Rasiercreme *shaving cream*
rasieren *to shave*
    sich rasieren *to shave oneself*
die Raststätte, -n *rest stop on an expressway*
das Rathaus, ⁻er *city hall*
der Raucher, - *smoker*
der Raum, ⁻e *room*
die Realität, -en *reality*
rechnen *to count*
die Rechnung, -en *check*
    Die Rechnung, bitte! *The check, please.*
das Recht, -e *right, law*
    Recht haben *to be right*
    ein Recht haben *to have a right*
rechts *to the right, on the right*
der Rechtsanwalt, ⁻e *lawyer (m.)*
die Rechtsanwältin, -nen *lawyer (f.)*
das Regal, -e *shelf*
regelmäßig *regular*
der Regen *rain*
der Regenmantel, ⁻ *raincoat*
regnen *to rain*
    Es regnet. *It's raining.*
der Reifen, - *tire*
die Reise, -n *trip, journey, travels*
    Gute Reise. *Have a nice trip.*
das Reisebüro, -s *travel agency*
der Reiseführer, - *travel guide (book)*
reisen *to travel*

der/die Reisende, -n, -n *traveler*
der Reisepass, ⁼sse *passport*
die Reisetasche, -n *travel bag*
das Reiseziel, -e *destination*
der Reißverschluss, ⁼sse *zipper*
rennen, rannte, ist gerannt
    to run
renovieren *to renovate*
reparieren *to repair*
reservieren *to reserve*
die Reservierung, -en *reservation*
das Restaurant, -s *restaurant*
    im Restaurant *in a restaurant*
das Rezept, -e *prescription, recipe*
die Rheintour *Rhine tour*
das Rindfleisch *beef*
der Rock, ⁼e *skirt*
die Rolle, -n *role*
die Röntgenaufnahme, -n *X-ray*
das Röntgenbild, -er *X-ray*
der Rosenmontag *Rose Monday (Monday*
    before Lent)
rot *red*
rötlich *reddish*
die Routine, -n *routine*
der Rückflug, ⁼e *return flight*
der Rucksack, ⁼e *backpack*
der Rücksitz, -e *backseat*
rufen, rief, gerufen *to call*
ruhig *calm, quiet; smooth*
die Ruine, -n *ruin*
die Runde *round, a little while*

S

die S-Bahn *city train*
die Sache, -n *thing*
    die Sachen *belongings*
sagen *to say*
die Sahne *cream*
    Schlagsahne *whipped cream*
der Salat, -e *salad*
die Salbe, -n *salve*
der Samstag *Saturday*
der Sand *sand*
sandig *sandy*
der Sänger, - *singer*
sauer *sour*
Schade! *Too bad. What a pity.*
der Schaden, ⁼ *damage*
der Schal, -s *scarf*
der Schalter, - *window (at post offices,*
    banks, etc.)

der Schalterbeamte, -n, -n *postal clerk at*
    the window
der Schauspieler, - *actor*
der Scheck, -s *check*
    einen Scheck einlösen *to cash a*
    check
das Scheckkonto *checking account*
der Schein, -e *bill (money)*
scheinen, schien, geschienen *to shine,*
    to seem
schenken *to give*
die Schere, -n *pair of scissors*
schicken *to send*
    schicken an *(+ acc.) to send to*
das Schiff, -e *ship*
das Schild, -er *sign*
schlafen, schlief, geschlafen *to sleep*
    schlafen gehen *to go to bed*
der Schlafsack, ⁼e *sleeping bag*
der Schlafwagen, - *sleeping car*
das Schlafzimmer, - *bedroom*
schlagen, schlug, geschlagen *to*
    beat
die Schlagfertigkeit *wit, ready wit*
schlecht *bad, badly*
    Es geht mir schlecht. *I'm not feeling*
    well.
schleppen *to haul*
schließen, schloss, geschlossen *to*
    close
der Schlüssel, - *key*
die Schmerzen *pain, hurt*
schmerzen *to hurt*
der Schnee *snow*
der Schneefall, ⁼e *snowfall*
schneiden, schnitt, geschnitten *to*
    cut
schneien *to snow*
    Es schneit. *It's snowing.*
schnell *fast*
der Schnellimbiss, -sse *snack bar*
das Schnitzel, - *cutlet*
der Schnurrbart, ⁼e *mustache*
die Schokolade *chocolate*
schön *beautiful, nice*
schrecklich *horrible*
schreiben, schrieb, geschrieben *to*
    write
    schreiben an *(+ acc.) to write to*
    schreiben über *(+ acc.) to write*
    about
schreien, schrie, geschrie(e)n *to*
    scream, to yell

die Schule, -n *school*

schwach *weak*

der Schwager, - *brother-in-law*

die Schwägerin, -nen *sister-in-law*

schwarz *black*

die Schwarzwälderkirschtorte, -n *Black Forest cake*

das Schweinefleisch *pork*

die Schweiz *Switzerland*

die Schwellung, -en *swelling*

die Schwester, -n *sister*

schwimmen, schwamm, ist geschwommen *to go swimming*

das Schwimmen *swimming*

schwindlig *dizzy*

schwül *muggy*

sechs *six*

sechzehn *sixteen*

sechzig *sixty*

der Seetang *seaweed*

der Segelanzug, ⁓e *sailing suit*

das Segelboot, -e *sailboat*

sehen (sieht), sah, gesehen *to see*

auf Wiedersehen *good-bye (pol.)*

die Sehenswürdigkeiten *sights*

die Sehne, -n *tendon*

die Seife, -n *soap*

sein *his; its*

sein, war, ist gewesen *to be*

frei sein *to be available*

fertig sein *to be ready*

seit *since; for (time expressions)*

der Sekretär, -e *male secretary*

selber *self, oneself, myself, themselves, etc.*

selbst *self, oneself, myself themselves, etc.; even*

selbstverständlich *of course*

seltsam *strange, odd*

senden, sandte, gesandt *to send*

senden, sendete, gesendet *to broadcast*

der Sender, - *station (radio, TV)*

der September *September*

servieren *to serve*

Servus *good-bye (Austrian)*

der Sessel, - *easy chair*

die Sesselbahn, -en *chairlift*

setzen *to set, to place, to put*

sich setzen *to sit down, to take a seat*

sicher *sure, safe, secure*

die Sicherheit *certainty, security, safety*

der Sicherheitsgurt *safety belt*

sicherlich *certainly*

die Sicht *view*

sie *she/it; they*

Sie *you (pol.)*

sieben *seven*

siebzehn *seventeen*

siebzig *seventy*

der Sieg, -e *victory*

siegen *to win*

sitzen, saß, gesessen *to sit*

der Sitzplan, ⁓e *seating plan*

die Sitzung, -en *meeting*

das Skilaufen, Skifahren *skiing*

die Skulptur, -en *sculpture*

sobald *as soon as*

die Socke, -n *sock*

ein Paar Socken *a pair of socks*

das Sofa, -s *sofa*

sogar *even*

der Sohn, ⁓e *son*

solche *such (usually pl.)*

sollen *to be supposed to, should (obligation)*

der Sommer, - *summer*

das Sonderangebot, -e *special offer*

die Sonderausstellung, -en *special exhibition*

sondern *but, on the contrary, rather*

nicht nur . . . sondern auch *not only . . . but also*

die Sonderschule, -n *special needs school*

der Sonnabend *Saturday*

die Sonne, -n *sun*

der Sonnenbrand, ⁓e *sunburn*

die Sonnenschutzcreme, -n *sunscreen lotion*

das Sonnenschutzöl, -e *sun protection oil*

der Sonntag *Sunday*

sonst *otherwise*

Sonst noch etwas? *Anything else?*

die Sorge, -n *care, sorrow*

Sorgen haben *to be worried, to worry*

sowieso *in any case, anyhow*

die Sozialdemokratische Partei Deutschlands (SPD) *the Social Democratic Party of Germany*

die Sozialwissenschaft *social sciences*

Spanien *Spain*

spannend *exciting, thrilling*

der Spargel *asparagus*

spät *late*

Wie spät ist es? *What time is it?*

das Sparbuch, ⁓er *passbook*

sparen *to save*

das **Sparkonto** *savings account*
der **Spediteur, -e** *mover, shipping agent*
die **Spedition, -en** *moving agency, shipping agency*
    speichern *to save; to load (on computer)*
die **Speisekarte, -n** *menu*
der **Speisewagen, -** *dining car*
das **Spiel, -e** *game*
der **Spieler, -** *male player*
das **Spielkasino, -s** *gambling casino*
die **Spielzeit, -en** *season*
die **Spitze, -n** *top*
die **Splitterpartei, -en** *splinter party*
der **Sport** *sport*
der **Sportverein, -e** *sports club*
    sprechen (spricht), sprach, gesprochen *to talk*
      sprechen uber *(+ acc.) to talk about*
das **Sprechzimmer, -** *consulting room*
die **Spritze, -n** *shot*
    eine Spritze setzen *to give a shot*
der **Staat, -en** *state*
das **Staatstheater, -** *federal theater*
die **Stadt, ̈e** *city; town*
das **Städtchen, -** *small city*
die **Stadtmauer, -n** *city wall*
die **Stadtmitte, -n** *city center*
der **Stadtplan, ̈e** *city map*
das **Stadttheater, -** *municipal theater*
das **Stadtzentrum, Stadtzentren** *city center*
    ständig *constantly*
    stark *strong*
    statt*finden, fand statt, stattgefunden *to take place*
    stecken *to stick, to put*
    stehen, stand, gestanden *to stand*
      Schlange stehen *to stand in line*
    stehen bleiben, blieb stehen, ist stehen geblieben *to stop, to stall*
    stehlen, stahl, gestohlen *to steal*
    steigen, stieg, ist gestiegen *to climb*
    steil *steep*
der **Stein, -e** *rock*
    stellen *to place, to put*
die **Steuer, -n** *tax*
die **Steuererhöhung, -en** *tax increase*
die **Steuersenkung, -en** *tax decrease*
die **Stimme, -n** *vote, voice*
    seine Stimme abgeben *to cast one's vote, to vote*
    stimmen *to be correct, to be true*
    Das stimmt. *That's right.*

der **Stock, ̈e** *floor*
    der erste Stock *the second floor*
der **Stoff, -e** *material*
der **Strand, ̈e** *beach*
    am Strand *at the beach*
der **Strandkorb, ̈e** *large wicker beach chair*
die **Straße, -n** *street*
das **Straßencafé, -s** *sidewalk café*
die **Straßenwachthilfe** *highway assistance service*
    streuen *to sprinkle*
der **Strom, ̈e** *electrical current, stream*
der **Strudel, -** *strudel*
das **Stück, -e** *piece*
der **Student, -en, -en** *student*
    studieren *to study, to go to college*
das **Studium, Studien** *studies*
der **Stuhl, ̈e** *chair*
    stundenlang *for hours*
der **Sturm, ̈e** *storm*
    stürmen *to storm*
      Es stürmt. *It's stormy.*
    stürmisch *rough, stormy*
die **Sturmwarnung, -en** *storm warning*
    stutzen *to trim*
    suchen *to search for, to look for*
    südlich *southerly*
    sündigen *to sin*
der **Supermarkt, ̈e** *supermarket*
    superschnell *superfast*
die **Suppe, -n** *soup*
    surfen *to surf*
    süß *sweet*
    sympathisch *likable*
      Er ist mir sympathisch. *I like him.*
    sympathisch sein *to be likable*
das **Symptom, -e** *symptom*
die **Szene, -n** *scene*

T

die **Tablette, -n** *pill*
der **Tachometer, -** *speedometer*
    der Tacho, -s *speedometer*
die **Tafel, -n** *announcement board*
    die Tafel Schokolade *bar of chocolate*
der **Tag, -e** *day*
    Guten Tag. *Hello. (pol.)*
    Tag. *Hello. (fam.)*
die **Tagesroutine** *daily routine*
die **Tagesschau** *daily news program*

täglich *daily*

   dreimal täglich *three times a day*

das **Tal, ̈er** *valley*

   tanken *to get gas*

die **Tanksäule, -n** *gasoline pump*

die **Tankstelle, -n** *gasoline station*

die **Tante, -n** *aunt*

die **Tapete, -n** *wallpaper*

   tapezieren *to hang wallpaper*

die **Tasche, -n** *bag, purse*

der **Taschenrechner, -** *pocket calculator*

die **Tasse, -n** *cup*

   eine Tasse Kaffee *a cup of coffee*

   tausend *thousand*

das **Taxi, -s** *taxi*

der/das **Teil, -e** *part*

der **Teilnehmer, -** *participant*

das **Telefon, -e** *telephone*

das **Telefonbuch, ̈er** *telephone book*

das **Telefongespräch, -e** *telephone conversation*

   telefonieren *to call, to telephone*

   telefonisch *by telephone, over the telephone*

   telefonisch erreichen *to reach by telephone*

die **Telefonkarte, -n** *telephone card*

die **Telefonnummer, -n** *telephone number*

die **Telefonzelle, -n** *telephone booth*

der **Teppich, -e** *rug, carpet*

der **Termin, -e** *appointment*

   einen Termin haben *to have an appointment*

die **Terrasse, -n** *terrace*

   teuer *expensive*

das **Theater, -** *theater*

der **Theaterbesucher, -** *theatergoer*

die **Theaterkasse, -n** *theater box office*

   an der Theaterkasse *at the theater box office*

das **Theaterstück, -e** *play*

der **Tisch, -e** *table*

der **Titel, -** *title*

die **Tochter, ̈** *daughter*

   toll *great (colloquial), terrific*

die **Tonaufnahme, -n** *audio recording*

der **Töpfer, -** *potter*

die **Töpferei** *pottery*

das **Tor, -e** *goal*

die **Torte, -n** *tart, fancy cake*

der **Tourist, -en, -en** *tourist*

die **Tracht, -en** *regional dress, costume*

   tragen (trägt), trug, getragen *to wear*

der **Transformator, -en** *transformer*

der **Transport, -e** *transport*

die **Transportmöglichkeit, -en** *means of transportation*

   treffen (trifft), traf, getroffen *to meet*

   sich treffen *to meet one another*

   treiben, trieb, getrieben *to do (an activity)*

   Sport treiben *to engage in sports*

   trennen *to separate*

   sich trennen *to part*

die **Treppe, -n** *stair*

   Nehmen Sie die Treppe! *Take the stairs.*

das **Treppenhaus, ̈er** *staircase*

   trinken, trank, getrunken *to drink*

das **Trinkgeld, -er** *tip*

   trocknen *to dry*

   sich die Haare trocknen *to dry one's hair*

der **Tropfen, -** *drop*

   trotz *in spite of*

   Tschau. *Good-bye. (fam.)*

   Tschüs. *Good-bye. (fam.)*

   tun, tat, getan *to do, to make*

   gut tun *to do good*

   Schwimmen tut ihr gut. *Swimming is good for her*

   weh tun *to hurt*

   Es tut weh. *It hurts.*

die **Tür, -en** *door*

der **Turm, ̈e** *tower*

   turnen *to do gymnastics*

das **Turnen** *gymnastics*

die **Tüte, -n** *bag*

U

   über *above, over, across*

   überall *everywhere*

der **Überblick, -e** *overview*

   überein*stimmen *to agree*

   nicht überein*stimmen *to disagree*

   überholen *to pass, overtake (another vehicle)*

   überflüssig *superfluous, unnecessary*

   überprüfen *to test, to check*

   übertragen, übertrug, übertragen *to broadcast*

   über*wechseln *to change, to transfer*

   überweisen, überwies, überwiesen *to transfer money*

die **Uhr, -en** *clock, watch*
    Wie viel Uhr ist es? *What time is it?*
um *around; at (time expressions)*
    Um wie viel Uhr . . .? *At what time . . .?*
um*bauen *to rebuild, to remodel*
um*buchen *to change reservations*
die **Umhängetasche, -n** *shoulder bag*
die **Umkleidekabine, -n** *fitting room*
um*schalten *to switch, convert*
um*setzen *to convert*
    in die Realitat um*setzen *to implement, realize (an idea)*
um*steigen, stieg um, ist umgestiegen *to change trains*
der **Umtausch, -e** *exchange*
umtauschen *to exchange*
die **Umwelt** *environment*
um*ziehen, zog um, ist umgezogen *to move (house)*
    sich um*ziehen *to change one's clothes*
der **Umzug, ⁻e** *move; parade*
unangenehm *unpleasant*
die **Unannehmlichkeit** *inconvenience*
und *and*
unglaublich *unbelievable*
uninteressant *uninteresting*
die **Universität, -en** *university, college*
unklar *unclear*
unmodern *old-fashioned*
unruhig *restless*
unser *our*
unter *under, beneath; among*
das **Unwetter, -** *violent storm*
der **Urlaub** *vacation*
    in Urlaub fahren *to go on vacation*
das **Urlaubsziel, -e** *destination*
die **Urne, -n** *ballot box*
    zur Urne gehen *to cast one's vote*
die **USA** *the U.S.A.*

V

der **Vater, ⁻** *father*
verabschieden: sich verabschieden *to say good-bye*
    Ich verabschiede mich. *I'm saying good-bye.*
die **Verabschiedung, -en** *good-bye, leave-taking*
der **Verbandkasten, -** *first-aid kit*
der **Verbandstoff** *bandage*

verbieten, verbot, verboten *to forbid*
verbinden, verband, verbunden *to connect*
    falsch verbunden *wrong number*
verbringen, verbrachte, verbracht *to spend time*
verdienen *to earn*
verdoppeln: sich verdoppeln *to double*
vergessen (vergisst), vergaß, vergessen *to forget*
das **Vergnügen, -** *pleasure*
    Viel Vergnügen! *enjoy yourself!*
die **Verhandlung, -en** *discussion, negotiation*
der **Verkäufer, -** *salesman*
der **Verkehr** *traffic*
die **Verkehrsregel, -n** *traffic rule*
das **Verkehrsschild, -er** *traffic sign*
der **Verkehrsstau, -s** *traffic congestion*
verlieren, verlor, verloren *to lose*
die **Verpackung, -en** *wrapping*
verpassen *to miss*
verschlafen (verschläft), verschlief, verschlafen *to oversleep*
verschreiben, verschrieb, verschrieben *to prescribe*
versichert *insured*
die **Versicherung, -en** *insurance*
versprechen (verspricht), versprach, versprochen *to promise*
    das Blaue vom Himmel versprechen *to promise the moon*
vertreten (vertritt), vertrat, vertreten *to represent*
der/die **Verwandte, -n, -n** *relative*
verwenden *to use*
die **Verwendung, -en** *use*
    für etwas Verwendung haben *to have use for something*
der **Vetter, -n** *cousin (m.)*
das **Video, -s** *video*
das **Videogerät, -e** *VCR*
viel *much, a lot*
    zu viel *too much*
vielleicht *perhaps*
vier *four*
vierzehn *fourteen*
vierzig *forty*
die **Vokabel, -n** *vocabulary word*
die **Vollbeschäftigung** *full employment*
das **Volt, -** *volt*

von *from; by (the agent of an action)*
  von morgens bis abends *from morning to evening*
vor *in front of; before; ago*
voraus *ahead*
vorbei*fahren (fährt vorbei), fuhr vorbei, ist vorbeigefahren *to drive by*
vorbei*kommen, kam vorbei, ist vorbeigekommen *to come by*
der **Vordersitz, -e** *front seat*
der **Vorderzahn, ⁓e** *front tooth*
  vorrätig *available*
    vorrätig sein *to be in stock*
    Die Ware ist nicht vorrätig. *The merchandise isn't in stock.*
der **Vorschlag, ⁓e** *suggestion*
  vor*stellen *to introduce*
    sich vorstellen *to imagine*
die **Vorstellung, -en** *introduction; performance*
  vorteilhaft *advantageous; flattering*

W

  wach halten (hält wach), hielt wach, wach gehalten *to keep awake*
  wachsen (wächst), wuchs, ist gewachsen *to grow*
der **Wagen, -** *car*
die **Wahl, -en** *choice, election*
die **Wahlbeteiligung** *voter turnout*
  wählen *to choose; to vote*
der **Wähler, -** *male voter*
die **Wählerin, -nen** *female voter*
das **Wahlergebnis, -se** *election result*
der **Wahlkampf, ⁓e** *political campaign*
das **Wahlrecht** *right to vote*
  wahr *true, genuine*
    Das ist wahr. *That's true.*
  während *(+ gen.) during, in the course of*
  wahrscheinlich *probably*
der **Wald, ⁓er** *forest, woods*
die **Wand, ⁓e** *wall*
  wandern *to wander, to walk*
die **Wanderung, -en** *hike*
die **Wandmalerei, -en** *mural*
  wann *when (as question)*

die **Ware, -n** *merchandise*
  warm *warm*
  warten *to wait*
    warten auf *(+ acc) to wait for*
das **Wartezimmer, -** *waiting room*
  warum *why*
  was *what*
  waschen (wäscht), wusch, gewaschen *to wash*
    mit der Hand waschen *to wash by hand*
    sich waschen *to wash oneself*
die **Waschküche, -n** *laundry room*
das **Wasser** *water*
    Wasser brauchen *to need water*
  weben *to weave*
der **Weber, -** *weaver*
die **Weberei** *weaving*
die **Web-Site, -n** *Web site*
der **Wechselkurs, -e** *exchange rate*
  wechseln *to change*
der **Wechselstrom** *alternating current (AC)*
die **Wechselstube, -n** *money changing establishment*
  wecken *to wake*
    Wecken Sie mich um . . . *Wake me at (time) . . .*
der **Wecker, -** *alarm clock*
der **Weg, -e** *way*
  wegen *(+ gen.) because of*
  weich *soft*
  Weihnachten *Christmas*
  weil *because*
die **Weile** *while, short time*
der **Wein, -e** *wine*
der **Weinberg, -e** *vineyard*
der **Weisheitszahn, ⁓e** *wisdom tooth*
  weiß *white*
  weit *wide, far*
  welcher *which*
die **Welle, -n** *wave*
  weltweit *worldwide*
  wem *whom*
  wenig *little*
  wenigstens *at least*
  wenn *if; when, whenever*
  wer *who*
die **Werbung, -en** *advertisement*
    der Werbeslogan, -s *advertising slogan*
  werden, wurde, ist geworden *to become*

der Wert, -e *value*
    wert sein *to be worth*
    westlich *westerly*
    weiter westlich *farther west*
das Wetter *weather*
    wie *how*
    wieder *again*
die Wiederholungsaufgabe *review quiz*
die Wiedervereinigung *reunification*
die Wiese, -n *meadow*
der Wind, -e *wind*
der Winter *winter*
    der Wintermorgen *winter morning*
    wir *we*
    wissen (weiß), wusste, gewusst *to know (a fact)*
    Das sollten Sie wissen. *You should know this.*
der Wissenschaftler, - *scientist*
    witzig *witty, funny*
    wo *where*
die Woche, -n *week*
die Wochenschau, -en *weekly news program*
der Wochentag, -e *day of the week*
    woher *from where*
    wohin *to where*
    wohl *probably*
    wohnen *to reside, to live*
die Wohnung, -en *apartment*
    sozialer Wohnungsbau *subsidized apartments*
das Wohnzimmer, - *living room*
die Wolke, -n *cloud*
    wollen *to want (intention)*
    Wie Sie wollen. *As you wish.*
    wünschen *to wish*
die Wurst, ⁔e *sausage*
die Wurzel, -n *root*
die Wurzelbehandlung, -en *root canal*
    wütend *furious*
    wütend sein *to be furious*

X

x-mal *many times*

Y

die Yacht, -en *yacht*

Z

die Zahl, -en *number*
    zahlen *to pay*
    zahllos *numerous*
der Zahn, ⁔e *tooth*
der Zahnarzt, ⁔e *male dentist*
    beim Zahnarzt *at the dentist's*
die Zahnärztin, -nen *female dentist*
der Zahnbelag *plaque*
die Zahnbürste, -n *toothbrush*
das Zahnfleisch *gum*
    zahnlos *toothless*
die Zahnmedizin *dentistry*
die Zahnpasta, Zahnpasten *toothpaste*
die Zahnschmerzen *toothache*
die Zehe, -n *toe*
    zehn *ten*
der Zehneuroschein, -e *ten euro bill*
    zeichnen *to draw*
die Zeichnung, -en *drawing*
    zeigen *to show*
die Zeit *time*
die Zeitschrift, -en *magazine*
die Zeitung, -en *newspaper*
das Zentrum, Zentren *center*
    das Stadtzentrum *city center*
    zerbrechen, zerbrach, zerbrochen *to break*
    zerren *to sprain, to tear*
die Zerrung, -en *sprain*
der Zettel, - *slip of paper*
das Zimmer, - *room*
das Zimmermädchen, - *maid*
die Zimmernummer, -n *room number*
die Zinsen *interest*
der Zinssatz, ⁔e *interest rate*
die Zivilisation, -en *civilization*
der Zoll *customs*
die Zollerklärung, -en *customs declaration*
    zu *to (with people and some places)*
der Zucker *sugar*
    zudem *besides, in addition to that*
    zuerst *at first*
der Zug, ⁔e *train*
    zu*greifen, griff zu, zugegriffen *to take the opportunity, to take advantage*
die Zündkerze, -n *spark plug*
der Zündschlüssel, - *ignition key*
die Zündung, -en *ignition*

zurück *back*

zurück*geben (gibt zurück), gab zurück, zurückgegeben *to return*

zurück*lassen (lässt zurück), ließ zurück, zurückgelassen *to leave behind*

zurück*zahlen *to pay back, to reimburse*

die Zusammenkunft, ¨e *meeting*

zusammen*legen *to lay together; to put together*

zusammen*liegen, lag zusammen, zusammengelegen *to lie together*

der Zuschlag, ¨e *surcharge*

zwanzig *twenty*

einundzwanzig *twenty-one*

zwei *two*

die Zweitstimme *second vote*

zwingen, zwang, gezwungen *to force*

zwischen *between*

zwölf *twelve*

ENGLISH–GERMAN

A

about *über*

above *über*

academy *die Hochschule, -n*

account *das Konto, Konten*

checking account *das Scheckkonto, das Girokonto*

savings account *das Sparkonto*

acquire (to) *erwerben*

across *über*

act (in a play) *der Akt, -e; der Aufzug, ¨*

actor *der Schauspieler, -*

actually *eigentlich*

add (to) *bei*fügen*

address *die Adresse, -n; die Anschrift, -en*

return address *der Absender, -*

admire (to) *bewundern*

advantageous *vorteilhaft*

advertising *die Werbung, -en*

advertising slogan *der Werbespruch, ¨e*

afford (to) *sich leisten*

after *nach*

afterward *danach*

again *wieder*

against *gegen*

ago *vor*

agree (to) *überein*stimmen*

ahead *voraus*

airplane *das Flugzeug, -e*

airplane passenger *der Fluggast, ¨e*

airport *der Flughafen, ¨*

airtight *luftdicht*

aisle *der Gang, ¨e*

middle aisle *der Mittelgang, ¨e*

album *das Album, -s*

alive (to be) *leben*

all *alle*

allergy *die Allergie, -n*

allow (to) *gestatten*

alone *allein*

alphabet *das Alphabet*

Alps *die Alpen*

always *immer*

amazing *erstaunlich*

America *Amerika*

among *unter*

and *und*

anesthesia *die Betäubung*

local anesthesia *die örtliche Betäubung*

animated *beweglich*

answer *die Lösung, -en*

answer (to) *antworten; beantworten*

antique (object) *die Antiquität, -en*

anyhow *sowieso*

anyway *ohnehin*

apartment *die Wohnung, -en*

subsidized apartments *sozialer Wohnungsbau*

apologize (to) *sich entschuldigen*

apple *der Apfel, ¨*

apple strudel *der Apfelstrudel, -*

appliance (electrical) *das Elektrogerät, -e*

appointment *der Termin, -e*

apprentice *der Lehrling, -e*

apprenticeship *die Lehre, -n*

April *der April*

apron *der Kittel, -*

area *die Fläche, -n*

arithmetic (mental) *das Kopfrechnen*

around *gegen; um*

around ten o'clock *gegen zehn Uhr*

arrange (to) *arrangieren*
arrival *die Ankunft, ⸚e*
arrive (to) *an*kommen; ein*treffen*
art *die Kunst, ⸚e*
   art museum *das Kunstmuseum,*
      Kunstmuseen
   work of art *das Kunstwerk, -e*
artist *der Künstler, -*
article *der Artikel, -*
ascent (to) *auf*steigen*
Ascension Day *Himmelfahrt*
ascent *der Aufstieg, -e*
Ash Wednesday *der Aschermittwoch*
asparagus *der Spargel*
aspirin *das Aspirin, -*
at *bei*
   at a place of business *bei*
   at the side of *an*
attach *bei*fügen*
attention *die Achtung*
attic *der Dachboden, ⸚*
audio recording *die Tonaufnahme, -n*
August *der August*
aunt *die Tante, -n*
Austria *Österreich*
author *der Autor, -en*
automatically *automatisch*
automobile *das Auto, -s*
   automobile mechanic *der*
      Automechaniker, -
   automobile repair shop *die*
      Autoreparaturwerkstatt, ⸚
autumn *der Herbst*
available *vorrätig*
average *der Durchschnitt*
awake (to keep) *wach halten*
aware *bewusst*
away (from) *entfernt*

B

back *zurück*
backpack *der Rucksack, ⸚e*
background *der Hintergrund, ⸚e*
bad *schlecht*
bag *die Tasche, -n*
   shoulder bag *die Umhängetasche, -n*
   sleeping bag *der Schlafsack, ⸚e*
bake (to) *backen*
balcony *der Balkon, -e*
bald (head) *die Glatze, -n*
ball *der Ball, ⸚e*
   costume ball *der Maskenball*

Baltic *die Ostsee*
band *die Kapelle, -n*
bandage *die Binde, -n; der Verbandstoff*
   elastic bandage *die elastische Binde*
bag *die Tüte, -n*
bank *die Bank, -en*
   bank transfer *die Banküberweisung, -en*
bar *die Bar, -s*
   snack bar *der Schnellimbiss, -e*
   chocolate bar *die Tafel Schokolade*
barbershop *der Frisiersalon, -s; der*
     Herrenfrisiersalon, -s; der Friseur
bargain (to) *handeln*
bath *das Bad, ⸚er*
   bath with mineral water *das*
     Mineralwasserbad, ⸚er
bathe (to) *baden*
bathrobe *der Bademantel, ⸚*
bathroom *das Badezimmer, -*
battery *die Batterie, -n*
be (to) *sein*
   to be available *frei sein*
   to be in stock *vorrätig sein*
   to be ready *fertig sein*
beach *der Strand, ⸚e*
   beach robe *der Bademantel, ⸚*
beaker *der Becher, -*
bean *die Bohne, -n*
beard *der Bart, ⸚e*
beat (to) *schlagen*
beautiful *schön*
because *denn; weil*
   because of *wegen*
become (to) *werden*
bed *das Bett, -en*
bedroom *das Schlafzimmer, -*
beef *das Rindfleisch*
beer *das Bier, -e*
before *bevor; davor; vor*
behind *dahinter; hinter*
   one behind the other *hintereinander*
believe (to) *glauben*
bellhop *der Hotelpage, -n*
belong to (to) *gehören*
belonging (personal) *der*
     Privatgegenstand, ⸚e
belongings *die Sachen*
belt *der Gürtel, -*
   baggage conveyor belt *das*
     Gepäckband, ⸚er
   seat belt *der Sicherheitsgurt, -e*
beneath *unter*
beside *neben*
besides *außer; zudem*

between *zwischen*
beverage *das Getränk, -e*
beyond *dahinter*
bicycle *das Rad, ̈er*
bicycle (to) *Rad fahren*
big *groß*
bill (money) *der Schein, -e*
bitter *bitter*
black *schwarz*
blond *blond*
blouse *die Bluse, -n*
blow (to) *blasen*
blue *blau*
board *die Tafel, -n*
body *der Körper, -*
book *das Buch, ̈er*
booked *ausgebucht*
bookshelf *das Bücherregal, -e*
booth *der Messestand, ̈e*
boot up (to) *hoch*fahren*
border *die Grenze, -n*
boring *langweilig*
borrow (to) *leihen*
bottle *die Flasche, -n*
box *der Karton, -s; die Packung, -en; die Kiste, -n*
    ballot box *die Urne, -n*
    box seat *der Logensitz, -e*
    factory packing *die Originalverpackung, -en*
boxing *das Boxen*
    boxing match *der Boxkampf, ̈e*
boyfriend *der Freund, -e*
brake *die Bremse, -n*
    brake pedal *das Bremspedal, -e*
brake (to) *bremsen*
brand-new *allerneuest-*
bread *das Brot, -e*
break (to) *zerbrechen*
breakfast *das Frühstück*
    including breakfast *inklusive Frühstück*
breakfast (to) *frühstücken*
breezy *luftig*
bring (to) *bringen*
    to bring along *mitbringen*
broadcast (to) *übertragen*
broken *kaputt*
brother *der Bruder, ̈*
    brother-in-law *der Schwager, ̈*
brown *braun*
brunette *brünett*
burden (to) *beschweren*
burn (to) *brennen*

bus *der Bus, -se*
    bus line *die Buslinie, -n*
business *das Geschäft, -e*
    business discussion *die Geschäftsbesprechung, -en*
busy *besetzt*
but *aber; sondern*
butter *die Butter*
buy (to) *kaufen*
buyer *der Abnehmer, -*
by *von*

C

café *das Café, -s*
    garden café *das Gartencafé, -s*
    sidewalk café *das Straßencafé, -s*
cake *der Kuchen, -; die Torte, -n*
calculate (to) *berechnen*
calculator (pocket) *der Taschenrechner, -*
call (telephone) *der Anruf —e*
    long-distance call *das Ferngespräch, -e*
call (to) *an*rufen; rufen*
called (to be) *heißen*
calm *ruhig*
calm (to) *beruhigen*
    to calm down *sich beruhigen*
camera *der Photoapparat, -e*
campaign (political) *der Wahlkampf, ̈e*
can (to be able to) *können*
Canada *Kanada*
candidate *der Kandidat, -en*
cap *die Mütze, -n*
    bathing cap *die Badenmütze, -n*
car *das Auto, -s; der Wagen, -*
    dining car *der Speisewagen, -*
    sleeping car *der Schlafwagen, -*
    used car *der Gebrauchtwagen, -*
card (credit) *die Kreditkarte, -n*
card (post) *die Postkarte, -n*
care *die Sorge, -n*
carnival *der Karneval; Fasching*
carpet *der Teppich, -e*
carport *das Dach, ̈er*
carrot *die Möhre, -n*
case (in any) *sowieso*
cash *das Bargeld*
cashier *der Kassierer, -*
casino (gambling) *das Spielkasino, -s*
castle *die Burg, -en*
catch (to) *fangen*
    to catch cold *sich erkälten*

cathedral *der Dom, -e; die Kathedrale, -n*
cavity *Karies*
ceiling *die Decke, -n*
celebrate (to) *feiern*
celebration *die Feier, -n; das Fest, -e*
cellar *der Keller, -*
center *das Zentrum, Zentren*
ceramics *die Keramik*
ceremony *die Feier, -n*
certain *bestimmt*
certainly *sicherlich*
chair *der Stuhl, ̈e*
  easy chair *der Sessel, -*
  large wicker beach chair *der
    Strandkorb, ̈e*
change *das Kleingeld*
change (to) *über*wechseln; um*steigen;
  wechseln*
  to change one's clothes *sich um*ziehen*
  to change reservations *um*buchen*
Channel Two *das Zweite Programm, ZDF*
charge *die Gebühr, -en*
  service charge *die Bearbeitungsgebühr,
    -en*
charge (to) *berechnen*
  to charge extra *einen Aufschlag berech-
    nen*
cheap *billig*
cheaper *billiger*
check *die Rechnung, -en; der Scheck, -s*
  to cash a check *einen Scheck einlösen*
check (to) *prüfen; überprüfen*
  to check the air *die Luft prüfen*
cheese *der Käse*
cherry *die Kirsche, -n*
chicken *das Huhn, ̈er*
child *das Kind, -er*
childlike *kindhaft*
chocolate *die Schokolade*
  bar of chocolate *die Tafel Schokolade*
choice *die Wahl, -en*
choose (to) *aus*suchen; wählen*
Christmas *Weihnachten*
  Christmas Eve *der Heiligabend*
city *die Stadt, ̈e*
  city center *die Stadtmitte, -n; das
    Stadtzentrum; Stadtzentren*
  city map *der Stadtplan, ̈e*
  city wall *die Stadtmauer, -n*
  small city *das Städtchen, -*
civilization *die Zivilisation, -en*
class *die Klasse, -n*
  first class *erster Klasse; die erste Klasse*

clean (to) *putzen; reinigen*
  to clean (brush) one's teeth *sich die
    Zähne putzen*
  to dry-clean *chemisch reinigen*
cleaning *die Reinigung, -en*
  dry cleaning *die chemische Reinigung*
  express dry cleaning *die
    Schnellreinigung*
  light dry cleaning *das Kleiderbad*
clear *klar*
clerk *der/die Angestellte, -n, -n*
  bank clerk *der Bankangestellte, -n, -n*
  postal clerk *der Schalterbeamte, -n, -n*
  reception clerk *der Empfangschef, -s*
climb (to) *auf*steigen; steigen*
clock *die Uhr, -en*
  alarm clock *der Wecker, -*
cloister *das Kloster, ̈*
close *nah(e)*
close (to) *schließen*
closed *geschlossen*
clothing *die Kleidung*
cloud *die Wolke, -n*
coach (through) *der Kurswagen, -*
coast *die Küste, -n*
coffee *der Kaffee, -s*
coins *das Kleingeld*
cold *die Erkältung, -en; die Kälte; kalt*
collar *der Kragen, -*
college *die Universität, -en*
  to go to college *studieren*
color *die Farbe, -n*
coloring *das Färben*
comb (to) *kämmen*
  to comb one's hair *sich kämmen*
come (to) *kommen*
  to come by *vorbei*kommen*
  to come for a visit *zu Besuch kommen*
  to come from (with locations) *kommen
    aus (+ Dat.)*
company *der Konzern, -e*
  large company *der Großkonzern, -e*
compartment *das Abteil, -e; das Fach, ̈er*
  inside compartment *das Innenfach, ̈er*
  nonsmoking compartment *das
    Nichtraucherabteil, -e*
  outside compartment *das Außenfach, ̈er*
competition *die Konkurrenz*
complain (to) *sich beklagen; sich
  beschweren*
computer *der Computer*
concern *der Konzern, -e*
  large concern *der Großkonzern, -e*

concert *das Konzert, -e*
   concert at a spa *das Kurkonzert, -e*
conductor *der Dirigent, -en*
confectionery *die Konditorei, -en*
conference *die Besprechung, -en; die*
    Konferenz, -en
connect (to) *verbinden*
connection *der Anschluss, ¨sse*
constantly *ständig*
consul *der Konsul*
consulate *das Konsulat, -e*
contents *der Inhalt, -e*
contrary (on the) *sondern*
contrast *der Kontrast, -e*
conversation *das Gespräch, -e*
converter *der Transformator, -*
cook (to) *kochen*
cooperate (to) *kooperieren;*
    zusammen*arbeiten
corner *die Ecke, -n*
correct (to be) *stimmen, recht*
    haben
cost (to) *kosten*
couchette *der Liegewagen, -*
cough *der Husten*
cough (to) *husten*
count (to) *rechnen*
country *das Land, ¨er*
cousin (female) *die Kusine, -n*
cousin (male) *der Vetter, -n*
cozy *gemütlich*
craft *das Handwerk*
cream (whipped) *die Schlagsahne*
crisp *knusprig*
cross *das Kreuz, -e*
crown *die Krone, -n*
   gold crown *die Goldkrone, -n*
crunchy *knusprig*
cup *der Becher, -; die Tasse, -n*
   a cup of coffee *eine Tasse Kaffee*
culture *die Kultur, -en*
curable *heilbar*
cure *die Kur, -en*
curl *die Locke, -n*
curly *lockig*
current (electrical) *der Strom, ¨e*
   alternating current (AC) *der*
     Wechselstrom
   direct current (DC) *der Gleichstrom*
current(ly) *aktuell; augenblicklich*
   current events *das Aktuelle*
customer *der Kunde, -n*
customs *der Zoll*

customs declaration *die Zollerklärung, -en*
cutlet *das Schnitzel, -*

D

daily *täglich*
   daily news broadcast *die Tagesschau, -en*
   daily routine *die Tagesroutine, -n*
damaged *beschädigt*
damaged (to be) *beschädigt sein*
dash off (to) *los*rennen*
daughter *die Tochter, ¨*
day *der Tag, -e*
   Good day. *Guten Tag.*
December *der Dezember*
deck (observation) *das Aussichtsdeck*
decompose (to) *zersetzen*
defeat *die Niederlage, -n*
delicious *lecker*
delight *die Lust, ¨e*
delivery *die Lieferung, -en*
   delivery van *der Lieferwagen, -*
democracy *die Demokratie, -n*
dentist (female) *die Zahnärztin, -nen*
dentist (male) *der Zahnarzt, ¨e*
dentistry *die Zahnmedizin*
deodorant *das Deodorant, -s*
depart (to) *ab*fahren*
   to depart by airplane *ab*fliegen*
department *die Abteilung, -en*
departure *der Abflug, ¨e*
deposit (to) *ein*zahlen*
descend (to) *ab*steigen*
descent *der Abstieg, -e*
describe (to) *beschreiben*
dessert *der Nachtisch, -e*
destination *das Reiseziel, -e; das Ziel*
detail *die Einzelheit, -en*
dialogue *der Dialog, -e*
difference *die Differenz, -en, der*
    Unterschied, -e
diploma *das Abitur, -s*
directions *die Gebrauchsanweisung, -en*
directly *direkt*
director *der Direktor, -en; der*
    Intendant, -en
disagree (to) *nicht überein*stimmen*
discussion *die Verhandlung, -en*
disease *die Krankheit, -en*
display (to) *an*zeigen*
district *das Viertel, -*
dizzy *schwindlig*

do (to) *machen; tun*
  to do calisthenics *Gymnastik machen*
  to do good *gut tun*
  to do someone's hair *frisieren*
door *die Tür, -en*
double (to) *(sich) verdoppeln*
download (to) *herunter*laden*
draw (to) *zeichnen*
drawing *die Zeichnung, -en*
dress *das Kleid, -er*
dress (to) *an*ziehen*
  local dress (costume) *die Tracht, -en*
  to get dressed *sich an*ziehen*
drill (to) *bohren*
drink (to) *trinken*
drive (to) *fahren; treiben*
drop *der Tropfen, -*
druggist *der Drogist, -en, -en*
drugstore *die Drogerie, -n*
  self-service drugstore *der Drogeriemarkt, ̈e*
dry (to) *trocknen*
  to dry dishes *ab*trocknen*
  to dry one's hair *sich die Haare trocknen*
  to dry oneself *sich ab*trocknen*
during *bei; während*
dye *die Farbe, -n*
dye (to) *färben*
dyeing *das Färben*

E

each *jeder*
earn (to) *verdienen*
Easter *Ostern*
easterly, eastern *östlich*
easy, easily *einfach*
eat (to) *essen*
egg *das Ei, -er*
election *die Wahl, -en*
  federal election *die Bundestagswahl, -e*
  local election *die Kommunalwahl, -en*
  state election *die Landtagswahl, -en*
elevator *der Aufzug, ̈e*
e-mail *die E-Mail*
emergency *der Notfall, ̈e*
  emergency call *der Notruf; -e*
  emergency exit *der Notausgang, ̈e*
employment *die Beschäftigung, -en; die Stellung, -en*
  full-time employment *die Vollbeschäftigung, -en; die Ganztagsbeschäftigung, -en*

part-time employment *die Teilzeitbeschäftigung, -en; die Halbtagsbeschäftigung, -en*
  temporary employment *die Aushilfearbeit*
empty *leer*
end *das Ende*
endless *endlos*
endure (to) *aus*halten*
England *England*
enjoy (to) *genießen*
  Enjoy yourself! *Viel Vergnügen!*
entrance *der Eingang, ̈e*
environment *die Umwelt*
even *sogar; selbst*
evening *der Abend, -e*
  Good evening. *Guten Abend.*
  in the evening *abends*
evenings *abends*
every *jeder*
everything *alles*
everywhere *überall*
examination (high school) *das Abitur*
example *das Beispiel, -e*
  for example *zum Beispiel*
examine (to) *prüfen*
excellent *ausgezeichnet*
except (for) *außer*
exchange *der Umtausch*
  exchange rate *der Kurs, -e; der Wechselkurs, -e*
exchange (to) *um*tauschen*
exciting *spannend, aufregend*
excuse *die Entschuldigung, -en*
excuse (to) *entschuldigen*
exhausted *erschöpft*
  to be exhausted *erschöpft sein*
exhibition *die Ausstellung, -en*
  special exhibition *die Sonderausstellung, -en*
  exhibition grounds *das Messegelände, -*
exit *der Ausgang, ̈e*
  highway exit *die Ausfahrt, -en*
to expect *erwarten*
expensive *teuer*
eye *das Auge, -n*
eyeglasses *die Brille, -n*

F

fable *die Fabel, -n*
fabulous *fabelhaft*
fair (trade) *die Messe, -n*
fall (to) *fallen*

family *die Familie, -n*
famous *berühmt*
fantastic *fantastisch*
far *weit*
fast *schnell*
father *der Vater, ∵*
February *der Februar*
fee (bank) *die (Bank)gebühr, -en*
feel like (to) *Lust haben*
festival *das Fest, -e*
few (a) *ein paar*
fight (to) *kämpfen*
file *Datei, -en*
fill (to) *füllen*
filling *die Füllung, -en*
  gold filling *die Goldfüllung, -en*
film *der Film, -e*
finally *endlich*
find (to) *finden*
first (at) *zuerst*
fish *der Fisch, -e*
fit (to) *passen*
flag *die Fahne, -n*
flattering *vorteilhaft*
flea market *der Flohmarkt, ∵e*
flight *der Flug, ∵e*
  return flight *der Rückflug, ∵e*
flirt (to) *flirten*
floor *der Boden, ∵; der Fußboden, ∵; der*
    Stock, ∵e
  first floor *das Erdgeschoss; das*
    Parterre
  second floor *der erste Stock*
flour *das Mehl*
flower *die Blume, -n*
flu *die Grippe, -n*
fly (to) *fliegen*
foggy *nebelig*
foot *der Fuß, ∵e*
for *für; seit*
forbid (to) *verbieten*
force *der Zwang, ∵e*
force (to) *zwingen*
forest *der Wald, ∵er*
forget (to) *vergessen*
form *das Formular, -e*
  deposit slip *das Einzahlungsformular,*
    -e
  registration form *das*
    Anmeldeformular, -e
  withdrawal slip *das*
    Auszahlungsformular, -e
former *ehemalig*

France *Frankreich*
freeze (to) *frieren*
fresh *frisch*
Friday *der Freitag*
  Good Friday *der Karfreitag*
friend (female) *die Freundin, -nen*
friend (male) *der Freund, -e*
frizzy *kraus*
from *aus; von*
  from morning to evening *von morgens bis*
    abends
front of (in) *vor*
fruit *die Frucht, ∵e; das Obst*
function (to) *funktionieren*
funny *witzig*
furious *wütend*
furious (to be) *wütend sein*
furniture *die Möbel (pl.)*
  furniture style *der Möbelstil, -e*

G

gallery *die Galerie, -n*
game *das Spiel, -e*
garage *die Garage, -n*
garland *die Girlande, -n*
gas (to get) *tanken*
gasoline *das Benzin*
  gasoline pedal *das Gaspedal, -e*
  gasoline pump *die Tanksäule, -n*
  gasoline station *die Tankstelle, -n*
gentleman *der Herr, -en, -en*
genuine *echt*
German *Deutsch (n.), deutsch (adj.)*
  High German *Hochdeutsch*
  Standard German *Hochdeutsch*
Germany *Deutschland*
get (to) *bekommen*
  to get up *auf*stehen*
gift *das Geschenk, -e*
  gift purchase *der Geschenkeinkauf,*
    ∵e
girlfriend *die Freundin, -nen*
give (to) *geben; schenken*
  to give a shot *eine Spritze setzen*
glacier *der Gletscher, -*
gladly *gern*
glass *das Glas, ∵er*
  glass blower *der Glasbläser*
glasses (eye) *die Brille, -n*
glorious *herrlich*
glove *der Handschuh, -e*

go (to) *gehen*
  to go by (means of) *fahren mit*
  to go on vacation *in Urlaub fahren*
goal *das Tor, -e*
gold *das Gold*
golden *golden*
good *gut*
good-bye *Ade; auf Wiederhören; auf Wiedersehen; Servus; Tschau; Tschüs*
gown *der Kittel, -*
grade *die Note, -n*
graduate (high school) *der Abiturient, -en, en*
gram *das Gramm, -e*
grammar *die Grammatik*
granddaughter *die Enkeltochter, :*
grandfather *der Großvater, :*
grandmother *die Großmutter, :*
grandson *der Enkelsohn, :e*
graphic *die Grafik, -en*
grass *das Gras, :er*
gratitude *der Dank*
gray *grau*
great (coll.) *toll*
Greece *Griechenland*
green *grün*
greet (to) *grüßen*
greeting *die Begrüßung, -en; der Gruß, :e*
groceries *die Lebensmittel*
ground *der Boden, :*
grow (to) *wachsen; an*bauen*
gums *das Zahnfleisch*
gymnastics *die Gymnastik; das Turnen*
gymnastics (to do) *turnen*

H

hair *das Haar, -e*
  hair color *die Haarfarbe, -n*
  hair dryer *der Haartrockner, -*
  hair growth product *das Haarwuchsmittel, -*
haircut *der Haarschnitt, -e*
hairdresser (female) *die Friseuse, -n*
hairdresser (male) *der Friseur, -e*
hairdresser's (shop) *der Friseursalon, -s*
hall *die Halle, -n*
  city hall *das Rathaus, :er*
hallway *die Diele, -n; der Flur, -en; der Gang, :e*
hand in (to) *ab*geben*

handicraft *das Handwerk, -e*
hang (to) *hängen*
  to hang up *auf*legen; auf*hängen*
  to hang wallpaper *tapezieren*
harbor *der Hafen, :*
hard *hart*
hat *der Hut, :e*
haul (to) *schleppen*
have (to) *haben*
  to have a right *ein Recht haben*
  to have an appointment *einen Termin haben*
  to have supper *zu Abend essen*
  to have use for something *für etwas Verwendung haben*
head *der Kopf, :e*
headache *die Kopfschmerzen*
headless *kopflos*
heal (to) *heilen*
healthy *gesund*
hear (to) *hören*
heaven *der Himmel, -*
hello *Grüetzi; Grüß Gott; Hallo*
help (to) *helfen*
  to help with *helfen bei (+ dat.)*
here (adverb) *da*
high *hoch*
highway *die Autobahn, -en*
  highway assistance service *die Straßenwachthilfe*
hike *die Wanderung, -en*
  hiking and climbing club *der Gebirgsverein, -e*
hill *der Berg, -e*
hole *das Loch, :er*
holiday *der Feiertag, -e; der Festtag, -e*
  national holiday *der Nationalfeiertag*
  religious holiday *der kirchliche Feiertag*
homeland *das Heimatland*
homework *die Aufgabe, -n*
hopefully *hoffentlich*
horn *die Hupe, -n*
horrible *schrecklich*
hot *heiß*
hotel *das Hotel, -s*
hour *die Stunde, -n*
hours (for) *stundenlang*
house *das Haus, :er*
how *wie*
however *aber*
hundred *hundert*
  one hundred one *hunderteins*
  two hundred *zweihundert*

hunger *der Hunger*
hurry *die Eile*
hurry (to) *sich beeilen*
hurt (to) *schmerzen; weh tun*
  to hurt somebody *schaden*
husband *der Mann, ⁻er*
hygiene (personal) *die Körperpflege*

I

ice (cream) *das Eis*
icy *eisig*
idea *die Idee, -n*
if *wenn*
ignition *die Zündung, -en*
  ignition key *der Zündschlüssel, -*
ill *krank*
illness *die Krankheit, -en*
imagine (to) *sich vor*stellen*
implement (to) *in die Realität umsetzen*
impressive *imposant*
in *in*
inconvenience *die Unannehmlichkeit, -en*
increase (to) *erweitern*
individual *individuell*
industrialist *der Industrielle, -n*
industry *die Industrie, -n*
inflammation *die Entzündung, -en*
inform (to) *informieren; orientieren*
  to inform oneself about *sich informieren*
    über
initial *die Initiale, -n*
injured *beschädigt*
inquire (to) *nach*fragen*
inside *in; innerhalb*
inspection *die Besichtigung, -en*
instead (of) *(an)statt*
instruct (to) *orientieren, lehren*
insurance *die Versicherung, -en*
insured *versichert*
interest *die Zinsen*
  interest rate *der Zinssatz, ⁻e*
interesting *interessant*
intermission *die Pause, -n*
Internet *das Internet*
intersection *die Kreuzung, -en*
interview *das Interview, -s*
  interview director *der Interviewleiter*
  interviewee *der/die Befragte, -n*
interview (to) *interviewen*
into *in*
introduce (to) *vor*stellen*
introduction *die Vorstellung, -en*

investment *die Anlage, -n*
iron (electrical) *das Bügeleisen, -*
issue (to) *aus*stellen*
Italy *Italien*

J

jacket *die Jacke, -n*
jam (to) *klemmen*
jam, strawberry *die Erdbeermarmelade, -n*
January *Januar*
journey *die Reise, -n*
July *der Juli*
June *der Juni*
just (now) *augenblicklich*
justice *die Gerechtigkeit*

K

key *der Schlüssel, -*
kilo *das Kilo, -s*
  half a kilo *das Pfund, -e*
kilometer (km) *der Kilometer, -*
kiosk *der Kiosk, -s*
kit (first-aid) *der Verbandkasten, ⁻*
kitchen *die Küche, -n*
know (to) *kennen* (a person); *wissen* (a
    fact)
knowledge *die Fachkenntnis, -se* (a particu-
    lar field); *das Wissen* (general)
known (well-) *bekannt*

L

lament (to) *beklagen*
lamp *die Lampe, -n*
  reading lamp *die Leselampe, -n*
land (to) *an*legen*
last (to) *dauern*
late *spät*
law *das Recht, -e*
lawyer *der Jurist, en, -en; der
    Rechtsanwalt, ⁻e*
lay (to) *legen*
  to lay together *zusammen*legen*
lead (to) *führen*
league *die Liga, -s*
learn (to) *lernen*
least (at) *wenigstens*
leather *das Leder, -*
  (made) of leather *aus Leder*

leave (to) *weg*gehen; lassen*
  to leave behind *zurück*lassen*
left (direction) *links*
leg *das Bein, -e*
lend (to) *leihen*
Lent *die Fastenzeit*
let (to) *lassen*
letter *der Brief; -e*
  express letter *der Eilbrief, -e*
  registered letter *das Einschreiben, -*
lie (to) *liegen*
lifesaver *der Lebensretter*
lift (chair) *die Sesselbahn, -en*
likable *sympathisch*
  to be likable *sympathisch sein*
  to like *mögen*
liked (well-) *beliebt*
limit (speed) *die Geschwindigkeitsbegrenzung*
line *die Leitung, -en*
listen (to) *hören*
liter *der Liter, -*
little *wenig*
  a little while *die Runde*
live (to) *leben; wohnen*
load (to) *auf*laden; ein*laden, laden*
lock (combination) *das Kombinationsschloss, -̈sser*
long *lang*
look (to) *gucken*
  to look at *an*sehen; an*schauen; besichtigen*
  to look at oneself *sich an*sehen*
  to look at something *sich etwas an*schauen*
  to look for *suchen*
lose (to) *verlieren*
lot (a) *eine Menge; viel*
loud *laut*
lounge *die Liegehalle, -n*
luggage *das Gepäck*
  luggage cart *der Gepäckwagen, -*
lunch *das Mittagessen, -*

M

magazine *die Zeitschrift, -en*
magnificent *großartig*
maid *das Zimmermädchen, -*
mail *die Post*
  air mail *die Luftpost*
mailbox *der Briefkasten, -̈*
make (to) *machen; tun*

man *der Mann, -̈er*
manager *der Geschäftsführer, -*
manual *handwerklich*
  manual dexterity *handwerkliches Geschick*
manufacturer *der Fabrikant, -en, -en*
March *der März*
march (to) *auf*ziehen*
mark *der Fleck, -en*
market *der Markt, -̈e*
mass media *die Massenmedien*
massage *die Massage, -n*
material *der Stoff, -e*
matinee *die Matinée, -s*
May *der Mai*
may (to be allowed to) *dürfen*
meadow *die Wiese, -n*
meat *das Fleisch*
medication *das Medikament, -e; das Präparat, -e*
medicine *das Mittel, -*
Mediterranean Sea *das Mittelmeer*
  Mediterranean island *die Mittelmeerinsel, -n*
meet (to) *treffen*
  to meet one another *sich treffen*
meeting *die Sitzung, -en: die Zusammenkunft, -̈e*
memory *die Erinnerung, -en*
  in memory of *zur Erinnerung an*
menu *die Speisekarte, -n*
merchandise *die Ware, -n*
messenger *der Bote, -n*
middle *die Mitte, -n*
  in the middle of *mitten auf (+ dat.)*
midnight *die Mitternacht, -̈e*
million *die Million, -en*
  a million *eine Million*
minute *die Minute, -n*
miss (to) *verpassen*
missing (to be) *fehlen*
mister *der Herr, -en, -en*
mixed *gemischt*
model *das Modell, -e*
modem *das Modem, -s*
molar *der Backenzahn, -̈e*
moment *der Augenblick, -e; der Moment, -e*
Monday *der Montag*
money *das Geld, -er*
month *der Monat, -e*
more *mehr*
morning *der Morgen*
  good morning *guten Morgen*
  in the morning *morgens*
mornings *morgens*

mother *die Mutter, ̈*
motorcycle *das Motorrad, ̈er*
mountain *der Berg, -e*
  the mountains *das Gebirge*
  mountain railway *die Bergbahn, -en*
mouse click *der Mausklick*
mouthwash *das Mundwasser, -*
move *der Umzug, ̈e*
move (to) *um*ziehen*
mover *der Spediteur, -e*
  moving company *die Spedition, -en*
movie *der Film, -e*
  movie fan *der Film-Enthusiast, -en, -en*
much *viel*
  too much *zu viel*
mud *der Lehm*
  mud pack *die Lehmpackung, -en*
muggy *schwül*
mural *die Wandmalerei, -en*
museum *das Museum, Museen*
musician *der Musiker, -*
must (to have to) *müssen*
mustache *der Schnurrbart, ̈e*
my *mein*

N

name *der Name, -n*
name (to) *nennen*
  to name a beneficiary *einen Nutznießer*
    ein*setzen
narrate (to) *erzählen*
narrow *eng*
near *bei; nah(e)*
neck *der Nacken, -*
need (to) *brauchen*
negotiation *die Verhandlung, -en*
nephew *der Neffe, -n*
Net (Internet) *das Netz*
new *neu*
  New Year *Neujahr*
news *die Nachricht, -en*
  news broadcast *die Nachrichten*
newspaper *die Zeitung, -en*
newsstand *der Kiosk, -s*
next to *neben*
nice *nett; schön*
niece *die Nichte, -n*
night *die Nacht, ̈e*
  at night *nachts*
  good night *gute Nacht*
no *nein*
noon *der Mittag, -e*

North Sea *die Nordsee*
northerly, northern *nördlich*
not *nicht*
  not only . . . but also *nicht nur . . .*
    sondern auch
note *die Notiz, -en*
notebook *das Notizbuch, ̈er*
nothing *nichts*
notify (to) *benachrichtigen*
November *der November*
now *jetzt*
nowadays *heutzutage*
numb (to) *betäuben*
number *die Nummer, -n; die Zahl, -en*
  room number *die Zimmernummer, -n*
  Wrong number! *Falsch verbunden!*
numerous *zahllos*

O

object *der Artikel, -; der Gegenstand, ̈e*
ocean *das Meer, -e*
occupied *besetzt*
October *der Oktober*
odd *seltsam*
  odd number *die ungerade Zahl*
of *von*
  of course *selbstverständlich*
  in the course of *während*
offer (special) *das Sonderangebot, -e*
offer (to) *an*bieten; bieten*
office *das Büro, -s*
  main post office *die Hauptpost*
  post office *die Post; das Postamt, ̈er*
official *der Beamte, -*
oil *das Öl, -e*
ointment *das Öl, -e: die Salbe, -n*
old *alt*
  old-fashioned *altertümlich: unmodern*
on *an; auf*
  on top of *auf*
  onto *auf*
once *einmal*
  once more *noch einmal*
oneself *selber; selbst*
open *geöffnet*
  to open an account *ein Konto*
    einrichten/eröffnen
opening *der Platz, ̈e*
or *oder*
orange *die Apfelsine, -n*
orchestra *das Parkett, -s*
order *die Ordnung, -en*

order (to) *bestellen*
orient oneself (to) *sich orientieren*
others *andere*
otherwise *sonst*
out of *aus*
outside *außerhalb (+ gen.)*
over *über*
oversleep (to) *verschlafen*
overview *der Überblick, -e*
own (their) *eigen*

P

package *das Paket, -e*
pain *die Schmerzen*
paint (to) *malen*
painter *der Maler, -*
painting *das Gemälde, -; die Malerei, -en*
pair *das Paar, -e*
  a pair of socks *ein Paar Socken*
pale *blass*
panorama *das Panorama, -s*
pants *die Hose, -n*
paper (slip of) *der Zettel, -*
parade *der Umzug, ̈e*
parade (to) *auf*ziehen*
parents *die Eltern*
parquet *das Parkett, -s*
part *der/das Teil, -e*
part (to) *sich trennen*
participant *der Befragte, -n, -n: der Teilnehmer, -*
participate (to) *mit*machen*
party *das Fest, -e*
party (political) *die Partei, -en*
  splinter party *die Splitterpartei, -en*
pass (to) *überholen*
  to pass by *vorbei*fahren*
  to pass one's time *verbringen*
passport *der Pass, ̈sse; der Reisepass, ̈sse*
  passport control *die Passkontrolle, -n*
pastry *das Gebäck*
path *der Pfad, -e*
pathological *krankhaft*
patience *die Geduld*
patient (female) *die Patientin, -nen*
patient (male) *der Patient, -en*
pay (to) *bezahlen; zahlen*
  to pay back *zurück*zahlen*
  to pay out *aus*zahlen*
pea *die Erbse, -n*
pedestrian *der Fußgänger, -*
  pedestrian zone *die Fußgängerzone, -n*

pedicure *die Fußpflege*
pedicurist (female) *die Fußpflegerin, -nen*
pedicurist (male) *der Fußpfleger, -*
penny *der Pfennig, -e, der Cent, -s*
Pentecost *Pfingsten*
people *die Leute*
performance *die Vorstellung, -en*
perhaps *vielleicht*
permanent wave *die Dauerwelle, -n*
permit (to) *gestatten*
perseverance *die Ausdauer*
pharmacist *der Apotheker, -*
pharmacy *die Apotheke, -n*
photo *die Aufnahme, -n; das Photo, -s*
photographer *der Fotograf, -en, -en*
physician (female) *die Ärztin, -nen*
physician (male) *der Arzt, ̈e*
pick (to) *aus*suchen*
picture *das Bild, -er*
piece *das Stück, -e*
pill *die Tablette, -n*
place *der Platz, ̈e*
place (to) *setzen; stellen*
plan *der Plan, ̈e*
  seating plan *der Sitzplan, ̈e*
plan (to) *planen*
plaque *der Zahnbelag*
platform *der Bahnsteig, -e*
play *das Theaterstück, -e*
player (female) *die Spielerin, -nen*
player (male) *der Spieler, -*
playwright *der Dramatiker, -*
pleasant *angenehm*
please (to) *gefallen*
pleasure *die Lust, ̈e; das Vergnügen, -*
plug (spark) *die Zündkerze, -n*
politician *der Politiker, -*
politics *die Politik*
popular *beliebt*
pork *das Schweinefleisch*
possibility *die Möglichkeit, -en*
postcard *die Ansichtskarte, -n*
potato *die Kartoffel, -n*
potter *der Töpfer, -*
pottery *die Töpferei*
pound *das Pfund, -e*
powder (dusting) *der Körperpuder, -*
preparation *das Präparat, -e*
prescribe (to) *verschreiben*
preserve (to) *erhalten*
president *der Präsident, -en, -en*
press *die Presse*
pretty *hübsch*

price *der Preis, -e*
  price range *die Preislage, -n*
print out (to) *aus*drucken*
probably *wahrscheinlich; wohl*
profession *der Beruf, -e*
program *das Programm, -e*
  cable program *das*
    Kabelfernsehprogramm, -e
promenade (to) *promenieren, spazieren*
  gehen
promise (to) *versprechen*
prospect (for a profession) *die*
  Berufsaussicht, -en
public *öffentlich*
punctual *pünktlich*
purchase *der Einkauf, ˝e*
purse *die Geldbörse, -n; die Tasche, -n*
put (to) *setzen; stecken; stellen*
  to put on (clothes) *an*ziehen*

Q

question *die Frage, -n*
quick *flink; schnell*
quiet *ruhig*
quiet (to) *beruhigen*
quiz (review) *die Wiederholungsaufgabe*

R

radio *das Radio, -s*
rain *der Regen*
rain (to) *regnen*
raincoat *der Regenmantel, ˝*
rare *rar*
rash *der Ausschlag*
rather *sondern*
razor (electric) *der Rasierapparat, -e*
reality *die Realität, -en; die Wirklichkeit, -en*
reasonable *preisgünstig*
rebuild (to) *um*bauen*
receipt *die Quittung, -en*
receiver *der Hörer*
receiver (of mail) *der Empfänger, -*
recipe *das Rezept, -e*
recognize (to) *erkennen*
recommend (to) *empfehlen*
recuperate (to) *sich erholen*
red *rot*
reddish *rötlich*
refreshing *erfrischend*
refrigerator *der Kühlschrank, ˝e*

register (to) *ein*tragen*
  to register oneself *sich ein*tragen*
regularly *regelmäßig*
reimburse (to) *zurück*zahlen*
relative *der/die Verwandte, -n, -n*
relax (to) *sich aus*ruhen; sich erholen*
remarkable *bemerkenswert*
remodel (to) *um*bauen*
renovate (to) *renovieren*
rent (to) *mieten*
repair (to) *reparieren*
replace (to) *ersetzen*
represent (to) *vertreten*
Republic (Federal) *die Bundesrepublik*
reservation *die Reservierung, -en*
reserve (to) *reservieren*
reside (to) *wohnen*
resident (local) *der/die Einheimische,*
  -n, -n
resort (health) *der Badeort, -e; der Kurort,*
  -e
respect *die Achtung*
rest (to) *sich aus*ruhen*
restaurant *das Restaurant, -s*
restless *unruhig*
result *das Ergebnis, -se*
  election result *das Wahlergebnis, -se*
return (to) *zurück*geben*
reunification *die Wiedervereinigung*
reward (to) *lohnen*
right *recht; das Recht, -e*
right (direction) *rechts*
right (to be) *Recht haben*
ring (to) *läuten*
rock *der Felsen, -; der Stein, -e*
role *die Rolle, -n*
roll *das Brötchen, -*
roof *das Dach, ˝er*
room *der Raum, ˝e; das Zimmer, -*
  child's room *das Kinderzimmer, -*
  consulting room *das Sprechzimmer, -*
  double room *das Doppelzimmer, -*
  fitting room *die Umkleidekabine, -n*
  laundry room *die Waschküche, -n*
  living room *das Wohnzimmer, -*
  single room *das Einzelzimmer, -*
  waiting room *das Wartezimmer, -*
root *die Wurzel, -n*
  root canal *die Wurzelbehandlung*
Rose Monday (Monday before Lent) *der*
  Rosenmontag
rough *stürmisch*
round *die Runde*
routine *die Routine, -n*

rub (to) *einreiben*
rug *der Teppich, -e*
ruin *die Ruine, -n*
run (to) *laufen; rennen*
run out of (to) *ausgehen*

S

sailboat *das Segelboot, -e*
salad *der Salat, -e*
sale *der Ausverkauf, ¨e*
salesman *der Verkäufer, -*
salve *die Salbe, -n*
sand *der Sand*
sandwich *das Butterbrot, -e*
sandy *sandig*
Saturday *der Samstag; der Sonnabend*
sausage *die Wurst, ¨e*
save (to) *sparen*
save (to) on computer *speichern*
say (to) *sagen*
   to say good-bye *sich verabschieden*
scarf *der Schal, -s*
scene *die Szene, -n*
school *die Schule, -n*
   high school *das Gymnasium, Gymnasien*
   special needs school *die Sonderschule, -n*
scientist *der Wissenschaftler, -*
scissors *die Schere, -n*
scream (to) *schreien*
sculptor *der Bildhauer*
sculpture *die Bildhauerei; die Plastik, -en;*
     die Skulptur, -en
sea *das Meer, -e*
   seashore *die Meeresküste, -n*
search for (to) *suchen*
season *die Jahreszeit, -en; (Sport) die*
     Spielzeit, -en
   vacation season *die Feriensaison*
seat *der Platz, ¨e*
   backseat *der Rücksitz, -e*
   front seat *der Vordersitz, -e*
seaweed *der Seetang*
secretary (female) *die Sekretärin, -nen*
secretary (male) *der Sekretär, -e*
see (to) *sehen*
self *selbst; selber*
send (to) *schicken; senden*
   to send off *ab*schicken*
   to send to *schicken an (+ acc.)*
sender *der Absender, -*
separate (to) *trennen*
September *der September*

serve (to) *servieren*
service *der Dienst, -e*
set (to) *setzen*
shall (to be supposed to) *sollen*
shave (to) *rasieren*
   to shave off *ab*rasieren*
   to shave oneself *sich rasieren*
   to shave the neck *aus*rasieren*
shaving creme *die Rasiercreme*
shelf *das Regal, -e*
shelter *die Hütte, -n*
shepherd (boy) *der Hirtenjunge, -n, -n*
shine (to) *scheinen*
ship *das Schiff, -e*
shirt *das Hemd, -en*
shop *das Geschäft, -e*
   coffee shop *das Café, -s*
   flower shop *das Blumengeschäft, -e*
   pizza shop *die Pizzeria, -s*
shop (to) *ein*kaufen*
shopping *Einkäufe machen*
   shopping list *die Einkaufsliste, -n*
shore *die Küste, -n*
short *kurz*
   on short notice *kurzfristig*
shot *die Spritze, -n*
show (to) *an*zeigen; zeigen*
shower *die Dusche, -n*
shower (to) *duschen*
   to take a shower *sich duschen*
sick *krank*
sights *die Sehenswürdigkeiten*
sightseeing *die Besichtigung, -en*
sign *das Schild, -er*
silly *dumm*
simple, simply *einfach*
sin (to) *sündigen*
since *seit*
Sincerely (letter) *Mit freundlichen Grüßen*
singer *der Sänger, -*
singly (piece by piece) *einzeln*
sink *der Ausguß, ¨sse*
sister *die Schwester, -n*
   sister-in-law *die Schwägerin, -nen*
sit (to) *sitzen*
   to sit down *sich setzen*
size *die Größe, -n*
skiing *das Skilaufen; das Skifahren*
ski (to) *ski laufen, ski fahren*
skirt *der Rock, ¨e*
sky *der Himmel, -*
slacks *die Hose, -n*
sleep (to) *schlafen*
   to go to bed *schlafen gehen*

small *klein*
smoker *der Raucher, -*
smooth *glatt*
snow *der Schnee*
snow (to) *schneien*
snowfall *der Schneefall, ⸚e*
soap *die Seife, -n*
soccer *der Fußball*
   soccer match *das Fußballspiel, -e*
social sciences *die Sozialwissenschaft, -en*
sock *die Socke, -n*
sofa *das Sofa, -s*
soft *weich*
sold out *ausgebucht; ausverkauft*
solution *die Lösung, -en*
some *manche*
sometimes *manchmal*
somewhere *irgendwo*
son *der Sohn, ⸚e*
soon *bald*
sorrow *die Sorge, -n*
soup *die Suppe, -n*
sour *sauer*
southerly, southern *südlich*
souvenir *das Andenken, -*
spa *der Badeort, -e; der Kurort, -e*
Spain *Spanien*
speed (to) *rasen*
speedometer *der Tacho, -s; der*
    Tachometer, -
spend (to) *ausgeben (Geld); verbringen*
    (Zeit)
spite of (in) *trotz*
splendid *glänzend*
splendor *die Pracht*
sport *der Sport*
   sports club *der Sportverein, -e*
   to engage in sports *Sport treiben*
spot *der Fleck, -en*
sprain *die Zerrung, -en*
sprain (to) *zerren*
spring *der Frühling; die Quelle, -n*
   medicinal spring *die Heilquelle, -n*
sprinkle (to) *streuen*
square *der Platz, ⸚e*
stage *die Bühne, -n*
stain *der Fleck, -en*
stair *die Treppe, -n*
staircase *das Treppenhaus, ⸚er*
stall (to) *stehen bleiben*
stamp *die Briefmarke, -n*
stand (to) *stehen*
   to stand in line *Schlange stehen*
start (to) *an*springen*

starter *der Anlasser, -*
state *der Staat, -en*
statement (bank) *der Kontoauszug, ⸚e*
station (train) *der Bahnhof, ⸚e*
station (radio or TV) *der Sender, -*
stay *der Aufenthalt, -e*
stay (to) *bleiben*
steal (to) *stehlen*
steam (to) *dampfen*
steamboat *der Dampfer*
   steamboat trip *die Dampferfahrt, -en*
steel (stainless) *der Edelstahl*
steep *steil*
stick (to) *stecken*
still *noch*
stomachache *die Magenschmerzen*
stop (to) *halten; stehen bleiben*
storage (room/space) *der Abstellraum, ⸚e*
store *das Geschäft, -e; der Laden, ⸚*
   department store *das Kaufhaus, ⸚er*
storm *der Sturm, ⸚e*
   storm warning *die Sturmwarnung, -en*
   violent storm *das Unwetter, -*
storm (to) *stürmen*
stormy *stürmisch*
stove *der Herd, -e*
straight *gerade*
   straight ahead *geradeaus*
strange *seltsam*
strenuous *anstrengend*
striking *eindrucksvoll*
stroll (to) *promenieren*
strong *stark*
strudel *der Strudel, -*
student *der Student, -en, -en*
studies *das Studium, Studien*
study (to) *studieren*
stupid *dumm*
subject *das Fach, ⸚er*
subway *die S-Bahn, -en*
such *solche*
suddenly *plötzlich*
suffer (to) *leiden*
   to suffer from *leiden an*
sugar *der Zucker*
suggestion *der Vorschlag, ⸚e*
suit (man's) *der Anzug, ⸚e*
   sailing suit *der Segelanzug, ⸚e*
suitcase *der Koffer, -*
summer *der Sommer*
summit *der Gipfel, -*
sun *die Sonne, -n*
   sun protection oil *das*
    Sonnenschutzöl, -e

sunburn *der Sonnenbrand, ∺e*
Sunday *der Sonntag*
sunscreen (lotion) *die Sonnenschutzcreme, -n*
suntan *die Bräune*
superfluous *überflüssig*
supermarket *der Supermarkt, ∺e*
supper *das Abendessen, -*
supplier *der Lieferant, -en, -en*
surcharge *der Aufschlag, ∺e; der Zuschlag, ∺e*
   spa surcharge *die Kurtaxe, -n*
surf (on) *surfen*
surface *die Fläche, -n*
swallow (to) *ein*nehmen; schlucken*
sweater *der Pullover, -*
sweet *süß*
swelling *die Schwellung, -en*
swimming *das Schwimmen*
swimming (to go) *schwimmen gehen*
switch (to) *um*schalten*
Switzerland *die Schweiz*
symptom *das Symptom, -e*

T

table *der Tisch, -e*
take (to) *bringen; ein*nehmen; nehmen*
   to take a picture *auf*nehmen*
   to take a seat *sich setzen*
   to take advantage *zu*greifen*
   to take off *aus*ziehen*
   to take place *statt*finden*
   to take the opportunity *zu*greifen*
talk *das Gespräch, -e*
talk (to) *sprechen*
   to talk about *sprechen über (+ acc.)*
task *die Aufgabe, -n*
tax *die Steuer, -n*
   tax decrease *die Steuersenkung, -en*
   tax increase *die Steuererhöhung, -en*
taxi *das Taxi, -s*
teach (to) *lehren*
teacher *der Lehrer, -*
team *die Mannschaft, -en*
tear (to) *zerren*
teeth (set of) *das Gebiss, -sse*
telephone *der Apparat, -e; das Telefon, -e*
   by telephone *telefonisch*
   coin-operated telephone *der Münzfernsprecher, -*
   over the telephone *telefonisch*
   telephone book *das Telefonbuch, ∺er*

telephone conversation *das Telefongespräch, -e*
telephone credit card *die Telefonkarte, -n*
telephone number *die Telefonnummer, -n*
telephone (to) *telefonieren; an*rufen*
   to reach by telephone *telefonisch erreichen*
television *das Fernsehen, -*
   television set *der Fernseher, -*
tell (to) *erzählen*
   to tell about *erzählen von (+ dat.)*
teller *der/die Bankangestellte, -n, -n*
tendon *die Sehne, -n*
terrace *die Terrasse, -n*
terrible *furchtbar*
terrific *toll*
test (to) *überprüfen*
thank (to) *danken*
   thank you *danke*
thanks *der Dank*
that *dass; jener*
theater *das Theater, -*
   court theater *das Hoftheater, -*
   federal theater *das Staatstheater, -*
   municipal theater *das Stadttheater, -*
   theater box office *die Theaterkasse, -n*
theatergoer *der Theaterbesucher, -*
theft *der Diebstahl, ∺e*
then *dann*
there *da; dort*
   over there *dort drüben*
   (to) there *hin*
   up there *da oben*
these *diese*
thief (male) *der Dieb, -e*
thief (female) *die Diebin, -nen*
thing *die Sache, -n*
think (to) *denken*
   to think of *denken an (+ acc.)*
this *dieser*
those *jene*
thought *der Gedanke, -n*
thousand *tausend*
threatening *bedrohlich*
thrilling *spannend*
throat *der Hals, ∺e*
   sore throat *die Halsschmerzen*
through *durch*
Thursday *der Donnerstag*
ticket *die Fahrkarte, -n*
time *die Zeit*
   closing time (store) *der Ladenschluss*
   half time *die Halbzeit, -en*
   many times *x-mal*

several times *mehrmals*
short time *die Weile*
three times a day *dreimal täglich*
tip *das Trinkgeld, -er*
tire *der Reifen, -*
tired *müde, erschöpft*
tiring *ermüdend*
title *der Titel, -*
to *an; nach; zu*
today *heute*
toe *die Zehe, -n*
toenail *der Fußnagel, ̈*
tomorrow *morgen*
tomorrow morning *morgen früh*
tooth *der Zahn, ̈e*
front tooth *der Vorderzahn, ̈e*
wisdom tooth *der Weisheitszahn, ̈e*
toothache *die Zahnschmerzen (pl.)*
toothbrush *die Zahnbürste, -n*
toothless *zahnlos*
toothpaste *die Zahnpasta, Zahnpasten*
top *der Gipfel, -; die Spitze, -n*
topical *aktuell*
torte *die Torte, -n*
tour (group) *die Gruppentour, -en*
tour (guided) *die Führung, -en*
tourist *der Tourist, -en, -en*
toward *nach*
towel (bath/beach) *das Badetuch, ̈er; das Handtuch, ̈er*
tower *der Turm, ̈e*
town *die Stadt, ̈e*
old town *die Altstadt, ̈e*
small town *die Kleinstadt, ̈e*
track (educational) *der Bildungsweg, -e*
track (and field) *die Leichtathletik*
trade *das Handwerk*
traffic *der Verkehr*
traffic congestion *der Verkehrsstau, -s*
traffic rule *die Verkehrsregel, -n*
traffic sign *das Verkehrsschild, -er*
trail *der Pfad, -e*
trailer *der Anhänger, -*
train *die Bahn, -en; der Zug, ̈e*
short-distance train *der Nahverkehrszug, ̈e; der Personenzug, ̈e*
transfer (money) (to) *überweisen*
transformer *der Transformator, -en*
transport *der Transport, -e*
transportation (means of) *die Transportmöglichkeit, -en*
travel *die Reise, -n*
travel agency *das Reisebüro, -s*

travel bag *die Reisetasche, -n*
travel guide (book) *der Reiseführer, -*
travel (to) *reisen*
traveler *der/die Reisende, -n, -n*
treat (to) *behandeln*
treatment *die Kur, -en*
trim (to) *stutzen*
trip *die Reise, -n*
round-trip *hin und zurück*
truck *der Lastwagen, -*
true *wahr*
true (to be) *stimmen*
Tuesday *der Dienstag*
turn on (to) *ein*schalten*

U

unbelievable *unglaublich*
uncle *der Onkel, -*
unclear *unklar*
uncomplicated(ly) *problemlos*
under *unter*
undress (to) *aus*ziehen*
to get undressed *sich aus*ziehen*
unemployment *die Arbeitslosigkeit*
uninteresting *uninteressant*
union *die Gewerkschaft, -en*
university *die Hochschule; die Universität, -en*
unload (to) *aus*laden*
unpleasant *unangenehm*
until *bis*
upholstery *die Polsterung*
usage *der Gebrauch, ̈e*
use *die Verwendung, -en*
use (to) *verwenden*

V

vacation *der Urlaub, -e; die Ferien (pl.)*
vaccination *die Impfung, -en*
valley *das Tal, ̈er*
value *der Wert, -e*
VCR *das Videogerät, -e*
veal *das Kalbfleisch*
vegetable *das Gemüse, -*
victory *der Sieg, -e*
video *das Video, -s*
view *der Ausblick, -e; die Sicht, -en*
view (to) *besichtigen*
village *das Dorf ̈er*

vineyard der Weinberg, -e
visit der Besuch, -e
visit (to) besuchen
visitor (spa) der Kurgast, -̈e
vocabulary die Vokabel, -n
volt das Volt, -
vote die Stimme, -n
vote (to) wählen
   right to vote das Wahlrecht
   election results das Wahlergebnis, -se
vote (to cast one's) seine Stimme
     ab*geben; zur Urne gehen
voter (female) die Wählerin, -nen
voter (male) der Wähler, -
   voter turnout die Wahlbeteiligung

W

wait (to) warten
   to wait for warten auf (+ akk.)
wake (to) wecken
   to wake up auf*wachen
walk (to) laufen; zu Fuß gehen
wall die Wand, -̈e
wallpaper die Tapete, -n
wander (to) wandern
want to (to) wollen
warm warm
warranty der Garantieschein, -e
wash (to) waschen
   to wash oneself sich waschen
watch die Uhr, -en
watch (to) beobachten
   to watch TV fern*sehen
water das Wasser
wave die Welle, -n
way der Weg, -e
   one-way einfach
weak schwach
weather das Wetter
weave (to) weben
weaver der Weber, -
weaving die Weberei
Web browser der Browser, -
Web page die Internetseite, -n
Web site die Web-Site, -s
Wednesday der Mittwoch
week die Woche, -n
   day of the week der Wochentag, -e
   weekly news broadcast die
     Wochenschau, -en
well gut; die Quelle, -n

westerly, western westlich
   farther west weiter westlich
wet nass
what warum
when als; wann; wenn
whenever wenn
where wo
   from where woher
   where (to) wohin
whether ob
which welcher
while die Weile; während
white weiß
Whitsuntide Pfingsten
who wer
whom wem
why warum
wide weit
wife die Frau, -en
willingly gern
win (to) siegen
wind der Wind, -e
window das Fenster, -
   window (bank, post office) der
     Schalter, -
wine der Wein, -e
winter der Winter
   winter morning der Wintermorgen, -
wish (to) wünschen
wit die Schlagfertigkeit
with bei; mit
without ohne
witty witzig, schlagfertig
woman die Frau, -en
woods der Wald, -̈er
word das Wort, -̈er
work die Arbeit, -en
work (to) arbeiten
worker (foreign) der Gastarbeiter, -
worldwide weltweit
worried (to be) besorgt sein
worry (to) Sorgen haben
worth (to be) wert sein
wrapping die Verpackung, -en
write (to) schreiben
   to write about schreiben über (+ acc.)
   to write to schreiben an (+ acc.)

X

X-ray die Röntgenaufnahme, -n; das
     Röntgenbild, -er

Y

yacht *die Jacht, -en*
yell (to) *schreien*
yellow *gelb*
yesterday *gestern*
yet *noch*
   not yet *noch nicht*

yogurt *das/der Joghurt*
young *jung*

Z

zip (code) *die Postleitzahl, -en*
zipper *der Reißverschluss, ̈-sse*

INDEX

THE GERMAN SPELLING REFORM

The educational ministries of all German states have agreed upon a spelling reform to make German spelling a little easier on students and natives alike. The spelling reform, mandatory in the year 2005, can be summarized as follows:

- After short vowels *ß* becomes *ss*. *ß* remains *ß* after long vowels, if the stem of the word shows no more consonants: *Fass* (keg) but *Straße* (street).
- Double consonants after a stressed short vowel: *nummerieren (to number), Ass* (ace), *Tipp* (tip).
- Always write in two separate words: verb combinations with *sein* such as *pleite sein* (to be destitute), combinations of two verbs such as *kennen lernen* (to get to know), combinations of verb and participle such as *gesagt haben* (to have said), combinations of verb plus noun such as *Rad fahren* (to ride on a bicycle), combinations of verb and adverb such as *beiseite legen* (to set aside), combinations of verb plus adjective such as *gut lesen* (to read well), and verb plus words ending on *-ig, -isch, -lich,* such as *lästig fallen* (to be a burden).
- Capitalize all nouns and derivatives of nouns: *Trimm-dich-Pfad* (fitness trail), *Leid tun* (to be sorry), *das Dutzend* (the dozen), *im Deutschen* (in German).
- Write out all letters that meet: *Schiff + Fahrt = Schifffahrt* (boat ride).
- The words *du* (you), *dir* (to you), *dein* (your), *eure* (your [pl.]), etc., in letters are written in lower case.
- Many foreign words receive a "Germanized" spelling: *Fotograf* (photographer), but the use is mostly optional.
- Words separate after spoken syllables: *Fens-ter* (window), *Bä-der* (bathroom), *A-bend* (evening).
- No more commas are necessary before *und* or *oder,* but should be used if the context would otherwise be unclear.

NOTES

NOTES

NOTES